Varieties of English

C000254692

English is a highly diversified language that appears in a multitude of varieties across the globe. These varieties may differ extensively in their structural properties. This coursebook is an introduction to the fascinating range of regional and social varieties encountered around the world. Comparing grammatical phenomena, the book analyses the varieties in depth, identifying patterns and limits of variation, and providing clear explanations. Using comparisons with other languages, the book identifies universal as well as language-specific aspects of variation in English.

This book is specially designed to meet the needs of students. Each chapter contains useful exercises targeted at three different ability levels, and succinct summaries and practical lists of key words help students to review and identify important facts.

PETER SIEMUND is Professor and Chair of English Linguistics at the University of Hamburg.

Varieties of English

A Typological Approach

Peter Siemund

CAMBRIDGE
UNIVERSITY PRESS

CAMBRIDGE UNIVERSITY PRESS
Cambridge, New York, Melbourne, Madrid, Cape Town,
Singapore, São Paulo, Delhi, Mexico City

Cambridge University Press
The Edinburgh Building, Cambridge CB2 8RU, UK

Published in the United States of America by Cambridge University Press, New York

www.cambridge.org
Information on this title: www.cambridge.org/9780521186933

© Peter Siemund 2013

First published 2013

Printed and bound in the United Kingdom by the MPG Books Group

A catalogue record for this publication is available from the British Library

ISBN 978-0-521-76496-4 Hardback
ISBN 978-0-521-18693-3 Paperback

For Georg, Cosima, and Johann

Contents

List of figures		*page* x
List of tables		xi
Acknowledgements		xiv
How to use this book		xv
Abbreviations		xvii
1	**Introduction**	**1**
	1.1 Background and aims	1
	1.2 Structure of the book and target audience	3
	1.3 Varieties of English: an overview	5
	1.4 Sociolinguistics and functional typology	10
	1.5 Summary and list of keywords	18
	1.6 Exercises	18
	1.7 References	20
	1.8 Further reading	22
2	**Reflexivity and reflexive marking**	**23**
	2.1 Overview	23
	2.2 Varieties of English	25
	2.3 Cross-linguistic comparison	33
	2.4 Summary and list of keywords	39
	2.5 Exercises	40
	2.6 References	42
	2.7 Further reading	44
3	**Pronominal gender**	**45**
	3.1 Overview	45
	3.2 Varieties of English	48
	3.3 Cross-linguistic comparison	55
	3.4 Summary and list of keywords	61
	3.5 Exercises	61
	3.6 References	63
	3.7 Further reading	64
4	**Pronominal case**	**65**
	4.1 Overview	65
	4.2 Varieties of English	71

4.3   Cross-linguistic comparison   78
4.4   Summary and list of keywords   81
4.5   Exercises   82
4.6   References   84
4.7   Further reading   85

5   Determiners   87
5.1   Overview   87
5.2   Varieties of English   91
5.3   Cross-linguistic comparison   100
5.4   Summary and list of keywords   105
5.5   Exercises   106
5.6   References   108
5.7   Further reading   109

6   Tense marking   111
6.1   Overview   111
6.2   Varieties of English   114
6.3   Cross-linguistic comparison   122
6.4   Summary and list of keywords   128
6.5   Exercises   129
6.6   References   131
6.7   Further reading   132

7   Aspect marking   134
7.1   Overview   134
7.2   Varieties of English   137
7.3   Cross-linguistic comparison   144
7.4   Summary and list of keywords   150
7.5   Exercises   150
7.6   References   152
7.7   Further reading   153

8   Modal verbs   155
8.1   Overview   155
8.2   Varieties of English   159
8.3   Cross-linguistic comparison   164
8.4   Summary and list of keywords   169
8.5   Exercises   169
8.6   References   171
8.7   Further reading   172

9   Negation   174
9.1   Overview   174
9.2   Varieties of English   177
9.3   Cross-linguistic comparison   183
9.4   Summary and list of keywords   190
9.5   Exercises   191
9.6   References   192
9.7   Further reading   193

10 Subject-verb agreement   195
    10.1 Overview   195
    10.2 Varieties of English   199
    10.3 Cross-linguistic comparison   208
    10.4 Summary and list of keywords   215
    10.5 Exercises   216
    10.6 References   217
    10.7 Further reading   218

11 Ditransitive constructions   219
    11.1 Overview   219
    11.2 Varieties of English   222
    11.3 Cross-linguistic comparison   229
    11.4 Summary and list of keywords   232
    11.5 Exercises   233
    11.6 References   235
    11.7 Further reading   236

12 Interrogative constructions   237
    12.1 Overview   237
    12.2 Varieties of English   241
    12.3 Cross-linguistic comparison   249
    12.4 Summary and list of keywords   253
    12.5 Exercises   254
    12.6 References   256
    12.7 Further reading   257

13 The formation of relative clauses   258
    13.1 Overview   258
    13.2 Varieties of English   262
    13.3 Cross-linguistic comparison   267
    13.4 Summary and list of keywords   273
    13.5 Exercises   274
    13.6 References   275
    13.7 Further reading   276

14 Summary and outlook   278
    14.1 Exceptional properties of English   278
    14.2 Universals, angloversals, and vernacular universals   280
    14.3 Variationist (sociolinguistic) typology   283
    14.4 Where to go from here   285
    14.5 Summary and list of keywords   285
    14.6 Exercises   287
    14.7 References   289
    14.8 Further reading   290

    General references   291
    Index of languages, varieties, and areas   295
    Index of names   299
    Subject index   304

Figures

3.1 Pronominal gender in standard English (Siemund 2008: 148).
Reproduced with permission. *page* 52

3.2 Distribution of *he*, *she*, and *it* in the southwest of England
(Siemund 2008: 62). Reproduced with permission. 53

3.3 Distribution of *he*, *she*, and *it* in Newfoundland English (Siemund
2008: 67 based on Paddock 1991: 133). Reproduced with
permission. 54

3.4 Distribution of *he*, *she*, and *it* in Tasmanian Vernacular English
(Siemund 2008: 100 based on Pawley 2002, 2004). Reproduced
with permission. 54

3.5 Distribution of *he*, *she*, and *it* in regional varieties of English
(Siemund 2008: 139). Reproduced with permission. 55

3.6 Morphosyntactic distinctions along a continuum of 'individuality'
(Sasse 1993: 659; Siemund 2008: 4). Reproduced with permission. 60

6.1 Correspondences between non-standard and standard tense use. 114

7.1 Aspectual oppositions (adapted from Comrie 1976: 25). 147

10.1 The ingredients of agreement (adapted from Corbett 2006: 5). 196

11.1 Map 'Give it me' taken from *An Atlas of English Dialects* by
Clive Upton and J.D.A. Widdowson (1996: 52). By permission of
Oxford University Press. 225

14.1 Visualisation of principal components of variance in the 76 × 46
database. Dotted boxes indicate group memberships (Kortmann
and Szmrecsanyi 2011: 276). Reproduced with permission. 286

Tables

1.1 Present tense paradigm of English verbs. *page* 2

1.2 Present tense paradigm of English verbs in areas of the Northern Subject Rule. 3

1.3 Structure of the book. 4

1.4 Order of subject, object, and verb (Dryer 2011a; n.d.o. = no dominant order). 13

1.5 Numeral bases (Comrie 2011). 14

1.6 Combined order of basic constituents and adpositions (based on Dryer 2011a, b; n.d.o. = no dominant order). 16

1.7 Logical types of universal statement (following Greenberg), taken from Evans and Levinson (2009: 437). 17

2.1 Constraints on the use of untriggered *self*-forms (Hernández 2002: 272). 32

2.2 Grammatical distinctions marked on reflexives (adapted from König and Siemund 2000b: 51). 36

2.3 Body-part nouns as lexical sources of reflexive markers (adapted from Schladt 1999: 120–4). 39

3.1 Gender distinctions in independent personal pronouns (Siewierska 2011). 56

3.2 Pronominal usage in standard English and a non-standard variety. 62

4.1 An illustration of Latin case suffixes. 66

4.2 Pronominal case forms in standard English (Quirk et al. 1985: 336). 68

4.3 Subject pronouns in Ghanaian Pidgin English (Huber 1999: 197). 76

4.4 Object pronouns in Ghanaian Pidgin English (Huber 1999: 199). 76

4.5 Number of cases in a sample of the world's languages (Iggesen 2011; e.b.c.m. = exclusively borderline case marking). 80

5.1 The pronominal paradigm of Bislama (Crowley 2004: 684). 97

5.2 Distance-oriented demonstratives in Hunzib (van den Berg 1995: 61, cited in Diessel 2011). 105

5.3 Person-oriented demonstratives in Japanese (Kuno 1973: 27, cited in Diessel 2011). 105

8.1 Deontic and epistemic meanings of English modal verbs
(adapted from Quirk et al. 1985: 221).   158
8.2 Interaction of modal verbs with negation (adapted from
Anderwald 2002: 38).   159
8.3 Token frequencies of *must* in the spoken subcorpora of
ICE-Singapore and *ICE*-Great Britain (Bao 2010: 1731).   162
8.4 The central modals in five Germanic languages (adapted from
Mortelmans et al. 2009: 13).   166
8.5 Modal verbs in Chinese (Li and Thompson 1981: 173–88;
Palmer 2001: 102).   166
8.6 The expression of deontic and epistemic possibility (adapted
from van der Auwera and Ammann 2011a, b).   167
8.7 The auxiliary verb – main verb scale (adapted from Quirk et al.
1985: 137).   168
8.8 Criteria for auxiliary verbs (adapted from Quirk et al. 1985: 137). 168
9.1 Auxiliary contraction and negative contraction (adapted from
Anderwald 2002: 28).   176
9.2 Asymmetrical paradigms (adapted from Anderwald 2002: 199).   183
9.3 Double negation in relation to other strategies of negation
(adapted from Dryer 2011).   188
10.1 The paradigms of the verb *be*.   197
10.2 *Committee* nouns in American English, Australian English, and
British English (Levin 2001: 108; Corbett 2006: 212).   199
10.3 Regularisation of the present tense paradigm.   200
10.4 *Were*-levelling.   205
10.5 *Was*-levelling.   205
10.6 *Was/were*-generalisation in relation to clause polarity.   206
10.7 Subject-verb agreement as triggered by different nouns (adapted
from Levin 2001: 166–9; Corbett 2006: 213).   207
10.8 Properties of canonical agreement (Corbett 2006: 9).   210
10.9 The effect of distance on the agreement of personal pronouns
with *committee* nouns (Levin 2001: 98; Corbett 2006: 236).   215
11.1 Distribution of the complementation patterns in ditransitives in
the Lancashire part of the *BNC* (adapted from Siewierska and
Hollmann 2007: 93).   226
11.2 Distribution of the complementation patterns in ditransitives in
the *Freiburg English Dialect Corpus* (adapted from Siewierska
and Hollmann 2007: 93).   226
11.3 Complementation patterns distinguished in Mukherjee and
Hoffmann (2006: 151).   228
11.4 Complementation of *give* and *send* in *ICE*-India and *ICE*-Great
Britain (adapted from Mukherjee and Hoffmann 2006: 172–3).   229

11.5 Ditransitive constructions as a function of the verb *give* (Haspelmath 2011). 231

12.1 Clause types and illocutionary force in English. 238

12.2 Properties of interrogative clauses in English. 239

12.3 *Wh*-words in English. 240

12.4 Inverted and uninverted main clause constituent interrogatives in the *ICE* (adapted from Davydova et al. 2011: 309). 243

12.5 Inverted and uninverted embedded constituent interrogatives in the *ICE* (adapted from Davydova et al. 2011: 308). 245

12.6 Inverted and uninverted embedded polar interrogatives in the *ICE* (adapted from Davydova et al. 2011: 310). 246

12.7 Some non-standard interrogative words. 247

12.8 Interrogative words in Sranan (adapted from Winford and Migge 2004: 494). 247

12.9 Non-standard tags (based on Kortmann et al. 2004). 248

12.10 Strategies for marking polar questions (Dryer 2011a). 251

12.11 Inverted and uninverted main clause constituent interrogatives in the *ICE* (adapted from Davydova et al. 2011: 309). 255

13.1 Non-standard relative markers based on a survey of Kortmann et al. (2004). 263

13.2 Strategies of relative clause formation (Comrie and Kuteva 2011a, b). 271

13.3 Frequency of relative clause forming strategies (Herrmann 2003: 133). 272

13.4 Resumptive pronouns in simple relative clauses (Herrmann 2003: 150). 273

14.1 Exceptional properties of standard English, as portrayed by Frans Plank in *Das grammatische Raritätenkabinett* (http://typo.uni-konstanz.de/rara/intro/). 279

14.2 Some additional exceptional properties found in standard English. 279

14.3 Exceptional properties of non-standard varieties of English. 280

14.4 Non-standard features of English that follow the cross-linguistic mainstream. 282

14.5 Angloversals (adapted from Kortmann and Szmrecsanyi 2004: 1154). 283

Acknowledgements

I would like to express my gratitude to the many students on my courses who accompanied me during the gestation process of this book and who served as guinea pigs for its content and the concomitant exercises. Their feedback, especially during the final stages of the project, was extremely helpful.

As we do not live in isolation and our thoughts and ideas are shaped by the daily input we receive, it is difficult to mention every source of inspiration that I drew on and that went into this book. A good number of colleagues deserve to be credited, even though I cannot recollect every aspect of their input. The following list makes no claims to completeness and could easily be extended: Julia Davydova, Florian Dolberg, Hans-Olav Enger, Markku Filppula, Volker Gast, Bernd Kortmann, Simone Lechner, Georg Maier, Heli Paulasto, Lukas Pietsch, Günter Radden, Monika Edith Schulz, Sali Tagliamonte, Katerina Stathi, Peter Trudgill, Johan van der Auwera, Donald Winford, and Bao Zhiming.

Georg Maier and Tayo Neumann helped me substantially to systematise the data. They deserve special mention for this labour-intensive job. Leonie Fölsing, Anika Lloyd-Smith, and Martin Schweinberger proved indispensable during the editorial process.

Moreover, I would like to thank the two anonymous referees who evaluated and commented on the initial book proposal. Their remarks prevented me from committing several blunders and helped avoid hidden pitfalls.

Last but not least, I owe a substantial debt of gratitude to Andrew Winnard of Cambridge University Press who encouraged me to pursue this project and who showed a lot of patience when I got severely distracted by serving as coordinator of the Collaborative Research Centre on Multilingualism (Sonderforschungsbereich 538) and the Research Centre on Linguistic Diversity Management in Urban Areas (LiMA).

How to use this book

The idea of the present book originated in a graduate course that I have taught several times over recent years at the University of Hamburg. It grew out of a dissatisfaction with widespread approaches to varieties of English that view these as national linguistic constructs (Indian English, Singapore English, Nigerian English, American English, Canadian English, etc.) without taking proper heed of the many structural commonalities that especially the non-standard varieties share. These commonalities have been referred to as 'vernacular universals' and also 'angloversals'.

The main difference from previous publications on varieties of English is that I do not proceed variety by variety, but phenomenon by phenomenon. I assume that varieties of English as far apart from one another as Shetland English and Torres Strait Creole or Appalachian English and Singapore English lend themselves to systematic structural comparison. To achieve this objective, I rely on the overall approach of functional typology and its methodology. In this approach, conceptual and structural differences are broken down to parameters of cross-linguistic validity, thus allowing us to compare highly different linguistic systems. Functional typology identifies the patterns and limits of variation and helps us locate individual varieties of English in the orchestra of other languages and language varieties.

This book can be used and read in different ways. Even though it has primarily been designed as a textbook for advanced undergraduate and graduate students, including their instructors, it may also be read as an introduction to structural variation across varieties of English. Each chapter is dedicated to one grammatical domain and offers a concise overview of this domain, a description of the structural variation encountered in this domain, and an assessment against known cross-linguistic parameters of variation.

Each chapter contains nine exercises at three levels (basic, intermediate, and advanced), with three at each level. The basic-level exercises are meant to recapitulate the contents of each chapter. More challenging exercises can be found at the intermediate level. The advanced-level exercises offer ideas for small research projects that you may tackle on your own.

The chapters are bracketed by succinct introductions, summaries, and lists of keywords that are meant as guidelines through the chapters. At the end of each chapter, you can find lists of references and suggestions for further reading. References that are relevant to several chapters are accumulated in the *General references* section at the end of the book.

Example sentences have been fitted with interlinear translations (glosses) where appropriate. As the examples and the glosses have been drawn from many different sources, there is some overlap and redundancy in the labels used (see the list of abbreviations, pp. xvii–xix). No confusion should arise, since the context disambiguates such cases.

Abbreviations

1	first person
2	second person
3	third person
ABS	absolutive
ACC	accusative
ASP	aspect
AUX	auxiliary
BNC	*British National Corpus*
CG	common gender
CL	classifier
CLF	classifier
COCA	*Corpus of Contemporary American English*
COMP	complementiser
COP	copula
CPL	complementiser
DAT	dative
DEM	demonstrative
DET	determiner
DO	direct object
ERG	ergative
F	feminine
FOC	focus
FUT	future tense
GEN	genitive
ICE	*International Corpus of English*
IO	indirect object
IMPF	imperfective
IMPFV	imperfective
INF	infinitive
INSTR	instrumental
INT	intensifier
INTR	intransitive

L2	second language
LOC	locative
M	masculine
MASC	masculine
NEC	necessity
NEG	negative
NEUT	neuter
NOM	nominative
NOT	not
NP	noun phrase
NPI	negative polarity item
NYT	*New York Times*
O	object
OBJ	object
OBL	olique
OED	*Oxford English Dictionary*
PART	partitive
PAST	past tense
PERF	perfective
PFV	perfect
PL	plural
PM	predicate marker
POS	possibility
POSS	possessive
PP	prepositional phrase
PRED	predicate marker
PREP	preposition
PRES	present tense
PRO	pronoun
Pro	pronoun
PROG	progressive
PST	past tense
PTCP	participle
Q	interrogative/question
REC	recipient
REFL	reflexive
REL	relative marker
RT	recipient-theme
S	subject
SG	singular
SMH	*Sydney Morning Herald*
SUBJ	subject

TH	theme
TOP	topic
TR	theme-recipient
TR	time of reference
TR	transitive
TSit	time of situation
TT	topic time
TU	time of utterance
TRANS	transitive
V	verb
VENT	ventive
WH	*wh*-word

1 Introduction

1.1 Background and aims

The present book aims to introduce the student of English and general linguistics to the fascinating world of morphosyntactic variation that can be encountered across varieties of English spoken around the world. At the same time, it presents and interprets the instances of structural variation found in English in the context of cross-linguistic variation, as discussed in typological studies of language. The book, thus, intends to build a bridge from sociolinguistics and variation studies to language typology.

Let me illustrate my general approach using a prominent example of morphosyntactic variation. Many regional, especially spoken or vernacular, varieties of English allow multiple negation of the type shown in the examples below.

(1) a. I couldn't find hardly none on 'em. 'I could not find hardly any on them.' [East Anglia, Trudgill 2004: 151]

   b. We didn't have no use for it noways. 'We had no use for it in any way.' [Appalachian English, Montgomery 2004: 258]

   c. I don't want no dinner. 'I want no dinner.' [Newfoundland English, Clarke 2004: 310]

   d. You've not heard of that nothing? 'You haven't heard of that?' [Irish English, Filppula 2004: 82]

   e. I couldn't see no snake. 'I couldn't see a snake.' [Australian Vernacular English, Pawley 2004: 634]

   f. Mi no bin toktok nating. 'I didn't talk at all.' [Bislama, Crowley 2004: 690]

   g. They didn't have no shirt. 'They had no shirt.' [Australian Creoles and Aboriginal English, Malcolm 2004: 670]

In this book – remaining with the example of multiple negation for a moment – I will give you an overview of the properties and the extent of multiple negation in varieties of English. As it turns out, many traditional dialects spoken in Great Britain and North America allow multiple negation. It is also attested in various Pidgin and Creole Englishes spoken in North America, the Caribbean,

Table 1.1 *Present tense paradigm of English verbs.*

	1	2	3
Singular	walk	walk	walk-s
Plural	walk	walk	walk

Africa, and Australia. In a preliminary way, we may characterise multiple negation as the agreement of indefinite expressions with the negative polarity of a clause. In addition, I will show that multiple negation is rather common cross-linguistically and that the function of multiple negation in varieties of English is very similar to its function in other languages. Similar examples of multiple negation can *inter alia* be found in Spanish and Russian. Many varieties of English here adopt a cross-linguistically pervasive pattern. Cross-linguistic comparison also reveals that multiple negation in varieties of English counts as an instance of 'negative concord' rather than 'double negation'. Since multiple negation is just one instance of non-standard negation, I will also provide a more general introduction to negation to facilitate the proper understanding of the non-standard phenomena.

The book will also familiarise you with morphosyntactic properties of English that are rather uncommon and exceptional from a cross-linguistic perspective. Such properties can be found both in the standard and in the non-standard varieties. A prominent example of standard English is the third person singular subject agreement marker on the finite present tense verb, as in Table 1.1, which is quite unique cross-linguistically and probably best interpreted as an historical relic.

Non-standard varieties also offer exceptional and rather surprising agreement patterns. In the north of England, for example, the verbal -*s* marker may appear on all finite verb forms – singular and plural – except when immediately preceded by a pronoun. Consider the examples in (2).

(2) a. the bird sings, the birds sings, I often sings
    b. they sing and dances

This agreement pattern is known as the Northern Subject Rule. The relevant verbal paradigm may be represented as in Table 1.2, even though it cannot capture the condition on adjacent pronouns, leading to examples like (2b). The agreement patterns found in standard and non-standard Englishes are quite exceptional and difficult to interpret from a cross-linguistic perspective.

Such examples make it clear that not all morphosyntactic properties that we find in varieties of English can readily be matched with cross-linguistic

Table 1.2 *Present tense paradigm of English verbs in areas of the Northern Subject Rule.*

	1	2	3
Singular	sing-s	sing-s	sing-s
Plural	sing-s	sing-s	sing-s

parallels. Languages and their varieties are the result of a multitude of forces, and we cannot expect that everything that we find is typical of language in general. Languages are full of historical accidents, and languages other than English, too, possess idiosyncratic properties. Nevertheless, the cross-linguistic approach adopted here will help us to separate the wheat from the chaff, as it were. Moreover, even such highly atypical phenomena as the Northern Subject Rule are interesting for the typologist, as they inform us about the scope of variation.

In the present book, we will adopt a perspective on varieties of English that takes a selection of grammatical domains as its point of departure. More precisely, it is the range of morphosyntactic phenomena in these domains that is of interest here and that will form the basis for our comparison of varieties of English. The book does not offer descriptive surveys of varieties of English understood as national entities (i.e. British English, American English, Australian English, Singapore English, Nigerian English, South African English, etc.). Such surveys can be found in Burchfield (1994), Kortmann et al. (2004), Siemund et al. (2012), and Trudgill and Hannah (2002), among others.

1.2 Structure of the book and target audience

As pointed out above, in this book we will approach varieties of English through a selection of grammatical domains and morphosyntactic phenomena, dedicating one chapter to each grammatical domain discussed. Thus, the book may also be read as a reference grammar of morphosyntactic variation in English. Each grammatical domain usually subsumes a handful of non-standard phenomena. For example, besides the phenomenon of multiple negation introduced in the previous section, the chapter on negation also includes discussions of non-standard sentential negators, negative contraction, negative tags, and categorial asymmetries under negation. It goes without saying that not all phenomena that are interesting and relevant in principle can be discussed within the covers of a book. A reasonable selection needs to be made, and I have made the selection on the basis of essentially three parameters.

Table 1.3 *Structure of the book.*

Level	Chapter	Grammatical domain
	1.	Introduction
Noun phrase	2.	Reflexivity and reflexive marking
	3.	Pronominal gender
	4.	Pronominal case
	5.	Determiners
Verb phrase	6.	Tense marking
	7.	Aspect marking
	8.	Modal verbs
	9.	Negation
Sentence level	10.	Subject-verb agreement
	11.	Ditransitive constructions
	12.	Interrogative constructions
	13.	The formation of relative clauses
	14.	Summary and outlook

Firstly, the phenomena representing the grammatical domains need to be prominent enough, where prominence may result from their being widespread in non-standard varieties, a high degree of grammatical sophistication, or substantial scholarly attention.

Secondly, the non-standard phenomena to be discussed here need to be relevant from a cross-linguistic point of view. Such relevance may be due to pervasive cross-linguistic parallels, or, conversely, a high degree of idiosyncrasy that stretches our assumptions on the limits of variation. The phenomena of multiple negation and the Northern Subject Rule may help to illustrate these points.

Thirdly, I have tried to cull phenomena from different linguistic domains so as to provide a good overview of the structural variation found across varieties of English. Rather than just focusing on, say, pronouns and determiners, I will here offer and discuss a selection of phenomena from the noun phrase, the verb phrase, and the sentential level.

The book is structured as follows. With the exception of the introductory chapter and the concluding chapter, which follow their own formats, all remaining chapters essentially have the same structure, each discussing a grammatical domain of English that shows remarkable and theoretically challenging instances of variation. I discuss twelve grammatical domains that should supply sufficient material to fill a university course. An overview of the grammatical domains discussed in this textbook can be found in Table 1.3.

Following a brief introduction, I will provide an overview of the relevant grammatical domain in each chapter, introduce the requisite empirical facts, and briefly discuss the major theoretical problems raised. The chapters will then outline the patterns and limits of variation pertaining to this grammatical domain across varieties of English. For the purposes of this textbook, the term 'varieties of English' is mainly, though not exclusively, understood in terms of its regional dimension. The third component of each chapter is formed by a systematic comparison of variation in English with cross-linguistic variation. The currently known cross-linguistic parameters of variation in the relevant grammatical domains serve as the conceptual grid against which this comparison is performed.

I will also try to provide explanations and motivations for the non-standard phenomena in varieties of English. Accepting the somewhat simplifying dichotomy between formal and functional modes of explanation, I will mainly provide functional explanations.

Each chapter concludes with a brief summary, a list of keywords, a list of references, and suggestions for further reading. In addition, they each contain nine exercises from three levels: basic, intermediate, and advanced. The exercises at the advanced level contain ideas for self-contained research projects that go beyond the scope of this book and require additional reading and empirical work.

This textbook mainly targets the graduate level, forming a basis for courses at the Master or even PhD level. It may also be suitable for advanced undergraduate courses provided that the students are part of a dedicated linguistics programme. Its organisation into fourteen chapters of which twelve address coherent grammatical domains makes it suitable for the European, the North American, and also the Asian market. It may be used in all institutions that offer terms of approximately twelve to sixteen weeks. Instructors who are under time pressure may choose to omit a few grammatical domains. Those who have ample time may include additional background reading.

1.3   Varieties of English: an overview

Even though this book focuses on a selection of morphosyntactic properties in varieties of English, we need to say something about the socio-cultural dimensions that determine and identify different varieties of English. This is necessary in order to understand and to approach varieties of English in their respective socio-cultural context.

To give an example, in terms of their socio-cultural histories, the traditional dialects of England have very little in common with Singapore English, which is essentially a product of language contact and second language acquisition strategies. We noticed above in Section 1.1 that negative concord (multiple negation) is a prominent feature of traditional dialects of English (both in Great Britain and the United States) as well as Pidgin and Creole varieties. Interestingly enough, it is much less widespread in post-colonial varieties (the so-called 'New Englishes'). Even though post-colonial varieties exhibit substantial influence from the relevant substrate languages (e.g. Chinese, Hindi), the traditional feature of negative concord apparently plays no important role in them. It would appear reasonable, then, to look for an explanation of this difference in the distinctive socio-cultural histories of these varieties, i.e. consider language-external factors. For example, we may hypothesise that multiple negation was not a prominent feature of the dialects exported to some colonies. Alternatively, we may assume that in some territories where post-colonial varieties are spoken, the pressure exerted by the standard varieties was too high for multiple negation to survive.

The issue may also be substantially more troublesome, as varieties of English that apparently have very little in common in terms of their socio-cultural histories may manifest very similar non-standard phenomena. A good example is furnished by what is known as 'embedded inversion', i.e. the occurrence of main clause interrogative word order (subject-auxiliary inversion) in embedded clauses. This is shown in (3). A more in-depth discussion of embedded inversion will be taken up in Chapter 12 on interrogative constructions.

(3) a. [Why's that?] I don't know why's – why's they uh done away with the one. [British English, Survey of English Dialects, cited in Paulasto et al. 2011]

   b. Now you could try by experiment to try and . . . allocate them to different variables at different times and see does it work out [Irish English, *ICE*-Ireland, cited in Paulasto et al. 2011]

   c. Witness can you tell the court what colour were your jerseys? [Singapore English, *ICE*-Singapore, cited in Paulasto et al. 2011]

   d. Now can you tell me what is short period? [Indian English, *ICE*-India, cited in Paulasto et al. 2011]

The above examples make clear that embedded inversion can be found in traditional English dialects (3a) and the historical contact variety of Irish English (3b), as well as the post-colonial Englishes of India and Singapore (3c, d). This is unexpected, as these varieties otherwise do not exhibit overlapping non-standard features. For shared phenomena such as embedded inversion, the literature on varieties of English gives us the labels 'vernacular universals' (Chambers 2004) and 'angloversals' (Mair 2003). The idea behind these labels is that vernacular speech and language characterised by second language acquisition processes may give rise to similar surface phenomena. Even though these notions are quite appealing, they carry the risk of oversimplification, as such angloversals may have different distributions, functions, and origins in each variety (Davydova et al. 2011). We will come back to these problems in Section 1.4.3, when discussing linguistic universals.

1.3.1 Classifying varieties of English

Varieties of English can be classified along several dimensions. The listing below contains the dimensions that are relevant for the present book. It is not exhaustive, and additional dimensions may easily be identified.
- region understood as national entities
- region understood as dialect areas
- historical expansion
- language contact
- language shift
- mode of language acquisition (first, second, third language acquisition)

For example, the distinction between written and spoken varieties is not addressed, as the data discussed here mainly comes from the spoken register. In a similar way, it is not necessary to distinguish between formal and informal (colloquial, vernacular) language, since we mainly deal with vernacular varieties. Moreover, sociolinguistic variables such as age or gender are largely ignored. The dimensions that do play a role for our purposes are region, language contact (resulting from historical expansion), and language acquisition processes.

1.3.2 National entities and dialect areas

Political borders are convenient constructs to identify regional varieties of English, as they are clearly identifiable and relatively stable. They allow us to distinguish British English (UK), American English (US), Canadian English, Australian English, New Zealand English, South African English, Nigerian English, Singapore English, Malaysian English, Indonesian English, i.e. the varieties of the inner and outer circle in the sense of Kachru (1988). Some of these political constructs are very young, even though English has a much longer history in the relevant territories.

We also find political boundaries below the national level, namely states, counties, cities, and similar constructs. They allow us to identify Somerset English, Scottish English, Ulster English, Texan English, Toronto English, Glasgow English, and so on and so forth. Such political classifications will frequently be made use of in the present book when relating non-standard phenomena and examples to specific regions.

Dialect areas, i.e. regions where specific linguistic systems are used within certain political entities, are more difficult to identify, as such decisions are typically based on linguistic features and not political argumentation. Linguistic features may be unstable, and not all speakers of a dialect area need share all representative features. The inclusion of dialect areas gives us varieties such as Appalachian English, Northern British English, Southern American English, Tyneside English, etc. Frequently, dialect areas overlap or are co-extensive with political boundaries below the national level.

1.3.3   Historical expansion

Without doubt, the development of the English language has been a success story. Starting from modest beginnings as a bunch of dialects spoken along the North Sea littoral, it turned into a global language within approximately 1,500 years. English exists in at least two standard varieties and numerous non-standard varieties. Over 400 million native speakers use it as their first language. An additional 500 million speakers can be assumed to use it as a second or foreign language. English enjoys the status of official or co-official language in many countries (Australia, the Bahamas, Barbados, Ghana, Jamaica, Liberia . . . Zimbabwe). According to Crystal (1988: 10), 'British English is now, numerically speaking, a minority dialect, compared with American, or even Indian, English.'

English was created when the Angles, Saxons, and Jutes arrived in the British Isles in the fifth century AD. The Anglo-Saxon Chronicle gives us the year 449, which appears astonishingly precise. Starting from the eastern and southern coast, they expanded to the north and to the west. Even Ireland saw English-speaking people as early as the twelfth century. The second big wave of historical expansion went to North America and the Caribbean, beginning in the sixteenth century and eventually resulting in the creation of two big English-speaking countries (i.e. the United States and Canada). A third wave can be tied to the boom years of the British Empire, when English-speaking people penetrated nearly every corner of the world, however remote. The Empire expanded, creating colonies in West, East, and South Africa, India, Australia, Southeast Asia, and the Pacific. Permanent settlements developed *inter alia* in South Africa, Australia, and New Zealand. The British Empire imported many valuable goods from these colonies. Among its top-selling products to the colonies was the English language.

To be sure, the fact that the English language has been a great success also means that other languages suffered, as it replaced many of the indigenous languages spoken in the territories to which English was exported. The Celtic languages of the British Isles nearly became extinct and have survived only due to dedicated affirmative action. Many of the languages spoken by the autochthonous populations in North America and Australia have been lost.

Many of the surviving languages are only spoken by a very few people and are bound to become extinct.

Looking at varieties of English in terms of their historical expansions yields the typology of varieties shown in the listing below. It is based on Burchfield (1994) and Algeo (2001), but it is also largely compatible with Kachru's (1988) circle model that distinguishes inner circle, outer circle, and expanding circle varieties (even though expanding circle varieties do not play a role here):

  i. English in England
 ii. English in the originally Celtic-speaking lands (Scotland, Ireland, Wales)
iii. the English of North America
 iv. the 'settler' Englishes of Australia, New Zealand, and South Africa
  v. the Englishes (largely non-native) of South and Southeast Asia
 vi. the Creole Englishes of Africa, the Caribbean, and the Pacific.

The Creole Englishes as well as the non-native Englishes of South and Southeast Asia (the so-called 'post-colonial Englishes') have a special status in this typology, as, besides processes of historical expansion, these Englishes were heavily shaped by processes of language contact and language shift, to which we will turn in the next section.

1.3.4 *Language contact and language shift*

English has always been a contact language, as our preceding remarks on its historical development have shown. It is perhaps the standardisation processes that set in with the advent of the Early Modern English period that cloud this fact and make us perceive English as a homogenous construct. In addition, the contact situation shifted away from the British mainland to other parts of the world.

In view of these historical facts, it would appear adequate to make language contact the primary prism for the analysis of varieties of English. This approach has attracted substantial scholarly attention over the past decade, as publications such as Filppula et al. (2009) attest. Peter Trudgill, in a number of recent publications (2009, 2011), even argues for a more general correlation between social structure, i.e. high-contact communities versus low-contact or isolated communities, and the type of language that these communities speak. As high-contact communities may plausibly be expected to be exposed to substantial levels of second language learning, the relevant contact languages may over time be developing into more analytic types. On that view, the appearance of highly fusional or even polysynthetic languages presupposes communities that lived in isolation for extensive periods of time.

The varieties of English that were probably exposed to the highest degree of language contact are English-based Pidgins and Creoles. As a matter of fact,

Pidgin and Creole languages are defined in terms of language contact. The inclusion of Pidgin and Creole languages into the set of varieties of English is not uncontroversial, as these are special languages developing in extreme social constellations. Be that as it may, I here follow Winford (2005, 2008), who holds that the processes of contact-induced change producing English-based Pidgin and Creole languages are similar to those found in other contact Englishes.

There are also less extreme cases, which are no less interesting. All so-called 'New Englishes' or post-colonial varieties involve second language acquisition or learning and are as such contact varieties, since English in these cases is in contact with the respective indigenous languages (Hindi, Bengali, Tamil, Malay, Chinese, Zulu, Xhosa, etc.). A special position in the context of contact varieties is taken up by what has come to be known as 'shift varieties', i.e. varieties of English that emerged through a population shifting from their first language to English for reasons of colonial pressure, language planning, or simply prestige. Varieties of English that belong in this group are Irish English, Welsh English, and partially Scottish English (the so-called 'Celtic Englishes'), but also Singapore English, which is emerging through substantial language shift of speakers of Chinese, Malay, and other languages to English.

Taking up the contact perspective also leads to a fundamental contrast between those varieties of English that are learnt as first languages (first language, or L1, varieties) and those that are primarily learnt as second languages (second language, or L2, varieties). It opposes the traditional varieties spoken in the United Kingdom, North America, Australia, and New Zealand to the New Englishes found in India, Pakistan, South Africa, Singapore, Nigeria, and comparable territories where English enjoys the status of an official language, but is learnt and used as a second language by the majority of speakers. One problem of this approach is that speaker populations are not uniform with respect to the distinction between first and second language acquisition and that in a society like, for example, that of Singapore both types of speaker live side by side. Pidgin and Creole varieties of English are also difficult to classify in such a scheme.

For that reason, Schneider (2003, 2007) offers a finer-grained typology of post-colonial Englishes, i.e. those varieties strongly influenced by language contact and L2 acquisition processes, distinguishing five phases in their development: Foundation (phase 1), Exonormative Stabilisation (phase 2), Nativisation (phase 3), Endonormative Stabilisation (phase 4), and Differentiation (phase 5).

1.4   Sociolinguistics and functional typology

Earlier in this chapter, I wrote that the present book aims to build a bridge from sociolinguistic research into functional typology. Both disciplines are crucially interested in linguistic variation, though they look for different types of variation using different methodologies.

Sociolinguistics – including its precursor, dialectology – typically explores structural variation as well as variable language use within a language. Sociolinguists may be interested in the distribution of multiple negation and the realisation of the verbal -*s* suffix in English dialects, investigating their linguistic and social conditioning factors. Their *tertium comparationis* is a linguistic variable (e.g. English negation), exploring the realisation of its values (e.g. simple negation versus multiple negation).

Functional typology explores cross-linguistic variation, trying to identify common marking strategies for the expression of different semantic domains. For example, typologists might want to develop a typology of the attested strategies for the expression of reflexive relations, possessive relations, temporal relations, and so on and so forth. Their *tertium comparationis* typically – though not exclusively – is a semantic or cognitive domain.

In this section, I will provide a brief summary of the major tenets held in sociolinguistics and functional typology, including a sketch of the historical development of the two disciplines. Moreover, I will also try to comment on the modes of explanation used in these disciplines, especially on the notion of 'linguistic universals' widely assumed in the typological literature.

1.4.1 Dialectology and sociolinguistics

Modern sociolinguistics explores the influence of social factors on language use. Social factors are diverse and include age, gender, ethnic background, religion, status in society, level of education, peer groups, and profession, as well as cultural norms. Sociolinguistics as a scientific field is related to and overlaps with dialectology, anthropological linguistics, and variation studies, and also pragmatics. We may view traditional dialectology as one important precursor to modern sociolinguistics.

Major dialectological projects were carried out in England, Germany, Italy, and France in the nineteenth and twentieth centuries, for example the *Deutsche Sprachatlas* coordinated by Georg Wenker, the *Survey of English Dialects* directed by Harold Orton, and the *Atlas linguistique de la France* by Jules Gilliéron. In addition, dialectological studies resulted in glossaries and grammars of rural dialects, as for example those distributed by the English Dialect Society in the second half of the nineteenth century. One of the milestones in English dialectology is Joseph Wright's *English Dialect Dictionary*, which appeared in 1898. Traditional dialectology had – and still has – a strong interest in regional variation, charting lexical and grammatical differences, including differences in pronunciation.

Modern sociolinguistics – even though just as interested in linguistic variation as traditional dialectology – gave an important reorientation to the field. Firstly, the focus of enquiry shifted from rural areas to cities and conurbations (Labov 1966; Trudgill 1974). Secondly, sociolinguistic studies consider all members of society and do not rely primarily on what is known as NORMS, i.e. non-mobile old rural male speakers. Thirdly, regional variation became just one parameter alongside the many social parameters mentioned above. Fourthly, the traditional questionnaire-based methods were complemented by sociolinguistic interviews and linguistic corpora. Fifthly, there has been an increasing theoretical sophistication in that sociolinguistics aims at developing models of language variation and change.

Besides sociolinguists, more recently scholars from other backgrounds have also developed an interest in linguistic variation – variation being understood as regional and social variation. This concerns theoretical linguists working in the Universal Grammar paradigm as much as functional typologists. As the present book primarily adopts the functionalist paradigm, I have little to say on Universal Grammar here. For that you may want to explore some of the following publications: Henry (1995), Cornips and Corrigan (2005), and Siemund (2011). Of course, when relevant, I will also discuss what these approaches have to say on the variation phenomena covered in the present book. Let us now turn to linguistic typology and observe how it can be connected to the study of regional and social variation.

1.4.2   Linguistic typology

Varieties of English, as we learnt above, find their origin in the colonial expansion of the British people and the British Empire. Incidentally, we may also link the emergence of linguistic typology as an academic field to European colonial expansion, as this triggered a strong interest in hitherto unknown languages, the discovery of new language families and genetic relationships, and, most importantly, new grammatical structures and ways of expression. Scholars of the nineteenth century like Wilhelm von Humboldt, Georg von der Gabelentz, August Schlegel, and August Schleicher worked on the classification of genetically unrelated languages into basic morphological types, from which still widely used labels such as 'analytic', 'synthetic', 'agglutinating', 'fusional', 'polysynthetic', 'incorporating', and related notions derive.

Just like sociolinguistics and dialectology, linguistic typology is interested in charting variation. However, the fine structural variants explored by sociolinguists are not the main focus of typology, even though they may matter. Moreover, social factors, which serve as the primary explanans in

Table 1.4 *Order of subject, object, and verb (Dryer 2011a; n.d.o. = no dominant order).*

Word order	SOV	SVO	VSO	VOS	OVS	OSV	n.d.o.	Total
Languages	565	488	95	25	11	4	189	1,377

sociolinguistics, play no role in linguistic typology. Typologists investigate structural differences, i.e. structural variation, between languages, working towards taxonomies of linguistic structures and their mutual relationships. Concerning its general aims and methods, linguistic typology is perhaps best compared to biology, the main difference being the object of enquiry (languages versus species). Traditional dialectology is closer to typology than sociolinguistics, as it examines structural differences between dialects, and the distinction between language and dialect is a relatively arbitrary one. Moreover, dialectology charts regional variation, which is a dimension present in much typological work (areal typology).

An important assumption underlying all typological work is that languages do not vary arbitrarily and hence do not differ from one another in completely unpredictable ways. This idea can be traced back at least to the nineteenth century, when classifications of languages in terms of distinct morphological types (synthetic, analytic, agglutinating) enjoyed great prestige. Such holistic typologies in the end turned out to be romantic ideals, as it became increasingly clear that mixed types are common and that linguistic subsystems may belong to different types. Platypus languages are not completely unheard of. Nevertheless, the belief that there are limits to structural variation and that there are clear patterns in the observable space of variation is still widely held among typologists.

Let me illustrate this general assumption using a simple example from the typology of word order, as the difference between what is logically possible and what is attested is clearly visible in this domain. On the assumption that all languages distinguish subject (S), object (O), and verb (V), we arrive at six word order permutations of these basic constituents. They are shown in Table 1.4, inclusive of the observable distributional differences. It is quite obvious that languages placing the subject before the object outnumber those that require the reverse order of these constituents.

We may procure another illustration of the same point using the numeral base of a language, where, for all practical purposes, languages fall into either of two major types, namely those with a decimal base (counting fingers) and those with a vigesimal base (counting fingers and toes). There are also some mixed

Table 1.5 *Numeral bases (Comrie 2011).*

Numeral base	Languages
Decimal	125
Hybrid vigesimal-decimal	22
Pure vigesimal	20
Other base	5
Extended body-part system	4
Restricted	20
Total	196

systems, as well as some completely different systems, which we ignore here. Table 1.5 shows the distribution of different numeral bases across languages. Again, it is obvious that the decimal base is vastly preferred over the other options.

Typological comparisons of the type shown in Table 1.4 and Table 1.5 have been carried out for many grammatical domains, thus identifying attested and prevailing phoneme inventories, word order patterns, word class systems, systems of encoding grammatical relations, and case systems, as well as many others. Linguistic typology, without doubt, has vastly increased our knowledge of the available structural options, possible grammars, typical grammatical properties, and so on and so forth. Moreover, it has shown that we can identify trends that hold across genetically unrelated languages. These are known as 'linguistic universals', to which we will turn in the next section.

1.4.3   Linguistic universals

Starting from the observation that all human beings basically share the same cognitive machinery (i.e. the brain or the wetware, as it were) and the same acoustic/articulatory apparatus, it would appear a reasonable conjecture that human languages also share certain characteristic traits as a consequence. This hypothesis is supported by another observation, namely that humans, independent of their ethnic or genetic background, are in principle able to acquire any language as their mother tongue. They acquire the language they are exposed to in the initial years of their lives.

The species-wide similarities concerning the cognitive apparatus and the acoustic/articulatory possibilities and constraints make us expect parallels in the structure of phonology, morphology, and syntax holding across languages. For example, we may hypothesise that all languages distinguish vowels and consonants, that all languages at least possess a word class distinction between nouns and verbs, and that all languages have constituent structure.

None of these hypotheses has been left completely undisputed, but there is compelling empirical evidence for their validity. For example, in his crosslinguistic investigation of vowel and consonant systems, Madison (2011) finds striking differences in the degree to which these systems are balanced between consonants and vowels. In Andoke, an isolate language spoken in Colombia, we find a high degree of balance, with ten consonants and nine vowels. In Abkhaz, a Caucasian language spoken in Georgia, fifty-eight consonants are opposed to just two vowels. Nevertheless, even though there are important differences in the vowel and consonant qualities distinguished, the basic contrast between vowels and consonants appears stable.

Similarly, word class systems display great variation cross-linguistically with there being minimal systems that merely distinguish between nouns, adjectives, verbs, and adverbs, and comparatively expanded systems – like English – recognising ten or even more word class distinctions. As a universal, we could propose, then, that languages at least distinguish the aforementioned four categories. However, it has also been argued that there are languages without adjectives and adverbs, rendering the universal contrast that between nouns and verbs. And if we can believe Evans and Levinson (2009: 434), even this contrast is not completely without exceptions, as a language like Straits Salish (spoken in Western Canada) only has predicates and requires nominalisations to appear as relative clauses.

As a final example of a linguistic universal, let us consider constituent structure. Much of current linguistic theorising assumes languages to have constituent structure. There is good reason for this, as for example syntactic operations such as passivisation or clefting typically operate on constituents, and not on isolated words. This is shown in (4) and (5).

(4) a. John ate the big red apple.
    b. The big red apple was eaten by John.
    c. *Apple was eaten the big red by John.

(5) a. John ate the big red apple.
    b. It was the big red apple that John ate.
    c. *It was apple that John ate the big red.

The idea of constituent structure as a linguistic universal seems compelling, as there appear to be no syntactic operations that would, say, reverse the word order of a clause for the expression of some function, even though a hypothetical passivisation operation as shown in (6b) would in principle be feasible.

(6) a. John ate the big red apple.
    b. *Apple red big the ate John.

Table 1.6 *Combined order of basic constituents and adpositions (based on Dryer 2011a, b; n.d.o. = no dominant order).*

	Postpositions	Prepositions	Inpositions	n.d.o.	No adpositions
SOV (565)	374	11	2	14	7
SVO (488)	33	303		28	6
VSO (95)	6	76		3	
VOS (25)		20		1	1
OVS (11)	8	3			
OSV (4)	3				
n.d.o.	54	50	5	8	15

For discontinuous constituents, as for example in secondary predications (*John ate the pizza tired.* 'John ate the pizza and John was tired.') or scrambling, syntactic theories typically offer some mechanism, like, for instance, small clauses in the case of secondary predication. The default assumption is that there are continuous constituents with exceptions being handled by the theory. However, as argued by Evans and Levinson (2009: 440–2), there are serious exceptions to the alleged universality of constituent structure, and, for some languages, dependency grammar may turn out to be the more reasonable approach.

Linguistic universals of the type just discussed are known as 'unrestricted absolute universals' or 'unrestricted tendencies' depending on whether they are exceptionless or not. Nowadays, most universals are regarded as tendencies, and not as absolute or exceptionless. Besides unrestricted or unconditional universals, linguistic typology has a strong interest in dependencies between grammatical properties. These are known as 'implicational universals', as shown in (7). Again, we can differentiate between absolute (7a) and statistical (7b) implicational universals.

(7) a. If a language has property X, it also has property Y.

  b. If a language has property X, it will tend to have property Y.

For example, in a classic article, Greenberg (1963: 78) claimed that 'Languages with dominant VSO order are always prepositional.' In other words, if the basic word order of a language is VSO, then it has prepositions rather than postpositions. We may test this hypothesis using the *World Atlas of Language Structures* (Dryer and Haspelmath 2011; http://wals.info), as it allows us to combine two grammatical features. The results are shown in Table 1.6. And indeed, languages with VSO word order nearly exclusively have prepositions. VOS languages are consistently prepositional. We can even identify another implicational universal in Table 1.6, as SOV languages very strongly tend to have postpositions. This implicational universal, too, had

Table 1.7 *Logical types of universal statement (following Greenberg), taken from Evans and Levinson (2009: 437).*

	Absolute (exceptionless)	Statistical (tendencies)
Unconditional (unrestricted)	Type 1. 'Unrestricted absolute universals' All languages have property X	Type 2. 'Unrestricted tendencies' Most languages have property X
Conditional (restricted)	Type 3. 'Exceptionless implicational universals' If a language has property X, it also has property Y	Type 4. 'Statistical implicational universals' If a language has property X, it will tend to have property Y

already been formulated by Greenberg (1963: 79). As implicational universals rarely come without exceptions, they mostly represent tendencies or statistical universals.

The linguistic universals discussed in the main chapters of the present book will mainly be of the implicational type. What we will encounter in various chapters is the stacking of conditional universals to what is known as 'implicational hierarchies' (see Croft 2004: ch. 5). The general principle is shown in (8). Such chains of implicational universals are usually represented as in (9).

(8) a. If a language has property P1, it also has property P2.
    b. If a language has property P2, it also has property P3.
    c. If a language has property P3, it also has property PM.
    d. If a language has property PM, it also has property PN.

(9)   PN > PM > P3 > P2 > P1

Implicational hierarchies make the prediction that if a language possesses a grammatical property at some point in the hierarchy, it will also possess all properties further to the left. For example, Hengeveld (1992: 68) hypothesises that the availability of word class distinctions follows the implicational hierarchy shown in (10). It predicts that if a language has a distinct class of adverbs, it will also distinguish the classes of verbs, nouns, and adjectives. In the minimal constellation, a language is assumed to have verbs or predicates.

(10) verb > noun > adjective > adverb

A summary of the types of universals discussed in the foregoing paragraphs is given in Table 1.7, the major dimensions being conditionality and absoluteness.

Let us at this point briefly return to the concepts of vernacular universals and angloversals, as introduced in Section 1.3 above. It is quite obvious, I think, that these conceptions of universals are different from typological universals, as the former try to capture phenomena relating to specific forms of language, namely non-standard spoken vernaculars, while the latter are meant to reflect fundamental properties of language that, almost by definition, are not tied to specific varieties.

1.5   Summary and list of keywords

Besides providing an introduction to the objectives and the structure of the present book, this chapter has aimed to achieve a concise overview of varieties of English and develop a set of criteria that can be used for their classification. We have learnt that traditional models, which classify varieties of English in terms of national entities and historical expansion, need to be complemented by models that include language contact and language acquisition. This is necessary to accommodate the many post-colonial Englishes, though also the Pidgin and Creole Englishes. Moreover, we were concerned with identifying the common ground and the differences between sociolinguistics and functional typology. Their common interest lies in identifying patterns in variation data based on formal and functional similarities, finding the relevant determinants of variation, and interpreting these in a theoretical framework (see Bisang 2004). The main difference is that sociolinguistics, and dialectology for that matter, consider variation data within a language, whereas typology investigates cross-linguistic variation, ideally across genetically unrelated languages. Their methodologies are similar, though. For the purposes of the present book, we make use of these methodological similarities and interpret English non-standard morphosyntactic phenomena as specimens of cross-linguistic variation. The overarching goal is to enlighten English variation data by cross-linguistic data and generalisations.

Keywords: absolute universals, agglutinating, analytic, angloversals, British Empire, colonial expansion, consonant systems, constituent structure, Creole Englishes, dialectology, embedded inversion, first language acquisition, functional typology, implicational hierarchies, language contact, language shift, linguistic universals, multiple negation, Northern Subject Rule, numeral bases, Pidgin Englishes, polysynthetic, post-colonial varieties, postpositions, prepositions, second language acquisition, sociolinguistics, statistical universals, subject-verb agreement, synthetic, *tertium comparationis*, third language acquisition, typology, vernacular universals, vowel systems, word class distinctions, word order.

1.6   Exercises

Basic level

1. The term 'variety' as in 'variety of English' serves as the cover term for different linguistic systems. It subsumes traditional notions such as 'dialect'.

Write a short essay (max. 500 words) in which you explain the term 'variety' and discuss the dimensions that give rise to different types of varieties.

2. Explain the term *tertium comparationis*.
3. Kachru (1988) introduced the terms 'inner circle varieties', 'outer circle varieties', and 'expanding circle varieties'.
   a. Explain what these terms mean.
   b. Identify three representative varieties of each circle.
   c. Which alternative classifications of varieties of English can you think of?

Intermediate level

1. The distinction between 'second language varieties' and 'shift varieties', as introduced in the foregoing sections, is an important one, though it is not easy to draw. Try to identify a few parameters that would allow us to capture this distinction.
2. Explain the terms 'analytic', 'synthetic', 'agglutinating', 'fusional', 'polysynthetic', and 'incorporating'. Illustrate each term with one example taken from a language of your own choice.
3. In Section 1.4.2 above, I introduced the term 'platypus language'. Try to explain what is meant.

Advanced level

1. a. Look up the term 'implicational universal' in Croft (2004) and familiarise yourself with this concept.
   b. It has been claimed that verb-initial languages tend to have prepositions, whereas verb-final language use postpositions. Try to provide evidence for this statement using the *World Atlas of Language Structures* (http://wals.info).
2. The distinction between languages, dialects, and other varieties is notoriously difficult to draw.
   a. Develop a set of criteria that allows you to draw this distinction in a systematic way.
   b. It has been claimed that a language is a dialect with an army and navy. Comment on this statement.
3. Explore the website of *Ethnologue*, which gives you an overview of the languages of the world (www.ethnologue.com).
   a. Take a look at English and the places in the world where it is spoken.
   b. Which status would you assign to the Englishes spoken in Tyneside, Zambia, Colorado, Singapore, Barbados, Brunei, Grenada, Malta, and the Seychelles?

1.7   References

Algeo, John (ed.). 2001. *The Cambridge History of the English Language: English in North America, volume VI.* Cambridge University Press.

Bisang, Walter. 2004. Dialectology and typology – an integrative perspective. In Bernd Kortmann (ed.), *Dialectology Meets Typology: Dialect Grammar from a Cross-Linguistic Perspective*, 11–45. Berlin: Mouton de Gruyter.

Burchfield, Robert (ed.). 1994. *The Cambridge History of the English Language. English in Britain and Overseas: Origins and Developments, volume V.* Cambridge University Press.

Chambers, Jack K. 2004. Dynamic typology and vernacular universals. In Bernd Kortmann (ed.), *Dialectology Meets Typology: Dialect Grammar from a Cross-Linguistic Perspective*, 127–45. Berlin: Mouton de Gruyter.

Comrie, Bernard. 2011. Numeral bases. In Matthew S. Dryer and Martin Haspelmath (eds.), *The World Atlas of Language Structures Online*. Munich: Max Planck Digital Library, chapter 131. Available online at http://wals.info/chapter/131. Accessed 22 December 2011.

Cornips, Leonie E. A. and Karen Corrigan (eds.). 2005. *Syntax and Variation: Reconciling the Biological and the Social*. Amsterdam: John Benjamins.

Croft, William. 2004. *Typology and Universals*. Cambridge University Press.

Crystal, David. 1988. *The English Language*. London: Penguin Books Ltd.

Davydova, Julia, Michaela Hilbert, Lukas Pietsch, and Peter Siemund. 2011. Comparing varieties of English: Problems and perspectives. In Peter Siemund (ed.), *Linguistic Universals and Language Variation*, 291–323. Berlin: Mouton de Gruyter.

Deutscher Sprachatlas. 1927–56. Based on Georg Wenker's *Sprachatlas des deutschen Reichs*, started by Ferdinand Wrede and continued by Walther Mitzka and Bernhard Martin. Marburg: Elwert.

Dryer, Matthew S. 2011a. Order of subject, object and verb. In Matthew S. Dryer and Martin Haspelmath (eds.), *The World Atlas of Language Structures Online*. Munich: Max Planck Digital Library, chapter 81. Available online at http://wals.info/chapter/81. Accessed 22 December 2011.

   2011b. Order of adposition and noun phrase. In Matthew S. Dryer and Martin Haspelmath (eds.), *The World Atlas of Language Structures Online*. Munich: Max Planck Digital Library, chapter 85. Available online at http://wals.info/chapter/85. Accessed 22 December 2011.

Evans, Nicholas and Stephen C. Levinson. 2009. The myth of language universals: Language diversity and its importance for cognitive science. *Behavioral and Brain Sciences* 32(5). 429–92.

Filppula, Markku, Juhani Klemola, and Heli Paulasto (eds.). 2009. *Vernacular Universals and Language Contacts: Evidence from Varieties of English and Beyond*. New York: Routledge.

Gilliéron, Jules and Edmond Edmont. 1902–14. *Atlas linguistique de la France*, 10 volumes. Paris: Ed. du Cths.

Greenberg, Joseph H. 1963. Some universals of grammar, with particular reference to the order of meaningful elements. In Joseph H. Greenberg (ed.), *Universals of Language*, 73–113. Cambridge, MA: MIT Press.

Hengeveld, Kees. 1992. *Non-Verbal Predication: Theory, Typology, Diachrony.* Berlin: Mouton de Gruyter.

Henry, Alison. 1995. *Belfast English and Standard English: Dialect Variation and Parameter Setting* (Oxford Studies in Comparative Syntax). Oxford University Press.

Kachru, Braj B. 1988. The sacred cows of English. *English Today* 16. 3–8.

Kortmann, Bernd, Kate Burridge, Rajend Mesthrie, Edgar W. Schneider, and Clive Upton (eds.). 2004. *A Handbook of Varieties of English, volume I: Phonology, volume II: Morphology and Syntax.* Berlin: Mouton de Gruyter.

Labov, William. 1966. *The Social Stratification of English in New York City.* Washington, DC: Center for Applied Linguistics.

Madison, Ian. 2011. Consonant–vowel ratio. In Matthew S. Dryer and Martin Haspelmath (eds.), *The World Atlas of Language Structures Online.* Munich: Max Planck Digital Library, chapter 3. Available online at http://wals.info/chapter/3. Accessed 22 December 2011.

Mair, Christian. 2003. Kreolismen und verbales Identitätsmanagement im geschriebenen jamaikanischen Englisch. In Elisabeth Vogel, Antonia Napp, and Wolfram Lutterer (eds.), *Zwischen Ausgrenzung und Hybridisierung,* 79–96. Würzburg: Ergon.

Orton, Harold and Eugen Dieth (eds.). 1962–71. *Survey of English Dialects,* 13 volumes. Leeds: E.J. Arnold & Son Ltd.

Paulasto, Heli, Elina Ranta, and Lea Meriläinen. 2011. *Syntactic Features in Global Englishes: How 'Global' are they?* Presentation given at the 2nd Conference of the International Society for the Linguistics of English, Boston, 17–21 June 2011.

Schneider, Edgar W. 2003. The dynamics of New Englishes: From identity construction to dialect birth. *Language* 79(2). 233–81.

2007. *Postcolonial English: Varieties around the World.* Cambridge University Press.

Siemund, Peter (ed.). 2011. *Linguistic Universals and Language Variation.* Berlin: Mouton de Gruyter.

Siemund, Peter, Julia Davydova, and Georg Maier. 2012. *The Amazing World of Englishes: A Practical Introduction.* Berlin: Mouton de Gruyter.

Trudgill, Peter. 1974. *The Social Differentiation of English in Norwich.* Cambridge University Press.

2009. Sociolinguistic typology and complexification. In Geoffrey Sampson, David Gil, and Peter Trudgill (eds.), *Language Complexity as an Evolving Variable,* 98–111. Oxford University Press.

2011. *Sociolinguistic Typology: Social Determinants of Linguistic Complexity.* Oxford University Press.

Trudgill, Peter and Jean Hannah. 2008. *International English: A Guide to Varieties of Standard English.* London: Hodder Education.

Winford, Donald. 2005. Contact-induced change: Classification and processes. *Diachronica* 22(2). 373–427.

2008. Processes of creolization and related contact-induced change. *Journal of Language Contact,* Second Thema Issue. 124–45.

Wright, Joseph. 1898–1905. *The English Dialect Dictionary,* 6 volumes. Oxford: Henry Frowde.

See *General references* for Clarke 2004; Crowley 2004; Dryer and Haspelmath 2011; Filppula 2004; Malcolm 2004; Montgomery 2004; Pawley 2004; Trudgill 2004.

1.8   Further reading

Bauer, Laurie. 2005. *An Introduction to International Varieties of English*. Edinburgh University Press.

Crystal, David. 2003. *English as a Global Language*. Cambridge University Press.

Davies, Diane. 2005. *Varieties of Modern English: An Introduction*. Harlow: Pearson Education Limited.

Jenkins, Jennifer. 2003. *World Englishes: A Resource Book for Students*. London: Routledge.

McArthur, Tom. 2003. *The Oxford Guide to World English*. Oxford University Press.

Melchers, Gunnel and Philip Shaw. 2003. *World Englishes: An Introduction*. London: Arnold.

2   Reflexivity and reflexive marking

Reflexive markers are expressions such as English *myself, yourself, himself,* and *herself*. As English reflexive markers are highly polysemous and compete with other expressions in the reflexive domain, we will distinguish very carefully between reflexive markers as form types and reflexive relations as a semantic concept. We will provide an overview of reflexive markers and reflexive relations in Section 2.1. This overview is based on well-known facts taken from the standard varieties. These will be contrasted with observations from non-standard varieties in Section 2.2, where we find astonishing differences both in terms of form and function. Our cross-linguistic comparison in Section 2.3 will provide a frame of reference for the interpretation of the observed phenomena.

2.1   Overview

We may define reflexive relations as the co-indexation of two constituents in a simple clause. In the typical case these constituents are the two arguments of a transitive predicate, i.e. subject and object. Co-indexation means that the two constituents are interpreted as referentially identical – they point to the same referent. In English we can use expressions such as *himself* to achieve this kind of co-indexation. Let us call the constituent that is co-indexed with the reflexive marker its 'antecedent'. A typical example is shown in (1). We may indicate co-indexation by a subscript letter, or by listing the antecedent in brackets behind the reflexive expression.

(1) a. John$_i$ sees himself$_i$ in the mirror.

   b. John sees himself (= John) in the mirror.

If a language has a dedicated marker for the expression of such relations (i.e. a special word or morpheme that is only or at least mainly used to express reflexive relations), we will call this a 'reflexive marker'. Standard English has an elaborate paradigm of reflexive markers that show agreement with the co-indexed noun phrase in terms of person, number, and gender. Moreover, we can distinguish between two series of reflexive pronouns depending on the pronominal form that is contained in them. This is a possessive pronoun in (2a), but an object form of the pronoun in (2b). We may list the form *herself* in either series. In addition to the forms listed in (2), there also is the indeterminate form *oneself* and the sex-neutral singular form *themself*. From a cross-linguistic perspective, this exuberance is quite exceptional.

(2) a. myself, yourself, ourselves, yourselves
    b. himself, herself, itself, themselves

Reflexive markers are used to indicate co-indexation within the boundary of a simple clause, but are not used in this function across clause boundaries, as shown in (3) below. Outside simple clauses, pronouns are used to express reflexive relations.

(3) a. John$_i$ saw himself$_i$ in the mirror.
    b. John$_i$ expected Mary to write a letter to him$_i$ / *himself$_i$.
    c. John$_i$ noticed that Mary saw him$_i$ / *himself$_i$ in the mirror.

The contrasts shown in (3), as well as the ensuing generalisations, are fairly robust in standard English, but we need to bear in mind that the distinctions are not completely categorical. Pronouns can be found in a co-indexing function within simple clauses, even as the co-arguments of a transitive predicate. In addition, reflexive markers can appear in this function across clause boundaries. We show the use of simple pronouns in a reflexivising function in (4). In metaphorical interpretations, reflexive pronouns are even inadmissible in these contexts, as in (5). Example (6) illustrates the use of a reflexive marker across clause boundaries. Huddleston and Pullum (2002: 1484) refer to cases such as (6) as 'override reflexives'.

(4) a. The hunter$_i$ noticed an ugly dragon near him$_i$.
    b. John$_i$ pulled a blanket over him$_i$.
(5) John$_i$ left his family behind him$_i$ / *himself$_i$.
(6) Marie$_i$ desperately wanted to be told what to do but there was no one but herself$_i$ to rely on. [*BNC*]

The distributional details of simple pronouns and reflexive markers in reflexivising functions are extremely complex and the amount of literature on this topic is vast. Since we cannot go into these details here, some suggestions for further reading are provided at the end of this chapter. However, we need to understand the difference between reflexivity as a function (i.e. co-indexation) and the means used for achieving this function (i.e. pronouns and reflexive markers). In fact, it is useful to refer to expressions such as *myself, yourself*, etc. as '*self*-forms' to avoid confusion.

We also need to bear in mind that reflexive relations can be understood without there being an overt marker expressing them. In English, this is prominently the case with so-called 'verbs of grooming' or 'verbs of bodily care', which are transitive and interpreted as semantically reflexive, even though the slot for the direct object may be left empty. This is shown in (7) below.

(7) a. John shaved. 'John shaved himself.'

    b. Mary dressed. 'Mary dressed herself.'

In addition to their reflexive function, complex *self*-forms in English also appear in a completely different function that is often referred to as 'intensive' or 'emphatic'. In this function, the *self*-forms appear as a modifier behind a noun phrase or verb phrase, as shown in (8), that is to say they occur in non-argument positions. Complex *self*-forms in these intensifying functions are always prosodically prominent.

(8) a. The president himself died in the aircraft accident.

    b. The bank robbers tried to open the stolen safe themselves.

In the adnominal function illustrated in (8a), where the intensifying *self*-form occurs in juxtaposition to the noun phrase modified, it evokes alternatives to the referent picked out by the noun phrase and characterises these alternative values as related, though somehow less important to the referent of the noun phrase. Plausible alternatives to the president in (8a) could be his ministers, his advisors, and similar entourage. In the adverbial function, as shown in (8b), the entire verb phrase is modified and contrasted with contextually salient alternatives. In the context of (8b), this could be a situation in which the bank robbers ask someone else to open the safe, resulting in a typical 'delegation reading'.

    In contrast with Spanish, German, and many other Indo-European languages, English reflexive markers are not widely employed as markers of middle situation types. Technically speaking, the middle is a voice distinction comparable to active and passive even though it ranges in between these established voice contrasts along many dimensions (e.g. the agentivity of the subject). English complex *self*-forms, nevertheless, can be found as markers of middle situations types, as shown in (9). The relevant middle interpretations predominantly occur in the context of certain verbs (Siemund 2010).

(9) a. An important idea suggested itself to me.

    b. The antidote produces itself very quickly.

2.2   Varieties of English

We will now turn to a discussion of reflexivity and reflexive marking in varieties of English. In this section, we will focus on non-standard varieties of English and largely exclude the standard varieties, only including them for contrastive purposes.

    The marking of reflexive relations in non-standard varieties differs from that in the standard varieties along a number of parameters. The most important of these concern the inventory of forms (Section 2.2.1), the use of simple pronouns for the expression of reflexive relations (Section 2.2.2), and the use of complex *self*-forms in non-reflexive contexts (Section 2.2.3).

2.2.1   Inventory of forms

In Section 2.1, we pointed out that there are two series of reflexive pronouns in English. One is formed on the basis of possessive pronouns (e.g. *myself*), whereas in the other series we find the object form of a pronoun used (e.g. *himself*). These differences notwithstanding, reflexive pronouns in English invariably consist of a pronoun and the form *self*, which also has a plural form (*selves*).

As far as this inventory of expressions is concerned, the most common type of morphological variation is the lack of number agreement between pronoun and *self*, as evidenced by the forms *ourself, yourself*, and *themself*. According to Kortmann and Szmrecsanyi (2004: 1158), this feature is especially prominent in L2 Englishes, as well as Pidgin and Creole varieties. Sakoda and Siegel (2004: 766) list it for Hawai'i Creole. Moreover, it is attested in the traditional dialects of the southeast and the southwest of England (Anderwald 2004: 177; Wagner 2004: 165), as well as in southern varieties of American English (Kautzsch 2004: 351; Montgomery 2004: 263). Examples of this phenomenon include those listed in (10).

(10) a. We keep it to *ourself*. [Jamaican English, *ICE*-Jamaica: S2A-047]
      b. Yes, we made that *ourself*. [Southwest of England, Wagner 2004: 165]
      c. They would've never forgiven *themself* for allowing me out on the deck. [Southeast of England, Anderwald 2004: 178]
      d. They'd all go and enjoy *themself*. [Appalachian English, Montgomery 2004: 263]
      e. Dang you ones. If you want them out, get in and get them *yourself*. [Appalachian English, Montgomery 2004: 263]

In Pidgin and Creole varieties, the number neutral forms of 'self' may appear as *sef* (e.g. Nigerian Pidgin English, Faraclas 2004: 850) and *selp* (e.g. Torres Strait Creole, Shnukal 1988: 33–4).[1] You can find examples in (11) and (12).

(11) Ai go   elpe *maiselp* apta.
      I   will help myself   later
      'I'll serve myself later.' [Torres Strait Creole, Shnukal 1988: 33]

(12) A si   ma *sef* for   glas
      I see my self LOC glass
      'I saw myself in the mirror.' [Nigerian Pidgin English, Faraclas 2004: 850]

---

[1] In Torres Strait Creole we also find dual reflexives: *Demtu pipi demtuselp*. 'The two of them wet the two of themselves.' (Shnukal 1988: 34).

Furthermore, it is noteworthy that many varieties of English rather consistently use possessive forms in reflexive pronouns, i.e. possessive pronouns occur in the entire paradigm. This is shown in (13) below, where (13a) gives the singular series and (13b) the plural series.

(13) a. *myself, yourself, hisself, herself, itsself*

    b. *ourselves, yourselves, theirself/theirselves*

The occurrence of this feature is a good indicator of traditional dialects spoken in Great Britain, Australia, and the United States (Cheshire et al. 1993: 77; Kortmann and Szmrecsanyi 2004: 1163). We may interpret the paradigm in (13) as the result of regularisation processes:

(14) a. [He] put his hand to steady *hisself* on top of the winch. [Southeast of England, Anderwald 2004: 178]

    b. He was just up there by *hisself*. [Appalachian English, Montgomery 2004: 263]

    c. And then they went and locked *theirselves* out of the trailer. [Colloquial American English, Murray and Simon 2004: 227]

    d. ... they call *theirself* A-1 Builders ... [Southwest of England, Wagner 2004: 165]

Another strategy for regularising the paradigm of *self*-expressions is the use of the object pronoun as the base form, resulting in the non-standard form *meself*. This feature seems to be especially common in Australia, as well as in the British Isles. In the relevant regions, *me* is often used as a possessive pronoun (Beal 1993: 205–6; Edwards 1993: 230; Burridge 2004: 1118; Kortmann 2004: 1097–8). We may interpret this use of *me* as an extension of the object form to possessive contexts. Alternatively, one might hypothesise that these cases of *me* did not participate in the Great Vowel Shift. (15) provides some illustration.

(15) a. No I want to do it *meself*. [Irish English, *ICE*-Ireland: S1A-088]

    b. I thought to *meself* 'Possession's nine points of the bloody law.' [Australian Vernacular English, Pawley 2004: 613]

    c. I had ten bob. Two bob for *meself* and eight bob for the board and lodging. [Southeast of England, Anderwald 2004: 178]

As reflexive relations may also be expressed by simple pronouns, we would in principle also have to discuss the variation across the paradigm of personal pronouns at this point. However, such a move would divert our discussion into a completely different domain. You can find some information on that in Chapters 3 and 4.

Let us now turn to another way of forming reflexive pronouns that is primarily found in English Pidgin and Creole varieties. There, reflexive markers may consist of a pronominal form followed by a noun describing a body part, such as 'head', 'body', or 'skin'. This is illustrated in (16)–(18). Notice that these examples easily allow for a literal interpretation besides the reflexive (i.e. grammatical) interpretation. Muysken and Smith (1995a: 272, 1995b: 46) also report the noun *skin* in reflexive uses for Saramaccan (*en sikin* 'he skin').

(16) Em i   hangamapim em yet.
     he PM hanged   he head
     'He hanged himself.' [Tok Pisin, Mühlhäusler et al. 2003: 19]

(17) Dì man bit   im bodi
     the man beat him body
     'The man beat himself.' [Nigerian Pidgin, Faraclas 1996: 103]

(18) wassi ju   skin na   beló tu.
     wash you skin LOC down too
     'Wash yourself at the lower part too.' [Sranan, van den Berg 2009: 6]

The use of body-part nouns to express reflexive relations is a typical process of metonymic construal relying on the well-known *pars pro toto* relationship where a part stands for the whole. This reflexivisation strategy is not only attested in English Pidgin and Creole varieties, but also in those that are based on other lexifier languages (Muysken and Smith 1995a, 1995b).

2.2.2   The use of simple pronouns for the expression of reflexive relations

Earlier on, I pointed out that it is important to distinguish between reflexive relations as a functional concept (i.e. the co-indexation or coreference of two nominal constituents) and the linguistic forms available in a language that can or must be used to express such coreference. The two types of expression that compete with one another in this functional domain in English are complex *self*-forms and personal pronouns.[2] In standard English, complex *self*-forms are obligatory for the expression of coreference between two argument positions of a transitive predicate (subject, object). Conversely, simple pronouns are compulsory if coreference is expressed across clause boundaries. The two types of expression may be used alternatively in adjunct positions (see example (4) above).

It is a matter of great debate as to how strictly the simple scenario sketched above is adhered to in standard English, as linguists have observed the use of simple pronouns in argument positions of transitive predicates and the use of complex *self*-forms for the expression of coreference across clause boundaries. To a certain extent, this debate is certainly due to a (necessarily) imprecise definition of standard English. Rather than try to make the notion of standard English more precise, we will here take a systematic look at non-standard varieties trying to evaluate the emerging patterns.

---

[2] For the sake of completeness, we also need to mention full noun phrases (*John criticised John*) and zero marking of reflexive relations (*John shaved*) at this point.

We may note, first of all, that non-standard varieties of English typically allow the use of simple pronouns for the co-indexation of subject and object position, even though their occurrence in indirect object position is more common than in direct object position. Example (19) below illustrates this with a line from a famous song text.

(19) When I was a young man, courting the girls, I played me a waiting game... [Christian 1991: 14]

Example (19) is taken from a study on Appalachian English (Christian 1991) in which the use of simple pronouns for such a reflexivising function in indirect object position is amply attested. Consider the examples in (20). Additional examples can be found in Montgomery (2004: 263). Two examples from Cape Flats English (spoken in Cape Town) are shown in (21).

(20) a. He was looking to buy *him* a house for his family.
  b. He wanted some straw to build *him* a house out of.
  c. I traded it, sold it for twenty-five dollars and bought *me* a pony.
  d. We'd head out up in them trees and roll that stuff up and make *us* cigarettes, you know, and smoke that.
  [Appalachian English, Christian 1991: 15–17]

(21) a. I'm going to buy *me* biscuits and chocolates.
  b. We all take *us* down to Hout Bay for the day.
  [Cape Flats English, McCormick 2004: 999]

We will come back to this 'benefactive dative' construction in Chapter 11 in the context of ditransitive and double-object constructions. In the present context, we may note that benefactive datives are more common in the first person than in the other persons, even though examples with third person pronouns are attested, as outlined in (20). In colloquial varieties of English that are not bound to a specific region, we can expect the preference ranking illustrated in (22), as perhaps the ambiguity in (22c) is too strong.

(22) a. I brewed me a cup of coffee.
  b. You brewed you a cup of coffee. (marginal)
  c. He brewed him a cup of coffee. (typically non-reflexive)

Let us now also take a look at personal pronouns encoding reflexive relations that occur in direct object position. Such usage of pronouns is attested for some of the traditional dialects, as shown in (23) and (24).

(23) a. He has cut him. (= himself)
  b. He went to bathe him. (= himself)
  [Yorkshire English, Wright 1898–1905: volume III, 164]

(24) He wouldn't shift 'im. [Bolton, Shorrocks 1999: 93]

These pronouns are most probably historical relics preserved from the times of Old English, i.e. from the varieties of English spoken between approximately 500 and 1100 AD, when dedicated reflexive markers did not exist and simple personal pronouns did double duty, serving as pronouns and as anaphors (reflexive markers). The example in (25) gives you a corresponding example from Old English.

(25) hine he bewerað mid wæpnum.

　　　him he defended with weapons

　　　'he defended himself with weapons' [Old English, Aelfric's Grammar 96.11, Zupitza 1966]

This reflexive use of personal pronouns in direct object position has also been reported from Pidgin and Creole Englishes, as shown in (26).

(26) bunne jorka kibri hem,

　　　good ghost hide him

　　　ougri jorka de   wakka va meki trobbi.

　　　evil   ghost ASP walk to make trouble

　　　'While the good ghost hides himself, the evil ghost goes out to make trouble.' [Sranan, van den Berg 2009: 5]

What I find noteworthy is that these pronouns occur in the third person, even though a clear ambiguity between reflexive and non-reflexive interpretation arises. This means that speakers can tolerate ambiguities – and hence rely on the context for disambiguation – even in the domain of reflexive marking where it would appear quite 'necessary' to distinguish between *hiding oneself* and *hiding someone else*. The ambiguity does not arise in the first person, so that examples like *I washed me* are easily interpretable, even in standard English.

2.2.3　The use of complex self-*forms in the position of simple pronouns*

In the previous section, we looked at the use of simple pronouns in positions where standard English requires complex *self*-forms. Let us now turn to an investigation of the opposite scenario, namely the use of complex *self*-forms in the position of simple pronouns. In these positions, complex *self*-forms are not used for the marking of coreference of two argument positions of a transitive predicate, nor are they used for the marking of coreference between two nominal arguments contained in the same minimal clause. The use of complex *self*-forms in a function similar to that of simple pronouns is a prominent feature of Irish English, where such *self*-forms can appear even in subject position. Consider (27):

(27) a. I'm afraid *himself* {the master of the house} will be very angry when he hears about the accident to the mare.

　　b. Is *herself* {i.e. the mistress} at home yet Jenny?

　　c. {Could fairies get back to Heaven?} Well, I wouldn't know now. Could *yourself* imagine they would?

　　[Irish English, Filppula 1999: 80–2]

Notice that the *self*-forms in (27) do not belong to the intensifying type, as introduced at the end of Section 2.1 above (i.e. *John cleaned the carpet himself*), since they occur in an argument position (the subject position) and are not used as adjuncts or adverbials. Nevertheless, a number of studies have pointed out that there are important semantic similarities between intensifying *self*-forms and the complex *self*-forms in subject position of Irish English (König and Siemund 2000a). For example, we noticed above that adnominally used intensifying *self*-forms (i.e. *the director himself*) characterise the referent of the noun phrase they modify as a contextually central point of reference. Subject uses of *self*-forms in Irish English have a semantics that is compatible with this general meaning. The *Scottish National Dictionary* – representing a variety of English in which such subject uses can also be found – describes the meaning of *himself* in such contexts as follows:

Himself: Applied to the head or chief person in any institution, e.g. a chieftain in a clan, the husband in a household, a minister in a congregation, an employer, the 'boss'. [Grant and Murison 1931–76: volume V, 142]

When we now compare the semantic characterisation of *himself* taken from the *Scottish National Dictionary* with the meaning of *himself* and *herself* in the examples given in (27), the semantic parallels are quite obvious. Moreover, although the use of third person *self*-forms is a prominent and distinct feature more or less exclusively attributed to Irish English, we also find instances of this usage, though not as frequently, in other varieties of English, as the following example in (28) illustrates.

(28) So I do hope Mr Speaker you will urge the honourable member to make the declaration of interest which *himself* has said he was going to make . . . [British English, *ICE*-Great Britain: S1B-051]

We are more likely, however, to encounter such subject uses of *self*-forms in the second and especially in the first person, rather than the third person. Some examples can be found in (29):

(29) a. . . . I trust in you Hon..r that you will be so kind as to Admit my Sister to go on this Passage ticket as my self is not Able . . . [Irish English, Filppula 1999: 81]

b. 'Oh, don't ask me that,' said the Crow, 'didn't yourself feel the cold and ill weather of last night?' [Irish English, Hyde Legend 58, Taniguchi 1972: 27]

It is a matter of some debate as to why first and second person *self*-forms are so prominent in subject position, but it appears that this observation can be related to their meaning as long as we analyse these instances as *self*-intensifiers. Given that the speaker is the most likely centre of perspective in a discourse situation, it is not entirely unexpected that a linguistic expression marking the centrality of a referent is used to pick out the speaker. The same reasoning holds, *mutatis mutandis*, for the addressee.

Table 2.1 *Constraints on the use of untriggered*
self-*forms (Hernández 2002: 272).*

#	Hierarchy
1	spoken > written (press texts > literary texts)
2	myself > yourself > other *self*-forms
3	coordinated NP > picture NP > PP > other contexts
4	non-initial position > initial position
5	long distance to verb / no verb > short distance to verb
6	referent is agent/subject > referent is patient/object

The use of complex *self*-forms in subject position, however, is only the tip of
the iceberg of a much more extensive phenomenon, as complex *self*-forms that
do not strictly co-index subject and object position of a transitive predicate can
be found in various other positions. In the relevant theoretical literature, such
occurrences of *self*-forms are frequently referred to as 'untriggered *self*-forms'
(as current theorising does not predict them) or 'not locally bound *self*-forms'
(as they are co-indexed with an NP from the wider context or are not co-indexed
at all).[3] Some illustration of this is provided in (30).

(30) a. The only English people there besides myself were a couple called
Keith and Doreen. [Longman/Lancaster Corpus]

b. You may be the one person to bring about improvements which will
benefit many others as well as yourself. [*BNC*]

c. At the same time he had the clearest image in his mind of the three of
them: Fred, Daisy, and himself, and it was a spectacle of nothing but
pleasure. [*BNC*]

The occurrence of such untriggered *self*-forms cannot be tied to specific regional
varieties of English (except for the subject cases being used more frequently
in Irish English than elsewhere), as they can also be found in the standard
varieties, albeit with a strong preference for the spoken registers. As regional
varieties typically exist as spoken registers, it is difficult to draw a boundary
between the spoken standard and spoken non-standard varieties. In a study
based on work with informants and digital corpora, Hernández (2002: 272)
identifies a number of contextual hierarchies constraining the occurrence of
such untriggered *self*-forms. They are summarised in Table 2.1.[4]

We have already introduced the first and the second hierarchy, or the preference for untriggered *self*-forms to occur in the spoken registers as well as in
the first person. Hierarchies number 3, 4, and 5 concern the syntactic position

---

[3] Huddleston and Pullum (2002: 1484) use the term 'override reflexives'; see (6) above.
[4] Additional frequency data of untriggered *self*-forms can be found in Siemund et al. (2012).

of untriggered *self*-forms. It is useful to consider some examples in order to understand what these hierarchies are about. These are given in (31).

(31) a. John and myself were invited.
     b. John noticed a picture of himself on the wall.
     c. a lot of young girls like herself
     d. it was myself; it was myself who . . .

As (31a) shows, the term 'coordinated NP' concerns coordinations of a *self*-form with another NP. The NP may also be a pronoun (*he and myself*), and the *self*-form may occur before or behind the other NP (*John and myself, myself and John*). Moreover, the coordination can occur in various grammatical functions in a clause (subject, object, adjunct). Example (31b) is really about the phrase 'picture of himself' and its inclusion is the result of an extended theoretical discussion of *self*-forms in such picture noun phrases in the Principles and Parameters Framework. In (31c) the *self*-form follows a preposition (not only *like*). Other contexts, as illustrated in (31d), can be subject complements and cleft constructions.

2.3   Cross-linguistic comparison

In this section, we will investigate reflexivity and reflexive marking from a cross-linguistic perspective. Of course, I am not able to offer an in-depth cross-linguistic survey here. The main idea is to compare the data from varieties of English, as introduced and discussed in the preceding sections, with cross-linguistic data, thus providing a better understanding of the relevant English facts in this domain. A cross-linguistic comparison of reflexivity and reflex-ive marking reveals a number of highly salient parameters of variation (i.e. dimensions along which languages can differ in this domain). We will here jointly explore which values of these parameters English, including its regional varieties, selects.

2.3.1   *Morphological form of reflexive markers*

The first parameter that we will look at is the morphological form of reflexive markers. This parameter presupposes that the relevant language has a special morphological form dedicated to the expression of reflexive relations. Notice that this does not have to be the case, as it is not necessary for a language to possess a dedicated reflexive marker. (The same holds for most, if not all, grammatical devices.) The relevant functions or semantic relations can also be expressed by other morphological elements or may simply be left unexpressed. In Section 2.2.2, I pointed out that Old English did not have a dedicated reflexive marker, with simple personal pronouns being used for the expression of reflexive relations. Another language that uses simple pronouns in a reflexive interpretation is shown in (32):

(32) xwâ bawii lohni   nen giwahn.
   Juan saw 3SG.PRO in   mirror
   'Juan saw him/himself in the mirror.' [Mitla Zapotec, Volker Gast]

It is also clear that the absence of a dedicated formal marker produces some vagueness of expression. In the example shown in (32), it is – at least without further context – not clear if the person described by the pronoun sees himself or someone else. Languages that possess a reflexive marker avoid this ambiguity.[5]

For those languages that have a dedicated reflexive marker we can draw a distinction between morphologically simplex reflexive markers on the one hand and morphologically complex markers on the other. German *sich*, Spanish *se*, and Dutch *zich* are simplex markers, because they consist of only one morpheme. Example (33) illustrates the use of German *sich*.

(33) Paul kritisierte   sich.
   Paul criticise.PAST REFL
   'Paul criticised himself.' [German, personal knowledge]

In addition, these markers are used only in the third person, while simple personal pronouns are used in the first and second person. The simplex reflexive markers of Polish (*sie*) and Russian (*-sja*), in contrast, are used in all persons.

(34) Ja umyl-sja.
   I wash.PAST-REFL
   'I washed myself.' [Russian, Julia Davydova]

The reflexive marker of English belongs to the complex morphological type, as it is composed of two morphemes: a pronominal element followed by the form *self*. Similar complex reflexive markers are found in Turkish (*kendi-*) and Greek *o eaftos tu*, as shown in (35).

(35) O Jórgos kritikári ton eaftó tu.
   the Jórgos criticises the self   his
   'Jórgos criticises himself.' [Greek, Katerina Stathi]

We noticed in Section 2.2.1 that there is substantial variation in the paradigm of *self*-forms across varieties of English. There are no reports of varieties in which forms for certain person/number combinations drop out of the paradigm so that, for example, *self*-forms are available only in the third person. However, it has been observed that pronouns of the first and second person may take

---

[5] Ambiguities or cases of vagueness are often considered a problem for the language user, because some function or semantic detail is not clearly expressed. It should be noted, however, that languages typically contain many such cases, since not everything that in principle can be expressed is or needs to be expressed. In our mother tongue, we do not normally notice ambiguities, and it is only when we meet other languages that they become obvious to us and we begin to think about them.

precedence over complex *self*-forms in indirect object positions, especially in colloquial varieties of English (e.g. *I sing me a song*). While such behaviour is attested for first and second person pronouns, it is not so widely found with third person pronouns.

We may compare these distributional facts of English varieties with cross-linguistic patterns of reflexive marking. These show that dedicated third person reflexive markers are more common than first and second person reflexive markers. Moreover, if a language has a dedicated reflexive marker for the first and second person, it also has one for the third person. This generalisation has the status of an implicational universal and is shown in (36).

(36) third person > second person > first person [Faltz 1985: 120]

2.3.2   *Inflecting and non-inflecting reflexive markers*

A second parameter of variation concerns the morphological variability of the reflexive marker. In some languages, the reflexive marker never changes its form and is in terms of its overt realisation independent of the context in which it occurs. The reflexive marker *sich* of German is such a candidate. It can be used with singular and plural antecedents, as well as in accusative and dative slots. Its form never changes and always remains *sich*. In contrast, the Turkish reflexive marker *kendi-* takes up inflectional endings marking person, number, and case, as shown in (37).

(37) Ali kendi-si-ni   sav-un-du.
      Ali self-3SG.POSS-ACC defend-PAST-3SG
      'Ali defended himself.' [Turkish, Yasemin Şahingöz]

Such inflecting reflexive markers can also be found in Slavic and Semitic languages, and also in Japanese the reflexive marker *jibun* takes a case suffix. Germanic languages typically have non-inflecting reflexives – with the exception of English, where the complex reflexives inflect for person, number, and gender. In other words, English does not pattern with its closest relatives on this parameter. Table 2.2 illustrates these marking patterns for a selection of languages.

2.3.3   *Identity and non-identity of reflexive markers with intensive* self-*forms*

The third parameter of variation that I would like to draw your attention to concerns the formal identity of reflexive markers with intensifying *self*-forms (also called 'emphatic reflexives'). English is among the languages that do not draw a formal distinction between these two functions, as shown in (38). Put differently, the function of co-indexing two argument positions of a transitive

Table 2.2 *Grammatical distinctions marked on reflexives (adapted from König and Siemund 2000b: 51).*

Language	Person	Number	Gender	Case
German	−	−	−	−
English	+	+	+	−
Turkish	+	+	−	+
Hungarian	+	+	−	+
Amharic	+	+	+	+
Arabic	+	+	−	+
Hebrew	+	+	+	+

verb and the intensifying function are taken over by the same expression (e.g. *himself*).

(38) a. The professor himself criticised the student. (intensive)
     b. The professor criticised himself. (reflexive)

In the context of other Germanic, even European, languages, English turns out to be quite exceptional in this respect. Most of the other European languages, with the exception of Basque, Finnish, Irish, and Hungarian, distinguish these functions on the level of expression, as shown in (39) for German. In this language, the reflexive marker *sich* contrasts with the intensifying *self*-form *selbst*, even though the reflexive marker may itself be modified by the *self*-intensifier.[6] In Irish, the two functions are collapsed in one form, as in (40).

(39) a. Der Professor *selbst* kritisierte den Studenten (intensive)
        the professor INT   criticised the student
        'The professor himself criticised the student.'
     b. Der Professor kritisierte sich   (selbst) (reflexive)
        the professor criticised REFL (INT)
        'The professor criticised himself.'
        [German, personal knowledge]

(40) a. Ghortaigh Seán é   féin (reflexive)
        hurt.PAST John MASC.SG self
        'John hurt himself.'
     b. Tháinig   Seán é   féin (intensive)
        come.PAST John MASC.SG self
        'John himself came.'
        [Irish, Lukas Pietsch]

---

[6] Notice that German *selbst* is etymologically related to English *self*, but *self* is not related to German *sich*. A cognate form of German *sich* did not exist even in Old English.

König and Siemund (2011) subjected this parameter of variation to a comprehensive cross-linguistic analysis investigating nearly 200 languages. The results show that about half of the world's languages use the same expression for reflexive marking and intensifying function, while the other half formally differentiate between the two functions. Nevertheless, there are striking areal clusters. For example, Europe is a linguistic area in which the two functions are typically differentiated. Asia, in contrast, is an area where the two functions are typically collapsed in the same expression.

Even though this parameter of variation is not immediately relevant for our discussion on varieties of English, as there appear to be no varieties that have a formally independent reflexive marker,[7] we mentioned earlier on in Section 2.2.2 that simple personal pronouns have been reported to appear in a reflexivising function in non-standard varieties of English. In using simple personal pronouns in a reflexivising function, these varieties effectively draw a formal distinction between intensifying and reflexivising function.

2.3.4   Binding domain

The term 'binding domain' refers to the structural distance between a reflexive anaphor and its antecedent. This term, as well as the underlying concept, is motivated by the observation that a reflexive pronoun can be co-indexed (i.e. be coreferential) with a noun phrase antecedent only within certain structural boundaries. This means that once a certain level of structural embedding has been surpassed, co-indexation becomes impossible. In English, a crucial boundary curtailing the co-indexing of a reflexive marker with an antecedent is the clause. Recall that we showed in Section 2.1 how a reflexive marker can find an antecedent in the same minimal clause, though not beyond it. In (41) below, the simple pronoun *her* can be coreferential with the subject of the matrix clause (*Mary*) while the *self*-form is co-indexed with the subject of the embedded clause (*Sarah*).

(41) Mary$_i$ realised that Sarah$_j$ criticised her$_{i/*j}$ / herself$_{j/*i}$.

Moreover, we also said that certain occurrences of English reflexive markers violate this clause-mate condition and may find their antecedent even across clause boundaries and across another subject (so-called 'untriggered reflexives'). Another such case is given in (42).

(42) John realised that everyone was happy except himself.

The binding domain or structural distance between reflexive marker and antecedent is a widely discussed cross-linguistic parameter of variation, as

---

[7] Varieties that use body-part nouns as reflexive markers may distinguish formally between reflexive and intensive expressions.

languages show substantial differences in this respect. As for standard English, simple pronouns and reflexive markers are in strict complementary distribution in the (direct) object position of transitive predicates, whereas the complementarity is less strict in other structural positions (indirect object, adjunct positions):

(43) a. John$_i$ criticised him$_{*i/j}$ / himself$_{i/*j}$.

   b. Mary$_i$ noticed the thief behind her$_{i/j}$ / herself$_i$.

In German, by contrast, the reflexive marker *sich* is obligatory for the expression of reflexive relations within the boundaries of a simple clause, including adjuncts, though never beyond it. In Icelandic, the reflexive marker can be co-indexed with the subject of the matrix clause even when it is contained in an embedded clause. This is shown in (44).

(44) Pétur bað Jens um að raka sig.

  Peter asked Jens for to shave REFL

  'Peter asked Jens to shave him/himself.' [Icelandic, Thráinson 1991: 51]

The so-called 'long-distance bound' reflexives of Icelandic have attracted enormous attention in the relevant theoretical literature, and over the years several other languages have been identified where the reflexive marker shows similar properties. In Mandarin Chinese, for instance, the reflexive marker *ziji* can find its antecedent across several clause boundaries:

(45) Zhangsan shuo Lisi chang piping ziji.

  Zhangsan say Lisi often criticise self

  'Zhangsan said that Lisi often criticised Lisi/Zhangsan.' [Mandarin, Huang and Tang 1991: 275]

The cross-linguistic comparison of reflexive markers has revealed that there can be considerable differences in the binding domain of these expressions that are difficult to capture by syntactic parameters alone. For example, it is undisputed by now that morphologically simplex and complex reflexives show a different behaviour in this respect and that the so-called 'long-distance binding' is influenced by the mood of the preceding verb form (subjunctive) and pragmatic constraints such as perspectivisation, meaning that the antecedent of long-distance bound reflexives is often the centre of perspective of the current textual passage.

  There have also been attempts to analyse the untriggered *self*-forms of English as cases of long-distance binding and to compare them with similar phenomena found in Icelandic and Mandarin, as shown above. Even though the pragmatic constraint on perspectivisation is clearly relevant for untriggered *self*-forms of English, too, and explains the dominance of first person *self*-forms in the relevant contexts (as the speaker is usually the centre of perspective), their high frequency in the spoken registers and in coordinations is difficult to make sense of and does not have obvious parallels in other languages.

Table 2.3 *Body-part nouns as lexical sources of reflexive markers (adapted from Schladt 1999: 120–4).*

Language	Reflexive marker	Lexical source
Georgian	*tav-*	'head'
Igbo	*ònwo*	'body'
Finnish	*itse*	'reflection on water'
Hebrew	*atsm-*	'bone'
Arabic	*nafs*	'soul'
Maba	*ndu*	'skin'
Tzotzil	*ba*	'face'

2.3.5 Body-part nouns as a lexical source of reflexive markers

In the context of our discussion of reflexive marking in Pidgin and Creole Englishes in Section 2.2.1, we have already encountered body-part nouns as a lexical source of reflexive markers. We may conjecture that in the relevant Pidgin and Creole Englishes (Tok Pisin, Nigerian Pidgin English, Sranan) the body-part reflexives have their origin in language contact processes. In other words, it is likely that the substrate languages of these Pidgin and Creole Englishes possess reflexive markers based on body-part nouns.

Table 2.3 shows languages from diverse families that have reflexives whose lexical source is a body-part noun. This strategy of forming reflexive markers is quite widespread cross-linguistically. Incidentally, a body-part etymology has even been proposed for English *self*.

2.4 Summary and list of keywords

In this chapter, we explored reflexive markers and the encoding of reflexive relations in non-standard varieties of English. Starting from an overview of this grammatical domain in the standard varieties, we learnt that non-standard reflexive markers may assume different forms and show different distributions. Many of these differences can be analysed as systematic extensions of the standard systems. We also interpreted the non-standard phenomena in terms of the major cross-linguistic parameters of variation in the domain of reflexivity. This comparison revealed many parallels between non-standard phenomena and cross-linguistically attested encoding strategies.

Keywords: adjuncts, anaphors, antecedent, argument, benefactive dative, binding domain, body-part nouns, co-argument, co-indexation, complex reflexives, coreference, emphatic reflexives, Great Vowel Shift, intensifying *self*-forms, long-distance reflexives, marker of middle situation types, metonymic construal, person hierarchy, perspectivisation, pronouns, reflexive markers, reflexive relations, untriggered reflexives.

2.5   Exercises

Basic level

1. Summarise the most important syntactic and semantic characteristics of argument reflexive *self*-forms, adnominal intensifying *self*-forms, adverbial intensifying *self*-forms, and untriggered *self*-forms as presented in the preceding chapter and try to come up with an example of your own for each category.
2. Collect the inventory of reflexive and intensive *self*-forms found across non-standard varieties of English.
3. Explain the grammatical concept of 'reflexive relations'.

Intermediate level

1. Take a look at the following sentences and try to determine whether the *self*-forms at hand are reflexive *self*-forms, adnominal intensifying *self*-forms, adverbial intensifying *self*-forms, or untriggered *self*-forms.

   a. *My girlfriend and myself went out last night.*
   b. *Much of what the accused himself said in court was an outright lie.*
   c. *The prisoner died after he had stabbed himself repeatedly in the leg with a pencil.*
   d. *According to the police, the hostage, who himself had limited training as a martial artist, could free himself from his hijackers.*
   e. *Placebos can be very effective, particularly if the patient believes in them herself.*
   f. *How, do you think, do teenagers define themselves and their role in society?*
   g. *I had to prepare dinner while himself sat in the front of the telly watching the football game.*
   h. *Mary would like to rename herself.*
   i. *Melvin and yourself are really the best friends I have.*
   j. *The minister made clear that one day he wants to become prime minister himself.*

2. This exercise represents a cloze test experiment, which basically is a context enrichment task. In the examples below, certain words are missing that need to be filled in.

a. Ask ten of your fellow-students (native speakers of English, if possible) to fill in the cloze test below.

b. Compare the results of your survey with the predictions of a reference grammar of English (e.g. Huddleston and Pullum 2002). Do your results and the predictions of the grammar book agree? Do they deviate? Explain.

a. *Mary pushed the offender away from* _____ *her / herself* (Mary).

b. *What can a boy like* _____ *me / myself do against it?*

c. *Sarah knows that Jim fancies* _____ *her / herself* (Sarah).

d. *I make* _____ *me / myself a sandwich.*

e. *I have to get* _____ *me / myself / ∅ a new drink.*

f. *The teacher told the student: 'You are not doing this exercise for me –* *you are doing it for* _____ *you / yourself.'*

g. *The professor supervised the exam* _____ *him / himself.*

h. *Jane, Jim and* _____ *I / me / myself want to go to the pub tonight.*

i. *Susan tried to ignore the alarm clock. She just pulled the blanket over* _____ *her / herself* (Susan) *again.*

3. You have learnt in this chapter that *self*-forms frequently occur in coordinations, i.e. in complex noun phrases conjoined by a conjunction (*and*, *or*). Let us devise a project that compares the frequency of occurrence of such *self*-forms in two varieties of English. Let us compare standard British English with Irish English along this parameter.

a. The *ICE* (http://ice-corpora.net/ice/) offers an empirical basis for the comparison of different varieties of English. Familiarise yourself with the structure of this corpus and procure the components of British English and Irish English.

b. Extract the *self*-forms in coordinations and sort them according to the person, number, and gender of the *self*-form. In addition, mark whether the *self*-form occurs in the initial or final position of the noun phrase.

c. Describe the differences you can find between British English and Irish English.

d. Try to interpret your findings.

Advanced level

1. In standard English *self*-forms are obligatory to indicate coreference in a local domain, as shown by the examples below:

a. *John$_i$ criticised himself$_i$ (*him$_i$).*

b. *John$_i$ made himself$_i$ a sandwich (*him$_i$).*

Non-standard varieties often admit simple pronouns to express coreference, but mostly in the first person and only in the position of indirect objects:

a. *I brewed me a cup of coffee.*
b. **He$_i$ brewed him$_i$ a cup of coffee.*
c. **He$_i$ criticised him$_i$.*

Cross-linguistic work on reflexive marking has revealed that dedicated reflexive markers typically exist in the third person, and less frequently appear in the first or second person. However, if a language has a reflexive marker in the first person, it also has such markers in the second or third person.

   a. Can you see parallels between these cross-linguistic generalisations and the data reported from non-standard varieties of English? Explain.
   b. Try to think of an explanation for the observed restrictions. You may consult Croft (2004: ch. 5) for inspiration on grammatical hierarchies.

2. English untriggered *self*-forms look like what is known as 'long-distance reflexives' since they can find their antecedent noun phrase outside the minimal clause they are contained in.
   a. Familiarise yourself with the concept of 'long-distance reflexives'. You may use the volume by Koster and Reuland (1991) as a starting-point.
   b. Compare English untriggered reflexives – especially those found in Irish English – against the properties identified for long-distance reflexives. Would it be justified to analyse them as long-distance reflexives?

3. In Section 2.3.5, we learnt that a typical lexical source of reflexive markers are body-part nouns (e.g. 'body', 'soul', 'skin', etc.). We also find these sources in non-standard varieties of English.
   a. Explain the linguistic process behind the use of body-part nouns as reflexive markers.
   b. Would you expect body-part nouns such as *toe* or *armpit* to grammaticalise into reflexive markers? Discuss.

2.6   References

Beal, Joan. 1993. The grammar of Tyneside and Northumbrian English. In James Milroy and Lesley Milroy (eds.), *Real English: The Grammar of English Dialects in the British Isles*, 187–213. London: Longman.

Cheshire, Jenny, Viv Edwards, and Pamela Whittle. 1993. Non-standard English and dialect levelling. In James Milroy and Lesley Milroy (eds.), *Real English: The Grammar of English Dialects in the British Isles*, 53–96. London: Longman.

Christian, Donna. 1991. The personal dative in Appalachian speech. In Peter Trudgill and Jack K. Chambers (eds.), *Dialects of English: Studies in Grammatical Variation*, 11–17. London: Longman.

Croft, William. 2004. *Typology and Universals*. Cambridge University Press.

Edwards, Viv. 1993. The grammar of southern British English. In James Milroy and Lesley Milroy (eds.), *Real English: The Grammar of English Dialects in the British Isles*, 214–42. London: Longman.

Faltz, Leonard M. 1985. *Reflexivization: A Study in Universal Syntax*. New York: Garland.

Faraclas, Nicholas G. 1996. *Nigerian Pidgin*. London: Routledge.

Filppula, Markku. 1999. *A Grammar of Irish English: Language in Hibernian Style*. London: Routledge.

Grant, William and David D. Murison. 1931–76. *The Scottish National Dictionary*, 10 volumes. Edinburgh: Neill & Co.

Hernández, Nuria. 2002. A context hierarchy of untriggered *self*-forms in English. *Zeitschrift für Anglistik und Amerikanistik* 50(3). 269–84.

Huang, C.-T. James and C.-C. Jane Tang. 1991. The local nature of the long-distance reflexive in Chinese. In Jan Koster and Eric Reuland (eds.), *Long-Distance Anaphora*, 263–82. Cambridge University Press.

König, Ekkehard and Peter Siemund. 2000a. Locally free 'self'-forms, logophoricity and intensification in English. *English Language and Linguistics* 4(2). 183–204.

2000b. Intensifiers and reflexives: A typological perspective. In Zygmunt Frajzyngier and Traci S. Curl (eds.), *Reflexives: Forms and Functions*, 41–74. Amsterdam: John Benjamins.

2011. Intensifiers and reflexive pronouns. In Matthew S. Dryer and Martin Haspelmath (eds.), *The World Atlas of Language Structures Online*. Munich: Max Planck Digital Library, chapter 47. Available online at http://wals.info/feature/47. Accessed 22 December 2011 (with Stephan Töpper).

Koster, Jan and Eric Reuland (eds.). 1991. *Long-Distance Anaphora*. Cambridge University Press.

Muysken, Pieter and Norval Smith. 1995a. Reflexives. In Jacques Arends, Pieter Muysken, and Norval Smith (eds.), *Pidgins and Creoles: An Introduction*, 271–88. Amsterdam: John Benjamins.

1995b. Reflexives in the creole languages: An interim report. In Dany Adone and Ingo Plag (eds.), *Creolization and Language Change*, 45–64. Tübingen: Niemeyer.

Mühlhäusler, Peter, Thomas E. Dutton, and Suzanne Romaine. 2003. *Tok Pisin Texts: From the Beginning to the Present*. (Varieties of English Around the World Text Series 9.) Amsterdam: John Benjamins.

Schladt, Matthias. 1999. The typology and grammaticalisation of reflexives. In Zygmunt Frajzyngier and Traci S. Curl (eds.), *Reflexives: Forms and Functions*, 41–74. Amsterdam: John Benjamins.

Shnukal, Anna. 1988. *Broken: An Introduction to the Creole Language of Torres*. Canberra: Research School of Pacific Linguistics, Australian National University.

Shorrocks, Graham. 1999. *A Grammar of the Dialect of the Bolton Area: Part II Morphology and Syntax*. Frankfurt am Main: Lang.

Siemund, Peter. 2010. Grammaticalization, lexicalization and intensification. English *itself* as a marker of middle situation types. *Linguistics* 48(4). 797–836.

Siemund, Peter, Georg Maier, and Martin Schweinberger. 2012. Reflexive and intensive *self*-forms. In Raymond Hickey (ed.), *Areal Features of the Anglophone World*. Berlin: Mouton de Gruyter.

Taniguchi, Jiro. 1972. *A Grammatical Analysis of Artistic Representation of Irish English*. Tokyo: Shinozaki Shorin.

Thráinson, Höskuldur. 1991. Long-distance anaphora and the typology of NPs. In Jan Koster and Eric Reuland (eds.), *Long-Distance Anaphora*. Cambridge University Press.

van den Berg, Margot C. 2009. Intensified! On reflexive expressions in Early Sranan. *Revue Roumaine de Linguistique* (Romanian Review of Linguistics), 54(3–4), 331–47. (Special volume on Pidgins and Creoles edited by Andrei A. Avram.)

Wright, Joseph. 1898–1905. *The English Dialect Dictionary*, 6 volumes. Oxford: Henry Frowde.

Zupitza, Julius (ed.). 1966. *Aelfrics Grammatik und Glossar*. Berlin: Weidmannsche Verlagsbuchhandlung.

See *General references* for Anderwald 2004; Burridge 2004; Faraclas 2004; Huddleston and Pullum 2002; Kautzsch 2004; Kortmann 2004; Kortmann and Szmrecsanyi 2004; McCormick 2004; Montgomery 2004; Murray and Simon 2004; Pawley 2004; Sakoda and Siegel 2004; Wagner 2004.

2.7   Further reading

Gast, Volker and Peter Siemund. 2006. Rethinking the relationship between *self*-intensifiers and reflexives. *Linguistics* 44(2). 343–81.

König, Ekkehard and Peter Siemund. 2000c. The development of complex reflexives and intensifiers in English. *Diachronica* 17. 39–84.

Siemund, Peter. 2000. *Intensifiers: A Comparison of English and German*. London: Routledge.

2002. Reflexive and intensive *self*-forms across varieties of English. *Zeitschrift für Anglistik und Amerikanistik* 50(3). 250–68.

2003. Varieties of English from a cross-linguistic perspective: Intensifiers and reflexives. In Britta Mondorf and Günter Rohdenburg (eds.), *Determinants of Grammatical Variation*, 479–506. Berlin: Mouton de Gruyter.

Webelhuth, Gert and Clare J. Dannenberg. 2006. Southern American English personal datives: The theoretical significance of dialectal variation. *American Speech* 81(1). 31–55.

3   Pronominal gender

The expression of gender in English is confined to pronouns of the third person (*he*, *she*, *it*). Therefore, we will here essentially be concerned with this pronominal domain. Nevertheless, we will see that varieties of English may differ with respect to the sets of referents for which they use these pronouns. Moreover, some varieties distinguish only two genders on third person pronouns, while others have only one pronominal form. We begin by providing some background information on the category of gender. Following that, we will explore gender-marked pronouns in varieties of English. Finally, we will embark on a cross-linguistic survey of pronominal gender systems, which will allow us to assess English pronominal gender from a wider perspective.

3.1   Overview

We can define gender as a relationship of covariance between two or more sentential elements and a so-called 'gender controller' that determines the shape of the other elements (the 'targets' of the gender).[1] Consider the examples from German in (1), where the relevant nouns (the gender controllers) determine the shape of the definite articles (the gender targets) that occur in front of them. In German, the controller of the gender also determines the shape of adjectives, pronouns, and some other elements.

(1) a. der Löffel   'the spoon' masculine gender
    b. die Gabel   'the fork' feminine gender
    c. das Messer 'the knife' neuter gender

Strictly speaking, English does not possess a comparable gender system, as only the pronouns of the third person show gender distinctions (*he*, *she*, *it*), though other sentential elements (e.g. adjectives) do not show gender marking.

---

[1] The term 'gender' is here used in its grammatical sense. It has at least two other prominent uses. On the one hand, it is frequently used in the same meaning as biological sex, i.e. male, female, unsexed. On the other hand, gender may refer to the cultural construction of sex, i.e. the development of a sexual identity different from the biological sex. None of these uses is at issue here, where the term exclusively refers to gender as a grammatical concept: masculine, feminine, neuter.

Moreover, the use of *he*, *she*, and *it* follows exclusively semantic principles, while in German and other languages with a gender system based on formal principles of gender assignment the occurrence of masculine, feminine, and neuter gender markers is primarily determined by the phonological and morphological properties of the gender-controlling noun (and therefore usually perceived as difficult to learn). The semantic principles regulating the distribution of *he*, *she*, and *it* are (i) humanness/animacy and (ii) sex, with male human referents triggering the use of *he* and female human referents the use of *she*, while all other referents take *it*, as shown in (2).

(2) a. man, boy   he
    b. woman, girl   she
    c. knife, table, stone it

An additional complication is that pronominal gender markers can occur without a preceding or following noun controlling their gender, since pronouns – besides their anaphoric uses – can also be used deictically. Hence, it is more correct to say that the distribution of these gendered pronouns is determined by the properties of the relevant referents, rather than the nouns encoding them. In the literature on gender marking, we find the term 'referential gender' used for these cases (Dahl 2000). This explains why one and the same noun can occur with different pronouns, here shown in (3), since in these cases the nouns encode different referents.

(3) a. doctor he, she
    b. nurse   he, she
    c. person he, she, they

It also explains why speakers may use alternative pronouns for picking out one and the same referent. As shown in (4), a cow may be referred to by *she* or *it*, even one and the same animal. The same holds for small children or babies, for whom the use of *he*, *she*, or *it* can be found. The observable variation in pronoun usage depends on the knowledge that the speaker has about the referent or the perspective they wish to adopt.

(4) a. cow   she, it
    b. bull he, it
    c. child he, she, it

3.1.1   *Gender as an agreement system*

Gender systems are typical agreement systems in which a controller element determines the form and distribution of one or more agreement targets. We have already introduced this terminology in the preceding section. The agreement relation between controller and target is based on features (formal or semantic) that are typically stored together with the lexical entry of the controller noun, and may take up different values, e.g. masculine, feminine, or neuter in German.

There are many other agreement relations, for example agreement in person, number, case, or grammatical function. English is not the best language to illustrate these agreement relations as it has a very small set of agreement (inflectional) morphemes. Nevertheless, there is some parsimonious agreement between subject and verb based on the features 'number: singular', 'person: third', and 'tense: non-past', as shown in (5).

(5) a. I eat fish.
    b. She eat-s fish.
    c. They eat fish.
    d. She ate fish.

We will come back to agreement systems and introduce additional aspects of them in Chapter 10, where we will discuss subject-verb agreement.

3.1.2 Principles of gender assignment

The gender system of English is best considered as a referential system where the properties of the referents directly determine the distribution of the pronominal gender exponents, i.e. male referents trigger *he*, female referents trigger *she*, and unsexed/inanimate referents trigger *it*. In such referential systems, nouns do not strictly speaking belong to a gender class, and hence it becomes void to speak about 'gender assignment' in such cases.

The term gender assignment is more adequate for gender systems in which the distribution of the gender exponents is determined by the formal and semantic properties of the controller noun, as in the German example shown in (1) above. Even though it is not obvious in these cases why the nouns for 'knife', 'fork', and 'spoon' have the gender they have, it is safe to assume that the gender is stored in the lexical entries of the relevant nouns. In such lexical gender systems, the assignment of a noun to a gender class may be motivated by the phonological properties of the noun (Spanish nouns ending in *-a* are feminine), by certain morphemes (German nouns ending in the diminutive suffix *-chen* are neuter), by certain semantic principles (German nouns for alcoholic beverages are mostly masculine), or by various combinations of these factors. Such gender assignment rules are clearly not relevant for Modern English, but we can find them in Old English – the language spoken in England between c. 500 and 1100 AD – which had a gender system quite similar to that of Modern German.

3.1.3 Dual gender and triple gender nouns

Handbooks of English typically acknowledge the special status of gender in this language. While Quirk et al. (1985: 314) assume a semantic categorisation of English nouns that is reflected in pronominal agreement patterns, Huddleston and Pullum (2002: 485) insist on the referential basis of English pronominal gender. Even though we here adopt Huddleston and Pullum's position, there is no denying the fact that pronominal agreement imposes an ordering pattern on English nouns. For example, nouns such as *doctor* and *lawyer* may occur together with masculine or feminine pronouns. A noun like *child* can be found with masculine, feminine, or neuter pronouns. In the handbooks mentioned above, we can find many largely self-explanatory labels for the resulting groups of nouns, as for example 'dual gender nouns', 'triple gender nouns', 'common gender nouns', 'collective nouns', and so on and so forth. These labels are not meant to suggest that English has nouns that belong to two or three genders, even though Quirk et al. (1985) may be interpreted in this way, but that certain nouns can be the antecedent of more than one pronominal form. Huddleston and Pullum (2002: 489) state that:

a dual gender noun is not to be interpreted as a noun which has two genders: it is a noun which can head the antecedent to a pronoun of either of two genders.

The assumption of referential gender is also supported by the observation that using one pronoun over another for the same referent can express a difference in perspective or stance: for instance, the use of the feminine pronoun for countries, cities, cars, ships, and other vehicles, but also for the sun and the moon, can be used to express affection or special emotional commitment. In doing so, speakers imbue these referents with qualities that are primarily attributed to humans and animates.

3.2   Varieties of English

Variation in the use of gendered pronouns is not as pervasive as in other domains of grammar and regionally quite restricted. However, non-standard forms and distributions of third person pronouns are attested for a number of varieties and have been the subject of extensive research (Pawley 2002, 2004; Siemund 2002, 2008; Clarke 2004; Wagner 2004).

Across varieties of English, pronominal gender basically differs along two dimensions. These are (i) the number of genders distinguished within the pronominal paradigm and (ii) the semantic distinctions introduced by the relevant genders. The semantic distinctions determine the scope of the referents that the pronouns can be used for.

3.2.1   *Three genders in the system of pronouns*

As in the standard varieties, the vast majority of traditional English dialects (native Englishes) draws a distinction between masculine, feminine, and neuter forms in the third person singular. This tripartite distinction is the norm for most English varieties. As we described it in Section 3.1, this point needs no further elaboration.

3.2.2   The complete lack of gender distinctions

In many Pidgin and Creole varieties of English, by contrast, we often find a complete lack of gender distinctions in third person singular pronouns. In other words, one form substitutes the three gender forms of the standard varieties. Moreover, there are varieties such as Tok Pisin, Bislama, and Solomon Islands Pijin that distinguish neither case nor gender, but use one form for all functions:

(6) a. *Em* harim wanpla dok singaut.
       3SG heard a   dog bark
       'He/she/it heard a dog barking.' [Tok Pisin, Smith 2004: 726]
   b. mi kam, yu kam, *em* i   kam.
      1SG come, 2SG come, 3SG PRED come
      'I come, you come, he/she/it comes.' [Tok Pisin, Smith 2004: 727]
(7) a. *Hem* i   holem rop i   taet.
       3SG PRED hold   rope PRED tight
       'He/she/it held the rope tightly.' [Bislama, Crowley 2004: 698]
   b. *Hem* i   kam from masket blong sutum man blo   smoke.
      3SG PRED come PREP gun   PREP shoot man PREP smoke
      'He/she came for a gun to shoot the smoker.' [Bislama, Crowley 2004: 695]

Even though the preceding examples may suggest that Pidgin and Creole varieties do not possess gender distinctions in general, such a conclusion would be too simplistic, as the level of decreolisation appears to determine the availability of gender distinctions to a considerable extent. For example, mesolectal speakers of British, Belizean, and Jamaican Creole are reported to exhibit a more differentiated gender categorisation than basilectal speakers of these varieties do (Escure 2004: 541; Patrick 2004: 428; Sebba 2004: 203).

3.2.3   Binary gender distinctions

Varieties exhibiting a binary gender system are not particularly widespread, most of the candidates for such a classification system coming from the domain of Pidgin and Creole Englishes. Moreover, such systems are difficult to detect, as speakers may master not only the basilectal level, where such distinctions are usually found, but also the mesolectal or even acrolectal level, and may switch between them.

Pure Fiji English appears a good candidate to illustrate a binary gender distinction, especially that of *he* versus *it*. The masculine form is used as a sex-neutral pronoun and may refer to men or women (Mugler and Tent 2004: 773).

(8) a. My mother, *he*'s a primary school teacher in Labasa.

　　b. That woman *he* hit *his* husband when *he* cut [i.e. was drunk].

　　[Pure Fiji English, Mugler and Tent 2004: 773]

In addition, Pure Fiji English possesses two distinct third person singular pronouns. On the one hand, there is the pronoun *fella* (< fellow), which is used for human referents, both male and female. On the other hand, we find the use of the noun *thing* as a pronoun (or incipient pronoun) in this variety, which serves as a pro-form for all non-human referents in place of *it* (Mugler and Tent 2004: 774):

(9) a. *Fella* was drinking grog [i.e. kava] there, during class. But his teaching
　　　is set [i.e. great, good]. But the way *fella* treat us, no good, èh?

　　b. When you on the alarm system you press this button. When you off *the
　　　thing* you press that one.

　　[Pure Fiji English, Mugler and Tent 2004: 774]

In Jamaican Creole, a similar situation obtains. Here, the pronominal form *im* corresponds to standard English *he, she, him, her,* and *it,* and is used as the default pronoun, as it were, that is not marked for gender or case. It may even be used as an expletive pronoun (dummy subject), especially in its reduced form *i.* The reduced form, however, is not used for human referents but only for non-human ones (Patrick 2004: 428).

(10) a. Dis wan swiit *im.*

　　　 this one sweet 3SG

　　　 'This one pleases her.' [Jamaican Creole, Patrick 2004: 415]

　　 b. *Him* lucky we never nyam *him* too...

　　　 3SG lucky we not　 eat　 3SG too

　　　 'It's [a chicken] lucky we didn't eat it too...' [Jamaican Creole, Patrick
　　　 2004: 413]

　　 c. *I* hard fi　　 kraas di　riba.

　　　 it hard PREP cross the river

　　　 'It's hard to cross the river.' [Jamaican Creole, Patrick 2004: 423]

In summary, although very many, perhaps even most, varieties of English draw gender distinctions using different third person pronouns, there are also varieties that show no contrast in this position of the pronominal paradigm. Moreover, pronouns of the third person are the only gender exponents. There appears to be no variety of English that has developed gender exponents that go beyond these pronominal forms. Some varieties show a binary contrast distinguishing between human (animate) and non-human (inanimate) referents through third person pronouns while relinquishing the contrast between male and female referents.

3.2.4 Variation in the use of masculine, feminine, and neuter pronouns

As we have just seen, varieties of English may differ with regard to the number of genders they distinguish within their pronominal paradigms. The second major dimension of variation concerns the scope of the referents for which the individual genders, i.e. masculine, feminine, or neuter pronouns, can be used. In this section, we will be especially concerned with the use of masculine and feminine pronouns for inanimate referents.

In general, such intra-paradigmatic variation of the gender-marking system, which has also been called 'gender animation', has been discussed as a prominent feature of the varieties of English spoken in Newfoundland, Tasmania, and the southwest of England, but it is also attested for Orkney and Shetland English, Irish English, and some varieties of American English (Kortmann 2004: 1097; Pawley 2004: 616–28; Schneider 2004: 1113; Siemund 2008; Wagner 2004). Even though the sporadic use of masculine and feminine pronouns for inanimate objects can in all likelihood be found in many varieties of English, deviations from the standard English system of pronominal gender that follow distinct classificatory principles have been described especially for the traditional dialects of southwest England (Somerset, Devon), Newfoundland English, and Tasmanian Vernacular English (Siemund 2008). The examples in (11) – (13) illustrate the usage of gendered pronouns in these varieties. We will concentrate on these varieties in what follows.

(11) a. [What's the matter with your hand?]
    Well, th'old horse muved on, and the body of the butt valled down, and *he* [the hand] was a jammed in twixt the body o' un and the sharps (bran-pollard).
  b. [Of an ash tree which was leaning over a road, a man said to me]
    Our Frank limb *un* last winter, but I don't never think *he*'ll never be able vor to be a-got upright.
  c. Thick farm on't suit me, *he*'s purty near all plough-land; idn meads 'nough to *un*.
    [Southwest of England, Siemund 2008: 43–5]

(12) a. I brought *he* [toaster] dere from da house.
  b. ... you got to find *he* [ring].
  c. Put the cover an the chest again an' ... locked *un* up screwed *un* up, however they had done with *un*.
    [Newfoundland English, Wagner 2004: 90, 274]

(13) a. What we'll be looking for is a tree with a straight barrel on '*im*.
  b. But this time I'm tell' yez about we was buildin' a garage. *She* was an excavation job.

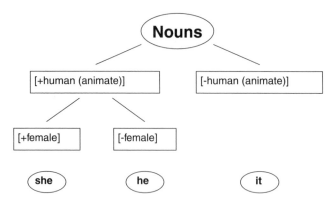

Figure 3.1 Pronominal gender in standard English (Siemund 2008: 148). Reproduced with permission.

  c. That timber gun, *she* splits the log open.
    [Australian (Tasmanian) English, Pawley 2004: 617, 620, 625]
For the sake of comparability, and also to portray these pronominal gender systems more vividly, we will make use of illustrations such as Figure 3.1, which summarises the principles governing pronominal usage in the standard varieties.

As the relevant rules have already been discussed, we will not be concerned with them any further and will now turn to the southwest of England. The examples given in (11) above suggest that masculine pronouns can generally be used for inanimate objects. This would be an oversimplification, though, as inanimate mass and abstract nouns trigger the inanimate pronoun *it* for referring back to them. Two examples of each domain are shown in (14) and (15).

(14) a. Thick there cask 'ont hold, tidn no good to put *it* [the liquid] in *he* [the cask].
    b. That there beef's to gross [too fat], our vokes 'ont ate *it*.
      [Southwest of England, Siemund 2008: 46]
(15) a. Well, that's a purty trick, sure 'nough! But howsomedever, zee nif I don't sar thee out vor *it*, 'vore thee art a twelmonth older, mind.
    b. I sure you, mum, 'twas a terble awkard job, and I widn do *it* ageean vor no such money.
      [Southwest of England, Siemund 2008: 35]
In other words, pronominal gender in these traditional dialects is based on the distinction between mass (abstract) nouns and count nouns. As one would expect, masculine and feminine pronouns are also used for male and female humans and animals, as these are countable. The overall pattern is shown in Figure 3.2.

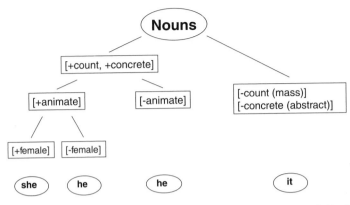

Figure 3.2 Distribution of *he*, *she*, and *it* in the southwest of England (Siemund 2008: 62). Reproduced with permission.

Pronominal gender in Newfoundland English was illustrated in (12) above. These examples look similar to those from the southwest of England – for good reason. Fishermen from the southwest of England used to travel to Newfoundland in summer, as the stock of salmon and cod was exuberant in the surrounding waters. Eventually they settled in Newfoundland, taking their dialects with them. For this reason, the pronominal gender system of Newfoundland English is largely parallel to that of the southwest of England.

There is one exception, though, which concerns the use of *she* for inanimates. In Newfoundland English, the feminine pronoun can be used for various mobile referents, such as ships, cars, and other craft. It is also found with some instruments. This usage is not attested in the southwest of England and may represent influence from North American English (Paddock 1991; Wagner 2004; Siemund 2008). Here are two examples:

(16) a. And when he'd come in in the evenings he'd never ask anyone to pull up his boat fer en, he'd always go, and wherever he was goin' to take *her*, take *her* up, take *her* hold bi the gunnels and take *her* ashore, turn *her* up. 'Tis no odds how heavy *she* was, he never need anyone. [Newfoundland English, Wagner 2004: 258]

b. Da man on top would be stearing *her* [pit saw] and da fellow dat was down under would be sawin'. You had dat line, you had dat stick lined now, *she* had to go faster den dat line to get your board fair see. Yes sir. [Newfoundland English, Wagner 2004: 255]

Since the use of *she* for inanimate mobile objects vastly outnumbers that for other inanimate objects, we may represent the pronominal gender system of Newfoundland English as in Figure 3.3.

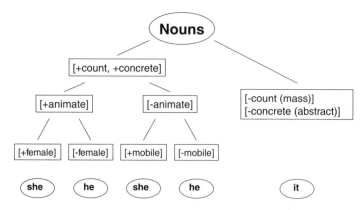

Figure 3.3 Distribution of *he*, *she*, and *it* in Newfoundland English (Siemund 2008: 67 based on Paddock 1991: 133). Reproduced with permission.

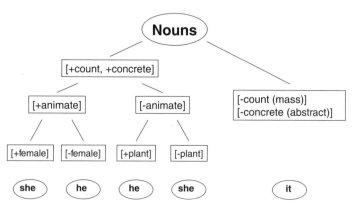

Figure 3.4 Distribution of *he*, *she*, and *it* in Tasmanian Vernacular English (Siemund 2008: 100 based on Pawley 2002, 2004). Reproduced with permission.

Let us finally also take a closer look at pronominal gender in Tasmanian Vernacular English, as described by Andrew Pawley in several papers (Pawley 2002, 2004; Siemund 2008). By and large, the relevant generalisations also carry over to Colloquial Australian English. There, the distribution of gendered pronouns may be summarised as in Figure 3.4.

In Tasmanian Vernacular English, we find masculine pronouns used with reference to trees and plants, whereas for other semantic domains of the inanimate world (e.g. human artefacts) feminine pronouns are mostly used. If we extend the animate universe so as to include trees and plants, which – in keeping with standard assumptions – is not done in Figure 3.4, but which, nevertheless,

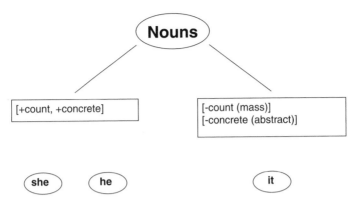

Figure 3.5 Distribution of *he*, *she*, and *it* in regional varieties of English (Siemund 2008: 139). Reproduced with permission.

appears intuitively plausible, we would obtain the generalisation that masculine pronouns cover all semantic domains that are [+animate], except for women and female animals of known sex. The examples in (13) above may help to illustrate these points.

The systems of pronominal gender described in the foregoing paragraphs correspond in their use of animate or personal pronouns (*he, she*) for nouns (as well as the corresponding referents) that are [+count] and [+concrete], as well as in their use of the neuter pronoun for nouns or referents that are either [−count] or [−concrete]. For example, we can expect *he* and *she* to be used for 'cars', 'tables', 'trees', 'houses', 'cups', 'knives', etc., whereas neuter *it* will be used for reference to materials, substances, and liquids, as well as to abstract referents like 'hate', 'joy', etc. This fundamental generalisation is illustrated in Figure 3.5.

Since descriptions of humans and animals are [+count, +concrete] as well, they can be easily subsumed under this generalisation. The division of labour between masculine and feminine pronouns across different domains of the inanimate world, however, varies from dialect to dialect.

3.3   Cross-linguistic comparison

In this section, we will compare the category of gender, as we observed it across varieties of English, with realisations of this category in other languages. As such a comparison can be based on various criteria which cannot possibly be pursued exhaustively here, we need to make a reasonable selection. In what follows, we will therefore restrict our discussion to systems of pronominal gender, as this is the domain where gender marking is pervasive in English.

Table 3.1 *Gender distinctions in independent personal pronouns (Siewierska 2011).*

3rd person + 1st and/or 2nd person	18 languages
3rd person only, but also non-singular	42 languages
3rd person singular only	61 languages
1st or 2nd person but not 3rd	2 languages
3rd person non-singular only	1 language
No gender distinctions	254 languages
Total	378

We will exclude from our discussion all noun phrase internal gender markers, such as determiners, adjectives, numerals, and the like.[2] As a consequence, our focus here will be on referential gender, by and large excluding lexical gender. In addition, we will pursue the question as to whether the well-known hierarchy of individuation (or animacy hierarchy) can be of use in the interpretation of pronominal gender systems, in English as well as in other languages.

3.3.1   Pronominal gender: person and semantic basis

The cross-linguistic study of pronominal gender exponents conducted by Siewierska (2011) reveals that the system of standard English, with gender distinctions drawn only in the third person singular, is the majority pattern. In her sample of 378 languages, gender distinctions in the pronominal systems are distributed as shown in Table 3.1.

It appears noteworthy that the dominant language sets invariably include gender marking on third person singular pronouns, even though other persons and numbers may be included, too. Apart from two exceptions, the great majority of languages in Siewierska's sample are consistent with Greenberg's (1963: 96) Universal 44: 'If a language has gender distinctions in the first person, it always has gender distinctions in the second or third person or in both.' Concerning the interaction with person and number, gender marking on pronouns in standard English follows the majority pattern. Most non-standard varieties behave alike. Gender distinctions on first or second person pronouns are unknown.

We may further note that many languages – the majority in Siewierska's sample – do not distinguish gender on independent personal pronouns. Thus, the English Pidgin and Creole varieties surveyed in Section 3.2.2 that draw no gender distinctions on third person pronouns follow the majority patterns.

---

[2] The interested reader is referred to Corbett (1991) and the relevant chapters in the *World Atlas of Language Structures* (Dryer and Haspelmath 2011; http://wals.info).

Siewierska's (2011) study does not per se reveal the semantic bases underlying the formal distinctions in the pronominal paradigms, even though she remarks that 'Most gender contrasts on personal pronouns are sex-based, i.e. pronouns used for male referents are masculine and those used for females are feminine.'

We may combine Siewierska's study with Corbett's (2011) survey of sex-based and non-sex-based gender systems.[3] According to Corbett, gender systems always have a 'semantic core' even when the arising agreement patterns seem to obey purely formal rules. A frequent semantic basis underlying gender systems is biological sex, and it is certainly not difficult to see why. In a typical situation, nouns describing male humans belong to one gender class, and those for female humans to another. These gender classes may also include some animals, especially animals that are useful for humans. Besides such sex-based systems, there are also gender systems whose semantic basis follows different principles, for example distinguishing animates from inanimates, animals from plants, or edible things from inedible things by putting them in different genders.

The combination of the two studies reveals 15 languages – out of 188 for which this feature combination can be established – that possess gender-marked third person pronouns and a non-sex-based gender system.[4] These contrast with fifty-five languages that have sex-based gender systems and draw gender distinctions on pronouns. An example of a language with a non-sex-based gender system is Plains Cree (a language spoken in Canada), in which gender is based on a contrast between animate and inanimate entities. The cross-linguistic studies do not mention gender systems with a mass/count basis. We will address this problem in the next section.

3.3.2   Mass/count systems

While the pronominal gender system of standard English squares with the majority pattern found across the world's languages (as long as genders are distinguished, that is), the dialectal systems introduced in Section 3.2.4, especially those based on the distinction between count nouns and mass nouns, do not find many parallels in the languages of the world. As a matter of fact, such systems appear to be unknown outside the group of West Germanic languages, and even there, they are confined to regional varieties and do not surface in the relevant standard languages (Siemund 2002, 2008).

---

[3] As described in the introductory chapter (Chapter 1), the online version of the *World Atlas of Language Structures* (http://wals.info) allows you to combine two features.

[4] Another four languages have a non-sex-based gender system, but do not distinguish gender on pronouns.

Pronominal gender systems based on the distinction between mass nouns and count nouns have been reported for many traditional dialects of Germanic languages spoken along the North Sea littoral. We find them in the southern Danish dialect of Jutland, in North Frisian, and West Frisian dialects (Wahrig-Burfeind 1989). For example, in the Jutland dialect, count nouns such as *æ man* 'the man', *æ hus* 'the house', and *æ træ* 'the tree' are pronominalised by the form *den*, whereas mass nouns and abstract nouns, as e.g. *det mælk* 'the milk', *det jord* 'the soil', *det luft* 'the air', and *det skrigen* 'the shouting', are replaced by the pronoun *det*. Consider the example in (17), where the use of the noun *træ* 'tree' results in different interpretations depending on the preceding determiner.

(17) a. *Den*   træ er stor.
        this.CG tree is high
        'This tree is high.'

     b. *Det*   træ er bedst til møbler.
        this.NEUT tree is best   for furniture
        'This wood is best for pieces of furniture.'

     [West Jutish, Gachelin 1991: 85]

These dialectal systems square nicely with the data reported from the traditional dialects of southwest England, as discussed above in Section 3.2.4. It remains a mystery, though, why we find nearly identical systems of pronominal gender in Jutland and in the southwest of England. There may be some sort of historical connection, but it is also conceivable that the systems developed independently of one another.

It is interesting to note in this connection that pronominal gender in modern spoken Dutch shows signs of developing into a mass/count-based system. Traditional written Dutch has a lexical gender system that distinguishes two gender classes called 'common gender' and 'neuter gender'. This gender system is similar to that of Modern German, or Old English for that matter, although it possesses only two gender classes and not three. Dutch gender classes are mainly signalled by articles, as shown in (18), where *de* precedes common gender nouns and *het* neuter nouns.

(18) a. de haring 'herring', de regering 'government', de zonde 'sin' (common
        gender)

     b. het diamant 'diamond', het voedsel 'food', het eigendom 'property'
        (neuter gender)

     [Dutch, Siemund 2008: 182]

The corresponding pronoun for the common gender is *hij*; that for the neuter gender is *het*. In current spoken Dutch, the pronouns frequently occur in conflict with lexical gender, and their distribution comes to be determined by the properties of the referents for which they are used. In other words, the pronouns establish a system of referential gender, with the pronouns being sensitive to the degree of individuation of the referents. This is illustrated in example (19), where the common gender nouns (*de tandpasta*, *de tube*) in (19a) and (19b) are taken up by different pronouns, namely *het* in (19a) and *hij* (19b). Evidently, this is due to the fact that toothpaste is a mass noun, while a tube of toothpaste is a count noun.

(19) a. Is de   tandpasta op?   Ja, *het*   is op.
          is the.CG tooth-paste finished yes 3.NEUT is finished
          'Is the tooth-paste finished? Yes, it is finished.'
      b. Is de   tube tandpasta   leeg ? Ja, *hij*   is leeg.
          is the.CG tube tooth-paste empty yes 3.MASC is empty
          'Is the tube of tooth-paste empty? Yes, it is empty.'
          [Dutch, Donaldson 1997: 62]

Audring (2009), based on a corpus of modern spoken Dutch, shows that this is no isolated phenomenon, but that many similar examples can be found. On the one hand, there are neuter count nouns that trigger the use of masculine pronouns: *gordijn* 'curtain', *masker* 'mask', *huis* 'house', *broodje* 'bun', *beeld* 'sculpture', *glas* '(drinking) glass', and some others. On the other hand, common gender mass nouns are replaced by neuter pronouns: *kaas* 'cheese', *soep* 'soup', *spinazie* 'spinach', *suiker* 'sugar', *gel* 'gel', *kleding* 'clothing', *koffiemelk* 'coffee milk', etc. Gender in spoken Dutch thus offers us a situation of on-going language change, though it must remain open where this process is headed.

3.3.3 The hierarchy of individuation

In order to motivate the differences between the varieties of English discussed in the present chapter, i.e. those of the southwest of England, Tasmania (Australia), and Newfoundland, and between these varieties and standard English, it is useful to take a brief look at the so-called hierarchy of individuation or 'animacy hierarchy' (Silverstein 1976; Croft 2004: 130).

It is well known that entities and the nouns referring to them may be ordered along a continuum, the so-called hierarchy of individuation (Figure 3.6). Proper names, as for instance *John*, *Anne*, and *Peter*, refer to entities that have a comparatively high degree of individuation, which means that they are easily distinguished as an individual, whereas the denotations of mass nouns, such as *homework* or *water*, are only little individuated or not individuated at all. Other noun classes with their relevant denotations lie in between these two extremes.

It has been shown (Siemund 2008) that the distributional differences of gendered pronouns across varieties of English can be linked to the hierarchy of individuation. Metaphorically speaking, masculine and feminine pronouns encroach upon this hierarchy from the left to the right, while neuter *it* proceeds in the opposite direction, i.e. from right to left. For example, masculine

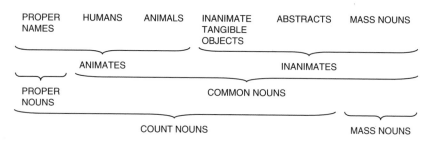

Figure 3.6 Morphosyntactic distinctions along a continuum of 'individuality' (Sasse 1993: 659; Siemund 2008: 4). Reproduced with permission.

and feminine pronouns are used for identifiable individuals (proper names), humans, and some animals in the standard varieties. For the other semantic domains on the hierarchy of individuation, the neuter pronoun is used. Thus, pronominal usage (*he/she* versus *it*) establishes a cut-off point roughly between humans and animals.

In many cases, the difference between standard and non-standard varieties is that the latter place this cut-off point slightly further to the right on this hierarchy. We learnt in Section 3.2.4 that the traditional dialects of southwest England use *he* and *she* for everything countable, whereas neuter *it* serves the domains of non-countables and abstracts. In other words, these varieties place the relevant cut-off point between inanimate tangible objects and abstracts in Figure 3.6.

Most of the cut-off points made available by the hierarchy shown in Figure 3.6 are attested in varieties of English. The use of animate pronouns for the entire continuum is not known, except for some Pidgin and Creole Englishes where only one form is used for the entire semantic territory. We may generalise that *he* and *she* are not normally found for reference to abstract concepts and non-individuated matter.[5]

You may be wondering why I consider the hierarchy of individuation such an important theoretical concept for the interpretation of pronominal gender systems. I am advocating this concept here since it has proved its usefulness and explanatory value for several other grammatical domains, including person marking, number marking, word order, and case marking (Croft 2004). Audring (2008) discusses several cross-linguistic examples of pronominal gender systems that neatly align themselves with the hierarchy of individuation. Siemund and Dolberg (2011) demonstrate its validity for historical processes of gender change. We will come back to the hierarchy of individuation in Chapter 4 in the context of pronominal case.

---

[5] Note, however, that such cases can be found in fictional texts (Svartengren 1927).

3.4   Summary and list of keywords

My principal aim in this chapter was to introduce you to paradigmatic and distributional differences of third person singular pronouns, as we find them across varieties of English. In English, third person pronouns encode gender contrasts, and these play out differently across varieties. We learnt that besides the familiar systems of three genders, some varieties draw a distinction between two genders, while others have no gender contrast at all. In addition, the gendered pronouns may be used for different categories of referents, in contrast to the standard varieties. For example, in the traditional dialects of southwest England, the opposition of animate (*he*, *she*) versus inanimate (*it*) pronouns encodes a contrast between countable and non-countable referents (mass versus count). We also compared the English non-standard systems of pronominal gender with data from other languages, finding surprising similarities. Finally, I introduced you to the hierarchy of individuation as a conceptual yardstick against which we can compare pronominal gender systems.

Keywords: abstract nouns, agreement, anaphoric uses of pronouns, animacy, controller, mass/count distinction, count nouns, deictic uses of pronouns, dual gender nouns, features, feminine, formal agreement, gender assignment, hierarchy of individuation, lexical gender, masculine, mass nouns, neuter, referential gender, semantic agreement, target, triple gender nouns.

3.5   Exercises

Basic level

1. Describe and analyse the gender system of standard English using the following categories: controller, target, agreement classes, gender assignment.
2. Gendered pronouns form a system of paradigmatic oppositions. How many members may these oppositions have in varieties of English? Provide examples.
3. Which semantic distinctions may be encoded by gendered pronouns? Draw up a list of the distinctions found and illustrate them.

Intermediate level

1. Take a look at the following list of nouns:

   bull, goddess, artist, waitress, queen, brother, parent, god, hen, heroine, monk, teacher, king, nun, dog, prince, hero, spinster, waiter, sister, cat, friend, bachelor, princess

Table 3.2 *Pronominal usage in standard English and a non-standard variety.*

Standard English		Variety X	
man	he	man	he
woman	she	woman	she
bull	he	bull	he
cow	she	cow	she
tree	it	tree	he
flower	it	flower	he
door	it	door	she
chair	it	chair	she
rock	it	rock	it
sand	it	sand	it

a. Try to determine with which pronominal gender form(s) – *he*, *she*, or *it* – each of the nouns above can be substituted. Note that some nouns may be replaced by more than one pronoun.

b. Try to assign these nouns to the following (self-explanatory) gender classes: male animal names, female animal names, animal names unspecified for sex, personal dual gender nouns, morphologically marked gender, male personal, female personal, personal unspecified for sex.

2. Consider the following data on pronominal usage taken from standard English and one of the varieties introduced in the preceding sections:

a. Describe the differences in pronominal gender distribution between standard English and the variety as given in Table 3.2. Which system of categorisation do the speakers of this variety of English use?

b. Try to determine from which variety the data in the right-hand column originates. Give reasons for your decision.

3. Take a look at the underlined personal pronouns in the sentences below and try to determine in which variety (-ies) these sentences might surface. Give reasons in favour of your opinion.

a. *Take care and don't break the bottle of lemonade that's in your bag. If he breaks, it will mess up all your stuff.*

b. *After you have hit the tree, you can tell if he's sound.*

c. *Dad made a very nice cake. She was really delicious, you know.*

d. *I really hate this job. It sucks big time.*

e. *She is not a really good bike. You should have bought the other one.*

f. *This coat is really beautiful. He certainly looks good on you.*

g. *Don't put the hammer back in the toolbox. Give her to me.*

h. *Park the car in the garage. I've just washed her.*

i. *You should see a doctor about your hand. He looks really bad.*

Advanced level

1. In the previous sections, I introduced to you the concept of a grammatical hierarchy, especially the hierarchy of individuation.
   a. Drawing on the explications in Croft (2004: ch. 5), describe the properties of grammatical hierarchies.
   b. Explain which predictions grammatical hierarchies make.
   c. Which domains of grammar have been found to be governed by grammatical hierarchies?
2. Reconsider what this chapter said about the hierarchy of individuation and pronominal gender systems. Summarise the predictions that the hierarchy of individuation makes for pronominal gender systems.
3. Audring (2009) analyses the gender system of Dutch and finds phenomena that are quite similar to those that we described for varieties of English in the preceding sections. Read Audring (2009) and identify the differences and similarities between pronominal gender in Dutch and in varieties of English. Write a short research paper of about five pages.

3.6   References

Audring, Jenny. 2008. Gender assignment and gender agreement: Evidence from pronominal gender languages. *Morphology* 18. 93–116.

2009. *Reinventing Pronoun Gender*. Utrecht: LOT dissertation series.

Corbett, Greville G. 1991. *Gender*. Cambridge University Press.

2011. Sex-based and non-sex-based gender systems. In Matthew S. Dryer and Martin Haspelmath (eds.), *The World Atlas of Language Structures Online*. Munich: Max Planck Digital Library, chapter 31. Available online at http://wals.info/chapter/31. Accessed 22 December 2011.

Croft, William. 2004. *Typology and Universals*. Cambridge University Press.

Dahl, Östen. 2000. Animacy and the notion of semantic gender. In Barbara Unterbeck and Matti Rissanen (eds.), *Trends in Grammar and Cognition, volume I: Approaches to Gender*, 99–116. Berlin: Mouton de Gruyter.

Donaldson, Bruce. 1997. *Dutch: A Comprehensive Grammar*. London: Routledge.

Gachelin, Jean-Marc. 1991. Gender and deixis in Southwestern Dialects. *Neuphilologische Mitteilungen* 92. 83–93.

Greenberg, Joseph H. 1963. Some universals of grammar, with particular reference to the order of meaningful elements. In Joseph H. Greenberg (ed.), *Universals of Language*, 73–113. Cambridge, MA: MIT Press.

Paddock, Harold. 1991. The actuation problem for gender change in Wessex versus Newfoundland. In Peter Trudgill and Jack K. Chambers (eds.), *Dialects of English: Studies in Grammatical Variation*, 29–46. London: Longman.

Pawley, Andrew. 2002. Using *he* and *she* for inanimate nouns in English: Questions of grammar and worldview. In Nick Enfield (ed.), *Ethnosyntax: Explorations in Language and Culture*, 110–37. Oxford University Press.

Sasse, Hans-Jürgen. 1993. Syntactic categories and subcategories. In Joachim Jacobs, Arnim von Stechow, Wolfgang Sternefeld, and Theo Vennemann (eds.), *Syntax: Ein internationales Handbuch zeitgenössischer Forschung / An International Hand-book of Contemporary Research* (Handbücher zur Sprach- und Kommunikation-swissenschaft / Handbooks of Linguistics and Communication, 9), 646–86. Berlin: Mouton de Gruyter.

Siemund, Peter. 2002. Mass versus count: Pronominal gender in regional varieties of Germanic languages. *Zeitschrift für Sprachtypologie und Universalienforschung* 55(3). 213–33.

2008. *Pronominal Gender in English: A Study of English Varieties from a Cross-Linguistic Perspective*. London: Routledge.

Siemund, Peter and Florian Dolberg. 2011. From lexical to referential gender: An analysis of gender change in medieval English based on two historical documents. *Folia Linguistica Historica* 45(2). 489–534.

Siewierska, Anna. 2011. Gender distinctions in independent personal pronouns. In Matthew S. Dryer and Martin Haspelmath (eds.), *The World Atlas of Language Structures Online*. Munich: Max Planck Digital Library, chapter 44. Available online at http://wals.info/chapter/44. Accessed 22 December 2011.

Silverstein, Michael. 1976. Hierarchy of features and ergativity. In Robert Malcolm Ward Dixon (ed.), *Grammatical Categories in Australian Languages* (Linguistic Series 22), 112–71. Canberra: Australian Institute of Aboriginal Studies.

Svartengren, T. Hilding. 1927. The feminine gender for inanimate things in Anglo-American. *American Speech* 3(2). 83–113.

Wagner, Susanne. 2004. *Gender in English Pronouns: Myth and Reality*. http://d-nb.info/97211100X. Accessed 22 December 2011.

Wahrig-Burfeind, Renate. 1989. *Nominales und pronominales Genus im südlichen Nordseegebiet: Eine areallinguistische Untersuchung*. Munich: Tūduv.

See *General references* for Clarke 2004; Crowley 2004; Dryer and Haspelmath 2011; Escure 2004; Huddleston and Pullum 2002; Kortmann 2004; Mugler and Tent 2004; Patrick 2004; Pawley 2004; Quirk et al. 1985; Schneider 2004; Sebba 2004; Smith 2004.

3.7   Further reading

Bechert, Johannes. 1982. Grammatical gender in Europe: An areal study of a linguistic category. *Papiere zur Linguistik* 26(1). 23–34.

Corbett, Greville G. 2006. *Agreement*. Cambridge University Press.

Curzan, Anne. 2003. *Gender shifts in the history of English*. Cambridge University Press.

Kruisinga, Etsko. 1905. *A Grammar of the Dialect of West Somerset: Descriptive and Historical*. (Bonner Beiträge zur Anglistik 18.) Bonn: P. Hanstein Verlag.

Mathiot, Madeleine and Marjorie Roberts. 1979. Sex roles as revealed through referential gender in American English. In Madeleine Mathiot (ed.), *Ethnolinguistics: Boas, Sapir and Whorf Revisited*, 1–47. The Hague: Mouton.

Stenroos, Merja. 2008. Order out of chaos? The English gender change in the southwest Midlands as a process of semantically based reorganization. *English Language and Linguistics* 12(3). 445–73.

4   Pronominal case

This chapter continues our exploration of pronominal forms, but approaches them from the perspective of case marking. In English, we find case-marked pronouns such as *I/me, he/him, she/her*, and so on and so forth. We begin with a general overview of case marking as a grammatical category, and then turn to a description of pronominal case in standard English. This will include a description of the distributional variation in the use of case forms, as such variation can be observed even in the standard varieties. The subsequent section will be devoted to pronominal case form variation across regional varieties, including an appraisal of what is known as 'pronoun exchange', i.e. the systematic replacement of subject forms by object forms and vice versa. Following this, there will be an assessment of English case marking against the backdrop of cross-linguistic variation.

4.1   Overview

The linguistic term 'case marking' concerns a specific kind of typically morphological marking in the nominal domain. In Table 4.1 we illustrate this point on the basis of Latin, which is often used for this purpose. You will probably be familiar with these examples, including the relevant terminology.

Nouns in Latin, when used in certain syntactic positions in a sentence, need to carry certain suffixes. In the examples provided above, these are the suffixes *-us*, *-um*, *-i*, and *-o*. These 'case markers' signal, in the order just given, the nominative, accusative, genitive, and dative cases respectively.

You have most probably seen such case marking tables, maybe even from languages other than Latin. They look complicated, especially as case marking may interact with other grammatical categories such as gender or number. In addition, they reveal very little about the function of case marking. So, what is case marking actually about?

Case markers signal that the noun bearing the relevant marker stands in some grammatical relation to another element in the clause. We may illustrate this using the English possessive suffix *'s*, even though its status as a case marker is

Table 4.1 *An illustration of Latin case suffixes.*

dominus		dominum		domini		domino	
domin	us	domin	um	domin	i	domin	o
master	NOM		ACC		GEN		DAT

not entirely undisputed, as this suffix may combine with noun phrases and not just individual nouns (*the man who lives next door's car*). Let us take a look at the example in (1).

(1) John's hat

The *'s* suffix in this example expresses that the nouns *John* and *hat* stand in a relation of possession, *John* being the possessor and *hat* the possessum (i.e. the possessed). More specifically, the noun *John* modifies the noun *hat*, because it characterises the hat more precisely (i.e. not just any hat but John's hat). In this construction, we may call the noun *hat* 'the head' and *John* 'the dependent', as the two nouns enter a relation of dependence mediated by the suffix *'s*.

For the other, more familiar case forms (nominative, accusative, dative) – and also for less familiar cases (allative, perlative, etc.) – we can equally postulate such a dependency relationship, although in these cases the relationship does not involve two nouns, but exists between verbal heads and nominal dependents, or prepositional heads and nominal dependents. This is shown for a verbal head in example (2), and for a prepositional head in example (3).

(2)   Poeta   fabulas   narravit.
       poet.NOM stories.ACC told
       'The poet told the stories.' [Latin]

(3)   auf dem   Tisch
       on   the.DAT table
       'on the table' [German]

Traditional, and also many current, introductions to linguistics are likely to tell you that the nominative is the case encoding the subject, while dative and accusative are object cases marking the indirect and the direct object respectively. This approach shifts the explanation to a different plane, as we now need to make clear what we mean by such notions as subject and object – and this may turn into a long story. As we cannot take up this challenge here, I propose an explanation in terms of so-called 'participant roles' represented by such labels as 'agent', 'patient', 'theme', 'recipient', and 'beneficiary', among others. This approach is useful, since these labels are by and large self-explanatory in that they describe the roles of the participant in the situation or scenario expressed through a sentence. Let us consider example (4) in this context, this time from Russian, which is another language with a case system.

(4) Masha   dala knig-u   Sash-e.
     Masha.NOM gave book-ACC Sasha-DAT
     'Masha gave Sasha the book.' [Russian, Julia Davydova]

In this example, we can say that the nominative encodes the agent or doer of
the giving-event. The accusative describes the object that changes its possessor, frequently referred to as the 'theme'. The dative case, finally, signals the
recipient. You need to bear in mind that the story offered here is not complete,
as it is not possible to capture case marking exhaustively simply on the basis
of participant roles, even though such frameworks as Case Grammar (Fillmore
1968) have tried to reduce all case marking systems to the underlying participant roles. Nevertheless, these roles provide a useful starting-point and have
the advantage of being a transparent and understandable concept.

4.1.1   Case forms in standard English

In the preceding section, we introduced case marking in terms of inflectional
affixes – suffixes, to be more precise – marked on nouns. Case marking may,
and usually does, also appear on other sentential elements such as adjectives,
articles, demonstratives, numerals, or personal pronouns, thus indicating which
elements of the nominal domain belong together and form one nominal group.
The case system of Old English illustrates nicely how case markers appear on
various sentential elements, thereby indicating their mutual dependence, as in
example (5).

(5) ac   ic   wille nu   [. . .] þara   þreora
     But 1.SG.NOM will   now [. . .] those.GEN.PL three.GEN.PL
     landrica   gemære   gereccan
     territory.GEN.PL boundary.ACC explain
     'But I will now [. . .] explain the boundary of those three territories' [Old
     English Orosius, book 1, chapter 1, page 9, line 18; Bately 1980]

Case marking in Modern English, by contrast, is extremely restricted and only
found in the system of pronouns (*I/me*, *he/him*, *she/her*, *we/us*, *they/them*).
The case suffixes shown in example (5) were lost in the transition from Old
to Middle English. As a consequence, nouns in Modern English do not carry
case markers, and the identification of syntactic functions (subject, object, etc.)
primarily depends on the position of a constituent in a clause.

The pronominal forms found in Modern English are shown in Table 4.2
below, based on Quirk et al. (1985: 336). We can ignore the reflexive forms,
as these represent a series of their own and do not offer case distinctions. The
central opposition that we are concerned with here involves the rows labelled
'subjective' and 'objective' in Table 4.2, giving rise to the formal distinctions
already mentioned in the preceding paragraphs. We may add that Table 4.2
contains instances of syncretism in the second person (both singular and plural)

Table 4.2 *Pronominal case forms in standard English (Quirk et al. 1985: 336).*

Subjective	*I*	*we*	*you*	*he*	*she*		*they*	*who*
Objective	*me*	*us*		*him*	*her*	*it*	*them*	*whom*
Possessive dependent	*my*	*our*	*your*	*his*			*their*	*whose*
Possessive independent	*mine*	*ours*	*yours*	*his*	*hers*	*its*		*theirs*
Reflexive	*myself*	*ourselves*	*yourself* *yourselves*	*himself*	*herself*	*itself*	*themselves*	

and the third person singular inanimate. Furthermore, there is a case contrast in the interrogative pronouns (*who/whom*), which, however, is by and large restricted to written language.

Table 4.2 introduces the terms 'subjective' and 'objective' to capture the underlying case contrast and avoids the classic terms introduced above (nominative, accusative), even though these labels can also be found in the discussion of English. This is a reasonable move, and we will adopt these conventions for our discussion, as terms like nominative and accusative were developed for Latin and do not easily carry over to English, especially Modern English. The term 'subjective', then, refers to the form that appears in subject position and 'objective' to that in object position, independent of the distinction between direct and indirect objects.

Table 4.2 also contains two series of possessive pronouns labelled there 'possessive dependent' and 'possessive independent'. The dependent forms occur in front of a noun phrase (*my new car*), while the independent forms function as pronouns (*You've got a nice car. Have you seen mine?*). It is not completely clear whether to include the possessive pronouns (*my, your*, etc.) and the *'s* genitive in the system of case marking.

4.1.2   Invariable usage of pronominal case forms

Even though it is widely believed that English distinguishes between subjective case and objective case in the pronominal system (see preceding Section 4.1.1), it has also been convincingly claimed that the so-called 'subjective forms' are mainly restricted to the position before the finite verb, while the 'objective forms' serve as default forms and can occur in all other positions (Hudson 1995). The main reason for these alternative theories is that we find widespread variation in the domain of case marking. In many environments there is competition between 'subjective forms' and 'objective forms', *inter alia* coordinations (*John and I/me*), left/right-dislocations, independent pronouns, copulative constructions, small clauses, gapping constructions, modified pronouns (*poor little me/I*), etc. Hence, the case contrast established by *I* versus *me*, for example, is not one between subjective and objective case – and not to mention between nominative and accusative – but one between default and non-default forms.

Let us consider a few typical environments where we only find subjective or objective forms. For example, the position left adjacent to finite verb forms is reserved for subjective forms, and objective forms are completely ruled out.

(6) He / *him ate the apple.

Subject positions of non-finite verbs, however, require objective forms. This happens in essentially three contexts, illustrated in (7). The example in (7a) represents a so-called 'exceptional case marking' construction (also known as 'accusativus-cum-infinitivo'), where the objective form of the pronoun may be analysed as either the object of the verb *see* or as the subject of the non-finite verb form *leave*. The example shown in (7b) is known as an 'absolute construction', a non-finite participial clause containing an independent subject juxtaposed with a finite clause. The pronominal form used in the subject position of the participial clause is the objective form. Example (7c), finally, is another use of the *-ing* form commonly referred to by the label 'gerund'. These forms have a strong nominal character, as they appear in sentential positions that are typical of nouns and noun phrases (e.g. subject and object position). Subjective forms are strictly excluded in the subject position of gerunds, while we also find possessive forms besides the objective forms (. . . *my opening the window*).

(7) a. Mary saw *he / him leave.
     b. With *he / him spending so much money, we will never be able to buy a house.
     c. Would you mind *I / me opening the window?

As a third structural environment where we find invariable usage of pronominal case forms in standard English, I would like to mention the object position of transitive verbs. No matter whether we consider direct object positions, indirect-object positions or prepositional objects, the only pronominal case forms permitted are objective forms.

(8) a. Mary criticised *he / him.
     b. Mary gave *he / him the book.
     c. Mary cannot rely on *he / him.

4.1.3   *Variable usage of pronominal case forms*

Having discussed the pronominal case forms available and the contexts requiring specific forms, while excluding all others, let us now focus our attention on those syntactic environments that permit more than one pronominal case form. As we will see in subsequent parapgraphs, competition arises mainly between subjective and objective forms and, to a lesser extent, between these and other available forms. Based on Huddleston and Pullum (2002: 459–61), we will survey the relevant syntactic structures successively.

To begin with, competition between subjective and objective case forms occurs in predicative constructions, where we find a relatively strong preference for the objective forms:

(9) Who said that? It was he / him.

Another competitive environment is furnished by coordinated NPs, both in subject and object/adjunct position. This is shown in (10). We also need to mention at this point that the order of the full noun phrase and the pronoun in these coordinations is not fixed and may be reversed.

(10) a. John and I / me have been invited.

      b. This was a great challenge for John and I / me.

In coordinations, pronominal case form variation occurs in varieties of English practically all over the world. Consider the examples in (11) to (13).

(11) a. Me and my mam and dad are going out for a meal.

      b. Him and me were there.

        [North of England, Beal 2004: 117]

(12) a. Ever since me and her was engaged, I've been true to her.

      b. Him and them dogs killed that bear.

        [Appalachian English, Montgomery 2004: 262]

(13) a. He gave it to Fred and me.

      b. He gave it to Fred and I.

        [Australian and New Zealand Vernacular English, Burridge 2004: 1118]

A third syntactic environment that we need to be aware of involves cleft constructions, as in (14) below. Cleft constructions or sentences can be thought of as the result of splitting (i.e. cleaving) one sentence up into two separate clauses. Let us assume that the source of the sentence in (14) is *He did it*. The operation of clefting turns this sentence into a predicative clause introduced by *it* and followed by an embedded clause (*who did it*). Pronominal case variation occurs in the so-called 'cleft position', i.e. the complement position of the *it*-predicative.

(14) It was he / him who did it.

Another syntactic environment where we find pronominal case variation relates to comparative and equative constructions, as shown in (15) and (16). In these constructions, the objective forms are preferred, presumably because the pronouns occur in clause-final position and are thus construed as objects.

(15) John is taller than I / me.

(16) John is as tall as I / me.

Again, it is impossible to tie the use of subjective or objective forms in these contexts to any specific regional variety. Two examples from Australian English can be found in (17). The contrast seems more sensitive to register, objective forms being preferred in spoken colloquial varieties.

(17) a. He had drunk far more than I and he was at least forty years older.

    b. The statue had become a boy some years older than me.

       [Australian English, Collins and Peters 2004: 605]

Pronominal case variation can also be found in answers to questions, as in (18).

(18) A: Who is there? – B: Me / I.

In Section 4.1.1 above, we introduced the pronominal forms that offer a contrast in terms of case. This also concerns the so-called 'wh-pronouns' that – at least in the more formal registers – realise a contrast between subjective and objective case which is subject to variation. Consider (19) and (20), the latter example illustrating the use of wh-pronouns as relative pronouns.

(19) Who / whom did you talk to?

(20) The man who / whom I talked to.

We also find variation in terms of pronominal case form usage after such indefinite pronouns as *nobody*, *everyone*, *all*, and *anybody* when these expressions are followed (not necessarily immediately) by *but* or *except*.

(21) a. Nobody but she can solve the problem.

    b. Nobody can solve the problem but her.

    c. Nobody said anything but me.

Moreover, pronominal case forms vary in prenominal position, as shown in (22). In this environment, variation especially concerns first person plural pronouns. This phenomenon occurs in many regional varieties, as e.g. shown in (23), but is probably best analysed as a feature of colloquial speech.

(22) We / us girls can always take a joke.

(23) a. Us kids used to pinch the sweets like hell. [Southeast of England, Anderwald 2004: 178]

    b. I remember us two boys was workin in the paddock. [Australian Vernacular English, Pawley 2004: 635]

4.2   Varieties of English

The pronominal case system of standard English appears in various modified forms across varieties of English, leading to simplified systems on the one hand and to more elaborate systems on the other. In addition, standard English pronominal case forms may appear in different functions and/or syntactic positions. We will provide a survey of these differences and alternative systems presently.

4.2.1   Retention and variation

We learnt in Section 4.1.1 that the standard English pronominal case system does not distinguish between subjective and objective forms in the second person singular and plural, nor does it draw this distinction for third person neuter pronouns. Earlier stages of English (Old English, Middle English) drew these distinctions (for example Old English *þu/þe* 'you', Middle English *thou/thee* 'you', cf. also *thy*, *thine*, and *thyself*). Some traditional dialects of the north and the west of England have preserved these formal contrasts (Wakelin 1984: 79; Trudgill and Chambers 1991: 7–8; Shorrocks 1999: 72–80; Beal 2004: 118–19). Consider the examples in (24).

(24) a. *Thou* weren't stood up. 'You weren't standing up.'
　　 b. I'll be seeing *thee* afore the week's over. 'I'll be seeing you before the week is over.'
　　 [Bolton, Shorrocks 1999: 122–4]

Another traditional dialect in which the distinction between subjective and objective forms for the second person singular has been noted is the variety spoken in Shetland. The relevant forms are *du* and *dee* (Melchers 2004: 42), as illustrated in (25).

(25) a. *Du* minds me aafil o dee grandfaider.
　　　 You remind me awful of you grandfather
　　　 'You remind me awfully of your grandfather.' [Shetland English, Melchers 2004: 38]
　　 b. Set *dee* doon.
　　　 Sit you down
　　　 'Sit down.' [Shetland English, Melchers 2004: 43]

Variation in terms of case-marked pronominal forms is, however, not restricted to the retention of earlier case distinctions. Another frequent feature is the use of objective forms in possessive functions. The most prominent exponent of this category is probably the so-called 'possessive *me*' (Anderwald 2004: 177).

(26) a. I sat down to have *me* tea as usual.
　　 b. I think *me* memory's getting bad now; somehow.
　　 [Southeast of England, Anderwald 2004: 177]

This double function of *me* serving both as objective and possessive pronoun appears especially common in Great Britain (Kortmann and Szmrecsanyi 2004: 1163). However, possessive *me* has also been reported from North American varieties, *inter alia* in Newfoundland English, the rural and ethnic varieties in the southeast of the USA, and Earlier African American English (Clarke 2004: 312; Kautzsch 2004: 351; Wolfram 2004a: 296).

(27) I lost *me* cap. [Southeast of the USA, Wolfram 2004a: 296]

Although an analysis of this phenomenon as an extension of the objective form to possessive contexts seems plausible from a synchronic point of view, it has been argued that this feature may also be interpreted as a remnant of Middle English *mi/my*. Being very frequent and unstressed, this form may have been exempt from the Great Vowel Shift. Thus, unstressed possessive *mi* and a weakened form of the objective pronoun *me*, pronounced as /mi/, could have merged into one form (Anderwald 2004: 177).

What speaks in favour of the extension hypothesis, however, is the fact that the use of the first person plural objective form in possessive function is likewise observed, notably in the north of England but also in the north and west Midlands, as well as in Earlier African American English (Wakelin 1984: 81; Trudgill and Chambers 1991: 7; Kautzsch 2004: 351; Kortmann 2004: 1096). The sentence in (28) shows an example.

(28) We like *us* town. [North of England, Trudgill and Chambers 1991: 7]

Interestingly enough, we also find the use of subjective pronouns in possessive functions. The possessive use of *they*, for example, is a robust and prominent feature of Urban African American Vernacular English (Wolfram 2004b: 333). An example can be found in (29).

(29) They want to do *they* own thing, and you steady talking to them. 'They want to do their own thing, and you're continuing to talk to them.' [African American Vernacular English, Green 2002: 103]

So far we have only discussed pronominal case features of traditional dialects. Let us now broaden our discussion so as to include Pidgin and Creole varieties. In the English spoken on St Helena – a perhaps controversial Creole English – we find the form *us* used both as subjective and as objective pronoun (Wilson and Mesthrie 2004: 1013).

(30) a. *Us* done finish the introduction.

　　 b. *Us*'s come pick you up.

　　 [St Helena English, Wilson and Mesthrie 2004: 1013]

Since the alternative form *we* is also in use, this feature seems similar to the phenomenon of 'pronoun exchange', as discussed in Section 4.2.3 below. We here leave this as a hypothesis that may be followed up in the future. Objective pronominal forms in subject positions can also be found in Hawai'i Creole (Sakoda and Siegel 2004: 766), as shown in (31).

(31) a. *hr* sik (her sick) 'She's sick.'

　　 b. *as* go (us go) 'We're going.'

　　 [Hawai'i Creole, Sakoda and Siegel 2004: 766]

Furthermore, Hawai'i Creole uses objective pronouns in contexts in which standard English requires subjective forms.

(32) a. Hu *him*? (who him) 'Who is he?'

　　 b. Huz san *him*? (whose son him) 'Whose son is he?'

　　 [Hawai'i Creole, Sakoda and Siegel 2004: 766]

Further non-standard uses of first person plural pronouns are attested in Liberian Settler English. In this variety, however, it is not the objective form, but the subjective form that has extended its range of application (Singler 2004: 889).

(33) a. When we done make *we* farm, we n't know nothing about sell, we keep it, to have to eat. 'After we made our farm, we didn't think at all about selling [the produce]; we kept it so that we would have something to eat.'

    b. Our people didn't learn *we* how to swim.

    [Liberian Settler English, Singler 2004: 889]

As the examples in (33) illustrate, *we* can be used instead of both *our* and *us*. This extension of the subjective form to cover other functions is reminiscent of the possessive use of *they* in Urban African American Vernacular English. And indeed, it has been suggested that the distribution of *we* is a feature with a long history in Liberian Settler English (Singler 2004: 889).

    In Butler English, non-standard uses of first pronoun case forms are also attested, though in this variety for the first person singular. Consider (34).

(34) a. *My* not eh English madam speaking. 'I am not eh speaking (do not
       speak) English (very well) madam.'

    b. Because *I* story . . . 'Because my story . . . '

    c. *Me* not drinking madam. 'I am not drinking (do not drink) madam.'

    [Butler English, Hosali 2004: 1035–36]

These examples show that *my* may be used for *I* and vice versa, and that the objective form *me* may be used for *I*. While some authors explain this variation in terms of simplification (Hosali 2004: 1035), others go so far as to say that individual speakers of Butler English behave idiosyncratically in their use of pronominal case forms, not only with regard to the first person singular but in general (Sebba 1997: 126).

4.2.2   Pidgins and Creoles: between simplification and innovation

In English-based Pidgins and Creoles, we can observe substantial variation in the use of pronominal case forms, the most common type being the complete absence of case distinctions, as in British Creole, Bislama, Solomon Islands Pijin, and Tok Pisin (Mühlhäusler 1997: 149–51; Crowley 2004: 684; Jourdan 2004: 707; Sebba 2004: 203; Smith 2004: 723). The examples in (35) and (36) help to illustrate this.

(35) a. *Mi* seleva nao   wakem.

    I   self   FOC make.TRANS

    'I did it by myself.' or 'I did it myself.'

    b. Bikfala dogi ia   fratem   *mi* tumas.

    big   dog DEM scare.TRANS me too much

    'This big dog scares me a lot.'

    [Solomon Islands Pijin, Jourdan 2004: 707, 710]

(36)   *em*   i   sindaun smail long *em*

    he/she PRED sit down smile at   him/her

    'He/she sat down smiling at him/her.' [Tok Pisin, Smith 2004: 732]

We need to bear in mind, however, that this lack of case distinctions holds primarily for the most basilectal forms of Creoles and that case distinctions can typically be observed in mesolectal varieties (Sebba 1997: 211; James and

Youssef 2004: 466; Patrick 2004: 428). Take a look at the contrast between
(37a) and (37b).

(37) a. *Im no   lov dem ting?*
       she NEG like DET thing
       'Doesn't she like those things?' [Jamaican Creole, Patrick 2004: 416]

   b. She had been ignoring it [a tumor] forever, you know forever. But we
      had another one we were doing our last exam . . . [Jamaican English,
      ICE-Jamaica: S1A-012]

Furthermore, there are Pidgin and Creole varieties that exhibit case distinctions
in their basilectal forms for some, but not for all, personal pronouns in their
paradigm. This is the case with some of the Creoles found in Australia and
Surinam, as well as Trinidad and Tobago (Shnukal 1988: 30–3; James and
Youssef 2004: 465–6; Winford and Migge 2004: 508–9):

(38) a. *Ai* go gibi nyu mabol.
       I   go give you marbles
       'I'll give you the marbles.'

   b. Lala bi   gibi *mi.*
      Lala PAST give me
      'Lala gave it to me.'
      [Torres Strait Creole, Shnukal 1988: 33]

(39) a. *Em   i   no   kolem prapa.*
       he/she PRED NEG call   proper
       'He/she didn't pronounce them (the words) correctly.'

   b. Yu mait bin   luk *em.*
      you might PAST look him/her
      'You may have seen him/her.'
      [Torres Strait Creole, Shnukal 1988: 32, 46]

As we can see in (38) and (39), the distinction between subjective and objective
form in Torres Strait Creole exists only in the first person. In Surinamese
Creoles, a case distinction can be observed for the third person singular, but not
for other persons (Winford and Migge 2004: 508–9). In Kamtok (Cameroon
Pidgin English), we find case distinctions in the first and third person singular
and the third person plural (Ayafor 2004: 916).

   Accepting the standard varieties as a reference point, we can conceive of
pronominal case as a continuum, with varieties lacking case distinctions at one
end of the continuum and varieties with more elaborate pronominal case systems at the other end. The examples from Solomon Islands Pijin and Tok Pisin
in (35) and (36) above illustrate the absence of case distinctions. Some of the
traditional dialects discussed in Section 4.2.1 provide examples of more elaborate pronominal case systems. Curiously enough, it is not only the traditional
dialects where we find more elaborate systems relative to the standard varieties.
Extensions of the pronominal paradigm can also be observed in Pidgin and

Table 4.3 *Subject pronouns in Ghanaian Pidgin English (Huber 1999: 197).*

Subject pronouns (free)			Subject pronouns (bound)		
	SG	PL		SG	PL
1	*mi*	*wi*	1	*à*	*wì*
2	*ju*	*ju*	2	*jù*	*jù*
3	*in* ([in ~ ī])	*dɛm* ([*dɛm* ~ *dɛ̃*])	3	*ì*	*dè*
					dɛm ([*dɛ̀m* ~ *dɛ̃̀*])

Table 4.4 *Object pronouns in Ghanaian Pidgin English (Huber 1999: 199).*

Object pronouns (free)			Object pronouns (bound)		
	SG	PL		SG	PL
1	*mi*	*wi, ɔs, ɛs, as*	1	*mì*	*wì, ɔ̀s, ɛ̀s, às*
2	*ju*	*ju*	2	*jù*	*jù*
3	*am*	*dɛm* ([*dɛm* ~ *dɛ̃*])	3	*àm*	*dè* ([*dɛ̀m* ~ *dɛ̃̀*])

Creole varieties, notably Ghanaian Pidgin English, Nigerian Pidgin English, the Surinamese Creoles, and the Creoles of Trinidad and Tobago (Huber 1999: 193–9; Faraclas 2004: 849–50; James and Youssef 2004: 465–6; Winford and Migge 2004: 508–9).

These varieties exhibit a distinction between emphatic and non-emphatic pronoun forms. For example, Ghanaian Pidgin English has sets of free and bound pronouns, where the free forms are used in emphatic contexts and the bound forms occur in neutral contexts. The bound forms always precede the verb. An overview of the subject forms is shown in Table 4.3.

Example (40) provides an illustration of bound and free forms. A similar opposition of emphatic and non-emphatic forms is also available for object pronouns, as shown in Table 4.4. Even though the emphatic forms do not yield additional case distinctions, they increase the inventory of pronominal case forms.

(40) ì   bì   dɛm   we dè   kam briŋ
     3.SG (BOUND) COP 3.PL (FREE) CPL 3.PL (BOUND) come bring
     dɛ   blaŋɛs
     DET blanket.PL
     'It was them who brought the blankets.' [Ghanaian Pidgin English, Huber 1999: 196]

4.2.3   *Pronoun exchange*

Let us now shift our attention to a phenomenon that is known as 'pronoun exchange' in the literature and that is particularly prominent in traditional English dialects (Kortmann 2004: 1096–7; Wagner 2004: 157–9). Pronoun exchange most often occurs as the use of a subjective personal pronoun in an object position or all other positions that would, according to the rules of standard English grammar, require the use of an objective case form:

(41) a. ... they always called *I* 'Willie', see.

   b. I did give *she* a 'and and she did give *I* a 'and and we did 'elp one another.

   [Southwest of England, Wagner 2004: 157]

The reversal of this exchange pattern, i.e. the use of bare uncoordinated objective forms in subject contexts, is also found, though this phenomenon appears more restricted than the use of subjective forms in object positions:

(42) a. *'er*'s shakin' up seventy. 'She is almost seventy.'

   b. *Us* don' think naught about things like that.

   [Southwest of England, Wagner 2004: 158]

As far as the regional distribution of pronoun exchange is concerned, this phenomenon is most often associated with the southwest of England. However, it is also attested for several other varieties, such as those spoken in East Anglia, the southeast of England, the north of England, and Newfoundland (Beal 2004: 117–88; Clarke 2004: 313; Trudgill 2004: 147–8), though with different distributions and frequency patterns.

The prevalent generalisation for the phenomenon of pronoun exchange is that the subjective pronoun forms are used in emphatic contexts, while the objective pronoun forms occur in all other contexts, even as subjects. In other words, the subjective pronoun forms were refunctionalised as emphatic forms in the relevant varieties. It is striking that in encoding emphasis or contrast in the pronominal paradigm, the traditional dialects display a functional distinction in their pronoun systems that is quite similar to that found in some Pidgin and Creole varieties (e.g. Ghanaian Pidgin English).

Furthermore, it is noteworthy that the distinction between emphatic and non-empathic forms can also be observed for the third person neuter pronoun, as shown in (43) below.

(43) a. *Thass* rainen. 'It is raining.'

   b. Ah, *that* wus me what done it. 'Yes, it was me that did it.'

   [East Anglia, Trudgill: 2004: 146]

In Appalachian English, we can find a similar distinction for the third person singular neuter: the historic form *hit* alternates with *it* and most often surfaces in stressed positions, usually as a subject (Montgomery 2004: 262).

(44) a. *Hit*'s been handed down to him, you see, so he's the third or fourth generation.
    b. They had to raise the young one and take care of *hit*.
    [Appalachian English, Montgomery 2004: 262]

4.3   Cross-linguistic comparison

Let us now also consider pronominal case systems of English in the light of some important cross-linguistic parameters of variation and generalisations. This discussion will primarily concern three areas. Firstly, we will evaluate case marking in English against two cross-linguistically dominant alignment types, namely nominative/accusative and ergative/absolutive. Secondly, we will take a look at the typical size of case systems, i.e. the number of case distinctions drawn, and see where English finds its place. And thirdly, we need to consider some curious asymmetries in the English case marking patterns and see how we can make sense of them.

4.3.1   Case marking alignment

The first parameter of cross-linguistic variation concerns what is known as 'case marking alignment'. It captures different strategies in the exponence of case marking on subjects and objects. The typological literature distinguishes between essentially two types of case marking alignment system, namely nominative/accusative systems and ergative/absolutive systems. They differ in the assignment of case markers to the arguments of transitive and intransitive predicates (i.e. subjects and objects). There are also some mixed systems, which we, however, can ignore here.

Nominative/accusative systems signal the subjects of transitive and intransitive predicates by the same case marker and use other case markers for objects. The subject case of such a system is traditionally called 'nominative', the object case 'accusative' (or dative). The example in (45) illustrates this system using Latvian.

(45) a. Putn-s   lidoja.
       bird-NOM fly.PAST.3
       'The bird was flying.'
    b. Bērn-s   zīmē   sun-i.
       child-NOM draw.PRES.3 dog-ACC
       'The child is drawing a dog.'
    [Latvian, Mathiassen 1997: 181, 187, cited in Comrie 2011]

By contrast, in ergative/absolutive alignment systems we find the case marker used for signalling the subject of intransitive predicates on direct objects, too. This is the absolutive case. The subjects of transitive predicates receive a different case exponent called 'ergative'. We may illustrate such a system using the example from Hunzib in (46), a Caucasian language spoken in Dagestan. In Hunzib, only the ergative has an overt exponent.

(46) a. kid y-ut'-ur
       girl CL2-sleep-PAST
       'The girl slept.'

    b. oždi-l   kid hehe-r
       boy-ERG girl hit-PAST
       'The boy hit the girl.'

    [Hunzib, van den Berg 1995: 122, cited in Comrie 2011]

Ergative/absolutive alignment systems – or ergative systems for short – grammaticalise the semantic roles of the sentential constituents with ergative case being used for the agentive noun phrase, and absolutive case for the non-agentive noun phrases (see Section 4.1). Accusative systems (i.e. nominative/accusative systems) encode syntactic functions such as subject and object.

The case system of English by and large belongs to the accusative type, even though the occurrence of the objective pronominal forms in various non-object positions does not make it a prototypical accusative system. But as it is clearly not ergative and quite consistent in its use of subjective and objective forms for subjects and objects, this appears the best categorisation. Pidgin and Creole varieties of English that do not distinguish between subjective and objective pronominal case forms may be termed 'neutral' (i.e. neither accusative nor ergative).

4.3.2   The size of case systems

Case systems can vary considerably in terms of the number of cases distinguished. At the one extreme, there are languages without case systems that encode grammatical relations primarily by word order. At the other extreme, we find languages with more than twenty cases. According to Iggesen (2011), Hungarian has twenty-one cases. This seems to be an extreme case. Of course, the number of cases distinguished depends on our theoretical assumptions and the relevant analyses.

Table 4.5 provides an overview of the size of case systems found in a cross-linguistic sample of 261 languages. We can see that many languages do not possess cases. With its two or perhaps three (if we include the genitive) case distinctions, standard English resides at the lower end of the attested spectrum. Binary case systems appear common.

As we saw in Section 4.2.2, many Pidgin and Creole varieties do not have case oppositions in the pronominal system – or elsewhere – and thus conform to the cross-linguistic majority pattern. There is no variety of English known

Table 4.5 *Number of cases in a sample of the world's languages (Iggesen 2011; e.b.c.m. = exclusively borderline case-marking).*

Case distinctions	0	2	3	4	5	6–7	8–9	≥10	e.b.c.m.	Total
Languages	100	23	9	9	12	37	23	24	24	261

to me that would have more cases than standard English, or show case marking on elements other than pronouns (disregarding possessive *'s*).

4.3.3   Asymmetrical case marking

There are some interesting asymmetries in the English case system that we will be looking at in this section. They concern the target types of case exponence and targets that fall outside the paradigm in not showing case exponence.

Let me first of all point out to you the remarkable fact that English pronouns instantiate a nominative/accusative case system, whereas full noun phrases do not participate in the case system. In other words, full noun phrases do not bear exponents of case. We agreed in Section 4.3.1 above to categorise standard English as accusative in terms of its alignment type, in spite of the default character of the objective case forms.

Given this discrepancy in the case marking of pronouns and full noun phrases, we may ask whether this is an accidental situation or whether there is some fundamental generalisation lurking behind it. We need to take seriously the fact that pronouns are case marked while full noun phrases are not, but not vice versa. This case marking pattern is compatible with the animacy hierarchy shown in (47). As the animacy hierarchy is an implicational hierarchy, its prediction for case marking systems is that if a noun class on this hierarchy receives case marking, all noun classes further to the left also show case marking. Even if we consider the possessive suffix *'s* as an exponent of genitive case relations, the implication still holds.

(47)   1 > 2 > 3 > proper nouns > human > animate > inanimate [adapted from Silverstein 1976: 122]

In the *Konstanz Universals Archive* (http://typo.uni-konstanz.de/archive/), these generalisations about case marking patterns are captured in terms of the absolute implicational universals quoted in (48) and (49).

(48)   If there is case-inflection on nouns, there is also case-inflection on some pronouns. [Konstanz Universals Archive 183, Moravcsik 1993]

(49)   In all languages, if a nominal possessor carries external case, so does the pronominal one. [Konstanz Universals Archive 20, Moravcsik 1995: 470]

In Chapter 3, we encountered the animacy hierarchy in a slightly different form. There, we referred to it as the 'hierarchy of individuation'. The two labels stand for essentially the same concept, as both hierarchies offer an ordering of nouns and their referents. Moreover, both hierarchies claim universality.

Although the case marking patterns that we find in standard and non-standard varieties of English appear fully compatible with the animacy hierarchy, there is an idiosyncrasy in the standard varieties, with second person pronouns showing no contrast in case (*you* versus *you*). This effectively runs counter to the predictions made by the animacy hierarchy and appears to be quite exceptional cross-linguistically. I can offer no explanation for it,[1] but it appears noteworthy that some traditional British dialects have preserved the Middle English *thou/thee*-distinction.

The situation in Pidgin and Creole Englishes is difficult to assess in this respect, as some of these varieties align themselves with the animacy hierarchy while others do not. For example, in drawing a distinction between subjective and objective forms in the third person, but not in the first or second person, the Surinamese Creoles are inconsistent with the animacy hierarchy. Conversely, Torres Strait Creole shows such a case distinction only in the first person and thus adheres to the animacy hierarchy.

4.4   Summary and list of keywords

We started this chapter with an overview of the parsimonious case system of standard English, whose key feature is the case marking on pronouns. Full noun phrases do not receive case marking, perhaps with the exception of the possessive marker *'s*. The introductory discussion also showed that the distribution of case-marked pronouns is subject to considerable variation, even in standard English. Non-standard varieties of English illustrate simpler case systems that may lack case distinctions altogether, but we also encountered more complex systems. Interestingly enough, the more complex systems are attested both in traditional dialects and in Pidgin and Creole varieties. In addition, non-standard varieties exploit the case system for drawing curious functional contrasts, as e.g. emphasis (pronoun exchange). In cross-linguistic terms, the English case system belongs to the nominative/accusative alignment type, even though its inherent variability blurs its status considerably. It is not uncommon for languages to have two (or three) cases. The existence of case marking on pronouns, but not on full noun phrases, turned out to be a well-known asymmetry that finds an explanation in the animacy hierarchy (or hierarchy of individuation).

---

[1] The distinction between subjective and objective forms in the second person was lost in Early Modern English as a result of an extension of the plural forms to singular contexts. The plural forms were also used as polite forms, and this use was generalised.

Keywords: absolutive, accusative, animacy hierarchy, asymmetries, case alignment, case marker, clefting, coordinations, dependent, emphasis, ergative, grammatical relations, head, hierarchy of individuation, nominative, object, participant roles, possessive *'s*, pronoun exchange, subject, syncretism.

4.5   Exercises

Basic level

1. Which function does grammatical case marking serve? Explain and give examples.
2. In the preceding sections, you encountered many non-standard pronominal case forms. Collect and systematise these forms.
3. In non-standard varieties of English, pronominal case forms may convey functional distinctions that are not expressed by pronominal case forms in the standard varieties. Describe and explain these additional functional distinctions.

Intermediate level

1. Insert what you consider to be the appropriate pronoun forms in the blanks below. Give reasons for your choice.

   a. *It was _____ she / her who was the most beautiful girl in the world.*
   b. *We are as good as _____ they / them.*
   c. *Well, I think James cheats on Margaret. But this is between you and _____ I / me.*
   d. *No one but _____ he / him can make me laugh.*
   e. *It is _____ she / her whom we do not like.*
   f. *John and _____ I / me have been a couple for seven years now.*
   g. *Who is the smartest student in class? _____ I / me.*
   h. *What? _____ She / Her a terrorist? Nonsense!*
   i. *It was very difficult for Claire and _____ I / me to cope with the new situation.*
   j. *It was not Annabelle who ate the whole cake. It was _____ he / him.*
   k. *_____ We / Us, we usually only buy fair trade coffee.*
   l. *He is much bigger than _____ she / her.*
   m. *It was _____ they / them I could not stand.*
   n. *_____ He / Him and Caroline will get married soon.*
   o. *A: Have you heard the news? Deborah left Patrick. B: Lucky _____ he / him!*
   p. *_____ We / Us English invented football.*

2. The sentences below differ from standard English in terms of pronominal case usage.
   a. Describe the differences using precise grammatical categories.
   b. From which region(s) might the sentences be?

   a. *We like us town.*
   b. *We used to drink a lot, didn't us?*
   c. *See how thou likes it.*
   d. *They want to do they own thing.*
   e. *Give me back me pen!*
   f. *Well, if they didn't know I, at least I knew they.*
   g. *Us old boys had really a good time.*
   h. *Our parents didn't learn we how to cook.*
   i. *If I were thee, I would not do it.*
   j. *Sees du yon boy?*

3. Take a look at the distribution of pronominal case forms in *it*-clefts in British English. In order to do this, go to Mark Davies' website at Brigham Young University and use the online version of the *BNC*, which can be accessed at http://corpus.byu.edu/bnc/

   By entering the search string 'it was [PRONOUN] who' into the search box for each of the possible options, consider the distribution of pronominal case forms in *it*-clefts for the first person singular and the third person singular (masculine or feminine).
   a. Which distribution for the first and for the third person can you detect? Enter your results in the following 2 × 2 chart.

	First person	Third person
No. of subjective forms		
No. of objective forms		

   b. Go to www.graphpad.com/quickcalcs/contingency1 and enter your numbers into the 2 × 2 table on this website. Using the chi-square test, check if there are statistically significant differences between the first and third person singular pronouns.
   c. Sum up your results in a short essay.

   Advanced level

1. Consider the distribution of so-called 'subjective pronouns' and 'objective pronouns' in the examples given below. Which generalisation can you infer from these examples regarding the distribution of subjective forms and objective forms?

    a. *Him, he's crazy.*
    b. *He doesn't drink beer, him.*
    c. *A: Who gave the book to John? – B: Him!*
    d. *Him wear a tuxedo? – He doesn't even own a clean shirt.*
    e. *Him free poses a greater risk than him behind bars.*
    f. *Why couldn't he be my age or me his?*
    g. *John might have wanted to leave, but not me.*
    h. *Perhaps any woman would, except me.*
    i. *Silly him / her.*

2. Take a look at the sentences listed below. According to Huddleston and Pullum (2002: 462–3), the sentences in (i) represent standard English, the sentences in (ii) are considered non-standard English, whereas the sentences in (iii) are forms of hypercorrection leading to non-standard English.

    a. Try to determine the underlying rationale for their classification.
    b. Discuss whether you think that this classification is convincing. Give reasons supporting your opinion.

    i.   a. *He and I have some of our biggest arguments over Conservative social issues.*
        b. *There has always been pretty intense rivalry between him and me.*
    ii. a. *Him and me fixed up the wagon while the others went to town.*
        b. *She and us are going to be good friends.*
    iii. a. *It would be an opportunity for you and I to spend some time together.*
        b. *There is a tendency for he and I to clash.*

3. Read Hudson (1995). Richard Hudson argues that the subjective forms of pronouns are essentially restricted to the preverbal position of finite clauses, while the objective forms may occur in any other position. Discuss Hudson's position in relation to the empirical evidence from varieties of English as introduced in this chapter.

4.6   References

Bately, Janet M. (ed.). 1980. *The Old English Orosius*. Oxford University Press.

Comrie, Bernard. 2011. Alignment of case marking. In Matthew S. Dryer and Martin Haspelmath (eds.), *The World Atlas of Language Structures Online*. Munich: Max Planck Digital Library, chapter 99. Available online at http://wals.info/chapter/99. Accessed 22 December 2011.

Fillmore, Charles J. 1968. The case for case. In Emmon Bach and Robert T. Harms (eds.), *Universals in Linguistic Theory*, 1–88. New York: Holt, Rinehart, and Winston.

Green, Lisa J. 2002. *African American English: A Linguistic Introduction*. Cambridge University Press.

Huber, Magnus. 1999. *Ghanaian Pidgin English in its West African Context: A Socio-historical and Structural Analysis*. Amsterdam: John Benjamins.

Hudson, Richard. 1995. Does English really have case? *Journal of Linguistics* 31(2). 375–92.

Iggesen, Oliver A. 2011. Number of cases. In Matthew S. Dryer and Martin Haspelmath (eds.), *The World Atlas of Language Structures Online*. Munich: Max Planck Digital Library, chapter 49. Available online at http://wals.info/chapter/49. Accessed 22 December 2011.

Mathiassen, Terje. 1997. *A Short Grammar of Latvian*. Columbus, OH: Slavica Publishers.

Moravcsik, Edith A. 1993. Government. In Joachim Jacobs, Armin von Stechow, Wolfgang Sternefeld, and Theo Vennemann (eds.), *Syntax: Ein internationales Handbuch zeitgenössischer Forschung, volume 1*, 707–21. Berlin: Mouton de Gruyter.

  1995. Summing up Suffixaufnahme. In Frans Plank (ed.), *Double Case: Agreement by Suffixaufnahme*, 451–84. Oxford University Press.

Mühlhäusler, Peter. 1997. *Pidgin and Creole Linguistics*. (Westminster Creolistics Series 3.) London: University of Westminster Press.

Sebba, Mark. 1997. *Contact Languages: Pidgins and Creoles*. Basingstoke and London: Macmillan.

Shnukal, Anna. 1988. *Broken: An Introduction to the Creole Language of Torres*. Canberra: Research School of Pacific Linguistics, Australian National University.

Shorrocks, Graham. 1999. *A Grammar of the Dialect of the Bolton Area: Part II Morphology and Syntax*. Frankfurt am Main: Lang.

Silverstein, Michael. 1976. Hierarchy of features and ergativity. In Robert Malcolm Ward Dixon (ed.), *Grammatical Categories in Australian Languages* (Linguistic Series 22), 112–71. Canberra: Australian Institute of Aboriginal Studies.

Trudgill, Peter and Jack K. Chambers. 1991. *Dialects of English: Studies in Grammatical Variation*. London: Longman.

van den Berg, Helma. 1995. *A Grammar of Hunzib*. Munich: Lincom Europa.

Wakelin, Martyn. 1984. Rural dialects in England. In Peter Trudgill (ed.), *Language in the British Isles*, 70–93. Cambridge University Press.

See *General references* for Anderwald 2004; Ayafor 2004; Beal 2004; Burridge 2004; Clarke 2004; Collins and Peters 2004; Crowley 2004; Faraclas 2004; Hosali 2004; Huddleston and Pullum 2002; James and Youssef 2004; Jourdan 2004; Kautzsch 2004; Kortmann 2004; Kortmann and Szmrecsanyi 2004; Melchers 2004; Montgomery 2004; Patrick 2004; Pawley 2004; Quirk et al. 1985; Sakoda and Siegel 2004; Sebba 2004; Singler 2004; Smith 2004; Trudgill 2004; Wagner 2004; Wilson and Mesthrie 2004; Winford and Migge 2004; Wolfram 2004a; Wolfram 2004b.

4.7   Further reading

Blake, Barry J. 1994. *Case*. Cambridge University Press.

Butt, Miriam. 2008. Modern approaches to case: An overview. In Andrej Malchukov and Andrew Spencer (eds.), *The Handbook of Case*, 27–43. Oxford University Press.

Hancock, Jan. 1991. St Helena English. In Francis Byrne and Thom Huebner (eds.), *Development and Structures of Creole Languages*, 17–28. Amsterdam: John Benjamins.

Paddock, Harold. 1994. From CASE to FOCUS in the pronouns of some Wessex-based dialects of English. In Elisabeth Engberg-Pedersen, Lisbeth Falster Jakobsen, and Lone Schack Rasmussen (eds.), *Function and Expression in Functional Grammar*, 255–64. Berlin: Mouton de Gruyter.

Quinn, Heidi. 2005. *The Distribution of Pronoun Case Forms in English*. Amsterdam: John Benjamins.

Shorrocks, Graham. 1992. Case assignment in simple and coordinate constructions in present-day English. *American Speech* 67(4). 432–44.

Spencer, Andrew. 2009. Typology of case systems: Parameters of variation. In Andrej Malchukov and Andrew Spencer (eds.), *The Oxford Handbook of Case*, 651–67. Oxford University Press.

5   Determiners

In this chapter, we will investigate the use of articles and demonstrative pronouns, as well as some other determiners across varieties of English. The relevant grammatical domain is often referred to as the 'determiner system' and is discussed in great detail in grammatical descriptions of standard English (see, for instance, Quirk et al. 1985: 253–81; Huddleston and Pullum 2002: 368–99). We will here be interested in special, non-standard determiner forms serving the functions of standard English determiners; standard determiners in non-standard functions; non-standard determiners in non-standard functions; and the overuse and underuse of determiners. In keeping with the general structure of the book, these findings will be interpreted against the backdrop of cross-linguistic observations and generalisations in this domain. Before discussing varieties of English and cross-linguistic data, let us first of all take a look at some important linguistic facts of this domain.

5.1   Overview

Determiners form a heterogeneous group comprising word classes such as articles, demonstratives, and quantifiers. Examples from (standard) English include *the*, *a*, *this*, *that*, *some*, *many*, *few*, and various others. What these words and word classes have in common is that they serve as modifiers of nouns and noun phrases, but, unlike adjectives, they are grammatical rather than lexical elements. This statement is based on the observation that these expressions form closed paradigms containing only a handful of elements, whereas the class of adjectives is open and forms a large set. Semantically, determiners modify the referential properties of the relevant noun phrases, again unlike adjectives, whose main function consists in the modification of certain qualitative aspects of the referents concerned. In what follows, we will take a more detailed look at the individual determiner classes.

5.1.1   *Definite and indefinite articles*

The terms 'definite article' and 'indefinite article', as you all know, are used for the expressions *the* and *a* (*an*), which can be found in front of many English noun phrases. The relevant forms are invariable apart from phonological differences so that their morphological aspects can hardly give rise to extensive discussions. In semantic terms, however, these expressions turn out to be rather tricky and have sparked sophisticated theoretical analyses (Hawkins 1978; Chesterman 1991).

Most of these analyses agree that the main function of the definite article is to signal 'identifiability'. In using the definite article, the speaker signals to the hearer (addressee) that the referent described by the relevant noun phrase should be identifiable (i.e. known, familiar) by him. Huddleston and Pullum (2002: 368) illustrate this function using the examples in (1), where using (1a) presupposes that the addressee can see the ladder or knows where it is conventionally stored, and (1b) strongly suggests that speaker and addressee agree on which car they are talking about.

(1) a. Bring me the ladder!
    b. Where did you park the car?

The notion of 'identifiability' appears to go a long way towards an adequate description of the function of the definite article even though it cannot explain why certain nouns and noun classes describing unique and usually identifiable referents (such as proper names) do not accept the definite article and why other such nouns almost demand its use (*the sun*, *the moon*). In English, the condition of identifiability on the use of definite articles carries over to plural NPs and non-count NPs:

(2) a. Bring me the ladders / the keys!
    b. Where did you put the milk / the sugar?

If it is correct to say that the definite article signals the identifiability of a referent, we may characterise the function of the indefinite article as one of signalling non-identifiability. We may illustrate this by using the indefinite article in the contexts introduced in (1), as shown in (3). In (3a) the referent (not the concept) of the noun *ladder* is now portrayed as unknown to speaker and hearer. Example (3b) is pragmatically odd, as the context strongly suggests the existence of a parked car.

(3) a. Bring me a ladder!
    b. Where did you park a car?

Although there are many additional facets of definite and indefinite articles that could be mentioned, let us turn now to the subject of demonstratives.

5.1.2   *Demonstrative pronouns*

Another important group of determiners is that of demonstrative pronouns. These expressions can be used to indicate the distance of a referent relative to a deictic centre, i.e. a centre of orientation. In English we find four forms of demonstrative pronouns (*this*, *that*, *these*, *those*) encoding a contrast between proximal (i.e. near the deictic centre) and distal (i.e. away from the deictic centre) referents and, on top of this, a contrast between singular and plural. The most common deictic centre is the location of the speaker. These basic contrasts are illustrated in (4).

(4) a. How about this book / these books?

    b. How about that book / those books?

The semantic contrasts encoded by demonstrative pronouns become explicit through combinatorial restrictions (Huddleston and Pullum 2002: 1505). We may successfully form phrases like *this book here* and *those flowers over there*, while a phrase such as **this book there* is perceived as ill formed. Furthermore, it is noteworthy that demonstrative pronouns have deictic (5a) and anaphoric (5b) uses (Huddleston and Pullum 2002: 1505–9).

(5) a. This apple looks riper than that one.

    b. I raised some money by hocking the good clothes I had left, but when *that* was gone I didn't have a cent.

5.1.3 Quantifiers

Another group of determiners that we need to introduce and discuss briefly at this point are quantifiers, i.e. expressions like *few*, *some*, *many*, *all*, *any*, etc., whose function consists in the specification of the size of a set. Cardinal numbers (*one*, *two*, *three*, etc.) can also be subsumed under this category.

As far as their formal properties are concerned, quantifiers yield a highly heterogeneous class, since we do not find either morphological or syntactic properties that all expressions of this class have in common. Morphologically, they look like completely unrelated lexical items. In syntactic terms, they can all occur in a prenominal modifying position – and hence fully deserve the label 'determiner' – but some quantifiers can also be used as pronouns (*I saw three* vs. **I saw every*; Gil 2001: 1281).

In view of the fact that quantifiers describe set sizes, it can come as no surprise that the main semantic difference between quantifiers lies in the set size described. It can range from the mere statement of existence (existential quantifier; *a*, *one*) to the quantification over all elements of a given set (universal quantifier; *all*), via various intermediate values (*few*, *some*, *many*, *most*). Cardinal numbers allow us to describe the size of a set in very precise terms.

5.1.4 Other determiners

Even though articles and demonstratives represent the prototypical members of the category of determiners, we also find a few less typical members, which will be briefly described here. Firstly, we need to mention prenominal possessive pronouns (*my*, *your*, *his*, *her*, etc.), as these belong to the category of determiners for syntactic reasons (and only marginally to the category of case-marked personal pronouns; see Chapter 4). Secondly, we also find the personal pronouns *we* and *you* in determiner function and position: *we Irish, you students*. This phenomenon was discussed in the context of variable usage of pronominal case forms in Chapter 4. And thirdly, we need to mention the interrogative words *which* and *what* that, besides their pronominal use (*Which did you buy?; What did you do?*), also appear in determiner function (*Which book did you buy?; What car did you choose?*).

5.1.5   Variable uses of articles

Even though the distribution of the definite article is in large parts predictable from the constraint on identifiability introduced in Section 5.1.1 above, there are a number of contexts in which the usage of the article varies for no apparent reason. We explicitly introduce these contexts here because some of them constitute domains where we can find differences between some regional varieties of English. A good overview of these variable contexts of definite article usage can be found in Quirk et al. (1985: 277–81). They are also addressed in English usage guides such as Swan (2005: 62–6), as they are difficult to understand for learners of English. It is also advisable to consider Hawkins (1978) and Liu and Gleason (2002).

We will here basically follow the exposition given in Quirk et al. (1985: 277–81). A first set of nouns showing variable article usage are institutions of human life and society such as *school, university, hospital*, etc., as shown in (6). Frequently, there is a semantic contrast such that omitting the definite article evokes the institutional reading of the relevant noun, whereas its usage brings up a particular building or place.

(6) a. be at school / visit the school
     b. go to town / The town is old.
     c. live on campus / live on the campus

Another area of variation concerns nouns describing means of transport and communication, as in (7). The usage of these nouns without articles is largely restricted to contexts in which they are preceded by the preposition *by*.

(7) a. travel by train / take the train
     b. communicate by telephone / Jill is on the telephone.

Nouns describing times of day and night and the seasons of the year yield another domain of variation. Examples are shown in (8) and (9). The definite article apparently yields a contrast between calendaric winter and seasonal winter in (9b) and (9c).

(8) a. at sunset / admire the sunset
     b. Evening approached. / in the evening

(9) a. in spring / in the spring
    b. The winter of 1963 was an exciting time. (calendaric)
    c. Winter in 1963 was not like last winter. (seasonal)

There is considerable free variation in article usage with nouns for meals and illnesses, as shown in (10) and (11).

(10) a. That day, (the) lunch was served on the terrace.
     b. have dinner / the dinner after the reception

(11) (the) flu, (the) measles, (the) chicken pox, etc.

The examples introduced above describe some noun classes where variation in article usage is well known to occur. They are referred to as 'situational uses' in Hawkins (1978: 111–23) and as 'cultural uses' in Liu and Gleason (2002: 7–8). Additional noun classes that in principle could be mentioned here are place names (*the Himalayas* versus *Mount Everest*), musical instruments (*play the oboe* versus *study oboe*), jobs and positions (*He was elected president* versus *I want to see the president*), and nouns following *both* and *all*, etc. In many of these cases we can probably detect subtle semantic differences between using the article and omitting it, offer historical explanations, or account for article usage in terms of loan translations (e.g. *The Hague*).

Here, the point of interest is a different one. We will see in the next section that article usage can be quite different in certain varieties of English, specifically in the so-called 'post-colonial Englishes' and 'learner Englishes' widely spoken in Asia. Interestingly, it will turn out that most of the variation in article usage observable in these varieties occurs in the contexts introduced above.

5.2   Varieties of English

As outlined in the previous section, we can observe a considerable amount of variation in terms of determiner use even for the standard varieties of English, especially with regard to the definite article. The susceptibility for variation in this domain is corroborated by data from non-standard varieties of English, as we can detect a huge scope of variation there. In what follows, we will focus on determiner systems of non-standard varieties of English. In Section 5.2.1, we will discuss differences in forms and functions observed across varieties of English, whereas in Section 5.2.2, we will mainly address the phenomena of overuse, underuse, and omission of determiner forms compared with standard English.

5.2.1   *Different forms and functions of determiners*

In investigating determiners across varieties of English, we need to be aware of three different scenarios:

  i. Non-standard varieties possess special determiner forms serving the functions of standard English determiner forms.

ii. Standard determiner forms occur in non-standard functions in non-standard varieties.

iii. Non-standard varieties have special determiner forms dedicated to functions unknown in the standard varieties.

In the following, we will take a look at each scenario, delimiting ourselves – for reasons of conciseness – to the most important aspects of variation.

Non-standard determiner forms in standard functions   A widespread phenomenon is the substitution of the initial dental fricatives in articles and demonstratives by an alveolar stop /d/. This phenomenon is amply attested in English-based Pidgins and Creoles, with the form *di*, for example, occurring in Jamaican and the Surinamese Creoles, as well as in Nigerian Pidgin English. The form *da* is found in Hawai'i Creole and Ghanaian Pidgin English (Faraclas 2004: 845; Huber 2004: 869; Patrick 2004: 433; Sakoda and Siegel 2004: 764; Winford and Migge 2004: 506).

Similar observations can be made in many of the post-colonial varieties (Indian English, Singapore English), even though in these varieties the standard and the non-standard forms usually co-exist side by side. In addition, the phenomenon carries over to many learner varieties of English where the dental fricative may also be replaced by other phonetically similar sounds (such as /s/ or /f/).

Many of the traditional dialects exhibit the form *them* used as a distal demonstrative, as shown in (12) below (Kortmann and Szmrecsanyi 2004: 1186).

(12) a. ... dont forget to get them boots [Irish English, *Hamburg Corpus of Irish Emigrant Letters*, Burke_03]

    b. That bloke used to cut them willows. [Southeast of England, Anderwald 2004: 179]

In addition, the distal demonstrative use of *them* is also attested in many Pidgin and Creole varieties, such as Jamaican Creole and Gullah, in which it may co-occur with the replacement of the initial dental fricative by the alveolar stop /d/ (Mufwene 2004: 362; Patrick 2004: 431).

(13) Lef *dem*   chiljren op a di   hoos.

    left those children up at the house

    '[I] left those kids up at the house.' [Jamaican Creole, Patrick 2004: 433]

Moreover, the third person subject pronoun *they* often occurs as distal demonstrative alongside the other variants *those* and *them* (Beal 2004: 119–20; Clarke 2004: 311).

(14) ... for to lanch ('launch') one of *they* schooners [Newfoundland English, Clarke 2010: 90]

Demonstratives across varieties of English may further be specified by a locative adverbial, as in (15). Such an additional specification may occur with basically all demonstrative forms, including standard forms such as *this*, *that*, and *these* (*this here*, *that there*) and non-standard forms such as *them*. We will see in Section 5.3.4 that this is a cross-linguistically common strategy to mark contrasts in distance.

(15) a. He had one of *these here* hog rifles.
 b. *That there* sawmill I worked at was there before I married.
 c. *Them there* fellows come through here, stealing horses and things.
 [Appalachian English, Montgomery 2004: 264]

In addition to differences in the form and complexity of demonstrative pronouns, we can also observe severely reduced demonstrative paradigms. In Bislama, for example, the form *ya*, which is historically derived from *here*, functions as general demonstrative and marker of definiteness, and indicates neither differences in number nor in distances or spatial relations (16). Notice that *ya* appears after the noun it modifies. The form *ya* may be further specified by *nao* or *lo(ng)we* to express proximity and distance.

(16) a. man ya
 man the/this
 'the man' or 'this man'
 b. trak ya nao
 car this
 'this car'
 c. ol trak ya longwe
 cars those
 'those cars'
 [Bislama, Crowley 2004: 687]

In contrast with such reduced determiner systems, we can also observe systems that exhibit finer-grained distinctions than the standard paradigm. In a number of Pidgin and Creole varieties spoken in Australia, Suriname, and Nigeria we can, for example, detect number-sensitive article forms. In other words, these varieties have different definite and indefinite article forms for singular and plural noun phrases. A good example illustrating this is Torres Strait Creole in Australia (Shnukal 1988: 24; Malcolm 2004: 661), as this variety has four different article forms: *da* 'the' (definite singular article), *dem* 'the' (definite plural article), *wan* 'a/an' (indefinite singular article), and *ol* (plural generic article). Other varieties, such as the Surinamese Creole Saamaka, however, possess only a singular–plural distinction for the definite article – distinguishing between *di* in the singular and *dee* in the plural – while Nigerian Pidgin English, for instance, has a number distinction only for the indefinite articles *wɔn* (indefinite singular) and *sɔm* (indefinite plural) (Faraclas 2004: 845; Winford and Migge 2004: 506).

With regard to indefinite articles, we can summarise that the most frequent non-standard feature in this domain is the use of forms that were historically derived from standard English *one* and that are most often manifested as *one* or *wan* in many Pidgin and Creole varieties, such as Ghanaian Pidgin English, Fiji English, and Indian South African English, as well as the Creoles of Hawai'i, Jamaica, and Suriname (e.g. Huber 2004: 870; Mesthrie 2004b: 985; Mugler and Tent 2004: 775; Patrick 2004: 433; Sakoda and Siegel 2004: 764; Winford and Migge 2004: 507). From a diachronic point of view, this is not surprising, as the standard English indefinite article *a/an* was itself grammaticalised from the numeral *one*, as will be further discussed in Section 5.3.3 below.[1]

Standard determiner forms in non-standard functions The second scenario introduced above, i.e. the use of standard English determiner forms in different functions in varieties of English, is much rarer than the use of special non-standard determiner forms serving functions available for standard English determiners.

The first determiner to be discussed in this context is the indefinite article *a*. In some traditional varieties, such as those spoken in the southwest of England and in the Orkney and Shetland Islands, as well as in the Appalachians, this article is used invariantly, i.e. it does not have its phonologically conditioned alternant *an* that occurs before vowels in standard English (Melchers 2004: 41; see (17)).[2]

(17) a. ... and naturally her father was *a* older man when she was a young girl ... [Southwest of England, Wagner 2004: 155]

  b. I had *a* uncle and *a* aunt that moved out there. [Appalachian English, Montgomery 2004: 266]

  c. *a* aafil flickament 'an awful state of excitement' [Orkney and Shetland English, Melchers 2004: 40]

The definite article *the* can also occur in different functions across varieties of English. In Newfoundland, for example, it may assume the function of the possessive pronoun *my* in certain idiomatic phrases (18a) and the function of the indefinite article (18b), as well as the function of the proximal demonstrative (18c)[3] (Clarke 2004: 311–12, 2010: 90–2).

(18) a. the wife 'my wife' [Newfoundland English, Clarke 2010: 91]

  b. when they'd get the cold 'when they'd get a cold' [Newfoundland English, Clarke 2004: 312]

  c. the fall, the year 'this (past or coming) fall, year' [Newfoundland English, Clarke 2004: 312]

In other traditional dialects, too, we can find the definite article premodifying temporal adverbials (Beal 2004: 129; Melchers 2004: 42; Miller 2004: 59–60).

---

[1] Variation concerning possessive determiners is discussed in Chapter 4.

[2] I view the form *a* as having extended its domain of use to that of *an*, and therefore this phenomenon is included here.

[3] Clarke (2010: 91) states that it remains unclear 'whether or not the origin of this use of *the* is the definite article or the preposition *to* (as in *tomorrow*, *today*)'.

(19) the day 'today', the morn 'tomorrow', the now 'now' [Scottish English, Milller 2004: 60]

(20) the/da day 'today', the/da nicht 'tonight', the/da mo(a)rn 'tomorrow' [Orkney and Shetland English, Melchers 2004: 42]

With regard to quantifiers, we observe that *less* and *much* may be found in an extended functional range in Scottish English. While these quantifiers are restricted to non-count nouns such as *water*, *patience*, or *time* in standard English, they can also be used with count nouns in Scottish English (see (21)).

(21) a. less cars 'fewer cars'

    b. much more cars 'many more cars'

    [Scottish English, Miller 2004: 50]

Moreover, standard English demonstratives may not show number marking in some varieties of English. Hence, the demonstratives *this* and *that* co-occur with plural nouns. This feature is prominent especially in Orkney and Shetland English and the varieties of English spoken in South Africa (see (22–4) and Mesthrie 2004b: 984):

(22) a. I'd better go and pick up *this* bags.

    b. It's because of *that* birds.

    [White South African English, Bowerman 2004: 956]

(23) *This* eens is better than *that* eens. 'These evenings are better than those evenings.' [Orkney and Shetland English, Melchers 2004: 44]

(24) a. He must take from *that* reserves.

    b. I've watched *this* children.

    [Cape Flats English, McCormick 2004: 997]

In these varieties, we observe a reduction of the formal inventory of demonstrative pronouns, as the standard English singular forms can be used to cover both singular and plural demonstrative function. However, non-standard varieties may also extend their inventory of demonstrative forms to cover functions unknown in standard English, as we will see in the following section.

Non-standard determiner forms in non-standard functions The forms to be discussed in this section are basically restricted to two subclasses of determiners, namely demonstrative pronouns and possessive pronouns. Each of these classes will be discussed below.

With regard to demonstrative pronouns, a first major non-standard feature concerning both form and function is the number of distances distinguished. Recall that the standard varieties draw a binary distinction (*this* versus *that*) indicating proximity to and distance from the speaker. Some traditional varieties of English, such as those in the north of England, Orkney and Shetland, as well as the Appalachians, have preserved an additional demonstrative that can be used to indicate remote distances (Beal 2004: 119–20, and see (25)). Although the meaning of *yan/yon/yonder* is slightly different in each of these varieties, we can generalise that in these systems *this* expresses proximity to the speaker and *that* distance from the speaker, while the forms *yan/yon* and/or *yonder* express remoteness. These systems may also be interpreted in such a way that *this* indicates speaker proximity, *that* hearer proximity, and *yan/yon/yonder* distance from hearer and speaker.[4]

(25) a. Middlesboro is on *yan* side of Cumberland Gap [Appalachian English, Montgomery 2004: 264]

     b. Sees du *yon* boy? [Orkney and Shetland English, Melchers 2004: 44]

Another remarkable deviation from standard English can be observed in the traditional dialects of southwest England, as these varieties also possess special demonstratives alongside the familiar forms. Moreover, all forms are equipped with highly unusual functions. In these dialects, we find the forms *thick*, *that*, *theäse*, and *this*. They encode the familiar proximal/distal distinction (*theäse/this* versus *thick/that*). What is more interesting, though, is the contrast established by *theäse/this* and *thick/that* respectively, as the relevant semantic opposition turns out to be one of countability. The forms *theäse* and *thick* are used together with countable nouns (or for picking out countable objects) while *this* and *that* are used to modify non-countable nouns, i.e. those denoting substances, liquids, and other masses (*thick book* but *that milk*).

(26) a. Come under *theäse* tree by *this* water.

     b. Teäke up *this* dowst in *theäse* barrow.

     c. Goo under *thik* tree, an' zit on *that* grass.

     d. Teäke *thik* pick, an' bring a little o' *that* haÿ.

     [Southwest of England, Siemund 2008: 24]

If you recall Chapter 3 on pronominal gender, you will notice, of course, that the mass/count distinction on demonstrative pronouns parallels exactly that on third person pronouns (*thick book – he* but *that milk – it*).

The other prominent domain in which we can detect marked differences from the standard – both in form and function – is the class of possessive pronouns or possessive determiners. To appreciate these differences, let us briefly take a look at number marking in standard English, where we find a distinction between singular and plural. The singular is used when we refer to one and only one entity. If we refer to more than one entity, we are required to use the plural (*one dog, two dog-s*). In some Pidgin and Creole varieties – especially those spoken in Australia and Oceania – we find finer-grained number distinctions, which are often the result of contact with the other languages involved in the formation of these varieties. In addition to singular and plural, these varieties may also have categories for dual and sometimes even trial number (e.g. Crowley 2004: 684–5; Malcolm 2004: 662–5). As these names already indicate, the dual makes reference to exactly two as opposed to either one or more entities, whereas the

---

[4] Systems of demonstratives with a tripartite distinction can also be encountered in Shakespeare's plays: *What light through yonder window breaks?* [Early Modern English, Romeo and Juliet, II, 2, 1]

Table 5.1 *The pronominal paradigm of Bislama (Crowley 2004: 684).*

Person	Singular		Dual	Trial	Plural
1	*mi*	Inclusive	*yumitu(fala)*	*yumitrifala*	*yumi*
		Exclusive	*mitufala*	*mitrifala*	*mifala*
2	*yu*		*yutufala*	*yutrifala*	*yufala*
3	*hem*		*tufala*	*trifala*	*ol(geta)*

trial marks exactly three referents as opposed to one, two, or more than three referents.

In Table 5.1, we see these number distinctions for the pronominal paradigm of Bislama, which is a variety that does not discriminate between subject, object, or possessive pronoun forms. You can see that Bislama distinguishes between singular, dual, trial, and plural forms for all persons and functions covered by the pronominal paradigm. Furthermore, Bislama also possesses an inclusive/exclusive distinction for the first person dual. This means that the first person dual also encodes whether the addressee of the utterance is included in the reference, i.e. inclusive dual, or whether the addressee is not included in the reference of the dual pronoun, i.e. exclusive dual.

5.2.2   Overuse and underuse

We have already stated, in Section 5.1.5, that the use of articles is variable in a number of contexts – both in standard English and across varieties of English. We have also mentioned that the variability of article use across varieties of English may best be conceived of as a continuum ranging from omission, sporadic uses, and standard use to overuse. In this section, we will now be looking at the following scenarios in detail: article overuse, article underuse, and general variability in the use of articles. Furthermore, we will address the lack of agreement with measure phrases.

With regard to the definite article *the*, an overuse of this form is attested for a number of varieties, such as Scottish, Irish, Appalachian, and Newfoundland English, and Singapore and Jamaican English, as well as for the varieties spoken on Orkney and Shetland and in the southwest of England. We find this phenomenon in traditional dialects, but also in post-colonial varieties. The examples in (27) to (29) illustrate the overuse of the definite article.

(27) a. ... for this, this is the poor people were starved with *the* hunger.

b. Well, now, I'll = I'll tell you this, the time *the* polio = came here into this country now, that's about ten twenty year ago, ...

c. We'd had a habit of playing football outside *the* George's Church, it being a big crescent, you know?
[Irish English, Filppula 1999: 59–60]

(28) a. ... but I stayed on until *the* Christmas.

   b. ... we had to walk a mile to *the* school and back.

   [Southwest of England, Wagner 2004: 155]

(29) a. The mother reminded her children at, eh, during *the* dinner to keep off their elbows off the table.

   b. I, eh, I saw *the* tigers at the zoo. *The* tigers are, I think that *the* tigers are very, are very beautiful animals.

   [Singapore English, own fieldwork]

In these varieties, the overuse of the definite article is associated with – or mostly restricted to – certain contexts, such as nouns describing institutions, diseases, geographical units, meals, seasons, etc., but also combinations with other determiners (Filppula 1999: 56–77; Miller 2004: 59–60; Montgomery 2004: 266; Patrick 2004: 432; Wagner 2004: 155–6). These are exactly those environments for which variable article use is also attested in standard English (the so-called 'cultural uses' discussed in Section 5.1.5). We can also observe the overuse of the definite article in Torres Strait Creole in Australia: *the las Sunday* 'last Sunday' (Malcolm 2004: 661).

   Let us now turn to the underuse or omission of articles in contexts where standard English requires them. This phenomenon is amply attested in a number of varieties, including Malaysian, Singapore, Indian South African, East African, and Butler English, as well as Gullah and Solomon Islands Pijin. It is quite typical of post-colonial varieties and Pidgin and Creole varieties. Consider the examples below:

(30) a. I don't have ticket.

   b. Maybe you better have microphone a bit closer.

   [Singapore English, Wee 2004: 1061]

(31) a. Main reason for their performance ...

   b. He is ∅ drug addict.

   [Malaysian English, Baskaran 2004: 1074]

(32) a. ... Because ball is going nearly 200/250 yards. '... Because the ball is going (goes) nearly 200 to 250 yards.'

   b. ... That is fore-carry. '... That is a fore-caddy's job.'

   [Butler English, Hosali 2004: 1034]

(33) a. You gwine cut it with knife? 'Are you going to cut it with a knife (not assumed known to the addressee)?'

   b. You ever see cat eat raw tato skin? 'Have you ever seen a cat eat raw potato skin?'

   [Gullah, Mufwene 2004: 362]

Although this phenomenon may superficially look the same in each variety, there may be different underlying reasons for the omission of articles or their general underuse. Regarding Solomon Islands Pijin, for example, Jourdan (2004: 704–5) argues that article omission is the result of an unstable system that has not yet developed a stable article paradigm. In East Anglia, as pointed out by Trudgill, 'the definite article could be omitted after prepositions of motion and before nouns denoting familiar domestic objects':

(34) a. he walked into house
      b. put th' apples into basket
      c. she come out of barn
          [East Anglia, Trudgill 2004: 146]

With regard to Singapore English, it has been suggested that this variety draws the boundary between count nouns and non-count nouns in a way different from standard English. Nouns that are classified and used only as count nouns in standard English can be used both as count and as non-count nouns in Colloquial Singapore English (Alsagoff and Ho 1998: 143–4), as shown in (35).

(35) She queue up very long to buy ticket for us. [Colloquial Singapore English, Wee 2004: 1061]

Conversely, some non-count nouns appear with plural marking and are apparently treated as count nouns: *luggages, equipments, staffs, furnitures*.

In a similar way, article omission is reported to occur before abstract nouns in Malaysian English (Baskaran 2004: 1074). However, articles can only be left out before abstract nouns that are modified, as in (31a) above, with the exception of concrete generic nouns in subject complement position, as in (31b).

Platt et al. (1984: 52–9) argue for a contrast between specific and non-specific reference expressed by the presence of the definite article in contrast with its absence. This is meant to hold for New Englishes in general. You can find some illustrations from East African English in (36).

(36) a. Give me beer. 'Give me any beer.' (unspecific)
      b. Give me the beer. 'Give me a certain beer.' (specific)
          [East African English, Schmied 2004: 933]

Even though there appear to be certain correlations between article overuse and omission and specific (regional) varieties, many varieties manifest these phenomena concurrently. In other words, there is general variability in the use of articles that we find mentioned explicitly in the descriptions of some varieties. For example, for Pakistani English, Mahboob gives us the following examples illustrating overuse and underuse of both the definite and indefinite article:

(37) a. The England is ∅ / a / the good place.
      b. He said that ∅ Education Ministry is reorganizing English syllabus.
      c. My father is ∅ lecturer.
          [Pakistani English, Mahboob 2004: 1052]

Similar remarks can be found for Ghanaian English. Huber and Dako (2004: 859) state that 'GhE omits articles that are required in BrE, inserts articles where there are none in BrE, and also ignores distinctions of definiteness that are made in BrE.' Consider the examples in (38). Such variability in the use of articles appears especially prominent in second language varieties.

(38) a. They are supposed to arrive at *the* Kotoka International Airport this
        evening.
     b. He called for ∅ abolition of the death penalty.
     c. I had *a* shock of my life yesterday.
        [Ghanaian English, Huber and Dako 2004: 860]

Finally, let me direct your attention to a phenomenon that is only marginally
relevant in the present context, but, as it falls within the domain of determiners,
we at least have to mention it. The phenomenon concerns the absence of plural
marking after measure nouns, i.e. nouns like *kilo*, *mile*, *meter*, etc. that are
premodified by a cardinal numeral. It is quite prominent in Pidgin and Creole
varieties, but may also be encountered in some traditional dialects. Examples
can be found in (39).

(39) a. He used to have four pound of butter a week every week. [Southwest
        of England, Wagner 2004: 157]
     b. I walked four mile yesterday. [Bahamian English, Reaser and Torbert
        2004: 398]

5.3   Cross-linguistic comparison

For a better understanding of the types of variation found in English and across
varieties of English in this domain, it is first of all necessary to point out that
definiteness is a cognitive notion that may receive overt marking, but can also
be left unmarked. Thus, we find languages without articles; languages with
definite articles; languages with definite and indefinite articles, definite articles
and demonstratives; and languages that mark definiteness in other ways (e.g.
word order). It is possible to draw a semantic map of definiteness and show
that markers of definiteness cover different areas on such a map in different
languages – and, by extension, in different varieties of English.

5.3.1   *The marking of definiteness*

In the introductory section to this chapter, we stated that definite articles are
grammatical expressions that mark the identifiability of a referent in discourse.
Using a definite article signals that the referent of the noun phrase thus modified
is known to the addressee and is thus identifiable.

As stated above, languages may have definite articles, but, of course, they
can also function without these devices. For example, Russian is a language
that does not mark definiteness in this way, as shown in (40).

(40) mal'chik   potseloval devochku
     boy.NOM kiss.PAST girl.ACC
     'The boy kissed the girl.' [Russian, Julia Davydova]

In a sample of 620 languages, Dryer (2011a) finds 198 languages that possess no definite or indefinite article. The majority of languages in this sample have a marker to signal definiteness, even though this does not necessarily have to be a definite article. We also find demonstrative pronouns used to signal definiteness, and also definite affixes. Languages with definite articles include English, German, Spanish, Lakhota, Malagasy, and many others; no definite articles are found in Greenlandic, Russian, Finnish, Kiowa, and Urdu, among others. Demonstrative pronouns in the function of definite articles are found in Latvian and Indonesian. The Scandinavian languages are suitable cases to illustrate definite affixes.

In cases where there is no dedicated definite article available, there are several alternative ways to express the identifiability of a referent, such as word order, stress assignment, indefinite and definite pronouns, or morphological case (Juvonen 2006: 485).

The absence of definite or indefinite articles in some languages may lead to changes in article usage in English when these languages come into contact with English, or, more precisely, when speakers of these languages begin to learn and use English. Such situations of language contact account for many of the cases of article overuse and article underuse as discussed in Section 5.2.2 above. Learners may impose the definiteness marking pattern of their first language on English, and they may also reinterpret the English article system when they learn English. It is certainly no accident that article usage in the relevant varieties shows differences in precisely those areas where article usage is variable in the standard varieties, i.e. with nouns for seasons, institutions, and the like (the 'cultural uses' in Liu and Gleason's 2002: 7–8 terminology). In the long run, these differences in article usage may stabilise and be passed on to the next generation of speakers, contributing to the nativisation of a variety.

5.3.2   Demonstratives and definite articles

It is not uncommon for definite articles formally to resemble or even be identical to demonstrative pronouns. In the sample of 620 languages compiled by Dryer (2011a), which I introduced in the previous section, there are 216 languages with definite articles that are formally distinct from the demonstrative pronoun, contrasting with 69 languages in which the demonstrative also serves the function of a definite article.

In historical terms, definite articles typically derive from demonstrative pronouns. For example, Old English was a language without definite articles, though it did have a series of demonstrative pronouns. These Old English demonstratives frequently come out as definite articles in today's English, as shown in (41). Evidently, they grammaticalised into today's definite article over time.

(41) hu   *ða* æþelingas ellen   fremedon
     how that nobles   courage did
     'how the nobles performed heroic acts' [Old English, *Beowulf* 3, van
     Gelderen 2006: 60]

Similar grammaticalisation processes appear to have been replicated in some
varieties of English. Although we do not find many clear cases illustrating such
processes, we can still name two good candidates here. For Tok Pisin, it is
reported that *dispela* 'this' is going through this grammaticalisation process
resulting in a new definite article. In the function of the definite article, it is
typically found in the reduced forms *displa*, *disla*, or *sla*. This is shown in
example (42).

(42) yu   kisim *sla*   buk.
     you take   this/the book
     'Take this/the book.' [Tok Pisin, Smith 2004: 734]

Hence, Tok Pisin seems to take the same grammaticalisation route as standard
English did. Another putative instance of an emerging definite article can be
observed in Solomon Islands Pijin. For this variety, it is reported that the
demonstrative pronoun *ia* 'this', which has historically been derived from
English *here*, is being used more and more to cover the functions of a definite
article. Thus – depending on the context – *ia* can be interpreted as either *the* or
as *this* (as in (43)).[5]

(43) Man *ia*   mi lukim long sip.
     man this/the I   see   on ship
     'I saw this/the man on the ship.' [Solomon Islands Pijin, Jourdan 2004:
     705]

The use of demonstrative pronouns in the function of definite articles is also
known from some post-colonial Englishes. Gil (2003: 474), for example,
discusses this phenomenon in the context of Singapore English, as illustrated
in (44).

(44) a. There was a rock in front. So he actually knock to *this*, eh, rock and he
        actually fall down.
     b. After that, eh, *this*, eh, the, the person who stole the, eh, pears actually
        cycle off.
        [Singapore English, own fieldwork]

5.3.3   *Indefinite articles and the numeral 'one'*

In Section 5.3.1 above, we learnt that languages may lack definite and/or
indefinite articles. While some languages only have definite articles, others just

---

[5] Example (43) also provides an interesting case of contact-induced word order variation.

have indefinite ones. Japanese and Persian, for example, only have indefinite articles. In the sample consulted by Dryer (2011a) there are forty-five languages that possess an indefinite, but no definite, article.

Indefinite articles frequently have the same form as the numeral 'one', and may derive from it in terms of their etymology. In German, the indefinite article and the numeral 'one' are not distinct, even though the former is typically unstressed.

(45) a. Paul hat *ein* neues Auto.
        Paul has a   new   car
        'Paul has got a new car.'
     b. Maria hat *EIN* Kind, nicht zwei.
        Mary has one child not   two
        'Mary has got one child, and not two.'
        [German, personal knowledge]

The standard English article *a/an* can also be traced back to the numeral 'one' historically. The examples in (46) from Old English show practically the same situation as in Modern German.

(46) a. ... for he was *an* yuel man...
            for he was an evil man
            '... for he was an evil man' [Old English, *Anglo-Saxon Chronicle* (Laud) (Peterborough contin.) anno 1140]
     b. se wer mot habban butan *an* wif.
        the man must have   but   one wife
        'man must have only one wife' [Old English, *Regula Canonicorum* (Corpus Cambr. 191) lxv. 305]

This formal correspondence of the numeral 'one' and the indefinite article is also common cross-linguistically. Dryer (2011b), relying on a sample of 534 languages, finds 112 in which the indefinite article is the same as 'one', and 102 that distinguish between the indefinite article and the numeral 'one'.

The historical grammaticalisation process leading from numeral 'one' to indefinite article appears to be replicated synchronically in some non-standard varieties of English. In this way at least we may interpret the occurrence of the numeral 'one' before nouns in some Pidgin and Creole varieties where it does not express the existence of one entity in contrast with two or more, but signals indefiniteness. Consider the examples in (47) through (49).

(47) Gani is *one* man who does not tell lies, he calls the spade a spade. [Nigerian English, Alo and Mesthrie 2004: 820]
(48) Ai gon bai *wan* pikap.
     I go buy a   pickup
     'I'm going to buy a pickup.' [Hawai'i Creole, Sakoda and Siegel 2004: 743]

(49) mipla wetim man bilong *wanpla* anti blong mi
     we   wait   man POSS one/an aunt POSS me
     'We were waiting for the husband of an auntie of mine.' [Tok Pisin, Smith
     2004: 734]

5.3.4   Distance contrasts in demonstrative pronouns

An important cross-linguistic parameter of variation concerns the number of
distances encoded by demonstrative pronouns. Recall from Section 5.1.2 that
standard English possesses a two-way contrast in the system of demonstratives,
permitting a distinction between proximal (near the speaker) and distal (away
from the speaker) entities.

   Cross-linguistically speaking, such a binary distinction is the typical case.
Based on a representative sample of 234 languages, Diessel (2011) shows that
no fewer than 127 possess such a proximal/distal contrast, while 88 have a
three-way contrast. Eight languages in the sample distinguish four distances,
and only four languages draw a distinction between five or more distances.
Seven languages in this sample have no distance contrast.

   These distributions make it clear that varieties of English boasting a three-
way contrast (*this*, *that*, *yon*) are not unexpected in cross-linguistic terms.

   In those cases where a language only has a distance-neutral demonstrative
pronoun, adverbial particles like 'here' and 'there' may be used to add distance
contrasts. For example, German and French are languages with distance-neutral
demonstratives (Diessel 2011), and hence such adverbial particles are used to
encode a contrast in distance: German *das hier* 'this here' versus *das da* 'this
there'; French *ceci* 'this here' versus *cela* 'this there'.

(50) Das   Bild   hier gefällt mir besser als   das   da.
     DEM picture here like   me better than DEM there
     'I like this picture better than that one (over there).' [German, Diessel
     2011]

From a functional perspective, this is an extremely transparent strategy, and
hence it can come as no surprise that we also find it in varieties of English, as
in (51).

(51) a. He had one of *these here* hog rifles.
      b. *Them there* fellows come through here.
      c. *That there* sawmill I worked at was there before I married.
         [Appalachian English, Montgomery 2004: 264]

Systems of demonstratives that distinguish three distances allow a division
into two distinct types (Diessel 2011). On the one hand, we find so-called
'distance-oriented systems' in which the paradigmatic contrast between the
demonstratives is tantamount to a difference in distance between the object and

Table 5.2 *Distance-oriented demonstratives in Hunzib (van den Berg 1995: 61, cited in Diessel 2011).*

Proximal	*bəd*
Medial	*bəl*
Distal	*əg*

Table 5.3 *Person-oriented demonstratives in Japanese (Kuno 1973: 27, cited in Diessel 2011).*

Near speaker	*kono*
Near hearer	*sono*
Away from speaker and hearer	*ano*

the deictic centre, for example proximal, medial, and distal. Such a system is shown in Table 5.2.

On the other hand, there are systems that allow one to signal speaker proximity and hearer proximity, in contrast with distance from both speaker and hearer. These systems are known as 'person-oriented systems' and are illustrated in Table 5.3.

The question arises as to whether the English non-standard systems of demonstratives that distinguish three distances belong to the distance-oriented type or the person-oriented type. To my knowledge, the literature on varieties of English contains no information to solve this question.

5.4   Summary and list of keywords

In the introductory sections to this chapter, we explored the functions of definite and indefinite articles, as well as those of demonstrative pronouns. Definite articles signal the identifiability of a referent, while the use of the indefinite article signals a non-identifiable referent. Demonstrative pronouns couple the notion of identifiability with the expression of distance, i.e. whether the relevant referent is close to a deictic centre or not. To a certain extent, article usage is variable even in the standard varieties. This variation concerns specific noun classes and may be captured as 'cultural uses' or 'situational uses'. In non-standard varieties of English, we encountered non-standard determiner forms that may also bear functions unknown in the standard varieties. We also examined phenomena of overuse and underuse of articles, assessed against the usage patterns found in the standard varieties. It emerged that the cultural uses are particularly prone to overuse and underuse. Demonstratives may assume the function of definite articles. Cross-linguistically, the expression of definiteness by articles is one strategy among several others, and it may also be left unmarked. Hence, there is nothing 'wrong' about varieties of English without articles. It is not uncommon that the functions of definite articles and demonstratives map onto one form – something we also encountered in varieties of English. Indefinite articles are typically derived from the numeral 'one', and this phenomenon, too, is attested in non-standard varieties. While standard English has only two distance contrasts in the system of demonstratives, non-standard varieties may have three.

Keywords: agreement, mass/count distinction, cultural/situational uses of definite articles, definite articles, definiteness, deictic centre, demonstrative pronouns, dental fricatives, distance contrasts, distance-oriented systems, dual, grammaticalisation, identifiability, indefinite articles, indefiniteness, locative adverbials, mass/count systems, measure nouns, numeral 'one', omission of articles, overuse and underuse of articles, person-oriented systems, possessive determiners, quantifiers, referential properties, trial, unique referents.

5.5   Exercises

Basic level

1. What are determiners? How do they differ from adjectives, and in which ways are they similar to adjectives? Explain.
2. Take a look at the following words:

   no, this, many, my, whichever, one, an, any, these, their, what, fewer

   a. Determine to which class of determiners, as introduced in Section 5.1, they belong.
   b. Can you find more examples for each of these categories?
3. Draw up a list of the non-standard determiners forms that we find across varieties of English. Can you detect any general trends?

Intermediate level

1. Take a close look at the following sentence pairs.

   i. a. *I met her at college.*
      b. *I met her at the college.*
   ii. a. *The summer of 1969 was an exciting time.*
       b. *Summer in 1969 was not like this summer.*

iii. a. *Measles is a very contagious disease.*
   b. *The Measles is a very contagious disease.*
iv. a. *Where are you having dinner tonight?*
   b. *The dinner yesterday was absolutely fantastic.*

   a. Determine whether there are differences in meaning between the sentences in a. and b. If there are, explain how they differ.
   b. The sentences above represent variable contexts of article use in standard English. Can you name them? Can you think of other contexts that are variable in terms of article use?
   c. Does the variability in article use in standard English have an impact on the use of articles across varieties of English? Explain.
2. Locative adverbials like *here* and *there* can be used to express or augment distance contrasts of demonstratives.
   a. Explain how this is possible.
   b. In which varieties of English do we find this phenomenon?
3. Huddleston and Pullum (2002: 372) analyse the pronominal forms in the examples below as determiners. Can you see why?

   a. *We supporters of federal Europe will eventually win the argument.*
   b. *You students should form a society.*

   Advanced level

1. The *World Atlas of Language Structures* (Dryer and Haspelmath 2011; http://wals.info) represents a cross-linguistic survey of grammatical domains based on extensive language samples. Chapter 41, by Holger Diessel, is concerned with distance contrasts encoded by demonstratives.
   According to chapter 41, out of a sample of 234 languages, 127 possess a demonstrative system that encodes two distance contrasts. Eighty-eight languages draw a three-way contrast, eight languages a four-way contrast, and four languages encode five or more distance contrasts. Seven languages have no distance contrasts in their system of demonstratives.
   a. Read chapter 41 and explain what is meant by 'distance contrast'. Which contrasts are typically encoded by languages; which contrasts are less typical?
   b. Draw a summary of the distance contrasts found across varieties of English. Which contrasts are encoded, and how do these compare against the cross-linguistic generalisations?
2. A good overview of variable article usage can be found in Quirk et al. (1985: 277–81). Let us hypothesise that varieties of English show differences in how they make use of these variable contexts, and test this hypothesis empirically.

    a. Procure the spoken sections of the *ICE* (http://ice-corpora.net/ice/) for the British component (*ICE*-Great Britain) and the Singapore component (*ICE*-Singapore).

    b. Extract the sentences containing the contexts where article usage may vary.

    c. Determine whether the two varieties differ in their article usage in these contexts, and interpret your findings.

3. Cross-linguistic work on grammaticalisation has revealed that demonstrative pronouns may develop into definite articles, and that the numeral 'one' may develop into an indefinite article (Heine and Kuteva 2002). A case in point is the English indefinite article *a/an*, which derives from the numeral 'one' in historical terms.

    a. You learnt in the preceding sections that the forms *one* or *wan* are employed in the function of indefinite articles in some varieties of English (e.g. Ghanaian English). Give reasons why the numeral has developed into an indefinite article, i.e. which properties has it adopted that characterise it as an indefinite article?

    b. Discuss why it is possible for the numeral 'one' to develop into an indefinite article. How can we explain this process?

5.6   References

Alsagoff, Lubna and Chee Lick Ho. 1998. The grammar of Singapore English. In Joseph Foley, Thiru Kandiah, Bao Zhiming, Anthea Fraser Gupta, Lubna Alsagoff, Ho Chee Lick, Lionel Wee, Ismail S. Talib, and Wendy Bokhorst-Heng (eds.), *English in New Cultural Contexts: Reflections from Singapore*, 175–200. Singapore: Oxford University Press.

Chesterman, Andrew. 1991. *On Definiteness: A Study with Special Reference to English and Finnish*. Cambridge University Press.

Clarke, Sandra. 2010. *Newfoundland and Labrador English*. Edinburgh University Press.

Diessel, Holger. 2011. Pronominal and adnominal demonstratives. In Matthew S. Dryer and Martin Haspelmath (eds.), *The World Atlas of Language Structures Online*. Munich: Max Planck Digital Library, chapter 42. Available online at http://wals.info/chapter/42. Accessed 22 December 2011.

Dryer, Matthew S. 2011a. Definite articles. In Matthew S. Dryer and Martin Haspelmath (eds.), *The World Atlas of Language Structures Online*. Munich: Max Planck Digital Library, chapter 37. Available online at http://wals.info/chapter/37. Accessed 22 December 2011.

2011b. Indefinite articles. In Matthew S. Dryer and Martin Haspelmath (eds.), *The World Atlas of Language Structures Online*. Munich: Max Planck Digital Library, chapter 38. Available online at http://wals.info/chapter/38. Accessed 22 December 2011.

Filppula, Markku. 1999. *A Grammar of Irish English: Language in Hibernian Style*. London: Routledge.

Gil, David. 2001. Quantifiers. In Martin Haspelmath, Ekkehard König, Wulf Oesterre-
icher, and Wolfgang Raible (eds.), *Language Typology and Linguistic Universals:
An International Handbook, volume II*, 1275–94. Berlin: Walter de Gruyter.
    2003. English goes Asian: Number and (in)definiteness in the Singlish noun phrase.
    In Frans Plank (ed.), *Noun Phrase Structure in the Languages of Europe*, 467–514.
    Berlin: Mouton de Gruyter.
Hawkins, John A. 1978. *Definiteness and Indefiniteness: A Study in Reference and
Grammaticality Prediction*. London: Croom Helm.
Heine, Bernd and Tania Kuteva. 2002. *World Lexicon of Grammaticalization*. Cambridge
University Press.
Juvonen, Päivi. 2006. Articles, definite and indefinite. In Edward Keith Brown (ed.),
Encyclopaedia of Language and Linguistics, volume I, 484–7. Oxford: Elsevier.
Kuno, Susumo. 1973. *The Structure of the Japanese Language*. Cambridge, MA: MIT
Press.
Liu, Dilin and Johanna L. Gleason. 2002. Acquisition of the article THE by non-
native speakers of English: An analysis of four nongeneric uses. *Studies in Second
Language Acquisition* 24(1). 1–26.
Platt, John, Heidi Weber, and Mian Lian Ho. 1984. *The New Englishes*. London: Rout-
ledge.
Shnukal, Anna. 1988. *Broken: An Introduction to the Creole Language of Torres*. Can-
berra: Research School of Pacific Linguistics, Australian National University.
Siemund, Peter. 2008. *Pronominal Gender in English: A Study of English Varieties from
a Cross-Linguistic Perspective*. London: Routledge.
van den Berg, Helma. 1995. *A Grammar of Hunzib*. Munich: Lincom Europa.
van Gelderen, Elly. 2006. *A History of the English Language*. Amsterdam: John Benjamins.
See *General references* for Alo and Mesthrie 2004; Anderwald 2004; Baskaran 2004;
Beal 2004; Bowerman 2004; Clarke 2004; Crowley 2004; Dryer and Haspelmath
2011; Faraclas 2004; Hosali 2004; Huber 2004; Huber and Dako 2004; Huddleston
and Pullum 2002; Jourdan 2004; Kortmann and Szmrecsanyi 2004; Mahboob 2004;
Malcolm 2004; McCormick 2004; Melchers 2004; Mesthrie 2004b; Miller 2004;
Montgomery 2004; Mufwene 2004; Mugler and Tent 2004; Patrick 2004; Quirk et
al. 1985; Reaser and Torbert 2004; Sakoda and Siegel 2004; Schmied 2004; Smith
2004; Swan 2005; Trudgill 2004; Wagner 2004; Wee 2004; Winford and Migge
2004.

5.7   Further reading

Abbott, Barbara. 2006. Definite and indefinite. In Keith Brown (ed.), *Encyclopaedia of
Language and Linguistics, volume III*, 392–9. Oxford: Elsevier.
Bauer, Brigitte L. M. 2007. The definite article in Indo-European: Emergence of a
new grammatical category? In Elisabeth Stark, Elisabeth Leiss, and Walter Abra-
ham (eds.), *Nominal Determination: Typology, Context Constraints, and Historical
Emergence*, 103–39. Amsterdam: John Benjamins.
Diessel, Holger. 1999. *Demonstratives: Form, Function and Grammaticalization*. Ams-
terdam: John Benjamins.

2006. Demonstratives. In Edward Keith Brown (ed.), *Encyclopaedia of Language and Linguistics, volume III*, 430–5. Oxford: Elsevier.

Haspelmath, Martin. 1999. Explaining article-possessor complementarity: Economic motivation in noun phrase syntax. *Language* 75(2). 227–43.

Sand, Andrea. 2003. The definite article in Irish English and other contact varieties of English. In Hildegard L.C. Tristram (ed.), *The Celtic Englishes, Volume III*, 413–30. Heidelberg: Winter.

2004. Shared morpho-syntactic features of contact varieties: Article use. *World Englishes* 23(2). 281–98.

Sankoff, Gillian and Claudia Mazzie. 1991. Determining noun phrases in Tok Pisin. *Journal of Pidgin and Creole Linguistics* 6(1). 1–24.

6 Tense marking

The grammatical category of tense relates to the expression of temporal relations and the linguistic embedding of real-world situations in time. It involves highly familiar categories such as the present tense, the present perfect, and the past tense, as well as several others. Tense marking has been widely researched in the grammar of English both in the standard varieties and in the non-standard varieties that are the topic of this book. Section 6.1 of this chapter will introduce the foundations of this category, while Section 6.2 will be concerned with tense in varieties of English. In Section 6.3, we will explore cross-linguistic variation in the realisation of this category.

6.1   Overview

Before we can concern ourselves with the study of tense in English and its varieties, we first of all need to achieve some clarification about this category. As scholarly interest in it has been exceptionally extensive, we can only mention the most important facts at this point (see Comrie 1985 and Klein 1994 for very readable introductions).

We can define tense as a grammatical category for the expression of temporal relations. Comrie (1985: 9) states that 'tense is grammaticalised expression of location in time'. I would like to emphasise the terms 'grammatical' and 'grammatical category', as temporal relations can also be expressed by a diverse set of lexical expressions (e.g. *before, after, yesterday, two minutes ago*, etc.). These will not be of interest here. We will define a linguistic expression as a 'grammatical marker' if its use is obligatory in certain contexts and it can be used together with a large number of lexical expressions. Grammatical markers, thus, belong to the regular and rule-based systems of language. An obvious candidate for a grammatical marker expressing temporal relations is the *-ed* suffix of English, which locates the situation described by the verb and its arguments before the moment of speaking:

(1) John walk-*ed* to school.

Tenses, we can generalise, thus establish a temporal relation between the time of utterance (TU), i.e. the moment of speaking, and the time at which the situation described by the sentence occurs (TSit). It is now easy to define past tense, future tense, and present tense, as shown in (2) below. Such schematic definitions can be found in practically all major treatments of tense (Reichenbach 1947: 287–98; Comrie 1985: ch. 6; Klein 1994: ch. 7).

(2) a. past tense: TU after TSit
    b. present tense: TU included in TSit
    c. future tense: TSit after TU

We take it that the description in (2) is largely self-explanatory, and hence it is sufficient to address briefly the 'included'-relation in (2b). This more special relation – rather than a simple relation of equality (TSit equals TU) – is necessary because the present tense is typically used for situations that began in the past and extend into the future, thus lying around the moment of utterance (e.g. *Paul lives in London*). We also find utterances in the present tense that are co-extensive with the moment of speaking (sports commentaries: *Rodrigo kicks and misses the goal*; performative utterances: *I hereby declare you husband and wife*); but these seem less frequent.

The description in (2) also shows that tense is a deictic category, as the time of situation is interpreted in relation to a point of reference (i.e. the moment of speaking). Tenses that relate the time of situation directly to the moment of speaking are called 'absolute tenses'. These, namely past, present, and future, contrast with tenses that require an additional reference point for their interpretation. Consider the past perfect example in (3a), where the event of leaving lies before the event of arriving, and the latter lies before the time of utterance. The corresponding formal representation is shown in (3b). The abbreviation 'TR' stands for the additional temporal reference point (time of reference).

(3) a. John had already left when Mary arrived.
    b. TSit before TR before TU

Tenses requiring an additional reference point for their interpretation are called 'relative tenses'. English relative tenses include the past perfect, as shown in (3a) above, the future perfect and the present perfect, even though the status of the present perfect is not completely clear as the additional reference point is usually indistinguishable from the time of utterance. In addition, the present perfect has properties that make it look like an aspectual category. A typical present perfect example, as in (4), expresses a result available at the moment of utterance caused by a situation that occurred prior to it. Many analysts therefore prefer to treat it as an aspect (Comrie 1976; Quirk et al. 1985).[1] The alternative

---

[1] On the differences between past tense and present perfect, see Comrie (1985: 78).

analysis, i.e. as a tense, is maintained in Declerck (1991) and Huddleston and Pullum (2002). Kortmann (1991: 19) views the perfect as a category *sui generis*. Apparently, it straddles the line of these categories. The perfect is here included in the chapter on tense marking, mainly for expository reasons.

(4) John has written the letter.

In the context of the present perfect, several finer-grained distinctions have been proposed that mostly result from the interaction of this category with the lexical aspect of the verb involved (also called aktionsart). Consider the examples in (5) below.

(5) a. existential perfect: I have met the Queen, but a very long time ago.
    b. resultative perfect: I have lost my keys.
    c. universal perfect: We have believed this for many years.

On the notional level, the so-called 'existential perfect' (experiential perfect) in (5a) is difficult to distinguish from the simple past, as the time of the situation lies completely before the moment of speaking, and, as a matter of fact, the present perfect could be replaced with the simple past in many of the examples involved. What the present perfect adds to such examples is a higher degree of relevance of the situation at the moment of speaking, i.e. meeting the Queen is still felt to have an impact at the moment of speaking. Resultative perfects, as in (5b), claim that the state described by the verb holds at the moment of speaking, while universal perfects (5c) describe states that began in the past and still hold at the moment of speaking. Accepting the danger of oversimplification, we may generalise that existential perfects arise in the context of verbs that describe punctual events. Resultative perfects, in contrast, can be found with change-of-state verbs, whereas universal perfects receive their specific interpretation from the state verbs involved.

Before turning to varieties of English, we finally need to discuss very briefly the future tense category, as several constructions compete for this category in English, with each of them tied to specific interpretations and contexts. Example (6) shows three categories that can be used for the expression of future time relations in English. The *will*-future expresses a strong prediction, whereas the *going-to*-future usually relies on some indicator available at the moment of speaking from which the prediction can be inferred. If the present progressive is used with future time reference, the situation is portrayed as unavoidable, i.e. necessarily going to happen. As the *will*-future imposes the fewest restrictions on its context of use and has the greatest diachronic depth, it is usually considered the typical future tense category of English, even though there is nothing wrong about assuming two such categories.

(6) a. *will*-future: You will win. (if you take that tonic.)
    b. *going-to*-future: You are going to win, as you have taken that tonic.
    c. present progressive: You are winning. (Nothing can stop you.)

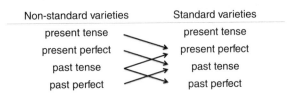

Figure 6.1 Correspondences between non-standard and standard tense use.

6.2   Varieties of English

The grammatical category of tense has been discussed widely in the study of English varieties, as it shows substantial variation. You are certainly aware that the use of the past tense and the present perfect differs even across the standard varieties. For example, (7a) is more likely to be encountered in British English, while (7b) has a greater chance of being heard in American English.

(7) a. Have you seen the movie?
      b. Did you see the movie?

Elsness (2009: 230) supports these intuitions by corpus evidence. For example, in present-day British English, the share of the present perfect in the set of all past-referring verb forms amounts to as much as 19.7 per cent, while the corresponding figure for present-day American English is only 9.8 per cent. Conversely, in British English, the past tense accounts for 61.9 per cent of all past-referring verb forms. In American English, the past tense is more widely used, with 76.2 per cent.

In addition to such distributional differences, we can also find genuinely different formal exponents and constructions in some varieties, as, for example, the *after*-perfect in Irish English:

(8) I'm after missing the train. 'I've just missed the train.'

In what follows, we will explore the category of tense across varieties of English along the two dimensions introduced above, starting with non-standard distributions of grammatical forms that are available in the standard varieties. In a second step, we will turn to grammatical forms that occur only in non-standard varieties of English.

6.2.1   Non-standard distributions

Variation concerning the use of standard tense forms is substantial, but certainly not overwhelming. We mainly find variation in the use of the present perfect and the past perfect, but also with regard to the present and the past tense. Figure 6.1 provides a summary of non-standard tense use in relation to standard (British) tense use. For example, the use of the present tense in non-standard varieties may correspond to that of the present perfect in standard varieties. We will explore these correspondences in what follows. The substitutions are variable features and typically are not obligatory.

Present tense in present perfect context The present tense may substitute the present perfect mainly in contexts that we referred to as the universal use of the present perfect, as introduced in (5c) above. Since the relevant examples, such as those shown in (9) and (10) below, describe a time period beginning in the past and still holding at the moment of utterance (and possibly continuing beyond this point), it is clear why the simple present tense is a reasonable alternative.

(9) a. I'm not in this [caravan] long { ... } Only have this here a few year. 'I haven't been [...] have had this here for a few years.'
     b. And = they're fighting out ten years in the North for an all-Ireland republic. ' ... they have been fighting ... '
        [Irish English, Filppula 1999: 122]
(10) a. I'm here for twenty years. [South African English, Mesthrie 2004c: 1134]
     b. I am here since two o'clock. [Indian English, Bhatt 2004: 1028]

This use of the present tense primarily occurs with state verbs in combination with temporal adverbials. It can be found in many post-colonial varieties of English (Indian English, Hong Kong English, South African English, etc.). It has also been described for Irish English – which may also be regarded as a post-colonial variety – and some historical English dialects (Filppula 1999: 122–8). This use of the present tense is not found in the standard varieties.

Present perfect in past tense contexts In some varieties we also find the present perfect in combination with time adverbials that clearly do not include the moment of utterance, as shown in (11). This domain is reserved for the simple past in the standard varieties. In the cross-linguistic section of this chapter (Section 6.3), we will learn that present perfects have a tendency to develop into narrative tenses (i.e. past tenses), and one is tempted to analyse the examples in (11) as such an instance of semantic change. However, there is usually not sufficient diachronic data available to substantiate such a claim.

(11) a. I have seen him yesterday. [Pakistani English, Mahboob 2004: 1046]
     b. It has been established hundreds of years ago. [Ghanaian English, Huber and Dako 2004: 855]
     c. It's been twenty year ago they offered me a house and land. [Appalachian English, Montgomery 2004: 251]

Past tense in present perfect context As illustrated in (12), the simple past tense may appear in present perfect contexts. We cannot really classify this phenomenon as a non-standard feature since it also occurs in the standard varieties, especially in North American English. Still, it is also widespread in non-standard varieties, both traditional dialects and Englishes emerging in post-colonial settings.

(12) a. We just saw her.

   b. Did you ever go to Tasmania?

With respect to our classification of present perfect contexts (see (5) above), the simple past can primarily be found in so-called existential contexts, i.e. in the context of event verbs.

(13) a. I never felt myself alien in Delhi, though I belong to Bihar.

   b. It's very nice and I studied Bible. Not very much but I have studied.
      [Mesolectal Indian English, *The Hamburg Corpus of Non-Native Varieties of English*, Davydova 2011]

(14) Were you ever in Kenmare? 'Have you ever been … ?' [Irish English, Filppula 2004: 74]

Past tense in past perfect contexts and vice versa There is also some variation in the use of the past tense and the past perfect, with either form occurring in the position of the other, even though this phenomenon is less well described and may also be encountered in the spoken or more colloquial forms of the standard varieties. I provide examples in (15), but I am hesitant to assign them to a specific variety of English.

(15) a. They had gone to the station and had taken the first train. 'They went to the station and took the first train.'

   b. He came before she left. 'He had come before she left.'

The past perfect, as a formal means to describe a past before the past, appears to be especially prominent in written language, as spoken language typically relies on the context and lexical expressions (*before, after*, etc.) to resolve sequential temporal settings. Hence, we can expect to find examples like (15) in many non-standard varieties, as these typically operate in the spoken register. You can find some authentic examples in (16).

(16) a. She said she came looking for me. 'She said she had come looking for me.' [Black South African English, Mesthrie 2004a: 964]

   b. … he … was angry I didn't stay in the café. 'He was angry that I hadn't stayed in the café.' [Scottish English, Miller 2004: 56]

   c. SIR – Sometimes back I had written a letter to this column about the deteriorating condition of the Vatuwaqa Cemetery Building and the filthy state of the toilets. [Fiji English, Mugler and Tent 2004: 781, Letters to the Editor, *Fiji Times*, 20 November 1996]

6.2.2   Special grammatical forms

Some varieties of English possess special grammatical forms dedicated to the expression of temporal relations. We can mainly find them for the expression of meanings associated with the standard English present perfect and for future time reference. We will survey them in the ensuing paragraphs.

The after-*perfect* The so-called '*after*-perfect' is a diagnostic feature of traditional Irish English that can also be encountered in Newfoundland English, as a significant part of the population there stems from Ireland. It is illustrated in (17) and (18).

(17) a. You're after ruinin' me. 'You have (just) ruined me.'
   b. And when the bell goes at six you just think you were only after going over, and you get out and up again.
      [Irish English, Filppula 2004: 75]

(18) a. I'm after havin' eleven rabbits eaten (by dogs) this last three months.
   b. I'm after burning now (in the sun) about three times.
      [Newfoundland English, Clarke 2004: 306]

You will probably agree that this construction looks highly unusual. It originated in Ireland as a consequence of language contact between English and Irish, which is the indigenous – and, today first official – language of Ireland. It is a more or less direct loan translation of an Irish syntactic structure. Consider (19).

(19) Tá sé tar éis imeacht.
   is he after going
   'He has just gone.' [Irish, Pietsch 2009: 540]

In Irish English, the *after*-perfect is primarily used for so-called 'hot-news perfects', i.e. perfects reporting events in the immediate pre-time of the moment of utterance. Note that the *after*-perfect can be found with either a present tense (17a) or a past tense auxiliary (17b).

Already and finish Another form to convey perfect meaning is the adverb *already*, as *inter alia* reported from Singapore English (Bao 1995, 2005). We frequently find this adverb in sentences with a present perfect in standard English, but its occurrence there is clearly not mandatory. What makes the use of this adverb special in non-standard varieties is that it occurs together with a verb in the present tense, or an untensed verb form for that matter, and assumes the function of perfect marking on its own. Hence, we may tentatively analyse it as a grammatical perfect marker, but a conclusive analysis would have to take additional criteria (distributional, phonological) into consideration. In the examples shown in (20), *already* does not express that the events described by the relevant sentences occurred earlier than expected, as it does in standard English.[2]

(20) a. Miss Lin eat cake already. 'Miss Lin ate / has eaten the cake.'
    b. I see the movie already. 'I saw the movie.'
    c. I wash my hand already. 'I have washed / washed my hand.'
    d. After it rain already, we can go out. 'After it has rained, we can go out.'
    [Singapore English, Bao 2005: 239–41]

Bao (1995, 2005) analyses these perfective or completive uses of *already* in Singapore English as substrate influence from Chinese (used as a cover term for various dialects such as Mandarin, Cantonese, Teochow, and Hokkien that are found in Singapore). As you can see in the examples shown in (21), Chinese has a particle (*le*) that is quite similar in terms of meaning and distribution to *already* in Singapore English.

(21) a. ta qu niuyue   le
    he go New York LE
    'He went to New York.' [Mandarin, Bao 1995: 185]
    b. Mary dǎ le dàn.
    Mary beat LE egg
    'Mary has beaten the eggs.' [Mandarin, Bao 2005: 243]

The substrate analysis gains further support from the fact that *already* in Singapore English has an additional inchoative use – marking the beginning of an event – that is part of the usage repertoire of the Chinese particle *le*. The initial three examples in (20) above also allow for this inchoative interpretation and could be translated as in (22). It is implied that the action started immediately before the moment of speaking.[3]

(22) a. Miss Lin eat cake already. 'Miss Lin is (now) eating the cake.'
    b. I see the movie already. 'I am (now) seeing the movie.'
    c. I wash my hand already. 'I am (now) washing my hand.'

You can find a corresponding inchoative example from Mandarin in (23) below. Bao (2005) argues for the so-called 'systemic substratist hypothesis', meaning that in situations of language contact complete grammatical subsystems are transferred from one language to another, with the transferred morphosyntactic exponents being required to obey the grammatical constraints of the receiving language.

---

[2] Singapore English also has an emphatic perfect constructed with *got*: *I got eat the peach.* 'I HAVE eaten the peach.' [Bao Zhiming, personal communication].

[3] Bao (1995: 187) states that for examples like *My son already go to school* and *My baby already speak* the inchoative interpretation is preferred. Here are some additional examples of the inchoative type: *This one enough already.* 'This is enough now.', *The wall white already.* 'The wall is already white.', *I eat the peach already.* 'I have started eating the peach.', *I want to go home already.* 'I need to go home.' [Bao Zhiming, personal communication].

(23) Zhāngsān kāi   ché móu sheng le.
   Zhangsan drive car for   live   LE
   'Zhangsan now drives for a living.' [Mandarin, Bao 2005: 242]

Such uses of *already* in combination with an untensed verb are not only attested in Singapore English, but can be found in other post-colonial varieties, too. Moreover, it is quite common in Pidgin and Creole varieties.

A similar strategy to convey the meaning of the present perfect is the use of the verb *finish*, which we find especially in Pidgin and Creole varieties of English. This strategy is illustrated in (24). In principle, we would also have to discuss the verbal form *done* at this point, as it signals the completion of an event in several non-standard varieties. However, as this form definitely crosses the border into the domain of aspect, we will defer its discussion to Chapter 7.

(24) a. mi kuk-im   pinis
      I   cook-TRANS FINISH
      'I have cooked it.' [Tok Pisin, Smith 2004: 730]

   b. You finish eat?
      'Have you eaten?' / 'Have you finished eating?' [Indian South African English, Mesthrie 2004b: 975]

Medial object perfects In the Englishes of Ireland, Scotland, Newfoundland, and the Appalachian mountain range, there is a perfect construction that looks nearly identical to the standard construction except that the position of direct object and perfect participle is reversed. Evidently, it only occurs in the context of transitive verbs. Consider (25).

(25) a. When your letter came to hand we had a letter prepared to send to you. [Irish English, Pietsch 2009: 546]

   b. You have access to a vein gained and a cardiac analysis done within one minute. [Scottish English, Miller 2004: 56]

   c. After he had the two of 'em killed. [Newfoundland English, Clarke 2004: 306]

   d. We had all our work done up and eaten a good camp supper. [Appalachian English, Montgomery 2004: 252]

The above non-standard examples position the direct object between *have* and participle, while the overall meaning of this aptly called 'medial object perfect' is more or less identical to that of the standard present perfect. As the medial object perfect primarily occurs in the Celtic Englishes and found its way from there to other parts of the world, an analysis in terms of language contact suggests itself and has been widely explored. The matter remains controversial, though, as similar constructions surface in historical English documents for which no case of language contact can be reconstructed.

Pietsch (2009) argues that both the standard *have*-perfect (participle-object-order) and the medial object perfect (object-participle-order) existed in the

English dialects spoken in Ireland in the eighteenth and nineteenth centuries, i.e. at a time when bilingualism in Ireland was strongest. However, the historical English medial object perfect was at best marginal and considerably less frequent than the standard construction. In contact with Irish, which has a perfect construction in which the object precedes the 'participle', we can assume that the historical English medial object perfect gained in frequency and became a regular perfect-construction in Irish English. Provided this account is correct, language contact would have resulted in a transfer of usage frequency, ultimately changing the grammatical status of a construction.

Perfect auxiliary be The final perfect construction that needs to be introduced at this point is illustrated in (26) and (27). Its diagnostic feature is the auxiliary *be*, instead of *have*. This so-called '*be*-perfect' is restricted to intransitive, mainly mutative verbs (i.e. verbs of motion: *arrive, come, return*, etc.). It has mainly been discussed in the context of Irish English, but has also been reported from Shetland, Scotland, and Newfoundland. We can safely interpret it as an historical feature that survived in dialects, as other Germanic languages possess it, too.[4]

(26) a. I think the younger generations are gone idle over it.

 b. {How many brothers and sisters you have, and what they're all doing?}
    They're not left school yet.
    [Irish English, Filppula 2004: 75]

(27) a. They're already left. [Newfoundland English, Clarke 2004: 306]

 b. I'm been dere twartree ('a couple of') times. [Shetland English, Melchers 2004: 39]

Past tense markers There are several attested past tense markers that occur as independent morphemes typically assuming the slot before the main verb. The most widespread markers are *bin*, *did*, and *wen*, evidently related to the standard forms *been*, *did*, and *went*. They are common in Pidgin and Creole varieties. Example (28) illustrates *bin* (*bi*) in three Creole Englishes.

(28) a. mi bin   witnesim long ai   bilong mi
     I   PAST witness   with eye POSS me
     'I witnessed it with my own eyes.' [Tok Pisin, Smith 2004: 722]

 b. Ai bin   klin ap mai pleis fo da halade.
    I   PAST clean up my place for the holiday
    'I cleaned up my place for the holidays.' [Hawai'i Creole, Sakoda and Siegel 2004: 743]

---

[4] Wolfram (2004a: 288) even reports an example with a transitive verb from the southeast of the United States: *I'm forgot the food yesterday.*

   c. Yesedey A bi   go fa maket.
      yesterday I PAST go to market
      'Yesterday I went to the market.' [Kamtok, Ayafor 2004: 921]

The form *did* is exemplified in (29). It is important to bear in mind that this use of *did* is unstressed and must not be confused with emphatic *do/did* of the standard varieties. In the relevant non-standard varieties, *did* simply marks past tense.

(29) a. Him did sing pure lovers rock tune. 'He sang only "Lover's Rock"
      tunes.' [British Creole, Sebba 2004: 200]

   b. If yu luk pan we Itla did du ina Jaamani. 'If you consider what Hitler
      did in Germany.' [Jamaican Creole, Patrick 2004: 413]

   c. Then after my daughter died, I did feel lonely inside the house.
      [St Helena English, Wilson and Mesthrie 2004: 1007]

The third past tense marker discussed here is *wen*, derived from the past tense of *go*. It appears less widespread, but the metonymic process through which this form becomes reinterpreted as a past tense marker is quite transparent. An example can be found in (30).

(30) Ai wen si   om.
    I   went see him
    'I saw him.' [Hawai'i Creole, Sakoda and Siegel 2004: 743]

In spite of these alternative past tense markers, we must not forget that many non-standard varieties choose to leave the past tense unmarked. Again, this is quite typical of Pidgin and Creole varieties. Example (31) illustrates such past time uses of bare verb forms.

(31) a. Yesterday they go to your office. 'Yesterday they went to your office.'
      [Nigerian English, Alo and Mesthrie 2004: 815]

   b. One time we go there. 'We went there once.' [Aboriginal English,
      Malcolm 2004: 669]

Markers of future time reference Another area that attests substantial variation concerns markers of future time reference. As outlined in Section 6.1, mainly three grammatical forms compete in this domain in standard English, namely the *will*-future, the *going-to* future, and the present progressive.

The verb *go* in its standard English base form or some derived form (*gon, gan, gwine, goin,* etc.), which are due to special pronunciations or heavy contractions of the form *going to*, is widely used as a marker of future time reference in many of the Creoles spoken in the Caribbean, and in the West African Englishes spoken in Ghana and Nigeria, as well as in the Creoles spoken in Australia or on Hawai'i. The main difference with respect to the standard varieties is a syntactic one: whereas standard English connects the marker of future time reference (*going*) and the main verb with the infinitival particle *to*, there is no connecting particle in the Creoles, resulting in a so-called 'serial verb construction', i.e. a juxtaposition of two or more verbs. Some examples can be found in (32).

(32) a. A go   waka.
    I FUT walk
    'I will walk.' [Nigerian Pidgin English, Faraclas 2004: 834]

 b. Ai gon bai wan pikap.
    I   FUT buy a   pickup
    'I'm going to buy a pickup.' [Hawai'i Creole, Sakoda and Siegel 2004: 743]

 c. you gwine cut it with knife?
    you FUT   cut it with knife
    'Are you going to cut it with a knife?' [Gullah, Mufwene 2004: 362]

 d. How he gan   come back home today?
    how he FUT come back home today
    'How is he going to come back home today?' [Liberian Settler English, Singler 2004: 884]

Another interesting development is attested through the future marker *bae/bai* in Bislama and Tok Pisin, which apparently derives from the adverbial 'by and by'. It occurs sentence-initially in (33a), though before the main verb in (33b). The position before the main verb is indicative of a higher degree of grammaticalisation, as the future marker forms one syntactic unit with the main verb.

(33) a. Bae mi pulum strong rop   ya.
    FUT I   pull   strong rope the
    'I will pull the rope hard.' [Bislama, Crowley 2004: 691]

 b. Me bai   kam.
    I   FUT come
    'I will come.' [Tok Pisin, Smith 2004: 728]

6.3   Cross-linguistic comparison

Cross-linguistic variation in the domain of tense and aspect has been thoroughly researched, and it appears that most of the dimensions along which varieties of English differ can be matched against the patterns of variation that have emerged from typological work. It is important to recapitulate at this point that languages do not necessarily possess grammatical exponents encoding temporal distinctions. In other words, there is no need for languages to have tenses, though many do have them. Temporal relations may be specified by lexical expressions or simply be recovered from the context. For instance, the Indonesian example in (34) is open with respect to an interpretation in the present or past time.

(34) Air   itu   dingin.
     water that cold
     'The water is/was cold.' [Indonesian, Dahl and Velupillai 2011a]

On the assumption that the cognitive representation of time and temporal relations is the same for all speakers, or at least largely similar, the question,
then, is how different languages divide up this pie using grammatical markers.
There is considerable variation, ranging from no distinctions to highly fine-
grained distinctions. In addition, there is an impressive set of morphosyntactic
options.

In our cross-linguistic assessment of tense marking in varieties of English, we
will mainly be concerned with three domains. Firstly, we will explore strategies
to express perfect meanings, which we may loosely define as past time events
with current relevance. In a second step, we will take a look at past tenses and
then, in a third step, turn to future tenses. On our way, we will also address the
grammaticalisation of tenses.

6.3.1   The encoding of perfect meaning

In the overview in Section 6.1, I introduced a commonly used typology of
perfect meanings (or use types) distinguishing resultative, existential (experiential), and universal perfects. These use types strongly correlate with the
aktionsart of the verb. What they have in common is the expression of current
relevance of the situation encoded by the verb for the moment of speaking (or
some other reference point).

In keeping with what we said about the necessity for languages to draw
grammatical distinctions, it is not surprising to find that many languages lack
the category of a perfect. In their cross-linguistic survey of 222 languages, Dahl
and Velupillai (2011b) identify 114 that do not possess this category. In other
words, more than 50 per cent of the languages sampled express the relevant
semantic territory in different ways. Against this background, it appears a great
luxury for Irish English to distinguish no fewer than three perfect categories in
addition to the standard *have*-perfect. These are summarised in (35), namely
the *after*-perfect in (35a), the medial object perfect in (35b), and the *be*-perfect
in (35c). Of course, they all have slightly different meanings and contexts of
use, but still, this degree of internal differentiation is surprising.

(35) a. John is after coming home from fishing. 'John has come home from
        fishing.'
     b. Mary has the cake finished. 'Mary has finished the cake.'
     c. Terry is arrived. 'Terry has arrived.'
        [Irish English, personal knowledge]

We may conjecture that those languages lacking a perfect in Dahl and Velupillai's (2011b) sample either do not encode tense distinctions grammatically or

employ the present or the past tense to cover the functional domains of the perfect. Here, varieties of English appear to give us the full range of cross-linguistic variation, with Pidgin and Creole varieties often lacking tense distinctions and many post-colonial varieties shifting the functional burden of the perfect to past and/or present tense. Examples are shown in (36) and (37). Notice that even the standard varieties fit into this general pattern, as North American Englishes have a clear tendency to use the past tense in present perfect contexts.

(36) a. We stay now here for twenty-four year. 'We have been staying here now for twenty-four years.' [Cape Flats English, McCormick 2004: 995]

b. {And do you go up to see it [a car race]?} I never went till it yet. 'I have never gone there.' [Irish English, Filppula 2004: 75]

(37) a. I'm staying this house seven years. 'I have been staying in this house for seven years.' [Indian South African English, Mesthrie 2004b: 975]

b. I am here since 2 o'clock. 'I have been here since 2 o'clock.' [Indian English, Bhatt 2004: 1028]

In terms of its construction type, the *have*-perfect found in the standard varieties, including the medial object perfect of Irish English, is not very common cross-linguistically. In Dahl and Velupillai's (2011b) sample, there are merely seven attestations of possessive perfects, and these are all from European languages (German, Swedish, Spanish, etc.). As such possessive perfects presuppose the existence of a verb expressing possession (i.e. *have*), and many languages lack such a verb, we have an explanation for the low number of *have*-perfects. Possessive perfects typically develop from dedicated resultative constructions (e.g. *I have the letter written.* 'I possess the letter and it is in a written state.'). You may wonder why the Irish English medial object perfect is not categorised as a resultative construction, and the reason is that it occurs with verbs that have no tangible result (e.g. *We have the dinner eaten*). Consider the examples in (38). Its historical predecessor, however, is a resultative construction.

(38) a. At this time I intended to go home and had passage agreed to go home. [Irish English, Pietsch 2009: 547]

b. I am sure you have them woods sold before this time. [Irish English, Pietsch 2009: 548]

Let me also briefly point out at this stage in our discussion that *have*-perfects have a tendency to develop into a narrative tense, i.e. a past tense. This can *inter alia* be observed in German and French, where the simple past is hardly used for telling a story. Such systematic extensions in function may be responsible for the observed use of the present perfect in past tense contexts in Australian English (*Then he's hit her on the head.* Collins and Peters 2004: 597). The phenomenon is also reported from post-colonial varieties, as shown in (39):

(39) a. And this all has not happened in the past and nowadays it's happening more and more. [Mesolectal Indian English, Davydova 2011: 202]

      b. Up to seventh class, I am in English medium school, after that I have taken my admission in Hindi medium government school. [Mesolectal Indian English, Davydova 2011: 218]

Besides the possessive perfect, another cross-linguistically recognisable construction type of the perfect is based on expressions meaning 'finish' or 'already'. Dahl and Velupillai (2011b) find twenty-one languages in their sample that can be subsumed under this type. There is an example in (40).

(40) Ó ti   ka iwe na.
      he PFV/already read book this
      'He has read this book.' [Yoruba, Dahl and Velupillai 2011b]

The parallels of the Yoruba example in (40) to what has been reported from some varieties of English are striking. Consider (41), where the example in (41a) is a perfect based on 'already' and that in (41b) on the verb 'finish'. Perfects based on 'finish' are also widespread in West African varieties. We need to bear in mind that examples like those in (41) are not ad hoc formations involving the lexical items 'already' and 'finish', but have systematic properties that give rise to the category of a perfect. Quite often, these perfects are transferred into English from the relevant substrate languages. You can find additional examples in Section 6.2.2.

(41) a. Before I married I know him, but I don't know I was going to marry him. I not yet born, they come to Singapore already. ' . . . they had come to Singapore.' [Singapore English, National Archives of Singapore, Collection of Oral History Recordings]

      b. Mi wakem gaden   blong mifala finis.
        I   work   garden POSS me   finish
        'I have completed my work in our garden.' [Solomon Islands Pijin, Jourdan 2004: 715]

6.3.2   The past tense and the number of remoteness distinctions

At the beginning of Section 6.3 I pointed out that languages may not have tenses and that the expression of temporal relations may be taken over by adverbials. It may also happen that temporal relations have to be recovered from the context. When we discussed the perfect in Section 6.3.1 we noticed that many languages do not possess this category and find other solutions to express the relevant nuances of meaning.

     We can make very similar observations in the domain of the past tense where, again, a substantial number of languages in a cross-linguistic sample turn out to have no grammatical opposition between past and present (or non-past).

Dahl and Velupillai (2011a), for example, scanned 222 languages for such a distinction and report that 88 of them lack it. Apparently, it is no problem for speakers to do without it.

Observations across non-standard varieties of English confirm this conclusion, as past tense marking is frequently dispensed with. Example (42) shows specimens from various parts of the English-speaking world. In some cases temporal relations are indicated by adverbials; in other cases they are left unspecified. We give here no explanation as to why the past tense is not used. Speakers may not have it in their grammatical system, but it may also be hidden due to phonological processes, which is likely in (42d). The effect is the same.

(42) a. And we look after those children like we look after our own. 'And we looked after those children like we looked after our own.' [St Helena English, Wilson and Mesthrie 2004: 1006]

b. One time we go there. 'We went there once.' [Aboriginal English, Malcolm 2004: 669]

c. Yesterday they go to your office. 'Yesterday they went to your office.' [Nigerian English, Alo and Mesthrie 2004: 815]

d. He live there for years. 'He lived there for years.' [Newfoundland English, Clarke 2004: 309]

The presence or absence of a past/present (non-past) distinction is perhaps the most important parameter for a cross-linguistic survey of this domain. Another parameter concerns the number of grammatical distinctions that are drawn in the domain of the past time, i.e. the domain before the moment of utterance. If such distinctions are available, they are referred to as 'remoteness distinctions'. According to Dahl and Velupillai (2011a), a common remoteness distinction is that between today and before today (hodiernal versus hesternal).

One may be tempted to analyse the contrast between the perfect, the past, and the past perfect of standard English in terms of remoteness distinctions. Intuitively, the past perfect appears to be used for events farthest away from the moment of speaking and the perfect for those that are closest to it, with the past tense ranging in between. Such reasoning, however, is difficult to substantiate.[5]

As far as non-standard varieties of English are concerned, we do find reports on remoteness distinctions in several of them, but it is currently not clear if the labels used in the literature on varieties of English match those encountered in cross-linguistic studies. I will list two potential examples here, but future research will have to show how robust such comparisons are.

---

[5] Using the sentences *This particle had been created 10^{-6} seconds before this other particle was created 10^{-9} seconds ago*, Comrie (1985: 68) argues that the past perfect does not signal remoteness from the moment of speaking. The past perfect simply requires another reference point.

A first example comes from Solomon Islands Pijin (43), where the expression *jes* (*des*) – derived from *just* – before the main verb signals that the situation occurred in the recent past. The problem is that it is not clear what is meant by 'recent'.

(43) Mi des   lukim kaen pipol   olsem.
     I   PAST see   kind people like
     'I have just seen this type of people.' [Solomon Islands Pijin, Jourdan 2004: 714]

The second example comes from Fiji English and is shown in (44). It is meant to illustrate the use of a remote past tense marker, in this case the expression *been*.

(44) You been tell me you gonna stop drinking grog [kava] because your work is going very badly. 'You had told me you would stop dinking grog because your work is going very badly.' [Fiji English, Mugler and Tent 2004: 780]

Remoteness distinctions are not uncommon. The cross-linguistic sample of 222 languages explored by Dahl and Velupillai (2011a) contains 38 languages that encode two or three degrees of remoteness. Two languages distinguish four or more such degrees.

6.3.3   The future tense

The expression of future time is subject to the same general considerations that we have identified in the previous sections. There may be grammatical markers available for situating events in the post-time of the moment of utterance, though adverbials can just as well take over this function. In the Finnish example in (45), for instance, future time reference is signalled by the present tense in combination with a lexical expression.

(45) a. Tänään on kylmää.
        today   is cold.PART
        'It is cold today.'
     b. Huomenna on kylmää.
        tomorrow is cold.PART
        'It will be cold tomorrow.'
        [Finnish, Dahl and Velupillai 2011c]

On this dimension, Finnish contrasts with French, where we find a dedicated future tense marker, namely a suffix on the verb, as in (46).

(46) a. Il fait   froid aujourd'hui.
        it do.PRES.3SG cold today
        'It is cold today.'

b. Il fera   froid demain.
   it do.FUT.3SG cold tomorrow
   'It will be cold tomorrow.'
   [French, Dahl and Velupillai 2011c]

According to Dahl and Velupillai (2011c), the probability of finding a dedicated future tense in a language lies at approximately 50 per cent, i.e. in a (more or less random) sample, we can expect half of the languages to possess a future tense while the other half use some other means of future time reference. This figure relates to inflectional futures; including other markers will yield higher numbers.

Standard English provides at least two marking strategies that we can count as future tenses (though not inflectional), namely the *will*-future and the *going-to*-future. The progressive does not count, as its main function lies in a different domain. The auxiliary *shall* as future marker has become rare.

Non-standard varieties of English, especially the various Pidgin and Creole varieties, quite consistently use the verb *go* as a future tense marker, as shown in (47). There are several attested phonological forms ranging from *gonna* via *gon* to just *go*, and there is great variation in the pronunciations of the vowel. You can find additional examples in (32) above.

(47) a. He gon build my house. 'He's going to build my house.' [Eastern Caribbean English, Aceto 2004: 446]
     b. Ngwing go go holide fo Limbe nex wik. 'Ngwing will go on vacation to Limbe next week.' [Kamtok, Ayafor 2004: 922]

It is very likely that the *go*-futures found in non-standard varieties have a higher degree of grammaticity relative to the standard English *going-to*-construction, as the non-standard forms are shorter and appear to be obligatory in more contexts. The latter point, however, must remain speculation until it has been empirically proved. In any event, in using the verb *go* as a future tense marker, non-standard varieties of English clearly replicate a cross-linguistically very common pattern.

6.4   Summary and list of keywords

We started this chapter by defining tense as the grammatical encoding of temporal relations, emphasising the notion of 'grammatical category'. This was followed by a discussion of the present perfect. We learnt that three major use types of the present perfect can be distinguished, and that it has been analysed as a tense, as an aspect, and even as a category *sui generis*. The standard English tense forms can be encountered in various non-standard uses across varieties. For example, the present tense frequently substitutes the present perfect. Non-standard varieties also give us several special tense forms, as documented by the

Irish English *after*-perfect and the Singapore English *already*-perfect. Moreover, there are distinct markers for past and future tense. Many non-standard features have striking cross-linguistic parallels. Perfects based on 'already' and 'finish' turned out to be a clearly recognisable cross-linguistic coding strategy. Future tenses grammaticalised from the verb 'go' are practically a universal.

Keywords: absolute tense, adverbials of time, *after*-perfect, aktionsart, *already*, aspect, *be*-perfect, change-of-state verbs, deixis, event verbs, existential perfect, experiential perfect, *finish*, future, grammaticalisation, inchoative, lexical aspect, medial object perfect, mutative verbs, narrative tense, past, past perfect, perfect, possessive perfect, present, present perfect, relative tense, remoteness distinctions, resultative perfect, state verbs, systemic substratist hypothesis, tense, tense marker, time, time of reference, time of situation, time of utterance, universal perfect.

6.5   Exercises

Basic level

1. In Section 6.1, we quoted Bernard Comrie (1985: 6) stating that 'tense is grammaticalised expression of location in time'.
   a. Look up and explain the notions 'grammaticalisation' and 'location in time'.
   b. Linguists carefully distinguish between tense markers (such as the English suffix *-ed*) and temporal lexical expressions (*yesterday*, *tomorrow*, etc.). Why do we need to draw this distinction?
   c. Develop a set of criteria to distinguish between tense markers and temporal lexical expressions.
2. Tense marking in varieties of English is mainly characterised by the occurrence of standard English tense markers in non-standard functions and to a lesser extent by special non-standard tense markers.
   a. Which non-standard functions do the present tense, the present perfect, and the past tense have in varieties of English?
   b. Draw up a list of the non-standard forms that we find used for tense marking.
3. Bao (1995) states that *already* in Singapore English has two functions. On the one hand, it can signal completion (a), while, on the other, it may express the beginning of an action (b).

   a. *I work about four months already.* '*I have (already) been working for four months.*'
   b. *My baby speak already.* '*My baby has started to speak.*'

a. Which use of *already* in Singapore English corresponds to the present perfect in standard English?

b. Read the article by Bao (1995). How does he explain the two functions of *already* in Singapore English?

Intermediate level

1. In the theoretical literature on the present perfect, we find at least three important use types distinguished, namely:
   a. existential use: *I have heard people speak Irish English.*
   b. universal use: *I have lived in Ireland all my life.*
   c. resultative use: *I have written the letter.*

   Non-standard varieties of English typically replace the present perfect of the existential use type by the simple past (*I heard people speak Irish English*) while the present perfect of the universal use type is substituted by the simple present tense (*I live in Ireland all my life*). In resultative contexts the present perfect is usually kept also in non-standard Englishes. The substitution of the present perfect by simple past and simple present appears well motivated – can you see why?

2. In Section 6.3.3 you learnt that the form *go* and its derivatives are widely employed as markers of future tense in varieties of English.

   Try to explain the process of semantic change that may turn a motion verb like *go* into a marker of future time reference and ultimately into a future tense marker.

3. It has often been observed that the present perfect is less frequently used in North American English in comparison to British English, as the simple past is used instead.

   Design a comparative corpus study to test this observation. You may base your analysis on the *BNC* and *COCA*. You can find these corpora at Mark Davies' website (http://corpus.byu.edu/).

Advanced level

1. Reichenbach (1947) introduced the categories 'time of speaking' (S), 'time of event' (E), and 'time of reference' (R) to analyse the temporal structure of a clause. Familiarise yourself with these notions.
   a. Compare the symbolic system introduced by Reichenbach (1947) with that of Klein (1994). Where do you see similarities? Where do you see differences?
   b. Reichenbach (1947: 290) analyses the English present perfect as E-S,R (event before reference point; reference point simultaneous with moment of speaking). In the preceding sections, you learnt that the simple present

tense may be found in present perfect contexts such that a sentence like *I live here all my life* comes to mean 'I have lived here all my life.' What consequences does this have for the analysis of the present tense and the present perfect in Reichenbach's system?

2. Below you can find an illustration of the tense/aspect system of Kamtok, a Pidgin English spoken in Cameroon. The illustration is based on O'Donnell and Todd (1980: 54).

   a. *kam*   come
   b. *i di kam*   he is coming
   c. *i bin kam*   he came
   d. *i bin di kam*   he was coming
   e. *i dong kam*   he has just come
   f. *i bin dong di kam* he had been coming

   a. Provide a syntactic and semantic analysis of the tense/aspect markers *bin*, *dong*, and *di*.
   b. The Kamtok paradigm does not look completely different from standard English. Where exactly does it differ?

3. Pietsch (2009) analyses the medial object perfect of Irish English as a case of contact-induced grammaticalisation.

   a. Read Pietsch (2009) and Heine and Kuteva (2003). Familiarise yourself with the concept of contact-induced grammaticalisation.
   b. Critically assess the validity of the analysis put forward by Pietsch (2009). Can you think of alternative ways to reconstruct the history of the medial object perfect?

6.6   References

Bao, Zhiming. 1995. *Already* in Singapore English. *World Englishes* 14(2). 181–8.
   2005. The aspectual system of Singapore English and the systemic substrate explanation. *Journal of Linguistics* 41(2). 237–67.
Comrie, Bernard. 1976. *Aspect*. Cambridge University Press.
   1985. *Tense*. Cambridge University Press.
Dahl, Östen and Viveka Velupillai. 2011a. The past tense. In Matthew S. Dryer and Martin Haspelmath (eds.), *The World Atlas of Language Structures Online*. Munich: Max Planck Digital Library, chapter 66. Available online at http://wals.info/chapter/66. Accessed 22 December 2011.
   2011b. The perfect. In Matthew S. Dryer and Martin Haspelmath (eds.), *The World Atlas of Language Structures Online*. Munich: Max Planck Digital Library, chapter 68. Available online at http://wals.info/chapter/68. Accessed 22 December 2011.
   2011c. The future tense. In Matthew S. Dryer and Martin Haspelmath (eds.), *The World Atlas of Language Structures Online*. Munich: Max Planck Digital Library, chapter 67. Available online at http://wals.info/chapter/67. Accessed 22 December 2011.

Davydova Julia. 2011. *The Present Perfect in Non-Native Englishes: A Corpus-Based Study of Variation.* Berlin: Mouton de Gruyter.

Declerck, Renaat. 1991. *Tense in English: Its Structure and Use in Discourse.* London: Routledge.

Elsness, Johan. 2009. The present perfect and the preterite. In Günter Rohdenburg and Julia Schlüter (eds.), *One Language, Two Grammars? Differences between British and American English*, 228–45. Cambridge University Press.

Filppula, Markku. 1999. *A Grammar of Irish English: Language in Hibernian Style.* London: Routledge.

Heine, Bernd and Tania Kuteva. 2003. Contact-induced grammaticalization. *Studies in Language* 27(3). 529–72.

Klein, Wolfgang. 1994. *Time in Language.* London: Routledge.

Kortmann, Bernd. 1991. The triad 'Tense-Aspect-Aktionsart': Problems and possible solutions. In Carl Vetters and Willy Vandeweghe (eds.), *Perspectives on Aspect and Aktionsart (Belgian Journal of Linguistics* 6), 9–29. Bruxelles: Editions de l'Université de Bruxelles.

O'Donnell, William Robert and Loreto Todd. 1980. *Variety in Contemporary English.* London: Allen & Unwin.

Pietsch, Lukas. 2009. Hiberno-English medial-object perfects reconsidered: A case of contact-induced grammaticalisation. *Studies in Language* 33(3). 528–68.

Reichenbach, Hans. 1947. *Elements of Symbolic Logic.* New York and London: Free Press.

See *General references* for Aceto 2004; Alo and Mesthrie 2004; Ayafor 2004; Bhatt 2004; Clarke 2004; Collins and Peters 2004; Crowley 2004; Faraclas 2004; Filppula 2004; Huber and Dako 2004; Huddleston and Pullum 2002; Jourdan 2004; Mahboob 2004; Malcolm 2004; McCormick 2004; Melchers 2004; Mesthrie 2004a; Mesthrie 2004b; Mesthrie 2004c; Miller 2004; Montgomery 2004; Mufwene 2004; Mugler and Tent 2004; Patrick 2004; Quirk et al. 1985; Sakoda and Siegel 2004; Sebba 2004; Singler 2004; Smith 2004; Wilson and Mesthrie 2004; Wolfram 2004a.

6.7   Further reading

Binnick, Robert. 1991. *Time and the Verb: A Guide to Tense and Aspect.* Oxford University Press.

Bybee, Joan and Östen Dahl. 1989. The creation of tense and aspect systems in the languages of the world. *Studies in Language* 13(1). 51–103.

Dahl, Östen. 1985. *Tense and Aspect Systems.* London: Blackwell.

Filppula, Markku, Juhani Klemola, and Heli Paulasto. 2009. Digging for roots: Universals and contact in regional varieties of English. In Markku Filppula, Juhani Klemola, and Heli Paulasto (eds.), *Vernacular Universals and Language Contacts: Evidence from Varieties of English*, 231–65. New York: Routledge.

Kortmann, Bernd. 2004. *Do* as a tense and aspect marker in varieties of English. In Bernd Kortmann (ed.), *Dialectology Meets Typology: Dialect Grammar from a Cross-Linguistic Perspective*, 245–75. Berlin: Mouton de Gruyter.

Lindstedt, Jouko. 2001. Tense and aspect. In Martin Haspelmath, Ekkehard Konig, Wulf Oesterreicher, and Wolfgang Raible (eds.), *Language Typology and Language Universals: An International Handbook, volume I*, 768–83. Berlin: Walter de Gruyter.

Miller, Jim. 2004. Problems for typology: Perfects and resultatives in spoken and non-standard English and Russian. In Bernd Kortmann (ed.), *Dialectology Meets Typology: Dialect Grammar from a Cross-Linguistic Perspective*, 305–34. Berlin: Mouton de Gruyter.

Pietsch, Lukas. 2008. Prepositional aspect constructions in Hiberno-English. In Peter Siemund and Noemi Kintana (eds.), *Language Contact and Contact Languages*, 213–36. Amsterdam: John Benjamins.

Rastall, Paul. 1999. Observations on the present perfect in English. *World Englishes* 18(1). 79–93.

Sharma, Devyani. 2001. The pluperfect in native and non-native English: A comparative corpus study. *Language Variation and Change* 13(3). 343–73.

2009. Typological diversity of New Englishes. *English World-Wide* 30(2). 170–95.

Siemund, Peter. 2004. Substrate, superstrate and universal: Perfect constructions in Irish English. In Bernd Kortmann (ed.), *Dialectology Meets Typology: Dialect Grammar from a Cross-Linguistic Perspective*, 401–34. Berlin: Mouton de Gruyter.

Velupillai, Viveka. 2003. *Hawai'i Creole English: A Typological Analysis of the Tense-Mood-Aspect System*. Basingstoke: Palgrave.

Winford, Donald. 1993. Variability in the use of perfect *have* in Trinidadian English: A problem of categorical and semantic mismatch. *Language Variation and Change* 5(2). 141–88.

7   Aspect marking

We opened the previous chapter with a description of the grammatical category of tense, which achieves a location of situations in time relative to the time of utterance (moment of speaking), or some other temporal reference point. We will continue this discussion in the present chapter, but will shift the focus to the *internal* temporal properties of the situation described by a sentence and the grammatical means available for portraying them. The label conventionally used for such grammatical marking is 'aspect'. Comrie (1976: 3) defines aspects as 'different ways of viewing the internal temporal constituency of a situation'. The temporal properties that we will be interested in involve central parameters of the situation described, especially such parameters as boundedness, completion, continuity, repetition, inception, and progressiveness, as well as some others. Moreover, these temporal properties are not objective, but, crucially, depend on how a speaker construes a real-world situation in their mind, or, put differently, how they view the situation. Aspect, thus, is a highly subjective category insofar as it allows the speaker to highlight different temporal properties of a situation, and to portray a situation in different ways.

7.1   Overview

We stated above that the term 'aspect' relates to grammatical exponents. As with tense marking, not all languages have aspects, but all languages can express aspectual distinctions by lexical means. For example, the contrast between perfective and imperfective situations in German may be expressed by a prepositional construction, as shown in (1), even though German lacks a corresponding grammatical aspect. We may translate (1a) into English using the simple past and render (1b) with the progressive aspect.

(1) a. Johann las   das Buch.
       John   read the book
       'John read the book.'

    b. Johann las   im   Buch.
       John   read in.the book
       'John was reading the book.'
       [German, Comrie 1976: 8]

Another strategy to express this semantic distinction without a proper grammatical aspect is shown in (2), where the use of the partitive case in (2b) yields an imperfective interpretation. Using the accusative case on the object noun phrase, as in (2a), results in a perfective interpretation. This contrast does not generalise to all verbs, though.

(2) a. Hän   luki kirjan.
        he/she read book.ACC
        'He read the book'.
    b. Hän   luki kirjaa.
        he/she read book.PART
        'He was reading the book.'
    [Finnish, Comrie 1976: 8]

Even though it is customary to assume that the use of grammatical categories is obligatory (i.e. if a situation happened in the past, the use of the past tense is obligatory), we need to relax this requirement a little in the case of aspect marking, as this category expresses the perspective of the speaker, which is open to different construals and hence to different verbalisations. Moreover, languages differ in how rigorously they enforce the use of aspectual distinctions. While the use of the progressive aspect in English is quite categorical for on-going situations, the use of the progressive in Spanish or Italian is mostly optional. In other words, non-progressive forms do not necessarily imply non-progressive meaning. The examples in (3) and (4) are all compatible with a progressive interpretation, though (3a) and (4a) are incompatible with a non-progressive interpretation.

(3) a. Juan está cantando.
        John is   singing
    b. Juan canta.
        John sings
        'John is singing.' [Spanish, Comrie 1976: 33]
(4) a. Gianni sta cantando.
        John   is singing
    b. Gianni canta.
        John   sings
        'John is singing.' [Italian, Comrie 1976: 33]

In the preceding chapter, we also briefly drew attention to the fact that the present perfect combines properties that make it difficult to categorise clearly as either a tense or an aspect. It locates the time of situation before the moment of speaking, as the simple past does, and also expresses the notion of current relevance, meaning that the situation described is portrayed as having an effect at the moment of speaking. The former property is indicative of a tense, while the latter suggests a categorisation in terms of an aspect.

Example (5a) in the present perfect illustrates these properties, as the writing of the letter occurred before the moment of speaking, but has a clear result or effect at the moment of speaking, since the letter exists. Expressing the same situation using the simple past, as in (5b), equally locates the situation before the moment of speaking, but removes the resultative interpretation. In other words, (5b) is compatible with a situation in which the letter does not exist at the moment of speaking.

(5) a. John has written the letter.

    b. John wrote the letter.

The 'correct' categorisation of the present perfect has led to extensive theoretical debate, and we can only mention this fact here as such without going into the details of the debate. As already mentioned in Chapter 6, I took the decision to discuss the perfect in that chapter, on tense marking. Hence, we will not discuss it any further in this chapter, but I would like to refer you back to the previous one for a more detailed discussion.

In contrast with tenses, aspectual categories are non-deictic, in that they do not relate the time of situation to some reference point, but rather provide information on the internal temporal constituency of the situation, and especially on how the speaker views it. Situations may be portrayed as ongoing, unbounded, repetitive, resultative, inceptive – to name just a few common realisations of this category. We will define some of these aspectual categories more clearly later.

The best exemplar of an aspectual category in English certainly is the so-called 'progressive form', whose most general semantic characterisation can be achieved in terms of on-goingness. We may paraphrase it as 'in the process of'. This is shown by the minimal pair in (6), where the paradigmatic contrast between the same sentence in the simple form and the progressive form yields a semantic contrast of boundedness (or: completion) and on-goingness (or: unboundedness, incompletion). Notice that only in the situation expressed by (6b) can the man be saved.

(6) a. The man drowned. (i.e. he is dead)

    b. The man was drowning. (i.e. he could be rescued)

To be sure, in a situation of drowning like that in (6) it would be infelicitous to use the progressive aspect if the man actually drowned, i.e. even though the speaker has a choice between simple past and past progressive – as a matter of fact, the speaker must take a decision – the external parameters of the situation enforce the use of the simple past. In situations like those described in (7), the speaker has greater freedom with respect to the construal of the situation, as both (7a) and (7b) would be adequate descriptions. Using the simple present suggests that the elevator usually does not work, whereas the progressive implies a disorder of limited duration.

(7) a. The elevator does not work.

    b. The elevator is not working.

Grammatical aspect such as the progressive (and also the perfect illustrated above) heavily interacts with the temporal properties inherent in the meaning of the verb and its arguments – often called lexical aspect or aktionsart. For example, stative verbs in the progressive aspect receive an interpretation of limited duration (8a), while certain punctual verbs receive an iterative interpretation (8b).

(8) a. John lives in London. / John is living in London.

    b. John kicks the ball. / John is kicking the ball.

Since the arguments of a verb influence its aktionsart, they interact with grammatical aspect, too. Thus, the interpretation of the progressive aspect in a sentence like *John was writing* is different from the interpretation in *John was writing a letter* (continuity versus unboundedness).

Linguists have invested a lot of thinking into the formal representation of aspectual systems, which is by no means trivial. As aspect is not a deictic category and to a considerable extent expresses the perspective of the speaker on a situation, this speaker perspective is often formalised as an additional temporal reference point that may lie at the beginning of a situation, in its middle, or at its end. It may also lie behind it, thus yielding a completed perspective of a situation. For example, the formalisation introduced by Klein (1994) distinguishes between time of utterance (TU), time of situation (TSit), and topic time (TT) that interact through the relation 'before', 'after', or 'is included in'. Crucially, tenses result from the interaction of topic time and time of utterance, whereas aspects relate the time of situation to a topic time. Thus, the temporal relations expressed by an English sentence in the past progressive, as in (9a), could be formalised as in (9b).

(9) a. John was playing tennis (when it started to snow).

    b. TT BEFORE TU AND TT INCLUDED IN TSit

7.2 Varieties of English

In the relevant descriptions and handbook articles, the reader is confronted with a plethora of labels that have been proposed to capture the aspectual distinctions encountered in varieties of English. For example, in the contributions to Kortmann et al. (2004), we find aspectual labels such as 'abilitative', 'attemptive', 'cessative', 'completetive', 'continuative', 'desiderative', 'dubitive', 'durative', 'inceptive', 'iterative', 'permissive', and 'repetitive', besides the more familiar categories of 'habitual', 'perfective', and 'imperfective'.

Far from belittling the scholarly effort that lies behind the analysis of non-standard systems of tense and aspect, which typically builds on highly heterogeneous data sets and conflicting speaker judgements, I would nevertheless like to issue a warning against using the aforementioned labels without a second thought, as their categorical status within the linguistic systems may not be fully clear. We find this uncertainty reflected in the literature. For example, Jourdan

(2004: 710) analyses the expression *save* of Solomon Island Pijin (encoding habituality or ability) shown in (10) as a modal verb (or a mood marker).

(10) a. Hem save sevis long sande. 'She (usually) goes to church on Sunday.'
     b. Pita no save draeva. 'Peter cannot drive.'
     [Solomon Island Pijin, Jourdan 2004: 710]

In contrast, the preverbal expression *stat* of Hawai'i Creole is interpreted as an inchoative aspect marker in Sakoda and Siegel (2004: 748). Their examples are shown in (11).

(11) a. Mai sist gon stat pleingsaka. 'My sister is going to start playing soccer.'
     b. And I wen' start eating the Raisinets all one time. 'And I started eating the Raisinets all at once.'
     [Hawai'i Creole, Sakoda and Siegel 2004: 748]

In a similar way, Shnukal (1988: 48–9) calls the following expressions of Torres Strait Creole aspect markers: *kip* (iterative), *nomo* (cessative), *oltaim* (habitual), *pinis* (completive), *stat* (inceptive), and *stil* (continuative). There is nothing wrong with these analyses, but in using such labels as 'modal verb' or 'aspect marker' we assign to these expressions different places in the grammatical system.[1]

As I cannot claim expert status on those varieties of English for which the lesser-known aspectual distinctions have been proposed, I will here focus on the more familiar categories (i.e. progressive, habitual, imperfective, etc.) whose status as aspectual categories is largely uncontroversial. Moreover, this more restrictive focus will facilitate our cross-linguistic survey in Section 7.3, as the comparison of highly analyst-specific categories is a difficult undertaking.

We will begin our survey of aspectual categories in varieties of English with non-standard distributions of forms and constructions found in the standard varieties. This mainly concerns the progressive aspect, i.e. V-*ing* + present participle, as I decided to treat the present perfect as a tense (see Chapter 6). In the second part of this section, we will turn to a description of special aspectual forms not found in the standard varieties.

7.2.1   *Non-standard distributions*

Scholars working on varieties of English have repeatedly reported that the distribution of the progressive aspect in non-standard varieties, i.e. the *be*+V-*ing*-construction, is different from that in the standard varieties. We can observe an extension of this construction to stative verbs (*think, know, believe*, etc.),

---

[1] Similar problems arise in the analysis of other grammatical subsystems, too. For example, we may analyse *will* as a modal verb or as a tense marker, *ago* as an adverb or a postposition, and so on and so forth.

with which it is not normally found in the standard varieties. This concerns verbs of mental and emotional states, verbs of sense perception, and verbs of possessing, among others. Some examples illustrating this restriction in the standard varieties can be found in (12).

(12) a. This book belongs to me. / *This book is belonging to me.
  b. The ship appears new. / *The ship is appearing new.
  c. I want to leave. / *I am wanting to leave.

Having said that, claiming that the progressive aspect is not found with stative verbs in the standard varieties would be misleading, as some of the afore-mentioned verbs have senses that are compatible with the progressive aspect. Consider the examples below taken from Swan (2005: 458).

(13) a. What are you thinking about? / What do you think of the government?
  b. The scales broke when I was weighing myself this morning. / I weighed 68 kilos three months ago – and look at me now!
  c. I'm just tasting the cake to see if it's okay. / The cake tastes wonderful.

It is against this background of variation in the standard varieties that we have to evaluate the more extensive use of the progressive found in non-standard varieties. I do not wish to downplay the phenomenon as such, but if we want to arrive at robust generalisations in this domain, we need to include the contexts and the senses in which the verbs are used, and cannot merely compare the number of progressive and non-progressive forms. I am saying this explicitly, because there is ample scope for such fine-grained studies.

The more extended use of the progressive aspect with stative verbs has been reported from Scottish English, Irish English, New Zealand and Australian English, Nigerian English, East African English, Indian English, and perhaps others. In terms of areal distribution, this appears to be a fairly general phenomenon. The examples in (14) show a few salient cases taken from the literature.

(14) a. Well, of course, Semperit is a, an Austrian firm ... They are not caring about the Irish people, they are only looking after their own nter-est ... [Irish English, Filppula 2004: 77]
  b. I am smelling something burning. 'I can smell something burning.' [Nigerian English, Alo and Mesthrie 2004: 815]
  c. You must be knowing him. 'You must know him.' [Indian English, Bhatt 2004: 1028]
  d. That bottle is containing sulphuric acid. 'That bottle contains sulphuric acid.' [Malaysian English, Baskaran 2004: 1078]
  e. People who are having time for their children ... 'People who have time for their children ... ' [Black South African English, Mesthrie 2004a: 963]

The examples in (15) show cases from Indian English produced by speakers whose command of English is on the acrolectal (i.e. near standard) level.

Such uses of the progressive are fairly widespread in the data recorded by Davydova (2011).

(15) a. I am thinking of going to Delhi.
     b. Sometimes I am easily falling ill.
        [Acrolectal Indian English, Davydova 2011: 37]

Apart from an overuse with stative verbs, the progressive aspect also appears in contexts in which it seems more aptly analysed as an habitual aspect. Consider the examples in (16), where non-progressive forms would be more likely in the standard varieties.

(16) a. Today, educational establishments are still trying to teach a standard. Many schoolchildren are not learning the standard outwith school. [Scottish English, Miller 2004: 55]
     b. He's going to the cinema every week. 'He goes to the cinema every week.' [Welsh English, Penhallurick 2004: 110]

As far as I can see, habitual uses of the progressive aspect across varieties of English are open for further enquiry, as the precise demarcation line to similar uses in the standard varieties is currently not clear to me. It is well known that the progressive occurs in habitual contexts there (Comrie 1976: 37; König 1994: 543), and even usage guides such as Swan (2005: 458) mention them, as e.g. shown in (17).

(17) a. These days, more and more people are preferring to take early retirement.
     b. We are going to the opera a lot these days.
     c. More people are dying of cancer this year than in previous years.

Davydova (2011: 178) mentions a less well-known use of the progressive aspect in Indian English that is tantamount to using the present perfect or the present perfect progressive, as in (18). It occurs in so-called 'universal' or 'extended-now contexts' (see Chapter 6 on tense marking) describing situations that began in the past and are still true at the moment of speaking. It is uncertain how widespread this phenomenon is.

(18) a. They've advantage because they are practising since May.
     b. He's explaining the difference between charming, graceful and beautiful for half an hour.
        [Mesolectal Indian English, Davydova 2011: 176]

7.2.2   Special grammatical forms

Let us now turn to non-standard grammatical forms used to encode aspectual distinctions. These can either express progressive meanings quite similar to the standard progressive (i.e. the *be*+V-*ing*-construction) or convey different aspectual distinctions (habituality, completion, iteration, etc.).

We begin this brief survey by mentioning '*a*-prefixing', which is an archaic way to express the present participle that occurs in the formation of the progressive. It can be found with elder speakers of Appalachian English and Newfoundland English, as well as the traditional dialects of southwest England. Being an archaic form, i.e. a conservatism preserved from traditional English dialects, this circumfixal strategy for deriving participles from verbs is very likely to disappear in the near future. Examples can be found in (19) below. Historically, the prefix originates in a locative preposition (*on*).[2]

(19) a. It just took somebody all the time *a-working*, *a-keeping* that, because it was *a-boiling*. 'It just took somebody all the time working, keeping that, because it was boiling.' [Appalachian English, Montgomery 2004: 256]

   b. They wasn't *a-doin'* nothin' wrong. 'They weren't doing anything wrong.' [Ozark English, Murray and Simon 2004: 234]

In White South African English, we can find a completely different way to express the progressive aspect, based on the adjective *busy*. Consider (20).

(20) a. I'm busy relaxing. 'I am relaxing.'

   b. I was busy losing my house. 'I was losing my house.'

   c. When I got to the car, he was busy dying. '. . . he was dying.'

   [White South African English, Bowerman 2004: 949]

This construction is not a traditional feature of English, but can be attributed to influence from Dutch or Afrikaans, which are spoken in South Africa. Example (21) shows the corresponding Dutch construction.

(21) Hij is bezig de fiets   te repareren.

   he is busy the bicycle to repair

   'He is repairing the bicycle.' [Dutch, Felser 1999: 206]

Pidgin and Creole varieties of English typically have an analytic progressive marker that occurs preverbally and can be combined with other markers of tense and aspect. Consider the examples in (22). The progressive marker also appears as *de*, *di*, or *da*, as, for example, in (27) or (28) below.

(22) a. Mi *a*   ron.

   I   PROG run

   'I am running.'

   b. Mi ben   *a*   ron.

   I   PAST PROG run

   'I was running.'

   [Jamaican Creole, Patrick 2004: 412]

Besides special forms to express the progressive aspect, there are also several grammatical constructions to convey habituality. Irish English is especially rich in habitual aspects and possesses no fewer than five or six different grammatical

---

[2] The structural scope of *a*-prefixing is more general, as it may also appear on participles derived from compound verbs and on adverbials: *People will up with their guns and go out a-rabbit-hunting, a-bird-hunting*; *I went back down a-Sunday* (Montgomery 2004: 256–7).

constructions in this domain, depending on how one counts. They are exemplified in (23) and stand in paradigmatic contrast with the simple form of the verb.

(23) a. Yeah, that's, that's the camp. Military camp they call it . . . They *do be shooting* there couple of times a week or so. 'They shoot there a couple of times per week or so.'

   b. They *does be lonesome* by night, the priest does, surely. 'They are lonesome . . .'

   c. Two lorries of them [turf] now in the year we *do burn*. ' . . . we burn.'

   d. {Where do they [tourists] stay, and what kind of pastimes do they have?}
   Well, they stay, some of them, in the forestry caravan sites. They bring caravans. They *be shooting*, and fishing out at the forestry lakes.

   e. {And who brings you in [to Mass]?}
   We get, Mrs Cullen to leave us in {ahah}. She *be's going*, and she leaves us in, too.

   f. {And what do you do in your play centre? Do you think it's a good idea in the holidays?}
   It's better, because you *be's bored* doing nothing {mm} at home.
   [Irish English, Filppula 2004: 78–9]

The examples in (24) offer a summary of the structural options. As you can see, we find the verbs *do* and *be* in various constructions and also in combination with one another.

(24) a. *do be* + V-*ing*

   b. *do be* + adjective

   c. *do* + INF

   d. *be* + V-*ing*

   e. *be's/bees* + V-*ing*

   f. *be's/bees* + *adjective*

A similar contrast between the verb *do*, which is always non-emphatic in these contexts and should not be confused with the *do* marking emphasis, and the simple form of the verb for marking habituality is found in Welsh English and the traditional dialects of southwest England, as shown in (25). The occurrence of *do* as such a marker in Irish English, Welsh English, and southwest English dialects prohibits a simple reconstruction of this aspectual marker in terms of contact with Celtic languages and has led to considerable scientific debate with regard to its origin.

(25) a. She beät the child. 'She beat the child at one time.'

   b. She did beät the child. 'She used to beat the child.'
   [Dorset, Barnes 1886: 23]

Various habitual aspects have also been reported from Appalachian English, Newfoundland English, African American English, Gullah, and several English

Pidgin and Creole varieties. These habitual aspects are mostly based on forms of *do* and *be*, as shown below:[3]

(26) a. Sometimes my ears be itching. 'Sometimes my ears itch.' [Bahamian English, Reaser and Torbert 2004: 394]

    b. How you duhz cook hog maw? 'How do you / did you use to cook hog maw?' [Gullah, Mufwene 2004: 366]

The formal and functional similarities between these aspectual markers in traditional dialects and English Pidgin and Creole varieties are remarkable. They are suggestive of input of dialectal speakers in the formation of these languages that are highly special with respect to the sociolinguistic circumstances of their genesis.

The markers of habitual aspect (i.e. *be* and *do*) can usually also be found in contexts where they would be more adequately referred to as incompletive aspect markers. The line between incompletion and habituality is not easy to draw (see Section 7.3.3). In addition, these markers occur in progressive contexts, as in (27) and (28).

(27) Tif   pipol dem bi   di   run foseka se polis bi   kam.
     thief people they PAST PROG run because the police PAST come
     'The thieves were running because the police came.' [Kamtok, Ayafor 2004: 922]

(28) yu   mada de   kaal yu
     your mother PROG call you
     'Your mother is calling you.' [Eastern Caribbean English, Aceto 2004: 449]

Besides the various markers of the imperfective domain (progressive, habitual, incompletive) discussed above, varieties of English offer a number of markers of completive aspect, typically derived from the verbs *done* or *finish*, that enjoy a wide dispersion. We can find them in Jamaican Creole, Bahamian Creole, African American English, Tok Pisin, and Nigerian Pidgin, as well as some others. The examples in (29) show such markers that express the completion of an event before the moment of speaking. In functional terms they straddle the line of the standard present perfect and simple past. I here list only the examples involving *done*, as we discussed the constructions based on the verb *finish* in the chapter on tense marking (in the context of the present perfect).

(29) a. He *done* asked her to marry him. 'He had asked her to marry him.' [Ozark English, Murray and Simon 2004: 235]

    b. She *done* sent the photographs. 'She has sent / sent the photographs (already).' [Bahamian English, Reaser and Torbert 2004: 395]

---

[3] An habitual aspect marker based on *got* is reported from Singapore English: *I got eat peach.* 'I eat peach.' [Bao Zhiming, personal communication].

   c. I *done* forget the year I born. 'I forgot / have forgotten the year I was born.' [Liberian Settler English, Singler 2004: 880]

   d. I *don* si dokta. 'He/she has seen the doctor.' [Kamtok, Ayafor 2004: 921]

Finally, I would like to make you aware of a less widely distributed strategy to signal progression (on-going situations) or iteration, namely the repetitive use of the verb that is known as 'reduplication'. This strategy is illustrated in (30) and is, I presume, more or less self-explanatory. It is very probably an effect of the substrate languages shining through the relevant forms of English.

(30) a. I walk-walk-walk then I fall down. 'I was walking...' [Singapore English, Wee 2004: 1067]

    b. Ay ben wed wed wed wed wed wed najing. 'I waited for ages, but nothing (came).' [Kriol, Malcolm 2004: 667]

7.3   Cross-linguistic comparison

Let us now turn to a cross-linguistic assessment of the major patterns of aspectual marking found in varieties of English. This assessment will show that the additional aspectual distinctions found in non-standard varieties are quite common cross-linguistically. Moreover, some of the marking strategies show great resemblance to cross-linguistically widespread patterns.

   In the subsequent discussion, we will again identify a number of dimensions on which a cross-linguistic comparison may be based, considering them one after the other. They concern typical marking strategies of aspectual distinctions, the distinction between perfective and imperfective aspect, aspectual distinctions related to the imperfective, and a brief excursion into locative expressions, as these represent a typical marking strategy.

7.3.1   Inflectional and periphrastic marking

Aspect as a grammatical category may be expressed by means of inflectional morphology, but it may also be expressed by periphrastic constructions. The English progressive aspect is a typical example of the periphrastic coding strategy, as the progressive aspect is marked by an auxiliary in combination with a special verb form (*-ing* form). It stands in paradigmatic opposition to the simple form of the verb, as shown in (31). Note that the non-progressive form in the past tense receives a perfective interpretation, while the non-past form expresses habituality (*John reads books*).

(31) a. John read the book.

    b. John was reading the book.

Spanish, in contrast, marks the imperfective aspect in the past tense by a verbal affix that stands in paradigmatic opposition to the perfective past tense marker.

(32) a. Juan le-yó   el libro.
      John read-PAST.PERF the book
      'John read the book.'
  b. Juan le-ía   el libro.
      John read-PAST.IMPERF the book
      'John was reading the book.'
      [Spanish, personal knowledge]

In Spanish and other Romance languages, the perfective/imperfective distinction is only available in the past tense. The English progressive construction can be used in all tenses, including the perfect. Spanish has a separate periphrastic progressive aspect that can also be used in all tenses (*Juan estaba leyendo el libro*).

To the best of my knowledge, there are no aspectual distinctions in non-standard varieties of English that would be expressed by inflectional affixes. This does not come completely unexpected, as there are no historical forms of English possessing inflectionally marked aspects. In addition, the general drift of English from a more synthetic to a more heavily analytic language makes us expect periphrastic marking.

Periphrastic marking of aspectual distinctions in non-standard varieties of English is based on a number of recurrent elements. They may be summarised as follows:[4]

(33) a. the auxiliary verb *do*
    b. different forms of *be*: *be, bi, bin*
    c. reduplication of the main verb
    d. the adjective *busy*
    e. various locative expressions.

The additional aspectual distinctions based on the verbs *do* and *be* use material originating in the English language itself, even though the expressed functions may at least in part be due to language contact. These auxiliaries typically occur immediately before the main verb. Reduplication as a means to signal progressive aspect mainly occurs in contact varieties and can probably be traced back to the relevant substrate languages. Here, a syntactic pattern was transferred to English, though no surface material. The special progressive form *busy* can be analysed as transfer from Afrikaans. Aspects based on locative expressions use material from English as well as from other languages. As

---

[4] The various forms of the auxiliaries *be* and *do* sometimes appear with what seems to be the verbal *-s* marker: *be's, bees, biz, does, doz, daz*. In Bahamian English, we find habitual examples like *We does be reading play every time* (Reaser and Torbert 2004: 394), in Newfoundland English *They bees sick* (Clarke 2004: 305), and in Irish English *They does be lonesome by night, the priest does, surely* (Filppula 2004: 79). It is not clear to me if these forms are invariable or if the *-s* marker could be analysed as a suffixal habitual aspect.

this is a prominent marking strategy cross-linguistically, we will discuss it in a separate section later on.

7.3.2   Perfective and imperfective aspect

Perhaps the most widespread aspectual distinction cross-linguistically is that of perfective and imperfective. The perfective signals bounded and completed events, usually in the past.[5] The imperfective aspect, in contrast, expresses incompletion and unboundedness. Perfective aspects present situations as bounded, as a whole, from the outside, and with a clear beginning and end. Imperfective aspects look at the situation from the inside, do not give beginning or end, and, crucially, are concerned with the internal structure of the situation. The Spanish example in (32) above is quite representative of this aspectual opposition. The aspectual system of Russian is also built around this major distinction, even though it is based on an extensive set of aspectual prefixes and suffixes that typically contribute some additional semantic component. You can find a minimal pair in (34) below. Notice that the imperfective verb translates as a progressive form in English.

(34) a. Ivan prochital   knigu vchera.
          Ivan read.PERF book yesterday
          'Ivan read the book yesterday.'
      b. Ivan chital,   kogda ja voshel.
          Ivan read.IMPERF when I entered
          'Ivan was reading when I entered.'
          [Russian, Comrie 1976: 3–4]

Dahl and Velupillai (2011) investigate the existence of a grammatical perfective/imperfective distinction in a sample of 222 languages and find relevant exponence in 101 of them. In other words, we can expect to find this aspectual distinction in approximately half of the world's languages. Moreover, this aspectual distinction appears to be relatively evenly spread around the world, with few genetic or areal clusterings (see Dahl and Velupillai 2011 for details).

It is hardly surprising against this background that several varieties of English possess grammatical marking that can be interpreted as a perfective/imperfective aspect, albeit periphrastically marked. There seem to be essentially two marking strategies. On the one hand, the periphrastic progressive aspect (i.e. the *be* + V-*ing* construction) acquires the more general meaning of an imperfective aspect. The examples in Section 7.2.1 illustrating an overuse of the progressive form may be interpreted in such a way. On the other hand, we

---

[5] The perfective is quite different from the perfect in that the former is a true aspectual category standing in opposition to the imperfective.

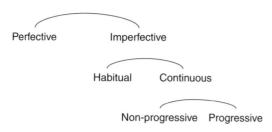

Figure 7.1 Aspectual oppositions (adapted from Comrie 1976: 25).

find dedicated markers of an imperfective aspect such as the particle *de* in West African Englishes, although in these cases, too, a precise demarcation from a progressive aspect is not easy to achieve. The main problem is that the label 'imperfective' really is a cover term for a number of more specific aspectual distinctions, which we will investigate in the next section.

7.3.3   Imperfective and related categories

The label 'imperfective' can be seen as a cover term for several semantically related aspectual distinctions, such as habitual, continuous, and progressive. Comrie (1976: 25) provides us with the taxonomy shown in Figure 7.1, where these additional aspectual distinctions are represented as subcategories of the more general imperfective aspect.

Habitual aspects indicate that a situation holds over an extended period of time. The notion also covers repeated events that, strictly speaking, do not hold at each point in a period of time. English arguably has a separate habitual aspect in the past (the form *used to*), as shown in (35). Fully dedicated imperfective aspects can usually also express habituality.

(35) a. The temple of Diana used to stand at Ephesus.
       b. Sally used to throw stones at my window in the morning.
          [Comrie 1976: 27–8]

Imperfective aspects typically also cover the semantic domain of progressivity, for which English has a separate marking strategy. However, such a progressive aspect does not cover the functional range of an imperfective aspect. True progressives mark a situation as 'on-going' and as such are incompatible with non-dynamic verbs. The progressive aspect in the English standard varieties is by and large incompatible with stative verbs, even though various extensions into this domain are attested. For example, the prototypical stative verb *be* can be combined with the progressive, but is recategorised as a dynamic verb as a consequence. This is shown in (36). But clearly stative verbs such as *see* and *understand* in (37) and (38) may also appear in the progressive aspect.

(36) a. Fred is silly.
     b. Fred is being silly (acting in a silly manner).
     [Comrie 1976: 36]

(37) a. *I am seeing you there under the table.
     b. I've only had six whiskies and already I'm seeing pink elephants.
     [Comrie 1976: 37]

(38) a. *I am understanding the problem.
     b. I am understanding more about quantum mechanics as each day goes by.
     [Comrie 1976: 36]

Two additional examples involving stative verbs can be found in (39) and (40), in which the use of the progressive results in an interpretation of limited duration that is quite incompatible with the idea of on-goingness. These and similar examples show that the more extensive use of the progressive aspect in certain varieties of English requires a finer-grained qualitative analysis. We cannot draw a categorical distinction that says the standard varieties do not permit the combination of stative verbs with the progressive while some non-standard varieties do. It is a continuum that requires further investigation.

(39) a. He suffers from a strong pain in his left leg.
     b. He is suffering from a strong pain in his left leg.

(40) a. I live in Berlin.
     b. I am living in Berlin.

In the standard varieties, we also find the progressive aspect in habitual contexts, as shown in (41), which again makes clear that the English progressive possesses a more general semantic profile than just 'on-goingness'. Examples carrying an emotive effect, as in (42), may be subsumed under the rubric of habituals.

(41) a. We are going to the opera a lot these days.
     b. At that time I was working the night shift.
     [Comrie 1976: 37]

(42) She is always buying far more vegetables than they can possibly eat.
     [Comrie 1976: 37]

Again, the bottom line of the foregoing discussion is that the various cases of progressive overuse in varieties of English still await an evaluation in relation to the less typical uses of the progressive aspect illustrated in the examples above. In addition, we need robust diagnostics to differentiate between competing interpretations in the imperfective domain (habitual, continuous, progressive, and possibly others).

7.3.4   Locative expressions

Let us conclude our cross-linguistic discussion of aspectual marking with a brief excursion into a fairly widespread marking strategy of the progressive aspect, namely in terms of locative expressions, as already briefly mentioned at the end of Section 7.3.1. According to Comrie (1976: 98),

In many languages, belonging to various genetic and geographical groupings, there is similarity between the formal expression of imperfective aspect, especially progressive aspect, and various locative adverbial phrases.

We may illustrate this statement using the examples shown below, even though it is not completely clear how tightly these constructions are integrated into the relevant grammatical systems. The grammatical status of the German example in (43), for instance, is not the same in all dialect areas.

(43) Paul ist am Lesen.
     Paul is at reading
     'Paul is reading.' [German, personal knowledge]

(44) Hij is aan het tuinieren.
     He is at   the gardening
     'He is gardening.' [Dutch, Comrie 1976: 99]

(45) sto   cantando
     stand singing
     'I am singing.' [Italian, Comrie 1976: 102]

(46) tá sé ag dúnadh an dorais
     is he at closing the door
     'He is closing the door.' [Irish, Comrie 1976: 100]

In view of these cross-linguistic observations, the interpretation of various progressives based on locative expressions in non-standard varieties of English becomes considerably more transparent. For instance, the example from Appalachian English in (47) reflects an earlier historical stage of English where the locative preposition *on* is still visible in the prefix *a-*. The examples from Hawai'i English in (48) contain a locative verb, which is probably due to influence from Romance languages. Moreover, the syntactic parallels between the Irish English example in (49) and the Irish substrate in (46) are clearly noticeable.

(47) He just kept a-beggin' and a-cryin' and a-wantin' to go out. [Appalachian English, Wolfram 1976: 45]

(48) a. What you stay eat? 'What are you eating?' [Hawai'i English, Platt et al. 1984: 72]

     b. Us stay playing basketball over here. [Hawai'i English, Nichols 1981: 86]

     c. One year I stay come up every day. [Hawai'i English, Bickerton 1980: 8]

(49) She is at the milking of the cow. [Irish English, Schlauch 1973: 172]

7.4   Summary and list of keywords

Aspect, in comparison with tense, is a non-deictic category that describes more closely the properties of the situation time. It may be used to portray situations as bounded or complete, as occurring habitually, or as on-going. Moreover, it may be used to focus on the initial or final phase of a situation, or on its middle part, thus masking beginning or end. The number of aspectual contrasts found across varieties of English is astonishing, even though there remains the problem of distinguishing between aspectual markers and modal verbs, or other lexical elements for that matter. Non-standard aspectual markers typically encode habituality, completion, or on-goingness. The progressive form of standard English is found in unexpected contexts in non-standard varieties. Aspectual marking in English is more or less exclusively periphrastic, thus restricting the marking options to one dominant type. Our cross-linguistic survey showed that the extension of the progressive aspect to habitual and imperfective contexts is not unexpected. Locative expressions turned out to be a widespread strategy for the formation of progressive aspects.

Keywords: aktionsart, analytic, *a*-prefixing, aspect, boundedness, completion, completive, construal, continuous, current relevance, *done*, *finish*, habitual, imperfective, inception, inchoative, incompletion, inflectional marking, iteration, lexical aspect, locative expressions, modal verbs, mood, obligatory marking, optional marking, perfect, perfective, periphrastic marking, progressive, reduplication, repetition, situation time, synthetic, time of situation, time of utterance, topic time.

7.5   Exercises

Basic level

1. Linguists take great pains to differentiate carefully between tense and aspect.
    a. Define the grammatical category of aspect in relation to tense. Where do the two categories exactly differ?
    b. Which standard English category is a tense? Which is an aspect? Explain your choice and provide examples.
2. Irish English is famous for possessing a remarkably large inventory of aspectual distinctions.
    a. Collect the formal inventory of aspectual distinctions reported from Irish English.
    b. Which recurrent functions do we find? Can you think of a reason why Irish English affords the luxury of having highly overlapping aspectual categories?
3. Explain the term '*a*-prefixing'. In which varieties do we find it?

Intermediate level

1. Go to your library and procure a copy of the *Handbook of Varieties of English, volume II: Morphology and Syntax*, edited by Kortmann et al. (2004).
   a. Identify the sections on tense and aspect in a set of varieties of your choice.
   b. Draw up a list of the aspectual distinctions encountered across varieties of English. Try to develop a taxonomy of those distinctions that form superordinate and subordinate categories.
2. English Pidgin and Creole varieties frequently signal the completed aspect by means of the verbs *finish* or *done*, as shown in the two hypothetical examples below.

   a. *He finish eat. 'He has eaten.'*
   b. *He done eat. 'He has eaten.'*

   Try to explain why speakers resort to these two verbs. You may base your explanation on the notion of aktionsart.
3. Kortmann (2004) offers a survey of the verb *do* as an aspectual marker, paying special attention to its usage in non-standard varieties of English.
   a. Read the article and establish a systematics of the aspectual functions of *do*, their contexts of use, and the varieties where these are found.
   b. Kortmann (2004) claims that the functions of *do* encountered across varieties of English tie in with well-known cross-linguistic paths of grammaticalisation. Explain.

Advanced level

1. It has often been claimed that the progressive aspect is commonly used with stative verbs in Indian English.
   a. Collect a list of stative verbs, drawing on grammars, usage guides, and dictionaries of English.
   b. Relying on the *ICE* (http://ice-corpora.net/ice/), Indian Component (*ICE-India*), devise a corpus study to test the above hypothesis.
   c. Carry out the analysis and interpret your results.
2. African American Vernacular English has an elaborate set of aspectual meanings that are typically rendered with the help of different forms of *be*. These are illustrated below (adapted from Rickford 1999; http://en.wikipedia.org/wiki/African_American_Vernacular_English).

   a. *He workin'.*
   b. *He be workin'.*
   c. *He be steady workin'.*
   d. *He been workin'.*
   e. *He been had that job.*

    a. Translate these sentences into standard English.

    b. Which aspectual meaning is rendered in each of these sentences?

    c. Which formal (morphosyntactic) means are employed to render that particular meaning?

    d. What do you think is the origin of the construction in example (b)?

3. Some languages such as Russian and Hindi draw the following aspectual distinction: perfective aspect versus imperfective aspect. This contrast is not rendered in English grammatically, though English has morphosyntactic means to express the notion of progressivity.

    a. What is the basic contrast implied in the aspectual distinction of perfective and imperfective?

    b. How is the concept of progressivity related to the perfective/imperfective distinction? Consult Comrie (1976) to find an appropriate answer.

7.6   References

Barnes, William. 1970 [1886]. *A Glossary of the Dorset Dialect with a Grammar.* Guernsey: The Toucan Press.

Bickerton, Derek. 1980. Creolization, linguistic universals, natural semantax and the brain. In Richard Day (ed.), *Issues in English Creoles. Papers from the 1975 Hawai'i Conference*, 1–18. Heidelberg: Julius Groos.

Comrie, Bernard. 1976. *Aspect.* Cambridge University Press.

Dahl, Östen and Viveka Velupillai. 2011. Perfective/imperfective aspect. In Matthew S. Dryer and Martin Haspelmath (eds.), *The World Atlas of Language Structures Online.* Munich: Max Planck Digital Library, chapter 65. Available online at http://wals.info/chapter/65. Accessed 22 December 2011.

Davydova, Julia. 2011. *The Present Progressive in Non-Native Englishes: A Corpus-Based Study of Variation.* Berlin: Mouton de Gruyter.

Felser, Claudia. 1999. *Verbal Complement Clauses: A Minimalist Study of Direct Perception Constructions.* Amsterdam: John Benjamins.

Klein, Wolfgang. 1994. *Time in Language.* London: Routledge.

König, Ekkehard. 1994. *English.* In Ekkehard König and Johan van der Auwera (eds.), *The Germanic Languages*, 532–65. London: Routledge.

Kortmann, Bernd. 2004. *Do* as a tense and aspect marker in varieties of English. In Bernd Kortmann (ed.), *Dialectology Meets Typology: Dialect Grammar from a Cross-Linguistic Perspective*, 245–75. Berlin: Mouton de Gruyter.

Nichols, Patricia. 1981. Creoles of the USA. In Charles A. Ferguson and Shirley Brice Heath (eds.), *Language in the USA*, 69–91. Cambridge University Press.

Platt, John, Heidi Weber, and Mian Lian Ho. 1984. *The New Englishes.* London: Routledge.

Rickford, John. 1999. *African American Vernacular English.* Malden, MA: Blackwell.

Schlauch, Margaret. 1973. *The English Language in Modern Times (since 1400).* London: Oxford University Press.

Shnukal, Anna. 1988. *Broken: An Introduction to the Creole Language of Torres.* Canberra: Research School of Pacific Linguistics, Australian National University.

Wolfram, Walt. 1976. Toward a description of *a*-prefixing in Appalachian English. *American Speech* 51(1/2). 45–56.

See *General references* for Aceto 2004; Alo and Mesthrie 2004; Ayafor 2004; Baskaran 2004; Bhatt 2004; Bowerman 2004; Clarke 2004; Filppula 2004; Jourdan 2004; Kortmann et al. 2004; Malcolm 2004; Mesthrie 2004a; Miller 2004; Montgomery 2004; Mufwene 2004; Murray and Simon 2004; Patrick 2004; Penhallurick 2004; Reaser and Torbert 2004; Sakoda and Siegel 2004; Singler 2004; Swan 2005; Wee 2004.

7.7 Further reading

Bao, Zhiming. 1995. *Already* in Singapore English. *World Englishes* 14(2). 181–8.

2005. The aspectual system of Singapore English and the systemic substratist explanation. *Journal of Linguistics* 41(2). 237–67.

Baugh, John. 1984. *Steady*: Progressive aspect in Black English. *American Speech* 50(1). 3–12.

Brinton, Laurel. 1988. *The Development of English Aspectual Systems: Aspectualizers and Post-Verbal Particles*. Cambridge University Press.

Collins, Peter. 2008. The progressive aspect in World Englishes: A corpus-based study. *Australian Journal of Linguistics* 28(2). 225–49.

Edwards, Walter F. 1991. A comparative description of Guyanese Creole and Black English preverbal aspect marker *don*. In Walter F. Edwards and Donald Winford (eds.), *Verb Phrase Patterns in Black English and Creole*, 240–55. Detroit: Wayne State University Press.

Harris, John. 1986. Expanding the superstrate: Habitual aspect markers in Atlantic Englishes. *English World-Wide* 7(2). 171–99.

Kallen, Jeffrey. 1989. Tense and aspect categories in Irish English. *English World-Wide* 10(1). 1–39.

Lindstedt, Jouko. 2001. Tense and aspect. In Martin Haspelmath, Ekkehard Konig, Wulf Oesterreicher, and Wolfgang Raible (eds.), *Language Typology and Language Universals: An International Handbook, volume I*, 768–83. Berlin: Walter de Gruyter.

McCafferty, Kevin. 2004. Innovation in language contact: *Be after* V-*ing* as a future gram in Irish English, 1670 to the present. *Diachronica* 21(1). 113–60.

Miller, Jim. 2004. Perfect and resultative constructions in spoken and non-standard English. In Olga Fischer, Muriel Norde, and Harry Perridon (eds.), *Up and Down the Cline – the Nature of Grammaticalization*, 229–46. Amsterdam: John Benjamins.

Miller, Jim. 2004. Problems for typology: Perfects and resultatives in spoken and non-standard English and Russian. In Bernd Kortmann (ed.), *Dialectology Meets Typology: Dialect Grammar from a Cross-Linguistic Perspective*, 284–311. Berlin: Mouton de Gruyter.

Pietsch, Lukas. 2008. Prepositional aspect constructions in Hiberno-English. In Peter Siemund and Noemi Kintana (eds.), *Language Contact and Contact Languages*, 213–36. Amsterdam: John Benjamins.

Siemund, Peter. 2004. Substrate, superstrate and universal: Perfect constructions in Irish English. In Bernd Kortmann (ed.), *Dialectology Meets Typology: Dialect Grammar from a Cross-Linguistic Perspective*, 401–34. Berlin: Mouton de Gruyter.

Van Rooy, Bertus. 2006. The extension of the progressive aspect in Black South African English. *World Englishes* 25(1). 37–64.

Winford, Donald. 1993. Variability in the use of the perfect *have* in Trinidadian English: A problem of categorial and semantic mismatch. *Language Variation and Change* 5(2). 141–87.

8   Modal verbs

Standard English has a closed class of central modal verbs (*can, may, must*, etc.) with highly specific properties. These modal verbs trigger the use of the bare infinitive, shun the otherwise obligatory third person -*s* suffix, possess no past tense forms, never occur together, do not trigger *do*-periphrasis – to mention just a few salient properties. In addition to the class of central modals, there are various so-called 'semi-modals' (*dare, need, ought to, used to, have to, be able to*, etc.) that have properties of both modal verbs and main verbs.

In this chapter, we will first of all familiarise ourselves with the special grammatical properties of the standard English modal verb system before considering their form, function, and distribution in non-standard varieties. In our cross-linguistic section, we will explore a broader array of strategies to encode modal meanings and also follow up the developmental paths of modal verbs, as the grammatical processes forming them are of wider significance.

8.1   Overview

In the standard varieties, the modal verbs *can, could, will, would, may, might, must, shall*, and *should* form a so-called 'closed class', as this group developed in the history of English – in the period known as 'Early Modern English' – and has remained largely unaltered since.

Modal verbs represent a subgroup of the wider category of auxiliary verbs with which they share many properties. Prototypical auxiliaries in English are *be, have*, and *do*, though these verbs may also be used as main verbs. 'Auxiliary' is the established term for a verb that assumes a function similar to that of verbal inflection (i.e. tense, mood, aspect, voice, etc.) and that does not form a predication of its own.

Auxiliaries and modal verbs are function words, as they belong to the grammatical system. Thus, they contrast with main verbs that express lexical meanings. The aforementioned class of semi-modals, i.e. verbs such as *need, dare, ought to, be able to, used to*, etc., are positioned between auxiliaries and main verbs, so to speak, expressing lexical meaning and possessing grammatical properties at the same time.

8.1.1   Grammatical properties of modal verbs

Modal verbs as a class can be recognised because they have special grammatical properties that all members of this class share (see Quirk et al. 1985: 136–48, 219–36; Palmer 2001: 100–3; Huddleston and Pullum 2002: 172–208). We will briefly investigate these here.

Modal verbs, being auxiliaries, cannot stand alone, but have to combine with a main verb to form a predication. When they combine with a main verb, they trigger the use of the bare infinitive and not the infinitive marked with the particle *to*, as shown in (1).

(1) a. I can go. / *I can to go.

   b. I can play tennis. / *I can tennis.

Moreover, modal verbs do not possess non-finite forms, such as infinitives or participles. The relevant contrast with main verbs is given in (2a). They take no inflection and hence do not mark person or number, as shown in (2b).

(2) a. *to can, *canning, *canned / to hope, hoping, hoped

   b. *She cans come. / She hopes to come.

In addition, modal verbs cannot be combined with one another. If there is a need to modalise modal verbs, periphrastic constructions are available in English (3).

(3) a. *We should can stay here.

   b. We should be able to stay here.

Modal verbs possess – at least in principle – oppositions of present and past tense forms. These, however, do not have present time or past time reference, as expected, but encode various modal meanings. Here, a former present/past opposition was refunctionalised and now encodes speaker perspective. This is shown in (4) to (6). For this reason, modal verbs are also referred to as 'preterite present' verbs.

(4) a. You could leave this evening. (not past time)

   b. You hoped to leave this evening. (past time)

(5) a. I think he may/might retire next May.

   b. *I think he retired next May.

(6) a. Will/would you phone him tomorrow?

   b. *Did you phone him tomorrow?

Modal verbs are highly restricted in terms of their contexts of use. In this way, they behave like the central auxiliaries *be*, *have*, and *do*. In declarative clauses, they invariably occur between the subject and the main verb, head the verb phrase before other auxiliaries, and occur before the negative element if one is present, and they can be the host for the contracted negative element.

(7) a. You must tell her the truth.

   b. She should have informed us.

   c. John may not like to travel to India.

   d. Mary wouldn't buy such expensive food.

Moreover, modal verbs partake in the inversion process that places the tensed element before the verb, as e.g. in interrogative formation (subject-auxiliary inversion). Since modal verbs express the perspective of the speaker, they are independent of the properties of the subject. These properties are illustrated in (8) and (9).

(8) Will he tell her? / May I leave?

(9) a. The man ought to be here at five. / The bus ought to be here at five.

b. The man hopes to be here at five. / *The bus hopes to be here at five.

Finally, we may notice that modal verbs, just like the other auxiliaries, do not require *do*-support (10).

(10) a. She cannot sing.

b. *She does not can sing.

8.1.2   Deontic and epistemic modality

Modal verbs in English may receive essentially two different interpretations, referred to as 'deontic' and 'epistemic'.[1] The difference is illustrated in (11). While both (11a) and (11b) involve the modal verb *must*, (11a) means that the addressee is under an obligation, namely to work harder. Sentence (11b) has no obligation meaning, but expresses a conjecture on the part of the speaker. The circumstances are such that the person not yet fully identified is very likely to be the postman.

(11) a. You must work harder. (deontic)

b. Speaker hearing the door bell ring: 'This must be the postman.' (epistemic)

Each modal verb has a special deontic meaning: obligation in the case of *must*, ability with *can*, volition with *will*, and so on and so forth. The deontic meaning of a modal verb is also called its 'root meaning', as it represents the basic meaning of the verb. Epistemic meanings arise through inferential processes on the part of the interlocutors and are thus more pragmatic in nature. Examples of *can* and *will* conveying epistemic meanings can be found in (12).

(12) a. (Reviewing a tax statement): 'This figure *can't* be correct.' 'From what I know, I deduce that this figure is not correct.'

b. The train is delayed. We *will* be late. 'From what I know, I deduce that we will be late.'

Table 8.1 provides you with a summary of the deontic and epistemic meanings found with English modal verbs.

---

[1] Alternative labels for 'deontic modality' are 'situational', 'circumstantial', or 'root modality'.

Table 8.1 *Deontic and epistemic meanings of English modal verbs (adapted from Quirk et al. 1985: 221).*

	Deontic meaning	Epistemic meaning
can	permission / ability	possibility
could	permission / ability	possibility
may	permission	possibility
might	permission	possibility
must	obligation	necessity
should	obligation	necessity
will	volition	prediction
would	volition	prediction
shall	obligation	prediction

8.1.3   Interaction with negation

Modal verbs show puzzling behaviour under negation, as the scope of negation – i.e. the elements of a clause that are negated – may either extend to the left or right of the negative element. Leftward scope of *not* negates the modal verb, while rightward negative scope negates the main verb. These alternative scope relations are illustrated in (13).

(13) a. It can't have been Tom.
          external: NOT > POS > it was Tom
      b. It may not have been Tom.
          internal: POS > NOT > it was Tom
          [König and Gast 2012: 111–12]

Modal verbs expressing deontic possibility are typically interpreted in the scope of negation, while epistemic possibility modals usually take scope over negation.

(14) a. You may not go home yet. (deontic, NOT > POS)
      b. He may not be home yet. (epistemic, POS > NOT)
          [König and Gast 2012: 112]

The necessity modal *must* always takes scope over negation in the standard varieties. Several non-standard varieties differ in this respect, as we will see below.

(15) You must not run away / use the elevator. (NEC > NOT) [König and Gast 2012: 112]

A brief summary of the interaction of modal meanings and negation can be found in Table 8.2.

Table 8.2 *Interaction of modal verbs with negation (adapted from Anderwald 2002: 38).*

Example	Modal meaning	Deontic / Epistemic	Scope of *not*
He may not enter the country.	'not permitted'	deontic	modal
You may not be here tomorrow.	'possible that not'	epistemic	main verb
People cannot openly speak their minds.	'not permitted'	deontic	modal
Democracy cannot be about giving politicians a blank cheque.	'not possible'	epistemic	modal
The price must not be excessive.	'necessary that not'	deontic	main verb
Thou shalt not steal.	'necessary that not'	deontic	main verb

8.2 Varieties of English

In what follows, we will survey the most important differences in the use of modal verbs between standard and non-standard varieties of English considering both their form and function. As we will see, some non-standard varieties possess distinctive modal verb forms, while other varieties tend to omit them completely. For some modal verbs, we encounter strikingly different usage patterns. Some varieties even permit the combination of modal verbs, a phenomenon known as 'double' or 'triple modals'.

8.2.1 Distinctive modal verb forms

Special forms of modal verbs, as a result of contractions and phonological differences, can be encountered mainly in traditional dialects of the British Isles. The northern and western varieties of the British Isles especially stand out in this respect. For example, in Scots there is a negative clitic *nae* that is regularly added to modals and auxiliaries, yielding the forms shown in (16a). In Welsh English we find the forms given in (16b).[2]

(16) a. *cannae, doesnae, dinnae, hinna* 'haven't', *isnae* [Scots, Miller 1993: 114–15]

  b. *anna* 'hasn't', *casn't* 'can't', *cust* 'could', *doona* 'doesn't', *inna* 'isn't', *munna* 'mustn't', *shanna* 'shan't' [Welsh English, Parry 1972: 151, Penhallurick 2004: 107]

Certainly, differences in pronunciation – in addition to cliticisation processes – may also be encountered in post-colonial varieties, as well as in Pidgin and Creole Englishes. The example in (17) illustrates the series of modal verbs

---

[2] Here is an example from other traditional British dialects: *I bet thee cansn' climb he* [he = tree]. [Southwest of England, Wagner 2004: 160]

found in Jamaican English, apparently the result of language contact in the Caribbean. However, we may conjecture that these forms are less stable than those of the traditional dialects.

(17) must: *mos(-a, -i)* or *hafi*; could: *kuda*; would: *wuda*; should: *shuda*; might, may: *mait(-a)*; will: *wi*; can: *kyan* [Jamaican Creole, Patrick 2004: 416]

The traditional dialects of Orkney and Shetland sport a distinct subjunctive form of the verb *be* that I choose to include in this section. It is shown in (18).

(18) a. Thoo'll git a sweetie if thoo bees good. 'You'll get a sweetie if you are good.'
      b. We'll can stert cuttan the morn if hid bees dry. 'We'll be able to start cutting tomorrow if it is dry.'
          [Orkney and Shetland English, Melchers 2004: 41]

8.2.2   Omission of modals and auxiliaries

Another difference from the standard varieties concerns the omission of modals and auxiliaries, shown in (19). Such omissions are frequent in Pidgin and Creole Englishes and can be subsumed under the more general phenomenon of function word omission.

(19) a. I no go Jesus. 'I won't go to Jesus.' [Butler English, Hosali 2004: 1039]
      b. What I do? 'What can I do?' [Butler English, Hosali 2004: 1040]

8.2.3   Subjunctive should

In our discussion of modal verbs, we also need to mention a phenomenon that is a relatively reliable diagnostic to distinguish between British and American English. We will briefly introduce it here, even though it concerns the two standard varieties. The relevant contrast is documented in (20) and (21).

(20) a. We recommend that he be released. [American English]
      b. It is necessary that she do it. [American English]
(21) a. We recommend that he should be released. [British English]
      b. It is necessary that she should do it. [British English]

The contrast surfaces in so-called 'subjunctive contexts', following subjunctive triggers such as verbs and adjectives of demanding and expressing obligation.[3] Strictly speaking, the use of the bare verb form in American English is not a dedicated subjunctive, as a completely unmarked form is used in a syntactic slot where an inflectional form would be expected. In this position it is just interpreted as a subjunctive. A similar use of another verb form conveying

---

[3] In more general terms, the term 'subjunctive' refers to verbal forms that appear in hypothetical contexts.

subjunctive meaning is the past tense of *be*, as in *I wish I were...* British English by and large prefers the use of the modal verb *should* in these contexts.

According to Collins and Peters (2004: 599), Australian and New Zealand English can be positioned between American and British usage with respect to this parameter.

8.2.4   *Deontic and epistemic modality*

Varieties of English also differ in the encoding of deontic and epistemic modality. As we learnt in Section 8.1.3, negative epistemic uses of *must* are not available in the standard varieties, i.e. uses of *must* as in *This mustn't be true* meaning 'This can't be true' are not acceptable there. As far as non-standard varieties are concerned, however, this phenomenon is not unknown, as the examples in (22) show.

(22) a. He mustn't have wanted the coupons because he came up and give them to me. '... can't have...' [Australian English, Collins and Peters 2004: 601]

   b. I mustn't have read the question properly. '... can't have...' [Scottish English, Miller 2004: 53]

   c. This mustn't be the place. '... can't be...' [Scottish English, Miller 2004: 53]

   d. The lift mustn't be working. '... can't be...' [North of England, Beal 2004: 127]

For the northern varieties of British English, it is reported that *must* is not found in deontic contexts. Deontic necessity is expressed by *have to* or *(have) got to* there:

(23) a. I'll have to write to Carol because she wrote to us six months ago. [Scottish English, Miller 2004: 52]

   b. Well you played the game, you got to pay the consequences. [North of England, Beal 2004: 127]

In Singapore English, by contrast, *must* is predominantly deontic, as shown in a recent study by Bao (2010). In Table 8.3, you can see that the share of deontic uses of *must* is much higher in Singapore English than in British English. The study is based on the relevant components of the *ICE*.

Bao (2010: 1731–6) discusses three factors that he holds instrumental in causing the high numbers of deontic *must* in Singapore English. Firstly, the Chinese lexical element expressing necessity (*bixu*) is not used in epistemic contexts. Secondly, typical epistemic contexts of *must*, such as the present perfect, are rare in Singapore English. And thirdly, as epistemic necessity is not expressed by *bixu* in Chinese but by a completely different lexical element, the metaphorical connection between deontic and epistemic *must* in English breaks down.

Table 8.3 *Token frequencies of* must *in the spoken subcorpora of* ICE-*Singapore and* ICE-*Great Britain (Bao 2010: 1731).*

	ICE-Singapore		*ICE*-Great Britain	
	Count	Per cent	Count	Per cent
Deontic	167	83.8	65	60.2
Epistemic	33	16.2	43	39.8
Total	200	100.0	108	100.0

8.2.5   Double and triple modals

The phenomenon in the domain of modal verbs that non-standard varieties of English are perhaps best known for is their multiple occurrence (double modals, triple modals). Such modal uses, which are strictly ungrammatical in standard English, have been observed across a wide range of varieties, including the traditional vernaculars of Orkney and Shetland, Scottish English, the English dialects in the north of England, Colloquial American English, Appalachian English, Urban African American Vernacular English, Gullah, Jamaican Creole, and perhaps others. A representative selection of double modal uses can be found in (24).

(24) a. He'll no can deu that. 'He won't be able to do that.' [Orkney and Shetland English, Melchers 2004: 41]

    b. You might should claim your expenses. 'You had better claim your expenses.' [Scottish English, Miller 2004: 53]

    c. If you folks don't have a cow barn, you might ought to build one. '... maybe you should build one.' [Appalachian English, Montgomery 2004: 253]

    d. We might could do with some more potatoes up here. 'It seems we could do ... ' [North of England, Beal 2004: 128]

    e. Dem gata must be coulda go fast. 'Those alligators must have been able to go/move fast.' [Gullah, Mufwene 2004: 365]

    f. Dem kuda kyan bai a bred. 'They would be able to buy a loaf of bread.' [Jamaican Creole, Patrick 2004: 417]

The examples in (25) give evidence for the existence of triple modals. In (26) another syntactic option is illustrated in which the second modal verb is connected via an infinitival structure.

(25) a. He'll might could do it for you. 'He might be able in the future to do it for you.' [Hawick Scots, Brown 1991: 75]

    b. John might should oughta be painting the barn. [Southern United States, Coleman 1975: 73]

(26) a. I would like to could swim. 'I would like to be able to swim.' [Hawick
         Scots, Brown 1991: 75]
     b. You have to can drive a car to get that job. [Scottish English, Miller
        2004: 54]

There appear to be restrictions on the combinatorial possibilities, in that not
all modals are equally likely candidates for the second or third position in
sequences of modal verbs. As the examples in (24) and also (25) document,
it is primarily the modal verbs *can*, *could*, and *should* that appear in the final
position in such sequences.

Double and triple modals pose challenging analytical problems, as the grammatical system of standard English emphatically rules out combinations of
modal verbs (see Section 8.1.1 above). And indeed, it is not immediately obvious how to analyse them. As far as I can see, there are mainly two ways to make
sense of the empirical observations we made in the foregoing paragraphs. On
the one hand, we may hold that the relevant examples contain only one modal
verb, and that all additional elements that look like modal verbs are in fact
adverbs. For instance, Miller (1993: 120; 2004: 53) holds that *might* in an
example like *he might no could do it* is in effect equivalent in meaning to
maybe. As the adverb-like modals do not look like adverbs morphologically
and behave like verbs in other respects, there is reason for scepticism with
respect to this analysis. On the other hand, we may argue that in those varieties
that allow double and triple modals, the modal verbs simply have a different
status in the verb phrase and do not form a distinct class of their own, as in
standard English. Notice that in standard English the juxtaposition of several
verbs is by no means ruled out per se, as evidenced by (27). Verbs like *want*,
like, *be able to*, etc. (so-called 'catenative verbs') may be combined with one
another and placed as a unit before the main verb.

(27) a. John might want to be able to play tennis.
     b. Mary would like to pass the test.

Consequently, we may want to say that varieties of English with double or
triple modal verbs simply have no class of modal verbs corresponding to that
of standard English. In syntactic terms, the modal verbs in these varieties
behave like other auxiliary verbs. It is revealing in this context to take a look
at languages that are genetically related to English, such as German in (28),
where combinations of modal verbs are readily available and form a distinct
complex of auxiliary verbs.

(28) a. Es scheint, dass er bald laufen können müßte.
        it seems   that he soon walk   can   must
        'It seems that he should be able to walk soon.'
     b. Paul sagt, dass man sich   wehren können dürfen muss.
        Paul says that one REFL defend can   may   must
        'Paul says that one must be allowed to be able to defend oneself.'
        [German, personal knowledge]

8.2.6   Politeness

Let us finally turn to some special uses of modal verbs that can loosely be captured under the heading of politeness. The following are cursory observations that have no claim to generality. They mainly show that modal verbs can be semantically reinterpreted, as illustrated by the data below.

A first such case of reinterpretation concerns the modal verbs *will* and *want*[4] that appear in the contexts of *would* and *would like to*, while the component of politeness expressed by the latter verbs in contexts like (29) is encoded by the dedicated politeness marker *please*.

(29) a. I will be happy, if you can come, please. 'I would be happy, if you can come.' [Nigerian English, Alo and Mesthrie 2004: 815]

b. I want to borrow your book, please. 'Could I borrow your book?' [Ghanaian English, Huber and Dako 2004: 856]

Another observation that we can make is that in the traditional Scottish and Irish dialects the verb *shall* is replaced by *will*, as in (30). Clearly, such evidence needs to be interpreted against the well-known fact that the usage of *shall* is declining in all varieties of English, gradually being replaced by *will*.

(30) a. Will I open the window? 'Shall I open the window?' [Scottish English, Miller 2004: 52]

b. Will I sing you a song? 'Shall I sing you a song?' [Irish English, Filppula 2004: 81]

8.3   Cross-linguistic comparison

Even though modal verbs appear to offer many interesting dimensions for cross-linguistic comparison, dedicated typologies of modal verbs, to the best of my knowledge, do not exist. Cross-linguistic studies in the domain of modality typically investigate the expression of modal meanings, and from such a perspective modal verbs represent one encoding strategy besides several others (see, for example, Palmer 2001). In Section 8.3.1 below I have tried to put together the sparse information on the typology of modal verbs that I have been able to find.

In the following we will also take a look at the grammaticalisation of modal verbs, as the processes leading to the emergence of groups of modal verbs with distinct grammatical properties are largely identical across languages.

8.3.1   The encoding of modal meanings

Modal verbs, i.e. auxiliaries expressing modality, are one of several possible strategies to convey modal meanings. Alternative marking strategies include

---

[4] For the sake of simplicity, I here subsume the verb *want* under the class of modal verbs.

suffixes, clitics, particles, and inflectional markers (Palmer 2001: 18). In addition, there is a host of lexical expressions and constructions (such as *necessary*, *possible*, *be required to*, *be allowed to*, etc. in English).

German, a West Germanic language closely related to English, possesses a set of modal verbs that is quite obviously related to that of English. This is shown in (31).

(31) können 'can', dürfen 'may', mögen 'want', müssen 'must', sollen 'shall', wollen 'will'

The modal verbs of German, however, do not form a separate class of auxiliary verbs in the same way as the English modal verbs do. They possess non-finite forms just like ordinary main verbs, as shown in (32). In addition, they take the inflectional markers of present and past tense, signalling present and past time in much the same way that they do on main verbs. German modal verbs can be combined, as is made clear by the examples in (28) above.

(32) a. infinitive: können
     b. past participle: gekonnt
     c. present participle: könnend

Nevertheless, German modal verbs also have properties that distinguish them from main verbs. For example, they do not take the requisite verbal affixes of the first and third person singular present tense (33). Moreover, like English modal verbs, they do not need the infinitival marker to connect to main verbs (34).

(33) a. ich will   'I will'   ich flieg-e 'I fly'
     b. du will-st 'you will'   du flieg-st 'you fly'
     c. er will   'he will'   er flieg-t 'he flies'
        [German, personal knowledge]

(34) a. Karl kann Violine spielen.
        Karl can violin play
        'Karl can play the violin.'
     b. Karl verspricht, mehr Violine zu spielen.
        Karl promises   more violin to play
        'Karl promises to play the violin more often.'
        [German, personal knowledge]

Table 8.4 offers an overview of the central modal verbs in five Germanic languages. Mortelmans et al. (2009: 11) define them as preterite present verbs that connect to a main verb using the bare infinitive. The modal verbs in parentheses are preterite presents, even though they do not trigger the bare infinitive. We can see that all Germanic languages have partially overlapping classes of modal verbs.

A class of modal verbs may also be postulated for Romance languages like Spanish, Italian, and French, but in these languages they seem to be even less clearly defined grammatically (see Palmer 2001: 101–2). Chinese possesses a class of verbs that appears to be by and large compatible with that of modal verbs in English (Table 8.5), even though these verbs differ in their potential to

Table 8.4 *The central modals in five Germanic languages (adapted from Mortelmans et al. 2009: 13).*

English	Dutch	German	Danish	Icelandic
can	kunnen	können	kunne	(kunna)
shall	zullen	sollen	skulle	skulu
may	mogen	mögen	matte	mega
will	willen	wollen	ville	(vilja)
must	moeten	müssen		
		dürfen	(turde)	(purfa)
				munu[5]
(ought)			(burde)	(eiga)

Table 8.5 *Modal verbs in Chinese (Li and Thompson 1981: 173–88; Palmer 2001: 102).*

yīnggāi, yīngdang, gāi	'ought to, should'
néng, nénggòu, huì, kěyi	'be able to'
néng, kěyi	'have permission'
gǎn	'dare'
kěn	'be willing to'
děi, bixū, bìyào, bíděi	'must, ought to'
huì	'will, know how'

express deontic and epistemic meanings (Bao 2010).

Van der Auwera and Ammann (2011a, 2011b) investigate the strategies for the expression of deontic and epistemic possibility in (overlapping) cross-linguistic samples of 234 and 240 languages respectively. They analyse the distribution of verbal constructions (i.e. modal verbs), verbal affixes, and some other word classes (adverbials, particles, adjectives, nouns) in these domains. Examples of each strategy can be found below. In (35) the verb meaning 'become' is interpreted as 'may'.

(35) Ní   d´uf-t-i   taa-t-i.
     FOC come-F-IMPF become-F-IMPF
     'She may come.' [Harar Oromo, Owens 1985: 78, cited in van der Auwera and Ammann 2011b]

---

[5] The Icelandic modal verb *munu* 'will' has no cognates (as modal verbs) in other Germanic languages except Old Swedish and some traditional dialects of northern England and Scotland (Hans-Olav Enger, Chris Jackson, personal communication).

Table 8.6 *The expression of deontic and epistemic possibility (adapted from van der Auwera and Ammann 2011a, b).*

	Verbal constructions	Affixes	Other markers	Total
Deontic	158	63	13	234
Epistemic	65	84	91	240

(36) Valai! Ngai a-vo-nen.
    how   I   1SG.SUBJ-come-POS
    'What? Can I come?' [Lavukaleve, Terrill 2003: 344, cited in van der Auwera and Ammann 2011a]

(37) Ija nu-ec   nu ihoc.
    I   go-INF for able
    'I am able to go.' [Amele, Roberts 1987: 265, cited in van der Auwera and Ammann 2011a]

As you can see in Table 8.6, verbal constructions are the dominant means of expression for deontic modality, followed by affixes and other markers, while the expression of epistemic modality appears to be rather randomly distributed across the strategies distinguished.

Verbal constructions for the expression of deontic modality are quite evenly distributed geographically and are by no means restricted to Europe. Their use for the expression of epistemic possibility, however, shows strong clusters in Europe, Africa, and South Asia.

8.3.2   Grammaticalisation processes

Today's properties of modal verbs are the result of historical grammaticalisation processes that can be assumed to be operative even in present times, even though our written cultures slow them down considerably. Over time, these processes, which essentially represent a bundle of phonological, morphosyntactic, and semantic changes, turn lexical expressions into grammatical exponents. Hence, it cannot be surprising that there is no simple opposition between modal auxiliaries and main verbs, but rather a cline with various intermediate categories, as shown in Table 8.7 below.

To be sure, there is extensive historical evidence documenting the path from main verbs to modal verbs in English. As it would not be adequate to review the relevant findings here, suffice it to say that today's modal verbs could still

Table 8.7 *The auxiliary verb – main verb scale (adapted from Quirk et al. 1985: 137).*

	Class of verbs	Examples
↑	central modals	*can, could, may, might, shall, should, will, would, must*
	marginal modals	*dare, need, ought to, used to*
	modal idioms	*had better, would rather/sooner, be to, have got to,* etc.
	semi-auxiliaries	*have to, be about to, be able to, be bound to, be going to, be obliged to, be supposed to, be willing to,* etc.
	catenatives	*appear to, happen to, seem to, get + -ed* participle, *keep + -ing* participle, etc.
↓	main verbs	*hope + to*-infinitive, *begin + -ing* participle, etc.

Table 8.8 *Criteria for auxiliary verbs (adapted from Quirk et al. 1985: 137).*

Modal auxiliary criteria	Modal auxiliary	Main verb
(i) bare infinitive	*I can go.*	**I hope go.*
(ii) no non-finite forms	**to can/*canning/*canned*	*to hope/hoping/hoped*
(iii) no *s*-form	**She cans come.*	*She hopes to come.*
(iv) abnormal time reference	*You could leave this evening.* (not past time)	*You hoped to leave this evening.* (past time)

be used as ordinary main verbs at the time of Shakespeare, i.e. in Early Modern English, as shown in (38).

(38) a. You must away to court, sir, presently; A dozen captains stay at door
for you. [Early Modern English, Shakespeare, *Henry IV part 2*, ii, 4]

    b. I stand aloof; and will no reconcilement... [Early Modern English,
Shakespeare, *Hamlet, Prince of Denmark*, v, 2]

Moreover, the so-called 'marginal modals' in Table 8.7 show properties of both main verbs and modal verbs, in that they can take *do*-support under negation, but can also directly be followed by the negation. Furthermore, they may take the *to*-infinitive, but may also occur with the bare infinitive (39).

(39) a. He needed / dared to escape.

    b. He doesn't need / dare to escape *versus* He needn't / daren't escape.

    c. Do we need / dare to escape? *versus* Need / dare we escape?

The scale from main verbs to auxiliary verbs in Table 8.7 is the result of the interaction of several criteria that allow to us distinguish between the two classes of verbs. These are shown in Table 8.8 (see also Section 8.1.1). As verbs fulfil these criteria to different degrees, intermediate positions between main verbs and auxiliaries arise.

Today's modal verbs find their origin in Proto-Germanic 'preterite present verbs', i.e. past tense forms with present tense meanings. The class of preterite present verbs was more extensive in Old English additionally including *uton* 'let's', *thurfan* 'need', and *witan* 'know' (Krug 2000: 45). The verb *will* does not stem from a preterite present verb.

8.4   Summary and list of keywords

English is quite unique among the Germanic languages in possessing a sharply defined closed class of modal verbs. We explored their properties in the overview section to this chapter. Non-standard varieties of English offer distinctive forms of modal verbs, show differences in the expression of deontic and epistemic modality, and permit the combination of modal verbs. Cross-linguistically speaking, modal verbs are one important strategy among several others to express modality. They can be found in many other languages, though mainly for the expression of deontic modality. Historically, modal verbs derive from preterite present verbs in the European languages and are grammaticalised to different degrees in the languages that have them.

Keywords: auxiliary verbs, bare infinitive, central modals, circumstantial modality, closed class, contraction, deontic modality, double modals, epistemic modality, epistemic *mustn't*, function words, grammaticalisation, main verbs, marginal modals, negation, negative modals, non-finite forms, politeness, predication, preterite presents, root modality, scope of negation, semi-modals, situational modality, subject-auxiliary inversion, subjunctive, verbal inflection.

8.5   Exercises

Basic level

1. Collect the central modals of standard English and put them together in a list. Identify the forms that belong together.
2. Look up the term 'preterito-presentia' and apply it to the modals collected in Exercise 1.
3. Modal verbs may assume special forms in varieties of English. Make a list of the non-standard forms of modal verbs.

Intermediate level

1. American English and British English are well known for differing in their use of subjunctive *should*. British English is claimed to show much higher rates of the use of this feature.

   a. Test this assumption on the basis of the *BNC* and the *COCA*. Mark Davies offers these corpora on his website (http://corpus.byu.edu/).

   b. Is the usage of subjunctive *should* a statistical or a categorical phenomenon?

2. Quirk et al. (1985: 137) propose a relatively elaborate taxonomy of verbs, ranging from 'central modals' to 'main verbs'.

   a. Investigate the criteria that underlie this taxonomy.

   b. Analyse the marginal modals *dare*, *need*, *ought to*, and *used to* in relation to these criteria.

3. The occurrence of double modals in non-standard Englishes is usually viewed as a highly puzzling phenomenon, since standard English does not tolerate the combination of modal verbs. Some examples of double modals are given below:

   a. *He should can go tomorrow.*

   b. *You might should claim your expenses.*

Interestingly enough, in a language like German, which is closely related to English historically, double modals are perfectly acceptable:

   c. *Paul <u>müsste</u> bald laufen <u>können</u>. 'Paul should be able to walk soon.' (lit. Paul must soon walk can.)*

What does such contrastive evidence mean for the analysis of double modals in non-standard Englishes, where they are usually analysed as combinations of modal verb and adverb?

Advanced level

1. In investigating modality in varieties of English, we usually adopt the class of modal verbs as a starting-point. In other words, we base our comparison on formal properties. Cross-linguistic studies, by contrast, depart from a conceptual definition of modality, asking which forms occupy the relevant conceptual space.

   a. Search for a conceptual definition of modality.

   b. Read Palmer (2001) and investigate the form types – in addition to modal verbs proper – that typically express modal meanings.

2. Some varieties of English allow epistemic uses of *mustn't*, as illustrated below.

   a. *This mustn't be the true story.*

   b. *Paul mustn't be in love with Sue.*

   a. Try to motivate the paraphrase of *mustn't* in terms of 'can't' typically found with these examples.

    b. In such examples, does the negation have scope over the modal verb or vice versa? Explain.

3. Although the use of double and triple modals is a distinctly non-standard phenomenon, a corpus of contemporary British English such as the *BNC*, which by and large represents standard language, contains several examples of this phenomenon.

    a. Using the access to the *BNC* offered by Mark Davies (http://corpus.byu.edu/), search for all combinations of double and triple modals. Do not forget to include negative contexts.

    b. The literature on double and triple modals mentions some combinatorial restrictions with respect to their patterns of use (see Section 8.2.5 above). Does the data drawn from the *BNC* confirm or disconfirm these hypotheses?

8.6   References

Anderwald, Lieselotte. 2002. *Negation in Non-Standard British English: Gaps, Regularizations and Asymmetries*. London: Routledge.

Bao, Zhiming. 2010. *Must* in Singapore English. *Lingua* 120. 1727–37.

Brown, Keith. 1991. Double modals in Hawick Scots. In Peter Trudgill and Jack K. Chambers (eds.), *Dialects of English: Studies in Grammatical Variation*, 73–103. Longman: London.

Coleman, William L. 1975. Multiple Modals in Southern States English. Bloomington, IN: Indiana University PhD dissertation.

König, Ekkehard and Volker Gast. 2012. *Understanding English–German Contrasts*. Berlin: Erich Schmidt Verlag.

Krug, Manfred. 2000. *Emerging English Modals: A Corpus-Based Study of Grammaticalization*. (Topics in English Linguistics 32.) Berlin: Mouton de Gruyter.

Li, Charles N. and Sandra A. Thompson. 1981. *Mandarin Chinese: A Functional Reference Grammar*. Los Angeles: University of California Press.

Miller, Jim. 1993. The grammar of Scottish English. In James Milroy and Lesley Milroy (eds.), *Real English: The Grammar of English Dialects in the British Isles*, 99–139. London: Longman.

Mortelmans, Tanja, Kasper Boye, and Johan van der Auwera. 2009. Modals in the Germanic languages. In Björn Hansen and Ferdinand de Haan (eds.), *Modals in the Languages of Europe: A Reference Work*, 11–69. Berlin: Mouton.

Owens, Jonathan. 1985. *A Grammar of Harar Oromo (Northeastern Ethiopia)*. Hamburg: Helmut Buske Verlag.

Palmer, Frank. 2001. *Mood and Modality*. Cambridge University Press.

Parry, David R. 1972. Anglo-Welsh dialects in South-East Wales. In Martyn F. Wakelin (ed.), *Patterns in the Folk Speech of the British Isles*, 140–63. London: Athlone Press.

Roberts, John R. 1987. *Amele*. (Croom Helm Descriptive Grammars.) London: Croom Helm.

Terrill, Angela. 2003. *A Grammar of Lavukaleve*. Berlin: Mouton de Gruyter.

van der Auwera, Johan and Andreas Ammann. 2011a. Situational possibility. In Matthew
S. Dryer and Martin Haspelmath (eds.), *The World Atlas of Language Structures
Online*. Munich: Max Planck Digital Library, chapter 74. Available online at http://
wals.info/chapter/74. Accessed 22 December 2011.

    2011b. Epistemic possibility. In Matthew S. Dryer and Martin Haspelmath (eds.), *The
World Atlas of Language Structures Online*. Munich: Max Planck Digital Library,
chapter 75. Available online at http://wals.info/chapter/75. Accessed 22 December
2011.

See *General references* for Alo and Mesthrie 2004; Beal 2004; Collins and Peters 2004;
Filppula 2004; Hosali 2004; Huber and Dako 2004; Huddleston and Pullum 2002;
Melchers 2004; Miller 2004; Montgomery 2004; Mufwene 2004; Quirk et al. 1985;
Patrick 2004; Penhallurick 2004; Wagner 2004.

8.7   Further reading

Battistella, Edwin. 1995. The syntax of double modal constructions. *Linguistica
Atlantica* 17. 19–44.

Bernstein, Cynthia. 2003. Grammatical features of southern speech: *yall, might could,
and fixin to*. In Stephen Nagle and Sara Sanders (eds.), *English in the Southern
United States*, 106–18. Cambridge University Press.

Boertien, Harmon S. 1979. The double modal construction in Texas. In Carlota Smith and
Susan F. Schmerling (eds.), *Texas Linguistic Forum* 13, 14–33. Austin: University
of Texas.

Boertien, Harmon S. 1986. Constituent structure of double modals. In Michael Montgomery and Guy Bailey (eds.), *Language Variety in the South: Perspectives in
Black and White*, 294–318. Tuscaloosa: University of Alabama Press.

Boertien, Harmon S. and Sally Said. 1980. Syntactic variation in double modal dialects.
Journal of the Linguistic Association of the Southwest 3. 210–22.

de la Cruz, Juan. 1995. The geography and history of double modals in English: A new
proposal. *Folia Linguistica Historica* 18(2). 75–96.

    1997. The history of double modals in the history of English revisited. In Raymond
Hickey and Stanisauw Puppel (eds.), *Language History and Linguistic Modeling:
Festschrift for Jacek Fisiak on his 60th Birthday, volume I*, 87–99. Berlin: Mouton
de Gruyter.

Di Paolo, Marianna. 1989. Double modals as single lexical items. *American Speech*
64(3). 195–224.

Dollinger, Stefan. 2008. *New-Dialect Formation in Canada: Evidence from the English
Modal Auxiliaries*. Amsterdam: John Benjamins.

Fennell, Barbara A. 1993. Evidence for British sources of double modal constructions
in Southern American English. *American Speech* 68(4). 430–36.

Fennell, Barbara A. and Ronald R. Butters. Historical and contemporary distribution of
double modals. In Edgar W. Schneider (ed.), *Focus on the USA*, 265–90. Amsterdam: John Benjamins.

Leech, Geoffrey. 1971. *Meaning and the English Verb*. London: Longman.

Mashburn, Carolyn. 1989. Multiple modals in an American English dialect. *CUNY
Forum* 14. 130–3.

Mishoe, Margaret and Michael Montgomery. 1994. The pragmatics of multiple modals in North and South Carolina. *American Speech* 60(1). 3–29.

Montgomery, Michael and Stephen J. Nagle. 1994. Double modals in Scotland and the Southern United States: Trans-Atlantic inheritance or independent development? *Folia Linguistica Historica* 14. 91–107.

Nagle, Stephen J. 1994. The English double modal conspiracy. *Diachronica* 11. 199–212.

  1995. English double modals: Internal or external change? In Jacek Fisiak (ed.), *Linguistic Change under Contact Conditions*, 207–15. Berlin: Mouton de Gruyter.

Plank, Frans. 1984. The modals story retold. *Studies in Language* 8(3). 305–64.

Tagliamonte, Sali and Alexandra D'Arcy. 2007. The modals of obligation and necessity in Canadian perspective. *English World-Wide* 28(1). 47–89.

9 Negation

For every descriptive statement that we make, we have to decide whether the truth-value of the proposition we wish to express is true or false, or, whether we wish to express that its truth-value is not fully known to us. We express – in our view – true propositions by affirmative sentences and false propositions by negative sentences, where 'negative' means that the sentence contains some overt negative element (e.g. *not*). Uncertain truth-values can be expressed by adverbials like *probably*, *likely*, *certainly*, etc., but in this chapter we will not be concerned with these. In English, as in the vast majority of other languages, affirmative sentences receive no special marking, while negative sentences are typically marked by one or more negative expressions. Apparently, we consider the making of positive statements the norm, and verbally express the absence of a positive truth-value.

Strictly speaking, the assignment of clear truth-values is only possible for what is known in the relevant literature as 'constative utterances' (Austin 1962; Searle 1969). These are, by and large, descriptive statements that contrast with performative utterances of the type 'I hereby christen this child "John".', i.e. utterances used for effectuating a change in the state in which the world is. Such utterances cannot be assigned a truth-value, as they require certain felicity conditions for their successful application. Some performative utterances, like the one just mentioned, are clearly odd when negated, but this should not be taken to mean that such utterances cannot in general be negated (*Don't move!*, *I do not apologise.*, etc.).

In the next section, I will introduce some essential facts about grammatical negation, but since this is a vast topic, we really have to restrict ourselves to those points that are necessary for handling the negation data found across varieties of English. In keeping with the general outline of each chapter, we will then assess the data from varieties of English against cross-linguistic data.

9.1 Overview

In using a negative element like English *not*, we can negate either the entire sentence or a specific constituent. This is known as 'sentence negation', in contrast with 'constituent negation'. The example in (1) is a case of sentence negation, which is made clear by the paraphrases.

(1) a. John is fifty years old. 'It is the case that John is fifty years old.'

    b. John isn't fifty years old. 'It is not the case that John is fifty years old.'

Constituent negation, as the name says, affects only constituents or their parts. This is shown in (2): for a quantifier in (2a), an adverbial in (2b), and a premodifying adjective in (2c). Notice that the negative element *not* does not need to be placed immediately in front of the constituent it negates, as illustrated in (2c), where the adjective *green* is negated.

(2) a. Not many people attended the conference (but a few did).

    b. Mary found a big treasure, but not alone.

    c. John did not want to eat the green apple, but the red one.

Let us call the domain within reach of the negative element the 'scope of negation'. The examples introduced so far show that *not* typically scopes to the right, as we would probably expect, but it may also have leftward scope. In the example in (3a), for instance, it may negate the universal quantifier *all*, provided the sentence is read with a slight intonational break after the first constituent and with final rising intonation. Sentence (3b) illustrates similar scope ambiguities. The 'minimal pair' in (4) shows how differences in scope lead to contrasting interpretations.

(3) a. All the men didn't go. 'None of the men went.' or 'Not all the men went.' [Jackendoff 1972: 352]

    b. Every boy didn't leave. 'Every boy did not leave.' or 'Not every boy left.'

(4) a. (Even) with no coaching he will pass the exam. 'He will pass the exam (even) without coaching.'

    b. With no coaching will he pass the exam. 'Whatever coaching is provided will not enable him to pass the exam.'
    [Quirk et al. 1985: 793]

Besides the negative element *not*, English has various additional negative expressions: *no, none, nobody, never, nothing*, as well as some others. Their presence negates a clause so that, as in (5), an additional clausal negation is not required.

(5) a. John called nobody.

    b. She never criticises you.

In combination with clausal negation, a special series of *any*-forms must be used, as in (6). These *any*-forms are referred to as negative polarity items (NPIs for short), since they mainly occur in negative contexts. There are many other negative polarity items you may be less aware of (*ever, give a damn, a bit, at all, yet*, etc.) whose occurrence is strongly restricted to negative contexts.[1]

---

[1] Negative polarity items may also occur in questions and some other contexts.

Table 9.1 *Auxiliary contraction and negative contraction (adapted from Anderwald 2002: 28).*

	Negative Form	
Positive form	Aux contraction	Neg contraction
am	'm not	–
is	's not	isn't
are	're not	aren't
was	–	wasn't
were	–	weren't
have	've not	haven't
has	's not	hasn't
had	'd not	hadn't
do	–	don't
does	–	doesn't
did	–	didn't
can	–	can't
could	–	couldn't
will	'll not	won't
would	'd not	wouldn't
shall	'll not	shan't
should	'd not	shouldn't
may	–	mayn't
might	–	mightn't
must	–	mustn't
need	–	needn't
ought	–	oughtn't

(6) a. John did not call anybody.

b. She did not criticise you at any time.

As a matter of fact, adding a clausal negation to sentences that already contain a negative expression (see (5) above) turns these into positive sentences, as in (7). In other words, two negative expressions cancel each other out. The interpretation of multiple negative elements in one clause is vastly different in non-standard forms of English, as we will see in Section 9.2.

(7) a. John did not call nobody. 'John called somebody.'

b. She never did not criticise you. 'She always criticised you.'

The English clausal negative element *not* has two peculiar formal properties that deserve mentioning. Firstly, clausal negation cannot occur on its own and requires the presence of an auxiliary verb. The default verb is *do* (*do*-support), but the auxiliaries *be* and *have*, as well as modal verbs, can also provide the requisite support:[2]

(8) a. John did not call. / *John called not. / *John not called.

   b. John could not call. / John is not ill. / John has not got a telephone.

Secondly, the negative element can cliticise to the preceding auxiliary, as illustrated in (9). This is known as 'negative contraction'.

(9) John didn't call. / John isn't ill. / John hasn't got a car. / John couldn't call.

Table 9.1 contains a summary of the contraction patterns that English auxiliary verbs produce. Negative contraction is possible with all forms of the auxiliaries and modal verbs except the first person singular present tense of the verb *be*, i.e. *I am not* does not contract to **I amn't*, apparently for phonological reasons.[3] Contraction of the auxiliary is less productive.

Anderwald (2002: 28) formulates the contraction patterns in Table 9.1 in terms of an implicational connection stating that the availability of negative contraction generally implies that of auxiliary contraction, except for the form *am*.

9.2   Varieties of English

In what follows, we will be taking a systematic look at negation phenomena across varieties of English from which many special properties have been reported for this domain. Section 9.2.1 concerns itself with non-standard sentential negators that typically co-exist side by side with standard English *not*. In Section 9.2.2, we will explore multiple negation (negative concord). The aforementioned contraction patterns will be discussed in greater detail in Section 9.2.3. Following that, there will be an analysis of negative tags in Section 9.2.4. We conclude our survey of variation phenomena with some remarks on asymmetries in Section 9.2.5.

9.2.1   Sentential negators

The standard English sentential negator *not* competes with at least three other expressions in non-standard varieties. These are *ain't*, which is perhaps the best known of the three, the temporal negative adverb *never*, and the preverbal negator *no*.

The most widely used non-standard marker for sentential negation is *ain't*. It can be found in various dialects of England, is a prominent feature of African

---

[2] Some modal verbs (*need*, *dare*) show optional *do*-support under negation, i.e. we find *you needn't pay* besides *you don't need to pay* or *he daren't do it* interchangeably with *he does not dare to do it*. What is also noteworthy is that *be* demands *do*-support under negation in imperatives: *Don't be stupid!* (**Be not stupid!*).

[3] However, in Northern Ireland the inverted form can appear as a question tag: *I'm here, amn't I?* (Kortmann 2004: 1094).

American Vernacular English, and can also be encountered in the Englishes of Newfoundland, Norfolk Island, and the Caribbean. The contracted form *ain't*, whose etymology lies in competing negative contracted forms of *have* and *be*, substitutes negative *have* or *be*, and in some vernaculars even replaces negative *do*.

(10) a. Well, *ain't* you the lucky one? 'Aren't you the lucky one?' [Colloquial American English, Murray and Simon 2004: 225]

   b. She *ain't* been here lately. 'She hasn't been here lately.' [Southeast of the USA, Wolfram 2004a: 295]

   c. You *ain't* asked me about makin' butter yet. 'You haven't asked me . . .' [Newfoundland English, Clarke 2004: 310]

   d. She *ain* tell um. 'She didn't tell him. / She hasn't told him.' [Gullah, Mufwene 2004: 367]

Interestingly enough, *ain't* may also replace *have* as a full verb:

(11) a. Mind you she *ain't* nobody to squash.

   b. Is she, she getting worse? Brain damage, *ain't* she?
      [*BNC*, Anderwald 2002: 144]

Non-emphatic *never* can be analysed as the sentential negation in some traditional dialects of England, Scottish English, Appalachian English, Newfoundland English, and Australian Vernacular English, but we also find it in varieties that fall into the categories of Pidgins and Creoles (e.g. Indian South African English, Cameroon English, Fiji English). The examples in (12) provide some illustration. Both say that a specific event in the past was not carried out, i.e. they do not negate the entire past time sphere. According to Ayafor (2004: 921), the negative past tense marker *noba* of Cameroon English stands in paradigmatic opposition to the positive past tense marker *don*.

(12) a. I never went to school today. 'I didn't go to school today.' [Southeast of England, Anderwald 2004: 188]

   b. I noba si dokta. 'He hasn't seen the doctor.' [Kamtok, Ayafor 2004: 921]

Preverbal *no* mainly occurs in English-based Pidgins and Creoles (e.g. Tok Pisin, Nigerian Pidgin, Jamaican Creole). Interestingly enough, preverbal *no* is also a well-known stage in second language acquisition, and apparently even in the acquisition process of English as a first language (Gass and Selinker 2008: 110).

(13) a. Yu no   go maket?
       you NEG go market
       'Didn't you go to the market?' [Nigerian Pidgin English, Faraclas 2004: 839]

   b. Laki na wanpela kar i   no   bin   kam.
      lucky and one   car PRED NEG PAST come
      'Luckily no cars came.' [Tok Pisin, Smith 2004: 728]

9.2.2   Multiple negation (negative concord)

Double or multiple negation refers to the occurrence of more than one negative expression in a sentence, as shown in the examples below.

(14) a. Yes, and no people didn't trouble about gas stoves then. [Southeast of England, Anderwald 2004: 188]

  b. We didn't have no use for it noways. [Appalachian English, Montgomery 2004: 258]

  c. He is not supposed to mention nobody's name. [Ghanaian English, Huber and Dako 2004: 857]

Such sentences receive an overall negative interpretation, i.e. the double occurrence of negative expressions does not cancel out the negative force, as the standard English example in (15) shows.

(15) I didn't see nobody. 'I saw somebody.'

The occurrence of multiple negative expressions is also known as 'negative concord', since other sentential elements – mainly quantifiers and indefinite expressions – *agree* with the overall polarity (positive, negative) of the sentence. As a matter of fact, it is more adequate to use the term 'negative concord', even though we encounter competing terminology in the literature. We will come back to this point in our cross-linguistic survey in Section 9.3.3. We can distinguish between preverbal and postverbal negative concord, as shown in (16) below.

(16) a. I couldn't find hardly none on 'em. [East Anglia, Trudgill 2004: 151]

  b. Nobody don't have none here. [Bahamian English, Reaser and Torbert 2004: 400]

According to Anderwald (2002: 109), preverbal negative concord is restricted to *nobody* or *no one*. The examples in (17) show two cases from her survey of the *BNC*.

(17) a. Nobody don't bother with them do they?

  b. No one didn't recognize her.

    [*BNC*, Anderwald 2002: 109]

The most frequent co-occurrence patterns of negative elements in Anderwald's (2002: 107) corpus survey are *-n't . . . no* (240 cases), *-n't . . . nothing* (178 cases), *-n't . . . none* (28 cases), and *never . . . nothing* (33 cases). Among the more typical negative elements participating in negative concord structures are *-n't, never, not*, and *no*. The elements *nobody, hardly, nor, no one, nowt*, and *none* are rarely attested in the corpus data.

Negative concord is widespread and occurs practically in all non-standard colloquial varieties. Even though it is probably best known as a prominent feature of African American Vernacular English (especially preverbal negative concord), we can find it in many traditional vernaculars and English-based Pidgins and Creoles, though it is less common in post-colonial Englishes. For example, Anderwald (2002: 110) shows for some dialect areas of England that negative concord can be found in over 30 per cent of the negative sentences in which it could in principle occur.[4]

Interestingly enough, some vernaculars also allow the use of negative polarity items of the *any*-series in positive contexts, i.e. without a preceding sentential negator. This especially concerns *anymore* and is aptly known as 'positive anymore'. In the respective affirmative contexts, *anymore* comes to be interpreted as 'nowadays' or 'from now on', as illustrated in (18). The phenomenon is common in vernacular forms of North American English, but is by no means restricted to them.

(18) Sam didn't useta eat red meat, but he sure does anymore. 'Sam didn't use to eat red meat, but he sure does nowadays.' [Colloquial American English, Murray and Simon 2004: 230]

Even though the use of positive *anymore* strikes speakers of standard English as ungrammatical, its semantic contribution to the overall interpretation of a sentence is quite predictable. On the assumption that standard occurrences of *anymore* that lie within the scope of the sentential negator describe a change from 'doing something' to 'not doing something', one may expect *anymore* outside negative scope to be interpreted as a change from 'not doing something' to 'doing something'.

9.2.3   Negative contraction and auxiliary contraction

Standard English allows the contraction of either the auxiliary to the preceding noun phrase or the negation to the preceding auxiliary. An overview of the contraction patterns was given in Table 9.1 above. Contraction describes a process of phonological reduction whereby a sentential element 'leans' on the preceding element, thus yielding a new complex unit. This is shown once again in (19).[5]

(19) a. John's not happy. (auxiliary contraction)
      b. John isn't happy. (negative contraction)

Table 9.1 presented some interesting restrictions: for example, the verbs *do*, *can*, *could*, *may*, *might*, *must*, *need*, and *ought* are not found with auxiliary contraction, but only with negative contraction (*we needn't*, **we'nd not*). As a general rule we said that wherever auxiliary contraction is possible, we also find negative contraction. However, there is one exception: the verb *be* resists

---

[4] Multiple negation is an historical feature of English that was abandoned in standard English around the time of Shakespeare but that has persisted in non-standard language to the present day (Anderwald 2002: 102–3).

[5] In English, such contraction or cliticisation invariably works to the left, the only exception being *do*: *D'you like her?*

negative contraction in the first person singular, even though it allows auxiliary contraction (*I'm not*, **I amn't*). This is the famous '*amn't* gap' widely discussed in the literature (Hudson 2000). Notice, though, that negative contraction in the first person is possible in interrogatives and tags, i.e. when the negated form of *be* precedes the pronoun. The contracted form is *aren't*:

(20) a. Aren't I your friend?
      b. I'm your friend, aren't I?
          [Hudson 2000: 308]

Varieties of English have been claimed to have differing preferences for negative or auxiliary contraction. For example, a widely accepted generalisation holds that negative contraction is more common in southern British dialects, while there is a preference for auxiliary contraction in the north of England and Scotland. You can find a good overview of these claims in Tagliamonte and Smith (2002: 253).

The more important predictor for the choice between auxiliary and negative contraction, however, appears to be the auxiliary involved. Both Anderwald (2002: 76) and Tagliamonte and Smith (2002: 271) report that *be* is generally found with higher rates of auxiliary contraction in comparison with other verbs, which favour negative contraction. Both studies concur that auxiliary contraction with *be* ranges between 40 and 100 per cent, with a clear tendency towards the higher percentages, and that the differences cannot be explained by regional factors. Anderwald (2002: 80) summarises these findings in terms of the following two hierarchies:

(21) BE: auxiliary contraction > negative contraction

(22) other verbs: negative contraction > auxiliary contraction

9.2.4   Negative tags

Standard English possesses so-called 'tag questions' or 'question tags' that can be added to declarative sentences for emphasis or to induce some kind of confirmation on the part of the addressee. They can be either positive or negative and typically have the opposite polarity to that of the main clause declarative.[6] Tags in English are full predications consisting of subject and verb, the verb agreeing with the subject according to the familiar rules. In addition, the subject of the tag question agrees with the main clause subject. This is shown in (23).[7]

(23) a. She eats too much, doesn't she?
      b. They do not like pasta, do they?

---

[6] This general rule, which has a strong prescriptive flavour to it, is by no means without exceptions.

[7] In principle, we could discuss tags just as well in the chapter on interrogatives (see Chapter 12). We could also treat them in the chapter on subject-verb agreement (see Chapter 10). They are included here since negative tags appear especially prominent.

The agreement properties found in standard English tag questions are often relaxed or simply non-existent in vernacular varieties. Let us take a look at the examples in (24). We may note that in sentence (24a) the subject of the tag question (*it*) is different from the main clause subject (*we*), even though the tag question is complete in all other aspects. Agreement inside the tag is consistent with the subject of the tag, but inconsistent with the main clause subject. We can say essentially the same about (24b), where the main clause subject is of the second person. Example (24c) is really interesting, as the tag question is reduced to the invariant form *inni* (also *innit*), which shows no agreement with the main clause subject. The form *innit* occurs with positive or negative main clause declaratives, as the contrast between (24c) and (24d) makes clear, and is insensitive to the tense of the main clause. Finally, there are also tags as in (24e), which are probably derived from the negative expression *not*.[8]

(24) a. We saw some the other day, isn't it? [Welsh English, Penhallurick 2004: 103]
   b. You said you'll do the job, isn't it? [Indian English, Bhatt 2004: 1022]
   c. Yall didn buy no clothes from town, inni? [Gullah, Mufwene 2004: 368]
   d. He gets upset quick, innit? [Southeast of England, Anderwald 2004: 191]
   e. I told you she will come, na? [Cameroon English, Mbangwana 2004: 905]

The reduced invariant tag *innit* does not seem to be an emblem of any particular regional variety, even though there are regional differences. Rather, it is a feature of colloquial speech that has been spreading into more formal registers for a considerable amount of time (Krug 1998).

It is interesting to note that these reduced tags are – at least in the majority of cases – derived from negative tag questions. In other words, a tag question like *isn't it* grammaticalises into an invariant tag that does not agree with the main clause any longer. As far as I can see, this does not happen with the corresponding positive tags, i.e. *is it* does not grammaticalise to *isit*.[9]

9.2.5   Asymmetries

Anderwald (2002: 198–201) argues that non-standard varieties show asymmetries in their verbal paradigms that, interestingly enough, result in simpler

---

[8] According to Bhatt (2004: 1022), non-agreeing tags serve important politeness functions in Indian English.

[9] The Englishes spoken in South Africa and Zimbabwe may be different, as *isit* seems to be used as a tag there, though in special meanings (see Siemund et al. 2012: 232 for authentic examples).

Table 9.2 *Asymmetrical paradigms (adapted from Anderwald 2002: 199).*

Positive	*am*	*is*	*are*	*has*	*have*	*do*	*does*	*was*	*were*
Negative	*ain't*					*don't*		*wasn't/weren't*	

paradigms under negation. In other words, several verb forms in the positive paradigm are collapsed into fewer forms – typically one invariant form – in the negative paradigm. Consider the data in Table 9.2.

As you can see, three forms of the positive paradigm of *be* and two forms of that of *have* correspond to the invariant negative form *ain't*. Similarly, positive *do* and *does* fall together in negative *don't*. This phenomenon is known as 'third person singular *don't*'. The past tense forms *was* and *were* are included, as levelling to either *wasn't* or *weren't* is most pronounced under negation.

We will come back to these asymmetries in Section 9.3.2 below. The generalisation of *was* and *were* to either of the two forms will be discussed in detail in Chapter 10. This chapter also contains some remarks on third person singular *don't*.

9.3 Cross-linguistic comparison

In the overwhelming majority of languages, negation is expressed through some additive mechanism on affirmative clauses, as already briefly mentioned at the beginning of this chapter. In the typological literature on negation, we encounter a few mentions of languages that apparently employ subtractive negation, i.e. an affirmative clause is negated by omitting some element rather than adding a negative morpheme. Such a strategy has been reported from South Dravidian languages (e.g. Tamil and Kannada) spoken in India. In example (25) below, clausal negation is expressed by omitting the tense affix on the verb, as shown in (26) and (27).

(25) noːḍ-em
  see-1SG
  'I do / did / will not see.' [Old Dravidian, Miestamo 2010: 170]

(26) noːḍ-uv-em
  see-FUT-1SG
  'I will see.' [Old Dravidian, Miestamo 2010: 170]

(27) noːḍ-id-em
  see-PAST-1SG
  'I saw.' [Old Dravidian, Miestamo 2010: 170]

On the whole, however, this marking strategy is extremely rare. The prototypical way of encoding negation consists in adding some material to the affirmative clause.

The first cross-linguistic parameter that we will investigate in this section concerns the attested marking strategies. Another parameter concerns asymmetries between affirmative and negative clauses with respect to the expression of other grammatical categories. The third cross-linguistic parameter captures the number of negative elements in a clause (single, double, triple negation). Finally, we will also explore the so-called 'Jespersen Cycle', which represents a common grammaticalisation path of sentence negation.

9.3.1   Strategies of negation

Following Dahl (1979), we may assume a very broad distinction between morphological negation and syntactic negation, both comprising various subtypes. Morphological negation may be prefixal, suffixal, or circumfixal. Example (28) shows a case of prefixal negation from Kolyma Yukaghir, a Siberian language spoken in Russia.

(28) met numö-ge   el-jaqa-te-je
      1SG house-LOC NEG-achieve-FUT-INTR.1SG
      'I will not reach the house.' [Kolyma Yukaghir, Maslova 2003: 492, cited in Dryer 2011]

We could analyse standard English clitic negation in combination with preceding auxiliaries as suffixal in a somewhat broader sense, as shown below:

(29) doesn't, didn't, couldn't, wasn't, weren't, etc.

The comparison is not completely robust, though, since such clitic negation competes with the negative particle *not*, which is usually analysed as primary. More convincing examples of suffixal negation are furnished by Scottish English and Irish English, where the negative suffixes (or clitics) not only appear on auxiliaries (e.g. *cannae, isnae*; Anderwald 2002: 47), but also on main verbs (*keenay* 'know not', *cairnay* 'care not', *looznay* 'loves not'; Anderwald 2002: 54). An authentic example sentence is shown in (30). Chapter 8 on modal verbs contains additional examples of suffixal negation.

(30) He didnae like cheese, e no? [Scottish English, Millar and Brown 1979: 33]

On the whole, however, morphological negation is not a big issue in varieties of English, be they standard or non-standard varieties. Syntactic negation is far more widespread. Here again, we may distinguish various subtypes that we will briefly discuss below.

Even though they are typically not recognised by typologies of negation, we will here mention the negation of sentences by negative words or negative quantifiers, i.e. expressions like *nobody*, *never*, *nothing*, *nowhere*, as these occur without the negative particle *not* in the standard varieties (for double and multiple negation, see Section 9.3.3 below). As shown in Section 9.2.1 above, the negative word *never* serves as the default sentence negation in various non-standard varieties of English, especially in the past tense. You can find some additional examples in (31). In a typology of negation, such examples would count as syntactic negation.

(31) a. I sat down to that tongue slips essay at 7 o'clock I never got it started till nine. '. . . I didn't get it started till nine.' [Scottish English, Miller 2004: 51]

      b. That time she never come up so far. '. . . she did not . . .' [Newfoundland English, Clarke 2004: 310]

      c. We never write yet. 'We haven't written [our exams] yet.' [Indian South African English, Mesthrie 2004b: 978]

A second strategy is negation by particles. It is the most widespread strategy in the cross-linguistic sample explored by Dryer (2011), being attested in approximately half of the languages in the sample. German, as illustrated in (32), is a typical language manifesting this marking strategy. Standard English also belongs in this group, for the reasons discussed above in Section 9.1.

(32) Johann isst die Suppe nicht.
      John   eats the soup not
      'John does not eat the soup.' [German, personal knowledge]

Some languages – clearly a minority – possess dedicated negative auxiliary verbs that serve as the main strategy of sentence negation. The Finnish example in (33) is a case in point. The negation is classified as a verb since it shows agreement with the subject in person and number. Dryer (2011) finds 47 languages with negative auxiliary verbs in his sample of 1,159 languages.

(33) e-n   syö-nyt   omena-a
      NEG-1SG eat-PTCP apple-PART
      'I didn't eat an apple.'
      [Finnish, Sulkala and Karjalainen 1992: 115, cited in Dryer 2011]

With some good will, we may interpret the standard English *do*-periphrasis as the negative auxiliary strategy, especially if the negator is cliticised. However, the comparison is more suitable for the invariant negative markers *don't* and *ain't* that clearly serve an auxiliary function, even though they do not show agreement with the subject. Some additional examples can be found in (34) and (35).

(34) a. If 'e don't work, 'e don't eat. [Australian Vernacular English, Pawley 2004: 633]

      b. She don't like it here in the courts and my dad well I'm not sure 'cause he don't live with us. [Chicano English, Bayley and Santa Ana 2004: 378]

(35) a. I telling you what the old people told me now. Because that one I ain't
see with my own eye. [Liberian Settler English, Singler 2004: 886]

b. She ain't but three years old. [Urban African American Vernacular
English, Wolfram 2004b: 332]

9.3.2   *Symmetric and asymmetric negation*

Negation in the standard varieties is asymmetric in the sense of Miestamo
(2011). The parameter of asymmetry captures possible category changes under
negation. For example, in the standard varieties, the option to express emphasis
by using the verb *do* is lost under negation, as this verb serves as the syntactic
host of the negator. Consider the contrasting affirmative sentences in (36),
where *did* in (36b) expresses emphasis, which is lacking in (36a). We cannot
express the same contrast in the corresponding negative sentence, as shown
in (37).

(36) a. Sue repaired the car by herself. (non-emphatic)

b. Sue did repair the car by herself. (emphatic)

(37) Sue did not repair the car by herself.

Disregarding emphasis marking, we could also say that negation in the standard
varieties is asymmetric, as it requires *do*-periphrasis and is thus structurally
different from the affirmative clause.

Miestamo (2011) distinguishes several ways in which negation can be asymmetric. The addition of a special finite element, i.e. the auxiliary verb *do* in the
English standard varieties, would be one important strategy. We encountered
something similar in the Finnish example in (33), even though the status of
the auxiliary is different in Finnish, in that it is not used for the expression of
emphasis in affirmative clauses.

Another prominent realisation of asymmetry is the addition of an element expressing hypothetical events in negative clauses (a so-called 'irrealis'
marker). The example from Imbabura Quechua in (38) illustrates this asymmetry nicely, as the verbal suffix *-chu* appears in negative and interrogative
clauses, though not in affirmative clauses.

(38) a. juzi iskay kaballu-ta   chari-n
José two   horse-ACC have-3
'José has two horses.'

b. ñuka wawki mana jatun wasi-ta   chari-n-chu
my   brother NEG big   house-ACC have-3-NEG/Q
'My brother does not have a big house.'

c. kan-paj   wawki jatun wasi-ta   chari-n-chu
you-POSS brother big   house-ACC have-3-NEG/Q
'Does your brother have a big house?'
[Imbabura Quechua, Cole 1985: 83, 94, cited in Miestamo 2011]

Furthermore, asymmetry may result from a category change that may involve any of the basic grammatical categories like tense, aspect, mood, person, number, or emphasis marking, as in the English example shown in (36) above. In addition, Miestamo (2011) distinguishes several types of asymmetry that result from combining the three types just introduced. For the sake of completeness, let me also give you an idea of the distributions of these types. Miestamo's (2011) cross-linguistic sample contains 297 languages, of which 40 use a special finite element under negation and 20 show some sort of irrealis marking, while 82 languages display a change in a grammatical category. The remaining languages in the sample show combinations of the basic types.

As far as non-standard varieties of English are concerned, we can observe the disappearance of several grammatical distinctions under negation, leading to an increased degree of asymmetry in relation to the standard varieties. We introduced the relevant facts in Section 9.2.5: the distinctions in grammatical person of the verbs *be* and *have* (i.e. *am, is, are, has, have*) are lost in negative clauses, as they are substituted by the invariant form *ain't*; the distinction between *be* and *have* is lost; and the contrast in person expressed by the opposition of *do* and *does* is frequently lost owing to the use of invariant *don't*. As Anderwald (2002: 198) puts it: 'Speakers will now have to remember to use *he does, she does, it does* in positive contexts, but *he don't, she don't, it don't* in negative ones.' In sum, non-standard varieties show more asymmetries under negation than standard varieties.

Negation in non-standard varieties of English, thus, falls into type three of the asymmetries distinguished in Miestamo's (2011) typology. Miestamo (2000: 78) argues that negative clauses show fewer grammatical distinctions than affirmative clauses, because non-occurring situations are typically less precise with respect to basic parameters such as *who, when, where,* and *why*. To put it in his own words:

In the asymmetric paradigms there is a 'vertical' analogy (or iconicity): the ontology of non-facts is less differentiated than the ontology of facts, and linguistic structure reflects this distinction.

9.3.3   Multiple negation

Of the fundamental strategies of negation introduced in Section 9.3.1 above, multiple negation deserves separate treatment. In the typological literature, the term 'double negation' is used to name the negation strategy of languages that employ two negative markers in a clause to indicate that the clause is to receive a negative interpretation. We may illustrate the phenomenon on the basis of French, as in (39), where the preverbal negator *ne* occurs together with the postverbal negator *pas*.

Table 9.3 *Double negation in relation to other strategies of negation (adapted from Dryer 2011).*

Strategy	Affix	Particle	Auxiliary	Double negation	Other	Total
#	396	502	47	120	94	1,159

(39) Je   ne   vois   pas   la   lune.
1SG NEG see.1SG NEG the moon
'I do not see the moon.' [French, Dryer 2011]

The problem with double negation in French is that the preverbal negative particle is optional in colloquial varieties. For this reason, Dryer (2011) does not include French in the group of languages with double negation. A more typical example of double negation is shown in (40). It is taken from Izi, a Niger-Congo language spoken in Nigeria, where a preverbal negative affix obligatorily co-occurs with a negative verbal suffix. We may also refer to this strategy of negation as 'circumfixal'.

(40) ó   tó-òmé-dú   ré
3SG NEG-do-NEG well
'He does not do well.' [Izi, Meier et al. 1975: 218, cited in Dryer 2011]

According to Dryer (2011), double negation is one of the more prominent strategies of negation. With 120 attestations, it is the third most frequent strategy in his cross-linguistic sample of 1,159 languages. You can find a summary of Dryer's findings in Table 9.3.

In Ma, another Niger-Congo language, this time spoken in the Democratic Republic of Congo, double negation is expressed by a preverbal affix in combination with a postverbal particle, i.e. here the joint occurrence of the affixal strategy and the particle strategy gives rise to double negation:

(41) tá-mù-sùbù-li   nɔ́ŋgbɔ́ nyɔ̀
NEG-1SG-eat-PAST meat   NEG.1SG
'I did not eat meat.' [Ma, Tucker and Bryan 1966: 130, cited in Dryer 2011]

In view of these examples of double negation, it becomes obvious that the term 'double negation' is, as a matter of fact, a misnomer for the phenomenon of multiple negation in varieties of English, because there we do not find two formally distinct negative markers, but the co-occurrence of the clausal negator with one or more negative quantifiers, i.e. expressions like *nobody*, *never*, *nothing*, etc. For this phenomenon, the term 'negative concord' is customarily employed. It suggests that quantifiers and other indefinite expressions agree in their polarity with the polarity of the clause. This is quite different from the cases of double negation shown above. Provided that this assessment of the English non-standard negation phenomena is correct, they more closely resemble negative concord in languages like Spanish or Italian, as shown in (42) and (43) below. Notice that Spanish is not coded as a language with double negation in Dryer (2011).[10]

(42) Nadie   dice nunca nada   a nadie.
nobody says never nothing to nobody
'Nobody says never anything to anybody.' [Spanish, Christoph Gabriel]

(43) Non è venuto nessuno.
NEG is come   nobody
'Nobody came.' [Italian, Miestamo 2007: 565]

To make this parallel perfectly clear, I offer two additional examples of negative concord from varieties of English, as shown in (44), where the example in (44a) comes from an historical variety.

(44) a. I thinke ye weare never yet in no grownd of mine, and I never say
no man naye. [Early Modern English, *Corpus of Early English Correspondence*, cited in Nevalainen 2006: 260]

b. Ain't nobody ever thought about picking up nothing. [African American Vernacular English, Martin and Wolfram 1998: 19, cited in
Nevalainen 2006: 260]

Cross-linguistically, negative concord is a rather widespread phenomenon. Drawing on a sample of 206 languages, Haspelmath (2011) identifies no fewer than 170 with negative concord. Only eleven languages in this sample prohibit the co-occurrence of predicate negation and negative indefinites.

9.3.4   The Jespersen Cycle

In concluding this brief cross-linguistic survey of negation, I would like to draw your attention to the historical development of negation in English, which, however, has wider typological significance. English negation underwent a process known as the Jespersen Cycle, after the Danish linguist Otto Jespersen.

According to Jespersen (1917: 9–11), the development of negation in English proceeded in essentially four steps, illustrated in (45) to (48) below. All exam-ples have been taken from Jespersen's original work. In Old English (45), the sentential negation was placed before the finite verb (particle negation). In Middle English (46), we often find a second negative element placed after the verb. At this historical stage, the expression of negation is doubled – has two exponents – even though the overall meaning remains negative. We can count this as a case of 'double negation' in the sense discussed in Section 9.3.3 above. The postverbal negative element itself is a contraction of the negative element

---

[10] If the negative indefinites in Spanish or Italian precede the verb, the sentential negator is omitted. Strict negative concord is found in Russian (Haspelmath 2011). Non-standard varieties of English appear to follow the Russian pattern.

na and the form *wiht*, meaning 'small person'. Jespersen (1917: 9) describes the development as from *nawiht/nowiht* via *noht* to *not*. The etymology of *nawiht* is similar to that of *nothing* (*not* + *thing*).

In Early Modern English (47), the preverbal negation drops out, while the postverbal negation remains. In another step, the negative element then moves to a position before the main verb in Modern English (48), with the additional requirement of *do*-support. In principle, this process may begin to repeat itself.

(45) Ic ne secge.   [Old English]
    I   not say
(46) I ne seye not. [Middle English]
    I not say   not
(47) I say not.   [Early Modern English]
(48) I do not say.   [Modern English]

Jespersen's Cycle receives its importance from the fact that it is not restricted to English. The development of negation in French follows a similar process (*ne* > *ne . . . pas* > *pas*), as is well known. Additional languages illustrating this general cycle in the development of negation can be found in van der Auwera (2010).

9.4   Summary and list of keywords

We began this chapter by introducing some essential properties of negation, as this is a sophisticated category that presupposes clarity on a number of background assumptions. It often takes some thinking to decide what exactly is negated in a clause. In the section on varieties of English, we explored non-standard sentential negators, multiple negation, negative and auxiliary contraction, negative tags, and asymmetries under negation. The highly stigmatised form *ain't* turned out to be a versatile sentential negator. We also found that contraction is lexically conditioned, and not governed by region. Moreover, it is striking to see that grammatical distinctions may be lost in negative contexts, leading to asymmetries in their expression. Such asymmetries are not uncommon cross-linguistically. The comparison of English non-standard patterns of negation with other languages also revealed that what is known as 'multiple negation' is more aptly referred to as 'negative concord', itself a widespread phenomenon that is by no means restricted to non-standard varieties. Finally, we explored the Jespersen Cycle, which can be described as a diachronic generalisation on the development of negation.

Keywords: agreement, *ain't*, asymmetries, auxiliary verbs, circumfixal negation, cliticisation, constative utterances, constituent negation, contraction, *do*-support, irrealis, Jespersen Cycle, morphological negation, multiple negation, negative auxiliaries, negative concord, negative indefinite expressions, negative polarity items, performative utterances, positive *anymore*, scope of negation, sentence negation, subtractive negation, syntactic negation, tags, truth-value.

9.5   Exercises

Basic level

1. The sentence below illustrates negative concord in non-standard English.

   He did not know nothing.

   a. Paraphrase the meaning of this sentence in standard English.
   b. What does the sentence mean in non-standard English?
2. Define and illustrate the term 'scope'.
3. Negation in standard English requires *do*-support, as you know. How about the requirement of *do*-support in non-standard varieties?

Intermediate level

1. The Jespersen Cycle represents a famous generalisation in the historical development of negation. It was first stated for English, but can also be observed for other languages.
   a. Explain the major empirical observations behind the Jespersen Cycle and illustrate them.
   b. Do data from varieties of English provide empirical evidence in support of the Jespersen Cycle?
2. Anderwald (2002) claims that multiple negation may be found at levels of more than 30 per cent. This claim is based on a survey of the dialect material contained in the *BNC*.

   Try to add to our knowledge of multiple negation (negative concord) by investigating this feature in other varieties of English. Make use of the *ICE* (http://ice-corpora.net/ice/) as an empirical basis.
3. Krug (1998) documents the emergence of the invariant tag *innit* in colloquial varieties of British English. Read the article by Krug (1998) and extend this analysis to up to three New Englishes of your choice. Use the *ICE* (http://ice-corpora.net/ice/) as an empirical basis.

Advanced level

1. In standard English the use of two negative expressions leads to a positive interpretation, i.e. negative elements cancel each other out: *I did not see nobody* means 'I saw somebody'. Such an effect does not arise in non-standard varieties of English, where several negative elements in one

sentence usually do not result in an overall positive interpretation. Sentences with several negative elements are negative semantically.

Since many languages use multiple negative expressions in a way similar to non-standard varieties of English, nothing can be 'wrong' with these varieties – but how can we make sense of the apparently 'superfluous' use of negative elements? Can you think of a convincing explanation?

2. In Section 9.3.3, we briefly discussed the distinction between 'double negation' and 'negative concord'. Write an essay of approximately three pages in which you develop criteria for drawing this distinction. Use sufficient exemplification to illustrate your discussion.

3. The term 'positive *anymore*' captures the use of *anymore* in affirmative clauses. It occurs in non-standard varieties. In standard English, *anymore* is confined to negative contexts:

   a. *She cannot stand it anymore.*
   b. *Everything we do anymore seems to have been done in a big hurry. (OED)*

   a. What does *anymore* mean in affirmative contexts?
   b. How can we semantically relate positive *anymore* to negative *anymore*?

9.6   References

Anderwald, Lieselotte. 2002. *Negation in Non-Standard British English: Gaps, Regularizations and Asymmetries.* London: Routledge.

Austin, John L. 1962. *How to Do Things with Words.* Oxford: Clarendon.

Cole, Peter. 1985. *Imbabura Quechua.* (Croom Helm Descriptive Grammars.) London: Croom Helm.

Dahl, Östen. 1979. Typology of sentence negation. *Linguistics* 17. 79–106.

Dryer, Matthew S. 2011. Negative morphemes. In Matthew S. Dryer and Martin Haspelmath (eds.), *The World Atlas of Language Structures Online.* Munich: Max Planck Digital Library, chapter 112. Available online at http://wals.info/chapter/112. Accessed 22 December 2011.

Gass, Susan M. and Larry Selinker. 2008. *Second Language Acquisition: An Introductory Course.* London: Routledge.

Haspelmath, Martin. 2011. Negative indefinite pronouns and predicate negation. Matthew S. Dryer and Martin Haspelmath (eds.), *The World Atlas of Language Structures Online.* Munich: Max Planck Digital Library, chapter 115. Available online at http://wals.info/chapter/115. Accessed 22 December 2011.

Hudson, Richard. 2000. *I amn't. *Language* 76(2). 297–323.

Jackendoff, Ray S. 1972. *Semantic Interpretation in Generative Grammar.* Cambridge, MA: MIT Press.

Jespersen, Otto. 1917. *Negation in English and Other Languages.* Copenhagen: Høst.

Krug, Manfred. 1998. British English is developing a new discourse marker, innit? A study in lexicalisation based on social, regional and stylistic variation. *Arbeiten aus Anglistik und Amerikanistik* 23(2). 145–97.

Martin, Stefan and Walt Wolfram. 1998. The sentence in African-American Vernacular English. In Salikoko S. Mufwene, John R. Rickford, Guy Bailey, and John Baugh (eds.), *African-American English*, 11–36. London: Routledge.

Maslova, Elena. 2003. *A Grammar of Kolyma Yukaghir*. Berlin: Mouton de Gruyter.

Meier, Ingeborg, Paul Meier, and John Bendor-Samuel. 1975. *A Grammar of Izi: An Igbo Language*. Norman, OK: Summer Institute of Linguistics.

Miestamo, Matti. 2000. Towards a typology of standard negation. *Nordic Journal of Linguistics* 23(1). 65–88.

2007. Negation – an overview of typological research. *Language and Linguistics Compass* 1(5). 552–70.

2010. Negatives without negators. In Jan Wohlgemuth and Michael Cysouw (eds.), *Rethinking Universals: How Rarities Affect Linguistic Theory* (Empirical Approaches to Language Typology 45), 169–94. Berlin: Mouton de Gruyter.

2011. Subtypes of asymmetric standard negation. In Matthew S. Dryer and Martin Haspelmath (eds.), *The World Atlas of Language Structures Online*. Munich: Max Planck Digital Library, chapter 114. Available online at http://wals.info/chapter/114. Accessed 22 December 2011.

Millar, Martin and Keith Brown. 1979. Tag questions in Edinburgh speech. *Linguistische Berichte* 60. 24–45.

Nevalainen, Terttu. 2006. Negative concord as an English 'Vernacular Universal': Social history and linguistic typology. *English Language and Linguistics* 34(3). 257–78.

Searle, John. 1969. *Speech Acts*. Cambridge University Press.

Siemund, Peter, Julia Davydova, and Georg Maier. 2012. *The Amazing World of Englishes: A Practical Introduction*. Berlin: Mouton de Gruyter.

Sulkala, Helena and Merja Karjalainen. 1992. *Finnish*. London. Routledge.

Tagliamonte, Sali and Jennifer Smith. 2002. NEG/AUX contraction in British dialects. *English World-Wide* 23(2). 251–81.

Tucker, Archibald N. and Margret A. Bryan. 1966. *Linguistic Analyses: The Non-Bantu Languages of North-Eastern Africa*. Oxford University Press.

van der Auwera, Johan. 2010. On the diachrony of negation. In Laurence R. Horn (ed.), *The Expression of Negation*, 73–101. Berlin: Mouton de Gruyter.

See *General references* for Anderwald 2004; Ayafor 2004; Bayley and Santa Ana 2004; Bhatt 2004; Clarke 2004; Faraclas 2004; Huber and Dako 2004; Mbangwana 2004; Mesthrie 2004b; Miller 2004; Montgomery 2004; Mufwene 2004; Murray and Simon 2004; Pawley 2004; Penhallurick 2004; Quirk et al. 1985; Reaser and Torbert 2004; Singler 2004; Smith 2004; Trudgill 2004; Wolfram 2004a; Wolfram 2004b.

9.7   Further reading

Anderwald, Lieselotte. 2003. Non-standard English and typological principles: The case of negation. In Günter Rohdenburg and Britta Mondorf (eds.), *Determinants of Linguistic Variation* (Topics in English Linguistics 43), 507–29. Berlin: Mouton de Gruyter.

Haspelmath, Martin. 1997. *Indefinite Pronouns*. Oxford University Press.

Horn, Laurence R. 2001. *A Natural History of Negation*. (The David Hume Series: Philosophy and Cognitive Science Reissues.) Stanford: CSLI Publications.

Howe, Darin M. 1997. Negation and the history of African American English. *Language Variation and Change* 9(2). 267–94.

Labov, William. 1972. Negative attraction and negative concord in English grammar. *Language* 48(4). 773–818.

1991. The boundaries of a grammar: Inter-dialectal reactions to positive *anymore*. In Peter Trudgill and Jack K. Chambers (eds.), *Dialects of English: Studies in Grammatical Variation*, 273–88. London: Longman.

Nolan, David W. 1991. A diachronic survey of English negative concord. *American Speech* 66(2). 171–80.

Payne, John R. 1985. Negation. In Timothy Shopen (ed.), *Language Typology and Syntactic Description, volume I: Clause Structure*, 197–242. Cambridge University Press.

Shields, Kenneth. 1997. Positive *anymore* in Southeastern Pennsylvania. *American Speech* 72(2). 217–20.

10   Subject-verb agreement

Agreement can be defined as a relationship of covariance between two or more sentential elements, as, for example, between subject and verb. In such a relationship, one element serves as the controller of the agreement relation, and one or more of the other sentential elements can be identified as the targets by virtue of some formal exponence that would not appear without this relationship. Handbooks of English usually agree that English has agreement between subject and verb at least in terms of person and number: *I leave, he leave-s, the house stand-s here, the houses stand here*. This agreement relation is only marked in the third person singular (non-past) by means of the suffix *-s*. We encountered another agreement relation in Chapter 3 in our discussion of systems of pronominal gender. Demonstrative pronouns show number agreement with their nominal heads (Chapter 5). Negative concord, as introduced in Chapter 9, may also be viewed as an agreement relation, though not a typical one. In the present chapter, we will be exclusively concerned with subject-verb agreement.

10.1   Overview

In his monograph on agreement, Corbett (2006: 1) begins his exposition by introducing a clearly false hypothesis – for didactic reasons, of course. According to this hypothesis, 'grammatical information will be found only together with the lexical item to which it is relevant'. Corbett continues by stating that '[t]his hypothesis suggests a situation which is iconic, functional, sensible and understandable'. By way of illustration, he introduces English plural marking (*dog/dogs*) and the marking of the past tense (*compute/computed*), which fulfil the above criteria. Subject-verb agreement, and agreement in general, blatantly violates such a commonsensical perception of language as that which lies behind the above hypothesis. The main 'problem' of agreement is that it expresses information originating in another constituent. The verbal third person *-s* suffix of standard English mirrors information on the subject constituent. Even though this fact is well known, it remains a puzzling phenomenon. We

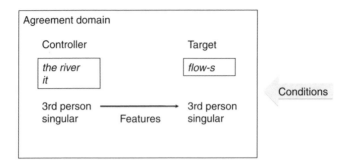

Figure 10.1 The ingredients of agreement (adapted from Corbett 2006: 5).

will see that non-standard varieties can add various complications to this simple scenario.

10.1.1   Agreement

Let us first of all try to make the term 'agreement' more precise. As stated above, we may tentatively define agreement as a relationship of covariance in which the formal properties of one (or more) sentential elements are determined by another element. Corbett (2006: 4–5) refers to the element that triggers the agreement relation as the 'controller' and the element (or elements) whose form is determined by the controller as the 'target' (Figure 10.1). The syntactic context in which the agreement relation can be observed is called the 'agreement domain'. The controller can trigger agreement on the targets in terms of various formal and semantic properties. These are called the 'agreement features'. In the case of the verbal suffix -s introduced above, the controller is the subject, the target is the finite verb, and the agreement features are person and number. The feature values that are overtly marked are 'third person' and 'singular'. Corbett (2006: 5) also points out that there may be additional conditions on the agreement relation, as it may only be realised provided further factors are fulfilled.

10.1.2   Canonical subject-verb-agreement

The sole formal exponent of subject-verb agreement in standard English is the well-known -s suffix that appears only in the third person singular and only with finite main verbs. Modal verbs do not take the -s suffix (*Mary live-s in London, Mary may live in London, *Mary mays live in London*; see Chapter 8). The verb *be* – both in its auxiliary and main verb uses – has different forms in the singular present tense, overlapping forms in the singular past tense,

Table 10.1 *The paradigms of the verb* be.

	Singular			Plural	
	Present	Past		Present	Past
I	*am*	*was*	we	*are*	*were*
you	*are*	*were*	you	*are*	*were*
he/she/it	*is*	*was*	they	*are*	*were*

and identical forms in the present and past plural paradigms, as shown in Table 10.1.[1] We will also subsume this phenomenon under agreement, even though the entire verb form agrees with the subject, so to speak, and is not just an affix.[2] This phenomenon is known as 'suppletion'.

The other auxiliary verbs *have* and *do* match the paradigms of main verbs, although they possess suppletive, or at least semi-suppletive, forms for the third person singular: *have – has, do* /dʊ/ *– does* /dʌz/) and the past tense (*had/did*).

10.1.3   Non-canonical subject-verb agreement

In spite of the fact that subject-verb agreement in the standard varieties is sparse and simple, we can identify a few areas where complications arise, especially concerning number agreement. For example, we can observe that subject noun phrases that are formally singular trigger plural agreement, and that plural marked noun phrases occur with singular agreement on the verb. Huddleston and Pullum (2002: 500) discuss the examples in (1), in which the verb forms do not agree with the preceding subject in number.

(1) a. It is part of one's linguistic competence to be able to control and interpret variations of word order and grammatical structure of the kind that *are* exemplified in the sentence above.

   b. A number of special units *are* available for patients requiring hospital-ization.

   c. The committee *were* informed that the proposal to close the canal had been made by the British Transport Commission.

We may interpret (1a) as a case of competition between singular and plural antecedent where the more salient plural antecedent wins. The plural verb form in (1b) may be explained in terms of agreement with the nearest noun

---

[1] This formal overlap, i.e. when one form appears in more than one cell of a paradigm, is known as 'syncretism'.

[2] In historical terms, the forms of the verb *be* belong to two different verbal paradigms (Old English *beon, wesan*), resulting in today's rather complicated paradigm.

phrase. This, in fact, is a fairly general phenomenon. Example (1c) shows plural agreement in the context of formally singular collective nouns.

Variation in terms of subject-verb agreement is rather common with collective nouns (*family*, *team*, *herd*, etc.). The condition triggering singular over plural agreement is generally held to be individuation: if the subject noun phrase referent is conceptualised as one undifferentiated unit, singular agreement will be strongly preferred; if it is viewed as a collection of individuals foregrounding the individuals, we are more likely to find plural agreement. This generalisation is illustrated in (2).

(2) a. A bunch of flowers was presented to the teachers.

    b. A bunch of hooligans were seen leaving the premises.

      [Huddleston and Pullum 2002: 503]

We may note as an interesting side issue that the option for singular or plural agreement is not available with noun phrase determiners, as shown in (3). Collective nouns are ungrammatical with plural determiners, unless they themselves are formally plural.

(3) a. The committee has decided. / The committee have decided.

    b. The committee has decided. / *These committee have decided.

      [Corbett 2006: 2–3]

Subject-verb agreement with collective nouns, thus, lies in the scope of the agreement hierarchy (Corbett 2006: 207), here shown in (4). It predicts a higher likelihood of semantic agreement with agreement targets located further to the right of the hierarchy. A summarising quotation can be found below the hierarchy. We will come back to this hierarchy in Section 10.3.3.

(4) attributive > predicate > relative pronoun > personal pronoun

    'For any controller that permits alternative agreement forms, as we move rightwards along the Agreement Hierarchy, the likelihood of agreement with greater semantic justification will increase monotonically (that is, with no intervening decrease).' [Corbett 2006: 207]

Levin (2001: 108), discussed in Corbett (2006: 211–13), provides quantitative information on English *committee* nouns that nicely confirms the agreement hierarchy. For his study, he sampled the *New York Times* (*NYT*, American English), the *Sydney Morning Herald* (*SMH*, Australian English), and the *Independent* (British English), as shown in Table 10.2 below. The data clearly show that semantic agreement increases monotonically as we move up the hierarchy. Moreover, the differences between the three varieties are substantial, British English favouring semantic agreement to a considerably greater extent than the other two varieties. American English disfavours semantic agreement by comparison, and Australian English ranges in between.

Variation in terms of subject-verb agreement can also be observed in a few additional contexts which shall briefly be mentioned in what follows. Firstly, the quantifying expressions *any* and *none* may be found with plural agreement,

Table 10.2 Committee *nouns in American English, Australian English, and British English (Levin 2001: 108; Corbett 2006: 212).*

	Verb		Relative pronoun		Personal pronoun	
	N	% plural	N	% plural	N	% plural
NYT	3,233	3	702	24	1,383	32
SMH	2,106	10	498	26	746	39
Independent	2,943	23	710	41	1,094	56

besides singular agreement, when quantifying over plural sets (Huddleston and Pullum 2002: 505). This is shown in (5).

(5) a. Please let me know immediately if any of the set texts are/is available.

    b. He made quite a few mistakes but none (of them) were/was very serious.

Secondly, we find singular agreement with both singular and plural noun phrases in cleft sentences, as in (6). Apparently, the expletive pronoun (*it*) assumes the subject function in these contexts (cf. also A: *Who was it?* – B: *It was them*).

(6) a. It is the key that got lost.

    b. It is the keys that got lost.

Thirdly, English shows singular agreement after measure phrases that are nominally plural, as in (7). We may explain such cases as reductions of more complex constructions of the type *Three eggs, this is plenty.*[3]

(7) Five miles is more than I want to walk this afternoon. / Three eggs is plenty.

    [Huddleston and Pullum 2002: 504]

Finally, there is substantial variation in coordinations (see Huddleston and Pullum 2002: 507–10).

10.2 Varieties of English

Across varieties of English, we often find subject-verb agreement systems that are different from the standard system. Many dialects of England, for example, have regularised subject-verb agreement and either have no agreement marker at all or use the -*s* suffix for all persons and numbers. In the north of England, parts of Scotland, and Northern Ireland there is an agreement system called the Northern Subject Rule, which places the -*s* marker on all finite verb forms except when immediately preceded by a pronoun (*birds sings, they sing*). In many other

---

[3] The following example from Hudson (1999: 182) is similar in character: *Two drops deodorizes anything in your house.*

Table 10.3 *Regularisation of the present tense paradigm.*

Singular			Plural		
I	you	he/she/it	we	you	they
go	*go*	*go*	*go*	*go*	*go*
goes	*goes*	*goes*	*goes*	*goes*	*goes*

varieties, we find variable occurrence of the *-s* marker across different persons and numbers, which apparently is conditioned by several factors (phonological, syntactic, semantic, lexical) and their complex interplay.

10.2.1   Regularisation processes

Varieties of English tend to regularise subject-verb agreement, as indicated above. The two main strategies to regularise the verbal paradigms are either to abandon agreement marking or to extend the *-s* suffix of the third person across the entire paradigm. Using the verb *go*, Table 10.3 illustrates these regularisation strategies.

In the dialects of East Anglia, for instance, the verbal paradigm of the present tense lacks the *-s* ending. Examples can be found in (8). According to Trudgill (2004: 142), East Anglia is the only area of Britain to show this pattern.

(8) a. He like her.
    b. She want some.
    c. That rain a lot there.
       [East Anglia, Trudgill 1999: 102]

This kind of regularisation, i.e. complete isolation, can also be found in English Pidgin and Creole varieties. Consider the examples in (9). As Pidgin and Creole Englishes are characterised by incomplete acquisition or learning processes, the lack of inflectional morphology is hardly surprising. In point in fact, Pidgins and Creoles in general are highly isolating languages.

(9) a. She look pretty though, and favour you too. [British Creole, Sebba 2004: 199]
    b. A laik fo wok. / I laik fo wok. 'I like to work.' / 'He/she likes to work.'
       [Kamtok, Ayafor 2004: 916]

Moreover, regularisation to zero marking is quite pervasive in post-colonial Englishes. Again, this is not to be unexpected, since these varieties are characterised by high levels of second language learning processes, leading to the suppression of inflectional markers. The examples in (10) provide an illustration.

(10) a. The teacher shout a lot. / The teachers shout a lot. [Singapore English, Wee 2004: 1059]

b. If somebody chop it then it fall down. [Cape Flats English, McCormick 2004: 997]

There may be important parallels between the zero marking found in East Anglia and that observed in Pidgin and Creole Englishes, as well as in post-colonial varieties. As argued by Trudgill (2004: 142), a significant number of Dutch and French speakers from what is now Belgium and Holland sought shelter in East Anglia in the sixteenth century to avoid persecution. They are known as 'the strangers' in East Anglia. This group of speakers learnt English as a second language, at that time mostly relying on untutored learning. It is to be expected that unmarked forms survive in such situations.

Zero marking in East Anglia is quite remarkable, especially as most, if not all, other dialect areas of Britain tend towards an overuse of the verbal -s marker. Regularisation processes that spread the -s suffix across the entire verbal paradigm are common in many western and northern dialects of England. Similar observations have also been made in the south of Britain, as example (11) shows. Arguably, using the -s suffix on all present tense verb forms helps to differentiate between past tense, present tense, and infinitival forms.

(11) I gets out of the car and walks down the street for a few yards before I sees them boys coming towards me. [Reading, Edwards 1993: 223]

As the factors governing dialectal verbal agreement are quite complex, we will investigate them in more detail in the following section. We will adopt a somewhat different point of view, though, looking at verbal agreement variation in general, comprising both the underuse and the overuse of suffixal agreement.

10.2.2 *Verbal agreement and the Northern Subject Rule*

Verbal agreement variation is quite pervasive in non-standard varieties of English and appears in a number of distinct contexts that we may refer to as 'conditioning factors' or 'variation attractors'. We will begin our discussion of agreement variation with a loose survey of the environments in which it has been documented. In this section, we will focus on suffixal verbal agreement variation. *Was/were*-generalisation will be discussed in Section 10.2.3.

A first context of verbal agreement variation, which is *inter alia* discussed in Pietsch (2005), concerns existential or presentational constructions, as shown in (12). They are referred to by these labels because they are typically used to introduce new discourse referents. The agreement conflict in (12) is quite obvious and needs no further comment. We should note, though, that these constructions in effect contain a relative clause that is not marked by an overt relative pronoun (see Chapter 13 for an in-depth analysis of relative clauses).

(12) a. There's people frae Castlerock owns that place.

    b. There's two priests teaches there all the time.

    [Northern Ireland, Pietsch 2005: 112]

In view of examples such as (12), we may expect to find agreement variation in the context of other relative clauses, too. Three example sentences are shown in (13). Two of them, namely (13a) and (13c), contain the relative marker *that*.

(13) a. He would have picked on the boys that wasn't working. [Northern Ireland, Pietsch 2005: 111]

    b. They had friends was in the building trade in Scotland. [Northern Ireland, Pietsch 2005: 111]

    c. Hedges that hasn't been done. [Leicestershire, Pietsch 2005: 86]

Another syntactic environment discussed in Pietsch (2005) concerns the inversion of subject and auxiliary. In non-standard data you may find examples such as (14). To avoid misunderstandings, let me point out again that this is not a categorical phenomenon. Such inverted contexts appear to be an attractor for agreement variation.[4]

(14) a. Is both you women wed? [Yorkshire, Pietsch 2005: 88]

    b. What does your parents do, your father do? [Northern Ireland, Pietsch 2005: 110]

Without any doubt, one of the most prominent contexts for agreement variation is the so-called '*they sing and dances* construction' that is illustrated in (15) below. This context, which has given rise to the Northern Subject Rule, contains two conjoined verb forms in which one of them is preceded by a pronominal subject. The striking observation is that the verb form preceded by the pronominal subject does not show the agreement marker, just as one would expect, while the verb form that is not preceded by a subject NP (due to coordination deletion) marks the verb as singular third person, even though the subject characterises it as third person plural. Especially in the traditional dialects of northern England and Scotland, this phenomenon is widespread and quite robust in the data. We will look more closely into the Northern Subject Rule below.

(15) a. They break into houses and steals. [Lancashire, Pietsch 2005: 90]

    b. They throw that down and picks another sheaf up. [Yorkshire, Pietsch 2005: 90]

According to Pietsch (2005), agreement variation is also conditioned by the subject type. For example, demonstrative pronouns in subject position (*they* and *them*), interrogative pronouns, indefinite quantifiers (*a lot of them*, *some of them*, *some*, *most*, etc.), and the pronoun *ones* favour singular agreement. This is illustrated in (16).

---

[4] Pietsch (2005) also mentions tag questions as syntactic environments that attract agreement variation.

(16) a. It was damp, them, all them old houses was damp.
      b. Thae girls takes them to bed.
      [Northern Ireland, Pietsch 2005: 115]

The examples in (17) show the verbal -s suffix in the context of the first person and the verb *say*. Even though the verbal suffix can also be found in the context of other verbs with a first person subject, its occurrence with the verb *say* appears especially idiomatic in northern dialects of the British Isles.

(17) a. And this lady come and asked me, and I says, well, I don't know about, or I don't know, I says, about the cooking, but . . .
      b. And then he came across to me, and he says, would you want one next Saturday night? And I says, well, if we're here, yes, I'll take one, if I'm here. And he says, I'll bring you a wee cabbage, as well. And I says, och, you needn't bother, I live on a farm.
      [Northern Ireland, Pietsch 2005: 98]

As already mentioned, the phenomena of verbal agreement variation described in the foregoing paragraphs have been condensed to the well-known Northern Subject Rule. A formulation of this rule that enjoys widespread currency can be found in (18). The rule states that verbal agreement is the default in the varieties participating in this system. Adjacency of the subject in combination with pronominal subjects pre-empts the default verbal agreement. This leads to the '*they sing and dances* construction' introduced above. The sentences in (19) provide some additional examples.

(18) *The Northern Subject Rule (A)*: [Pietsch 2005: 5]
      Every agreement verb takes the -s form, except when it is directly adjacent to one of the personal pronouns *I*, *we*, *you*, or *they* as its subject.

(19) a. They peel 'em and boils 'em. [Lancashire, Pietsch 2005: 90]
      b. They go in and cuts 'em down. [Yorkshire, Pietsch 2005: 90]

Categorical systems as described by the formulation in (18), however, are rarely found, except perhaps in pockets of highly traditional dialects. In most studies that investigate the Northern Subject Rule in data sets collected throughout the twentieth century it manifests itself as a statistical rule governed by two constraints that concern the type of the subject and the position of the subject. An alternative formulation of the Northern Subject Rule in terms of a statistical tendency is shown in (20).

(20) *The Northern Subject Rule (B)*: [Pietsch 2005: 6]
      a. All third singular subjects (and, where preserved, the old second singular *thou*) always take verbal -s.
      b. *Type-of-Subject Constraint:* All other subjects except the personal pronouns *I*, *we*, *you*, *they* (and, where it exists, *youse*) take verbal -s variably.
      c. *Position-of-Subject Constraint*: Non-adjacency of subject and verb favours verbal -s.

Pietsch (2005: 6) interprets the statistical Northern Subject Rule in the formulation given in (20) as the result of competition between two categorical systems, namely the traditional Northern Subject Rule (18), on the one hand, and the agreement pattern found in standard English, on the other (21).

(21) *The Standard English Agreement Rule:* All third singular subjects take verbal -*s*, all other subjects do not.

In a similar way, Godfrey and Tagliamonte (1999: 106) formulate the Northern Subject Rule as a statistical problem. Their analysis is based on data from Devon, where they find examples such as those in (22). In each of these examples, the verb appears with and without verbal -*s* in practically the same contexts. Moreover, this variation is found for all person/number combinations and with full noun phrases and pronouns.

(22) a. Her gives me a hug and a kiss, when I *comes* in and one when I *go*.
  b. People says 'yeah but look at your weather, you *gets* it freezing cold in the winter, you *get* all the rain.'
  c. He *comes* every- three times a week he *come*.
  d. Kiddies *come* over . . . and they'm talking to the animals and that. And the animals *looks* down, you know. And there's a fantastic thing – animals and kiddies.
  [Devon English, Godfrey and Tagliamonte 1999: 89]

Notice that in the Devon data not even third person singular subjects trigger verbal -*s* consistently. Godfrey and Tagliamonte (1999) show that phonological, lexical, semantic, and syntactic factors condition the distribution of the -*s* suffix. For example, the verb *say* triggers comparatively more instances of verbal -*s* than other verbs. In addition, habitual contexts favour the use of verbal -*s* (compare Chapter 7). Godfrey and Tagliamonte (1999: 108–11) also find support for the Northern Subject Rule in their data, in that full noun phrases are more likely to trigger verbal -*s* than pronouns, with non-adjacent noun phrases showing higher effects.

10.2.3   Was/were *generalisation*

Another important context for agreement variation concerns the verb forms *was* and *were* (the past tense forms of the verb *be*, as summarised in Table 10.1), which can be found interchangeably in several varieties of English. This means that *was* occurs in the position of *were* and vice versa. The phenomenon is known as '*was/were*-generalisation' (also '*was/were*-levelling') and can be regarded as an instance of analogical extension of one form into the domain of the other.

  The following examples provide some illustration of the phenomenon. The sentences in (23) exemplify *was*-generalisation; those in (24) show *were*-generalisation. They all come from the British Isles. The phenomenon has

Table 10.4 Were-*levelling*.

	Singular			Plural	
I	you	he/she/it	we	you	they
were	*were*	*were*	*were*	*were*	*were*

Table 10.5 Was-*levelling*.

	Singular			Plural	
I	you	he/she/it	we	you	they
was	*was*	*was*	*was*	*was*	*was*

also been reported from other areas of the English-speaking world, including several North American dialects, South African English, and Australian English. It has hardly ever been reported from post-colonial Englishes.

(23) a. Shops was open while ten. [Yorkshire, Pietsch 2005: 91]
   b. Them pidgeons was there. [Cheshire, Pietsch 2005: 91]
   c. They was very cheap, clay pipes was. [Cheshire, Pietsch 2005: 80]
(24) a. That were a game we invented.
   b. I were broke on a Monday.
   c. It weren't very satisfactory.
      [York English, Tagliamonte 1998: 155]

In view of the dominance of the form *were* in the past tense paradigm, which occurs in all person/number combinations except for the first and third person singular, we would expect primarily '*were*-levelling', namely the extension of the form *were* to the entire paradigm. You can find the result of this levelling strategy in Table 10.4.

According to Anderwald (2001: 9, 19), however, this option is not widely attested.[5] What is more, we probably should not expect it, as the first and third person forms of *be* (i.e. *was*) are more frequently used in contrast with the other forms. In other words, even though the form *were* is more prominent in the paradigm, we may expect the generalisation of *was*, as this form is more prominent in terms of its frequency of use. The outcome of this generalisation strategy is shown in Table 10.5.

---

[5] For similar observations, see Schilling-Estes and Wolfram (1994).

Table 10.6 Was/were-*generalisation in relation to clause polarity.*

	Singular			Plural		
I	you	he/she/it	we	you	they
was	*was*	*was*	*was*	*was*	*was*
weren't	*weren't*	*weren't*	*weren't*	*weren't*	*weren't*

Generalisation to *was* appears to be more frequent than generalisation to *were*. However, usage data suggest that *was/were*-generalisation heavily interacts with negation, such that *was* is generalised in positive clauses and *were* in negative clauses. Evidently, this is a statistical generalisation, not a categorical one. The examples in (25) and (26) help to illustrate this generalisation pattern.[6]

(25) a. I weren't able to answer.

 b. She weren't that close to you.

(26) a. Aye, I thought you was a scuba diver.

 b. We played on the beach until we was tired.

Table 10.6 portrays the system in idealised fashion, although it probably exists nowhere in this idealised form.

It has also been observed that *was/were*-variation depends on the subject of the clause. Some subject types trigger *was/were*-variation more often than others. For example, existential *there* frequently triggers *was* even if the noun phrase with which the verb formally agrees is plural. This phenomenon can even be found in the standard varieties:

(27) There was ten people in the room.

Chambers (2004: 133) posits a near-universal subject type hierarchy, with the third person plural pronoun *they* triggering non-standard *was* least often and existential *there* most often. Other subject types range in between. This hierarchy is shown in (28); it applies only to *was/were*-variation, not to agreement variation in general. The examples in (29) illustrate the hierarchy.

(28) there > you > we > NP$_{pl}$ > they

(29) a. they: They was all born in Georgia, mama and my daddy both.

 b. NP$_{pl}$: All the student teachers was comin' out to Wellborn.

 c. we: We was in an ideal place for it.

 d. you: You was a majorette?

 e. there: There was about twenty-somethin' boys and just four girls.

---

[6] The examples come from Nevins and Parrott (2010: 1145, 1148), even though these authors use them to make a different point.

Table 10.7 *Subject-verb agreement as triggered by different nouns (adapted from Levin 2001: 166–9; Corbett 2006: 213).*

	American		Australian		British		British	
	NYT		*SMH*		*Independent*		*BNC*	
	N	% plural	N	% plural	N	% plural	N	% plural
government	191	0	345	0	365	5	383	18
committee	149	0	123	5	137	9	104	26
team	154	1	161	7	145	37	97	37
family	162	4	118	16	173	37	102	43

10.2.4 Lexical differences

Even though the most widely discussed conditioning factors of the verbal *-s* marker are type of subject and adjacency of subject and verb, there is also evidence of the influence of lexical factors. Recall from our discussion of the Northern Subject Rule in Section 10.2.2 that the verb *say* is a prominent attractor of verbal *-s* in contexts other than third person singular. Non-standard verbal *-s* marking may be lexically conditioned to a much greater extent than we assume, but little is known about that.

Agreement in the context of *committee* nouns is also subject to lexical choice. For example, speakers strongly prefer the agreement chosen in (30a) and (30b), even though in principle plural agreement should be feasible in (30a) and singular agreement in (30b). Apparently, agreement is determined by the noun in subject position.

(30) a. More than one person has failed this exam.
  b. Fewer than two people have failed this exam.
    [Morgan 1984: 235, cited in Corbett 2006: 2]

Table 10.7 shows the results of a comparison of four English *committee* nouns in four major varieties of English (Corbett 2006: 211–13). It is scarcely surprising to find differences between varieties, especially between British and American English. This is well known. However, there are also important differences between the four nouns investigated, with *family* and *team* triggering considerably more plural agreement in British English than *government* and *committee*. American and Australian English appear to follow this trend.

10.2.5 Third person singular don't

The verb *do* has been observed to abandon subject-verb agreement in negative contexts. This is known as 'third person singular *don't*'. The phenomenon appears to be related to the consistent omission of verbal -*s* in East Anglia, as discussed in Section 10.2.1, but it enjoys a much wider regional spread than that (Anderwald 2002: 154). Some examples are provided in (31). Additional examples are discussed in Anderwald (2002: 151–70).

(31) a. Well, it sure don't help things none when we get hail like that. [Colloquial American English, Murray and Simon 2004: 224]
   b. He don't live in there. [Southeast of the USA, Wolfram 2004a: 292]
   c. If 'e don't work, 'e don't eat. [Australian Vernacular English, Pawley 2004: 633]
   d. My husband don't like this district. [Cape Flats English, McCormick 2004: 996]

Anderwald (2002: 151–70) tries to identify specimens of regular behaviour in her data sample drawn from the *BNC*. For instance, she observes that all dialects that permit *she don't* also permit *he don't* and hypothesises that there is an underlying implicational connection for third person *don't*. In a similar way, third person *don't* appears to interact with the clause type in which it occurs. It appears to be most widely used in declarative clauses, less widely in tag questions, and least widely in interrogative clauses. It would be interesting to see whether these hypotheses can be confirmed by other data sets.

10.3   Cross-linguistic comparison

Let us now approach the phenomena that we encountered across varieties of English from a cross-linguistic perspective, thereby assessing their position in the matrix of variation opened up by other languages. For the ensuing discussion, we will accept agreement in general as the basis for our comparison, even though our treatment of varieties of English was more narrowly concerned with subject-verb agreement.

To keep things manageable, we will structure this section as follows. To begin with, we will establish a cross-linguistically valid definition of agreement and delimit it from related phenomena. In a second step, we will introduce the major parameters of variation that have been observed in this domain, relying on the canonical approach introduced by Corbett (2006). Subsequently, we will take up these parameters one by one and assess subject-verb agreement in varieties of English against them.

10.3.1   Defining and delimiting agreement

We introduced the major defining parameters of agreement in Section 10.1.1. These are 'agreement domain', 'agreement controller', 'agreement targets', 'agreement features', and 'conditions on the agreement relation' (recall

Figure 10.1). These parameters are also appropriate to capture agreement as a cross-linguistic phenomenon. A more important problem is to delimit agreement from related phenomena that look similar or that possess overlapping properties.

Even though subject-verb agreement, i.e. the triggering of formal exponents on the verb by certain features of the subject constituent, is only one particular realisation of a more general phenomenon (Corbett 2006: 27–30), it seems to be something like a prototype that is accepted as typical by many linguists. The domain of subject-verb agreement, as its name implies, covers the subject constituent and the verb phrase, and thus operates beyond the phrase boundary. We also find agreement within phrase boundaries, typically inside the noun phrase, where the nominal head triggers agreement on determiners and adjectives. We may illustrate this kind of agreement using the examples in (32), although English has no agreement between noun and adjective, unlike, for example, Spanish or German. The chapter on determiners in this book (Chapter 5) illustrates these phenomena in some detail without making 'agreement' the central yardstick in this discussion.

(32) a. the book – these books
b. the books – *these book

Another agreement relation is furnished by anaphoric pronouns in which the agreement domain can even extend beyond clause boundaries. The example in (33) documents such agreement between pronouns and preceding noun phrases. Since such agreement may give rise to fairly extensive agreement domains – in principle spanning several clauses – and the agreement target is not inflectional, one may decide to treat such anaphor-antecedent relations as something separate. Within the confines of this book, agreement between anaphoric pronouns and antecedent noun phrases is treated in Chapter 3 on pronominal gender.

(33) Mary told John that she (she = Mary) did not want to marry him (him = John).

It is possible to include several other grammatical phenomena under agreement, some of which also fall within the scope of the present book. For example, in the chapter on negation (Chapter 9), we learnt that some varieties of English show negative concord, as shown in (34).

(34) I don't want no pork and I don't need no beer.

In this and similar cases one could argue that the first negative element triggers the appearance of the second, but although this is evidently the case, negative concord does not involve 'systematic covariation' of features, as Corbett (2006: 29) points out. It is probably better kept separate and treated as a concord phenomenon.

There are a few additional phenomena discussed as potential candidates of agreement in Corbett (2006: 27–30). These are sequence of tense, switch

Table 10.8 *Properties of canonical agreement (Corbett 2006: 9).*

Agreement	Properties
controller:	is present, has overt expression of features, and is consistent in the agreement it takes; its part of speech is not relevant
target:	has bound expression of agreement, obligatory marking, doubling the marking of the noun, marking is regular, alliterative, productive; the target has a single controller and its part of speech is not relevant
domain:	agreement is asymmetric (the gender of the adjective depends on that of the noun), local, and the domain is one of multiple domains
features:	lexical (in one instance), matching values, not offering any choice in values
conditions:	no conditions

reference, preposition doubling, and classifiers. As these have no relevance for the present book, I will not take them up for discussion, but refer the interested reader to the relevant pages in Corbett (2006).

10.3.2   Canonical and non-canonical agreement

In his cross-linguistic study of agreement, Corbett (2006) introduces the notion of 'canonical agreement' and opens up a cline ranging from canonical to non-canonical agreement. As canonical agreement is defined by a number of parameters that concern the major components of an agreement relation (i.e. controller, target, domain, features, and conditions), they unfold a space of variation that we can use to position and assess the phenomena from varieties of English, as introduced in Section 10.2.

Corbett (2006: 11) states that 'canonical agreement is redundant rather than informative'. Thus, it violates the hypothesis on informativity introduced at the beginning of Section 10.1. The properties of canonical agreement are sum-marised in Table 10.8.

A non-canonical agreement system at the end point of the cline from canon-ical to non-canonical would have the opposite properties to those shown in Table 10.8. We will investigate these properties in some detail in the para-graphs to follow. We may notice in passing that subject-verb agreement in standard English, as shown in (35), gives a fairly canonical impression, as the controller is always overt, the target shows a bound and obligatory agreement marker, and there are no additional conditions on the agreement relation. We will have to qualify this first impression later on.

(35) The child / she teases the dog.

Agreement relations may be based on form and/or meaning (syntactic versus semantic agreement). In example (35), we find both syntactic and semantic agreement, i.e. the two coincide, as the subject is notionally singular and is not marked for plural. The third person singular marker on the verb is consistent with the meaning and the form of the subject.

More complicated cases are furnished by *committee* nouns (Corbett 2006: 156), as these allow semantic agreement besides syntactic agreement. The subject in (36a) is notionally plural, but is not marked as such. In showing the third person singular marker, the verb signals syntactic agreement. The verb in (36b) lacks the relevant marking and thus yields a case of semantic agreement. Going back to the properties shown in Table 10.8, syntactic agreement would qualify as more canonical than semantic agreement.

(36) a. The committee has decided. (syntactic agreement)
     b. The committee have decided. (semantic agreement)

Having equipped ourselves with the theoretical notions introduced in the preceding paragraphs, we may now attempt a first assessment of non-standard agreement systems. Concerning the verbal -*s* suffix, we learnt in Section 10.2.1 that some varieties drop it completely, while others generalise it across the entire paradigm, i.e. it occurs in all persons and numbers in the present tense. As for the first type of system, subject-verb agreement has evidently broken down. The second type is trickier, as the -*s* suffix stands in paradigmatic opposition to the past tense marker -*ed*. This means, however, that the -*s* suffix is a pure tense marker, since it does not reflect any properties of the subject. In other words, subject-verb agreement has also broken down in these varieties.

10.3.3   Parameters of variation

Let us now consider the factors contributing to canonical agreement in more detail. This will give us a grid of parameters of variation with cross-linguistic validity. Moreover, this grid allows us to position variety phenomena in the logically possible space of variation.

Corbett (2006: 8–27) breaks canonical agreement down to properties of the controller, target, domain, and features, plus conditions on them (Table 10.8 above). Taking all together, he distinguishes no fewer than twenty criteria that identify canonical agreement. As not all of these criteria are relevant for English varieties, I will here mainly focus on those that inform the analysis of English subject-verb agreement.

Properties of the agreement controller As for the controller, a first parameter of variation is its presence or absence. Traditional dialects of English, including the standard varieties, do not allow the omission of the subject (i.e. they are not 'pro-drop' languages like Italian or Spanish). Those varieties of

English, however, that are strongly influenced by second language acquisition phenomena (including Pidgin and Creole varieties) may show subject omission, especially if the substrate language is pro-drop. The problem is that in these varieties subject-verb agreement is usually not realised, and hence the discussion of this parameter may become vacuous.

In the standard varieties, the controller agreement features are by and large overtly expressed (*dog/dogs*, *he/them*). Some varieties do not realise the plural marker on full noun phrases, losing in canonicity in this respect.

Corbett (2006: 11) describes a consistent controller as one that triggers the same agreement pattern on different targets. The best exemplar of an inconsistent controller in English may be *committee* nouns, as these can trigger singular agreement inside the noun phrase, though plural agreement on the verb. The relevance of this parameter for non-standard varieties is currently not completely clear.

In most varieties of English, it does not matter whether the controller is nominal or pronominal, as they trigger the same agreement. An exception are those varieties of northern Englishes in the British Isles that have the Northern Subject Rule. There, full NPs trigger agreement on the verb, while pronouns do not (cf. *they sing and dances* versus *birds sings*). Agreement under the Northern Subject Rule is less canonical than standard subject-verb agreement. As the part of speech of the controller is not the only conditioning factor of the Northern Subject Rule, we will have to return to it. Another non-standard phenomenon that needs mentioning here is Chamber's (2004: 133) subject type hierarchy, according to which it is observed that *was*-generalisation is most frequent with the subject *there* and least frequent with *they* (*there* > *you* > *we* > NP_{pl} > *they*), i.e. the controller type influences the agreement pattern.

Properties of the agreement target In principle, agreement markers may be bound, free, or have clitic status. As for the subject-verb agreement we are interested in here, the -*s* suffix on the verb is bound. Pronominal gender agreement, as investigated in Chapter 3, involved free forms. Clitic agreement exponents can be found in some Slavonic languages (Corbett 2006: 13). No variety of English has clitic agreement exponents for subject-verb agreement.

Another parameter relevant for agreement targets concerns the obligatoriness of the relevant exponents. According to Corbett (2006: 14), agreement is obligatory in the canonical case, and this is what we find in the standard varieties. Non-standard varieties, in contrast, often manifest marking patterns that appear inconsistent, as the agreement marker may not be realised. Sociolinguistic studies (e.g. Godfrey and Tagliamonte 1999) have shown that such optional subject-verb agreement is conditioned by various factors, as discussed in Section 10.2.2 above. Corbett (2006: 14) states that optional agreement marking is rare cross-linguistically, but then we have to bear in mind that we usually lack fine-grained sociolinguistic studies for the more exotic languages.

The obligatoriness of the agreement marking is closely related to its productivity, i.e. whether it occurs on all potential targets. In the standard varieties, the -*s* suffix is productive for all verbs except *be*. If subject-verb agreement is not obligatory, as described above, this also means that it is not fully productive, even though productivity is not a function of the target type, but is instead constrained by other factors. Corbett (2006: 17) quotes several languages in which agreement marking on the target is not fully productive.

Agreement marking may be regular or suppletive. Corbett (2006: 15) assumes that suppletive agreement is less canonical than regular agreement. Standard English shows suppletive agreement in the paradigm of the verb *be*; otherwise agreement marking is regular. We saw in Section 10.2.3 that the paradigm of *be* may be regularised in various ways in non-standard varieties (levelling, generalisation), especially in the past tense. Complete generalisation to either *was* or *were* effectively means giving up subject-verb agreement. The generalisation of *was* to positive clauses and *were* to those that have negative polarity would not count as an agreement phenomenon.

Corbett (2006: 16) remarks that 'English has a particularly opaque system... in having -*s* and allomorphs as the marker of the plural on controllers, but as the marker of the singular on verb targets'. Agreement systems gain in canonicity if the marking on controller and target coincides. Such alliterative agreement systems can be found in various African languages (e.g. Swahili).

Properties of the agreement domain Corbett (2006: 19–23) identifies three parameters that help to define an agreement domain. The first parameter characterises the agreement domain as either symmetric or asymmetric. Canonical agreement is asymmetric, as the controller triggers the agreement on the target. The second parameter concerns the locality of the agreement relation. In English, determiner-noun agreement is more local than subject-verb agreement. The agreement between gendered pronouns and their antecedent noun phrases is even less local. The third parameter captures whether a certain agreement domain belongs to a larger set of agreement domains in a given language. The canonical case is that agreement is asymmetric and local, and that several domains co-exist. Subject-verb agreement in English – including its varieties that have such agreement – thus represents a fairly canonical case.

Properties of agreement features Let us now briefly consider the properties of agreement features and a few parameters along which they can vary. In the typical case, we expect the features of the controller to correspond to those of the target. In English, this is so in the great majority of cases of subject-verb agreement. In (37a), the singular subject triggers singular agreement on the verb. For examples like (37b), we need to assume non-matching feature values, as the subject is syntactically singular while verbal agreement is plural. Corbett (2006: 24) introduces the notion of semantic agreement to handle cases like (37b), contrasting with syntactic agreement in (37a).

(37) a. This dog bites.

      b. This family are happy.

We may also interpret the kind of agreement triggered by the Northern Subject Rule as a case of non-matching feature values, provided that the -*s* suffix on the verb signals a singular third person subject. This assumption is consistent with the formulation of the Northern Subject Rule in (20) above (version B of this rule). As pronominal subjects – especially *I, we, you, they* – take verbal -*s* variably, such agreement would be based on non-matching features. Similarly, plural marked subjects triggering verbal -*s* may be analysed in terms of non-matching features. Nevertheless, as the Northern Subject Rule is stochastic rather than categorical, it becomes difficult to assess a categorical concept such as 'non-matching features'.

In addition to feature matching, Corbett (2006: 25) also distinguishes feature choice, where agreement varies even though controller, target, domain, and the features of the controller are identical. According to Corbett (2006: 25), it is more canonical for agreement not to offer feature value choice. Evidently, the statistical Northern Subject Rule also represents a case of feature choice.

Conditions on agreement We need agreement conditions to capture a residue of phenomena that remains if agreement relations have been exhaustively described in terms of controllers, targets, domains, and features. Corbett (2006: ch. 6) discusses such conditions as the animacy of the controller, the position of the controller relative to the target, individuation, definiteness, and even information structure.

As far as the English standard varieties are concerned, we do not expect conditions on agreement, but it turns out that the choice between semantic and syntactic agreement with *committee* nouns is constrained both by the type of agreement target (verb, relative pronoun, personal pronouns) and the distance between target and controller. We have already discussed the influence of the target type, in Section 10.1.3, in the context of Table 10.2 and the agreement hierarchy. If we keep the target type constant and focus our attention on personal pronouns, we can see that the distance between controller and target influences the resulting agreement. This is shown in Table 10.9. The first row gives the distance in terms of intervening words.

Certainly, Table 10.9 does not illustrate subject-verb agreement, but pronoun-antecedent agreement. As for subject-verb agreement, the Northern Subject Rule offers a nice illustration of a condition on distance or adjacency, as the

Table 10.9 *The effect of distance on the agreement of personal pronouns with committee nouns (Levin 2001: 98; Corbett 2006: 236).*

	0–4		5–9		10–14		15+	
	N	% plural	N	% plural	N	% plural	N	% plural
NYT	739	19	398	39	144	51	102	69
SMH	431	26	211	49	64	64	40	82
Independent	624	47	290	66	113	72	67	82

non-adjacency of subject and verb leads to higher frequencies of verbal -*s*. In the categorical form of this rule, a pronominal subject immediately preceding the verb suppresses the verbal suffix. Since pronominal subjects behave differently from other subjects (i.e. full noun phrases), we can also observe a condition on the subject type.

Another condition worth mentioning is clause polarity, as it has been shown to influence the distribution of *was* and *were* in many non-standard varieties. Recall that the form *was* may be generalised to the second person singular and all persons in the plural. Alternatively, we may find *were* for all person/number combinations. This is a statistical phenomenon that interacts with clause polarity, with *was* being more often found in affirmative clauses and *were* in negative clauses.

10.4 Summary and list of keywords

Even though subject-verb agreement appears to be an unpretentious phenomenon, this chapter should have convinced you that it involves substantial sophistication, especially as non-standard varieties offer intriguing agreement patterns. Coming to grips with this much variation necessitates a robust theory of agreement, which we introduced in Section 10.1, relying on Corbett (2006). In the sections on English varieties, we encountered various regularisation processes pertaining to the verbal -*s* marker and the past tense forms of *be* and negative *do*. It transpired that regularisation is never complete and is typiclly conditioned by a host of factors that in some cases converge to yield such phenomena as the Northern Subject Rule. Using Corbett's (2006) canonical agreement framework, itself developed for carrying out cross-linguistic comparisons of agreement phenomena, we then assessed the degree of canonicity of agreement in the varieties of English surveyed. Among several other findings, it became clear that the Northern Subject Rule is highly non-canonical, as both subject type and adjacency influence the resulting agreement pattern. Many of the non-standard patterns may be explained as competing historical processes.

If we wish to understand where the English agreement patterns come from, a closer look into these processes is inescapable.

Keywords: adjacency, agreement hierarchy, canonical agreement, clause polarity, clause type, cleft sentences, collective nouns, conditions on agreement, controller, covariance, domain, features, levelling, locality, negative concord, non-canonical agreement, Northern Subject Rule, productivity, regularisation, semantic agreement, subject type, subject type hierarchy, suppletion, syncretism, syntactic agreement, target, third person singular *don't*, *was/were*-generalisation, zero marking.

10.5   Exercises

Basic level

1. Compile a list of the verbal exponents that signal agreement with the subject in English. Don't forget to include cases of suppletion!
2. Describe and illustrate the Northern Subject Rule.
3. The paradigms of the verb *be* in the present tense and the past tense look strikingly different. Consulting Baugh and Cable (2002), take a look into the history of English and find out why they are so different.

Intermediate level

1. So-called 'corporate' nouns in English can trigger either singular or plural agreement, even though the noun is formally singular, as shown by below examples:

   a. *The team is happy.*
   b. *The team are happy.*

   However, plural agreement is not possible inside the noun phrase:

   c. **These team are happy.*

   Can you explain why plural agreement is not possible inside a noun phrase? Consult Corbett (2006) for an appropriate answer.
2. In Section 10.2.4, we stated that agreement variation in English is conditioned by lexical differences.
   a. Investigate the agreement profiles shown by the verbs *say, go, give, come, feel, travel,* and *assume.* You may use the corpora provided on Mark Davies' website (http://corpus.byu.edu/).
   b. The above verbs show vastly different agreement profiles. Can you see a way to explain these differences?
   c. Can you think of any additional verbs that prefer non-standard agreement? Test your hypotheses.

3. Corbett's (2006) monograph on agreement relies on the notions of 'canonical agreement' and 'non-canonical agreement'.
   a. Explain under which conditions an agreement relation is canonical or non-canonical. Which parameters influence canonicity?
   b. Compare the agreement patterns of standard English and the Northern Subject Rule in terms of canonicity.

Advanced level

1. Pietsch (2005: 6) analyses the statistical Northern Subject Rule as a case of competition between the traditional Northern Subject Rule and the agreement system of standard English. Can you explain why?
2. In the present chapter, we introduced two implicational hierarchies:
   a. the *agreement hierarchy* (Corbett 2006: 207)
   b. the *subject type hierarchy* (Chambers 2004: 133)
   In a short essay, describe the similarities and differences of the two concepts.
3. Subject-verb agreement has been extensively investigated in some of the traditional dialects of Great Britain and North America. We know much less about this phenomenon in post-colonial Englishes (Singapore English, Hong Kong English, etc.).
   Devise a pilot study to investigate subject-verb agreement in one of the post-colonial varieties using one of the components of the *ICE* (http://ice-corpora. net/ice/). Try to answer the following questions.
   a. Which non-standard agreement patterns do you find?
   b. How frequent is non-standard agreement?

10.6   References

Anderwald, Lieselotte. 2001. *Was/were* variation in non-standard British English today. *English World-Wide* 22(1). 1–21.

2002. *Negation in Non-Standard British English: Gaps, Regularizations and Asymmetries*. London: Routledge.

Baugh, Albert C. and Thomas Cable. 2002. *A History of the English Language*. London: Routledge.

Chambers, Jack K. 2004. Dynamic typology and vernacular universals. In Bernd Kortmann (ed.), *Dialectology Meets Typology: Dialect Grammar from a Cross-Linguistic Perspective*, 127–45. Berlin: Mouton de Gruyter.

Corbett, Greville G. 2006. *Agreement*. Cambridge University Press.

Edwards, Viv. 1993. The grammar of southern British English. In James Milroy and Lesley Milroy (eds.), *Real English: The Grammar of English Dialects in the British Isles*, 214–42. London: Longman.

Godfrey, Elizabeth and Sali Tagliamonte. 1999. Another piece of the verbal -*s* story: Evidence from Devon in southwest England. *Language Variation and Change* 11(1). 87–121.

Hudson, Richard. 1999. Subject-verb agreement in English. *English Language and Linguistics* 3(2). 173–207.

Levin, Magnus. 2001. *Agreement with Collective Nouns in English*. (Lund Studies in English 103.) Stockholm: Almquist and Wiksell.

Morgan, Jerry. 1984. Some problems of agreement in English and Albanian. In Claudia Brugman, Monica Maccauley, Amy Dahlstrom, Michele Emanatian, Birch Moonwoman, and Catherine O'Connor (eds.), *Proceedings of the Tenth Annual Meeting of the Berkeley Linguistics Society*, 233–47. Berkeley Linguistics Society, University of California.

Nevins, Andrew and Jeffrey K. Parrott. 2010. Variable rules meet impoverishment theory: Patterns of agreement leveling in English varieties. *Lingua* 120(5). 1135–59.

Pietsch, Lukas. 2005. *Variable Grammars: Verbal Agreement in Northern Dialects of English*. Tübingen: Niemeyer.

Schilling-Estes, Natalie and Walt Wolfram. 1994. Convergent explanation and alternative regularization patterns: *Were/weren't* leveling in a vernacular English variety. *Language Variation and Change* 6(3). 273–302.

Tagliamonte, Sali. 1998. *Was/were* variation across the generations: View from the city of York. *Language Variation and Change* 10(2). 153–91.

Trudgill, Peter. 1999. *The Dialects of England*. Oxford: Blackwell.

See *General references* for Ayafor 2004; Huddleston and Pullum 2002; McCormick 2004; Murray and Simon 2004; Pawley 2004; Sebba 2004; Trudgill 2004; Wee 2004; Wolfram 2004a.

10.7   Further reading

Hay, Jennifer and Daniel Schreier. 2004. Reversing the trajectory of language change: Subject-verb agreement with *be* in New Zealand English. *Language Variation and Change* 16(3). 209–36.

Jantos, Susanne. 2009. Agreement in Educated Jamaican English: A Corpus Investigation of ICE-Jamaica. University of Freiburg PhD dissertation.

McCafferty, Kevin. 2003. The Northern Subject Rule in Ulster: How Scots, how English? *Language Variation and Change* 15(1). 105–39.

2004. '[T]hunder storms is verry dangese in this countrey they come in less than a minnits notice . . . ': The Northern Subject Rule in Southern Irish English. *English World-Wide* 25(1). 51–79.

Smith, Jennifer and Sali Tagliamonte. 1998. We was all thegither, I think we were all thegither: *Was* regularization in Buckie English. *World Englishes* 17(2). 105–26.

Trudgill, Peter. 1974. *The Social Differentiation of English in Norwich*. Cambridge University Press.

1998. Third person singular zero: African American vernacular English, East Anglian dialects and Spanish persecution in the Low Countries. *Folia Linguistica Historica* 18. 139–48.

11 Ditransitive constructions

In this chapter on ditransitive constructions, we will be looking at verbal complementation patterns that involve two objects, i.e. verbs that take two objects, such as *give* or *sell*. Simple transitive clauses contain one object that we refer to as the 'direct object'. The additional object found in clauses with two objects is called the 'indirect object'. Varieties of English show diverging preferences concerning the ordering of the objects, especially when the objects are realised as pronominal forms. Some of the factors influencing this ordering relation can also be identified in other languages. In the usual manner, we will begin with an introductory survey of ditransitive constructions, followed by a discussion of English varieties in this domain, and a cross-linguistic comparison.

11.1   Overview

For sentences with two objects, standard English offers two competing constructions. On the one hand, the indirect object may precede the direct object, as in (1a). This is the classical double-object construction in which the syntactic status of the objects is exclusively determined by their position. On the other hand, there is a prepositional ditransitive construction in which the indirect object is marked by the preposition *to*. This is shown in (1b). In comparison with the double-object construction, the ordering of direct and indirect object is reversed in the prepositional construction.

(1) a. John gave Mary the book.
     b. John gave the book to Mary.

The word order in the double-object construction, i.e. the relative position of direct and indirect object, is fixed. The examples in (2) show quite clearly that reversing the position of the two noun phrases changes the interpretation in predictable ways (Huddleston and Pullum 2002: 248). In other words, there is a correlation of sentence position with syntactic function, and this correlation is similar to that of subject and object.

(2) a. They offered all the overseas students one of the experienced tutors.
     b. They offered one of the experienced tutors all the overseas students.

We can capture this functional difference in terms of semantic roles. Indirect objects in double-object constructions typically encode a recipient argument, while direct objects describe theme arguments.

11.1.1 Transitivity

In a chapter on ditransitive constructions, we also need to take a brief look at the concept of 'transitivity'. As a grammatical notion, transitivity may be defined both in syntactic and semantic terms. While the syntactic definition hinges on the presence of object noun phrases, transitivity can also be given a purely semantic interpretation in which it refers to the degree of affectedness of the object referent as a result of the action carried out by the subject referent. The sentences in (3) are transitive both in the syntactic and the semantic sense, as the situations of eating and biting involve two participants, and their degree of affectedness is relatively high.

(3) a. John was eating an apple.

    b. The dog bit the man.

The corresponding verbalisations in (4) are transitive only on the level of semantics, as the events are construed with two participants, even though these are not realised in syntax. In syntactic terms, the sentences in (4) count as intransitive.

(4) a. John was eating.

    b. This dog bites.

We can also find the opposite scenario where situations are expressed transitively in syntax, although they are notionally intransitive, i.e. involve only one participant. Some examples are shown in (5). Such sentences express one-participant events (some predication about a participant), but the situations are expressed transitively in syntax.

(5) a. John leads a quiet life.

    b. Mary took a shower.

A good diagnostic for transitivity is passivisation. If a sentence can be passivised, the sentence is likely to be transitive. The sentences in (3) above can be easily passivised, as expected; those in (5) yield less acceptable passives (*?A shower was taken by Mary*).

What we have said so far about the realisation of arguments in simple transitive clauses is also relevant for ditransitive clauses, as not all of the participants in situations with three participants need to be realised syntactically, even typically. For example, the verbs *sell*, *show*, and *tell* describe situations that involve three participants, namely an agent, a source or recipient, and a theme. A situation of showing implies a 'shower' (the person showing) and the thing shown, as well as the person shown to (the 'showee'). Still, as the examples in (6) make clear, the recipient may be left unexpressed with these verbs.

(6) a. John sold Mary a car. / John sold a car.
     b. John showed the kids a movie. / John showed a movie.
     c. John told the audience a story. / John told a story.

Other ditransitive verbs apparently impose stricter demands on the expression of the participants, as the verbs *give* and *hand*, for example, are typically found with two syntactically realised objects:

(7) a. Mary gave her daughter some money. / ?Mary gave some money.
     b. Mary handed her daughter the keys. / *Mary handed the keys.

11.1.2 Differences between the double-object construction and the prepositional construction

We said above that ditransitive constructions in English can be realised in basically two different ways, namely as the mere juxtaposition of two objects (double-object construction), or with a prepositional construction. This is shown again in (8). The opposition of the two constructions in (8) is also known as the 'dative alternation' (see Levin 1993: 45–8). Several classes of verbs participate in this alternation, for instance verbs of giving, verbs of sending, and verbs of throwing.

(8) a. John sent Mary a book. (double-object construction)
     b. John sent a book to Mary. (prepositional construction)

There are interesting differences between the two constructions, which shall be briefly surveyed in what follows (Krifka 2004; Rappaport Hovav and Levin 2008). To begin with, the distribution of the two constructions is influenced by the language affiliation of the verbs involved, as verbs of Latinate or Romance origin largely eschew the double-object construction. Verbs like *explain*, *donate*, and *transmit*, as shown in (9) below, can only be used in the prepositional object construction.

(9) a. *Alice explained them the problem. / Alice explained the problem to them.
     b. *The mayor donated the university a large sum. / The mayor donated a large sum to the university.
     c. *They transmitted them the message. / They transmitted the message to them.

Secondly, there are selectional restrictions on the recipient argument in the double-object construction in which only animate recipients seem to be allowed. Consider the contrast in (10).

(10) a. Ann sent a package to London.
      b. ??Ann sent London a package.

A third factor concerns the meaning of the verb, as, for instance, verbs of depriving are not admitted in the prepositional construction, though they can occur in the double-object construction. The relevant contrast is shown in (11).

(11) a. Ann denied Beth the ice-cream.

   b. *Ann denied the ice-cream to/from/of Beth.

In addition, information structure influences the distribution of the two constructions. A well-known principle of information structuring is that given information precedes new information. Since pronouns typically encode given information, they tend to be placed before full noun phrases. As a consequence, the distributions shown in (12) arise.

(12) a. John gave them some money. / ?John gave some money to them.

   b. John sent it to his relatives. / *John sent his relatives it.

Information structure also interacts with the length (or heaviness) of the noun phrases involved. In English, there is a general principle according to which shorter (lighter) noun phrases precede longer (heavier) noun phrases. In the examples in (12), the requirements from information structure are in harmony with the light-heavy principle, as pronouns are generally lighter than full noun phrases. The situation is different in (13), where the prepositional object construction would be preferred even if the recipient represented discourse-old information.

(13) a. Ann wrote a letter to the boy she met last summer in Italy.

   b. ?Ann wrote the boy she met last summer in Italy a letter.

Several additional differences between the two constructions have been discussed in the literature (see Krifka 2004). We need to bear these differences in mind when investigating these constructions in varieties of English.

11.2   Varieties of English

In non-standard varieties of English, we encounter differences in the ordering of direct and indirect object in the double-object construction. They are especially pervasive with pronominal objects. We will investigate these in Sections 11.2.1 and 11.2.2. Following that, in Section 11.2.3, we will explore a rather special double-object construction that is primarily found in southern dialects of the United States (the 'Southern Double-Object Construction'). To conclude our discussion of ditransitive constructions, we will study the complementation patterns of selected ditransitive verbs in varieties of English (Section 11.2.4).

11.2.1   The alternative double-object construction

In the standard varieties, the noun phrase encoding the recipient occurs before that encoding the theme in the double-object construction. As this ordering is regarded as the canonical case, the label 'canonical double-object construction' is found in the literature. It contrasts with the term 'alternative double-object construction', in which the order of direct and indirect object is reversed, i.e. the theme is positioned before the recipient (Gast 2007: 34). This is shown in (14).

(14) a. She gave the man a book. (canonical)
      b. She gave a book the man. (alternative)

According to Hughes et al. (2005: 19), the alternative double-object construction can be found in northern England, even though it 'is not especially common'. It is not clear, though, exactly how common the alternative ordering is there. Siewierska and Hollmann (2007: 93), in a sample of over 300 cases, found no examples of theme-recipient order with full noun phrase objects, though they did find cases with pronominal objects (see below).

Based on *ICE*-Great Britain and for the verb *give*, Mukherjee and Hoffmann (2006: 172) report 404 canonical cases contrasting with merely one alternative case. *ICE*-India contains 3 alternative and 407 canonical cases.[1]

11.2.2 Pronominal objects

Differences in the relative order of theme and recipient are more pervasive with pronominal objects. We need to distinguish scenarios with one or two pronominal objects. In examples with one pronominal object, either the theme or the recipient may be pronominal. This is shown in (15). The example in (15b) is usually considered ungrammatical, as the pronominal direct object occurs in a position associated with discourse-new information. As previously stated, pronouns typically encode discourse-old information.

(15) a. She gave him a book. (canonical)
      b. She gave the man it. (canonical)

The alternative orderings to those in (15) are shown in (16). Hughes et al. (2005: 19) state that (16a) is 'very common in the north of England, but is not found in the south'. Example (16b) is less common, but can 'be heard in the north of England, particularly if there is contrastive stress on *him*'.

(16) a. She gave it the man. (alternative)
      b. She gave the book him. (alternative)

If both direct and indirect object are pronominalised, the alternative ordering appears no less common than the canonical construction, as in (17). To quote Hughes et al. (2005: 19) again, the alternative double-object construction 'is very common indeed [in the north of England], and is also quite acceptable to many southern speakers'.

(17) a. She gave him it. (canonical)
      b. She gave it him. (alternative)

Speakers of all varieties appear to reject the reversal of recipient and theme in the prepositional construction (Siewierska and Hollmann 2007: 86–7):

---

[1] This study does not distinguish between full noun phrases and pronominal objects.

(18) a. *She gave to the man it.
  b. *She gave to him it.

With respect to the distribution of objects in ditransitive constructions, Gast (2007: 37–8) distinguishes three major types of variety:

  i. varieties that have only the canonical (but not the alternative) double-object construction, but that do not use it when both objects are pronominal (*gave me it, *gave it me, gave it to me; e.g. standard British English);

  ii. varieties that have only the canonical double-object construction and that do allow it in sentences with two pronominal objects (gave me it, *gave it me, gave it to me; e.g. some north-eastern varieties of British English);

  iii. varieties that have both the canonical and the alternative double-object construction and that use the latter when both objects are pronominal (*gave me it, gave it me, gave it to me; e.g. some (north)western varieties of British English). [Gast 2007: 37–8]

Gast (2007: 38) postulates the implicational hierarchy in (19) assuming that it governs the distribution of objects in double-object constructions. It has the status of a hypothesis that still awaits testing.

(19) $[V \, PRO_{TH} \, PRO_{REC}] > [V \, PRO_{TH} \, NP_{REC}] > [V \, NP_{TH} \, NP_{REC}] > [V \, NP_{TH} \, PRO_{REC}]$

Figure 11.1 illustrates the areal distribution of ditransitive constructions with two pronominal objects across England. The map is based on the *Survey of English Dialects* (Orton and Dieth 1962–71). In the northwest of England, we can see a clearly defined area where the alternative double-object construction is prominent (*give it me*).

Siewierska and Hollmann (2007: 93) undertook a corpus study to investigate the distribution of object noun phrases (full noun phrases and pronouns) in the dialect of Lancashire (i.e. northwest England). A selection of their results can be found in Table 11.1 and Table 11.2. The two tables follow the same format, but the figures therein come from different corpora.

In both data sets, the double-object construction outnumbers the prepositional construction (PP) by a wide margin. Moreover, the canonical order of recipient before theme (RT) is clearly the dominant one. The data suggest a slight preference for an order of theme before recipient (TR) when two pronominal objects are involved. However, as the numbers are very low, they certainly do not support the clearly defined isogloss in Figure 11.1.

In Siewierska and Hollmann's (2007) study, only three verbs occur in the alternative double-object construction. These are *give*, *send*, and *show*. All theme objects are third person non-human (*it/them*).

(20) a. I gave it him.
  b. Give it her for next time.
  c. So send it me.
  d. I'll give it you.
     [Siewierska and Hollmann 2007: 95]

Figure 11.1 Map 'Give it me' taken from *An Atlas of English Dialects* by Clive Upton and J.D.A. Widdowson (1996: 52). By permission of Oxford University Press.

11.2.3   The Southern Double-Object Construction Let us now turn to a phenomenon that we have already encountered in our discussion on reflexivity and reflexive marking (Chapter 2). It concerns a double-object construction that is regionally restricted and primarily occurs in southern dialects of the United States, especially in the Appalachian mountain range. Examples of this construction are shown in (21).

Table 11.1 *Distribution of the complementation patterns in ditransitives in the Lancashire part of the BNC (adapted from Siewierska and Hollmann 2007: 93).*

	2 Pro	ProNP	NPPro	NPNP	Total
TR	6	2			8
RT	4	71		7	82
PP	11	16	4		31
Total	21	89	4	7	121

Table 11.2 *Distribution of the complementation patterns in ditransitives in the* Freiburg English Dialect Corpus *(adapted from Siewierska and Hollmann 2007: 93).*

	2 Pro	ProNP	NPPro	NPNP	Total
TR	6	2			8
RT	4	171	1	12	188
PP	5	16	1	6	28
Total	15	189	2	18	224

(21) a. She went into the store to get her a pair of shoes.
   b. I got me a pole and got up this drift, laid down my gun, and commenced punching down through where the drift was hollow.
   c. And then you'd get you a bowl of ice-water.
   [Southern American Vernacular English, Webelhuth and Dannenberg 2006: 34]

As the first object noun phrase in this construction is obligatorily coreferential with the subject, i.e. reflexive, it may be considered a special reflexive construction. This was the perspective taken in Chapter 2. The reflexively used pronoun may be interpreted as a 'reflexive dative', as it adds a recipient or goal role to the subject. In the present chapter, we will approach it as a double-object construction trying to make its special properties explicit.

Interestingly enough, the Southern Double-Object Construction can also be found with predicates that are unexpected in ditransitive contexts. For example, the verb *have* in (22a) is a transitive verb taking a possessor argument in subject position and a possessum in object position. In the Southern Double Object Construction, we find it as a ditransitive predicate. The example in (22b) is even more remarkable, as the verb *send* occurs together with three object arguments, namely *her*, *a letter*, and *Sue*. It would appear, then, that the argument structure of a predicate may be extended in the Southern Double-Object Construction.

(22) a. I have me a theory of the Southern Double-Object Construction.

 b. Cindy sent her a letter to Sue yesterday.
[Southern American Vernacular English, Webelhuth and Dannenberg 2006: 34]

According to Webelhuth and Dannenberg (2006: 37–43), the Southern Double-Object Construction has five properties that distinguish it from the standard double-object construction.

Firstly, pronominal coreference happens in violation to Binding Principle B (Chomsky 1981: 188). Principle B says that pronouns cannot be coreferential with a subject in the same minimal clause (see also Chapter 2, Section 2.3.4).[2] The Binding Principles correctly predict the distribution of pronouns and anaphors (reflexives) in argument positions of transitive predicates. Consider (23):

(23) a. John bought himself (= John) some candy.

 b. John bought him (= John) some candy. (ungrammatical in the standard varieties, though grammatical in Southern American English)

Secondly, the Southern Double-Object Construction has a special meaning that distinguishes it from the standard double-object construction. The pronominal form coreferential with the subject intensifies the role of the subject referent in the predication (Webelhuth and Dannenberg 2006: 36, 40):

(24) a. I love me some baked beans.

 b. Fran likes her a day off every now and again.
[Southern American Vernacular English, Webelhuth and Dannenberg 2006: 39]

Thirdly, the noun phrase right adjacent to the verb must be a pronoun that is coreferential with the subject. This position cannot be filled by a full noun phrase or a pronoun that is not coreferential with the subject.

Fourthly, the pronominal noun phrase must appear right adjacent to the verb. It cannot be topicalised or passivised. Consider the contrast between (25) and (26).

(25) a. I gave him a watch and I gave her a bracelet.

 b. Him I gave a watch and her I gave a bracelet.

(26) a. He bought him a watch and she bought her a bracelet.

 b. *Him he bought a watch and her she bought a bracelet.

---

[2] The technical definition says that pronouns must be free in their governing category, where governing category is defined as the smallest clausal unit that contains a governor for the pronoun (the verb) and a subject.

Table 11.3 *Complementation patterns distinguished in Mukherjee and Hoffmann (2006: 151).*

Pattern	Example
NP_{IO} NP_{DO}	On Tuesday members of Parliament gave the government their overwhelming support <*ICE*-Great Britain: S2B-030 #54>
NP_{DO} to NP_{IO}	I meant to give it to you earlier <*ICE*-Great Britain: S1A-022 #176>
NP_{DO} $\emptyset_{IO}$	he wanted physical love and I couldn't give that <*ICE*-Great Britain: S1A-050#184>
$\emptyset_{IO}$ $\emptyset_{DO}$	The other major point he raises is in addressing the question of 'why give in the first place?' <*ICE*-Great Britain: W1A-011 #94>
NP_{IO} $\emptyset_{DO}$	I didn't give Lakshmi I had just given Sumi you know <*ICE*-India: S1A-098 #69–70>

The fifth property that makes the Southern Double-Object Construction special is that the second noun phrase requires a determiner (**Mary would love her (= Mary) flowers*).

We can summarise that Southern American dialects possess a double-object construction with highly idiosyncratic properties. Its origins presumably lie in Germanic benefactive datives that were generalised to a distinctive construction in southern American English. The history of this construction appears to be unknown.

11.2.4   Ditransitive verbs in varieties of English

We can also observe diverging complementation profiles of ditransitive verbs across varieties of English. Even though relatively little is known about such usage differences and their causes, we can use the study by Mukherjee and Hoffmann (2006) to shed some light on this matter.

Mukherjee and Hoffmann (2006) compared the complementation patterns of the verbs *give* and *send* in a corpus of British English and a corpus of Indian English (*ICE*-Great Britain and *ICE*-India respectively). The comparison is based on the five complementation patterns listed in Table 11.3. The authors did not distinguish between full noun phrases and pronominal objects, but they did include empty object positions.

The distributional differences between British English and Indian English are summarised in Table 11.4. We can identify clear differences. For example, speakers of Indian English, in contrast with British English speakers, use the double-object construction less often. They prefer the prepositional construction for *send*, though the double-object construction for *give*.

The figures in Table 11.4 represent percentages. They do not add up to 100 per cent, as only the main patterns are shown.

Table 11.4 *Complementation of* give *and* send *in* ICE-*India and* ICE-*Great Britain (adapted from Mukherjee and Hoffmann 2006: 172–3).*

	give		*send*	
Pattern	*ICE*-India	*ICE*-Great Britain	*ICE*-India	*ICE*-Great Britain
NP_{IO} NP_{DO}	22.6	38.0	15.4	21.8
NP_{DO} to NP_{IO}	17.3	11.6	22.3	22.5
NP_{DO} $\emptyset_{IO}$	29.4	23.2	37.1	24.2
$\emptyset_{IO}$ $\emptyset_{DO}$	1.3	0.9	2.0	0.7
NP_{IO} $\emptyset_{DO}$	0.3	0.0	0.0	0.4

Moreover, speakers of Indian English have a higher tendency to omit the indirect object in the double-object construction. They also omit both objects more often than British English speakers, even though the differences are very small.

In Indian English, several verbs show unusual complementation patterns, sporting the double-object construction with verbs that do not permit it in the standard varieties.

(27) a. The employee is also required to inform the appointed authority the amount of monthly instalment.[3]

      b. She said she wanted to gift him a dream.

      c. I advised him some technical changes like using both hands while stopping the ball.

      [Indian English, Mukherjee and Hoffmann 2006: 163–4]

11.3 Cross-linguistic comparison

The typological literature knows several ditransitive constructions and draws a distinction between 'indirect-object constructions' (the English prepositional construction), 'double-object constructions', and 'secondary-object constructions', in which the theme argument receives special coding. The latter construction is not attested in English.

From a typological perspective, it is highly interesting to note that pronominal objects often behave differently from full object noun phrases as far as the ordering of direct and indirect object is concerned. The kind of variability

---

[3] As Mukherjee and Hoffmann (2006: 166) point out, the non-standard complementation pattern of some of the verbs in their study is attested in historical varieties of English: *I informed him the account I had got from John Hutson.* [Israel D. Rupp. 1847. *History and Topography of Northumberland, Huntingdon, Mifflin, Centre, Union, Columbia, Juniata, and Clinton Counties, Pa.* Lancaster, PA: G. Hills.]

found in non-standard varieties of English is thus nicely paralleled by cross-linguistic data.

11.3.1   Alignment types

Cross-linguistic studies of ditransitive constructions have shown that languages may employ basically three strategies to encode them (Malchukov et al. 2010; Haspelmath 2011). Firstly, there is the so-called 'indirect-object construction', in which the indirect object receives special marking, while the direct object is encoded in the same way as in a monotransitive clause. Example (28) illustrates this coding strategy on the basis of Krongo, an African language spoken in Sudan.

(28) a. N-àpá-ŋ   à?àŋ káaw   y-íkkì.
        1-PFV.hit-TR I   person M-that
        'I hit that man.'

    b. N-àdá-ŋ   à?àŋ bìitì   à-káaw.
        1-PFV.give-TR I   water DAT-person
        'I gave water to the man/woman.'
        [Krongo, Reh 1985: 267–8, cited in Haspelmath 2011]

Secondly, we may distinguish the double-object construction whose main diagnostic is that the two objects are coded in the same way. Moreover, they receive the same marking as the object in a monotransitive clause. This is shown in (29) using an Australian language.

(29) a. Ngunha parnka ngarna-rta mantu-yu.
        that   lizard eat-FUT   meat-ACC
        'That lizard will eat the meat.'

    b. Ngatha yukurru-ku mantu-yu yinya-nha.
        I.NOM dog-ACC   meat-ACC give-PST
        'I gave the dog meat.'
        [Panyjima, Dench 1991: 193, cited in Haspelmath 2011]

Thirdly, we find ditransitive constructions in which the recipient argument is marked in the same way as the object of the monotransitive construction. These are referred to as 'secondary-object constructions', as shown in (30).

(30) a. Ha   tuge' i   kannastra.
        he.ERG weave ABS basket
        'He wove the basket.'

    b. Ha   na'i i   patgon ni   leche.
        he.ERG give ABS child   OBL milk
        'He gave the milk to the child.'
        [Chamorro, Topping 1973: 241, 251, cited in Haspelmath 2011]

In both standard and non-standard varieties of English, we find the double-object construction and the indirect-object construction, as the English prepositional construction corresponds to the latter type. Therefore, English in

Table 11.5 *Ditransitive constructions as a function of the verb* give *(Haspelmath 2011).*

Indirect-object construction	Double-object construction	Secondary-object construction	Mixed	Total
189	83	66	40	378

all its varieties may be considered a mixed language in this respect. Mandarin Chinese is another mixed language, just like English. You can find the double-object construction in (31a). The indirect-object construction in (31b) is based on a secondary verb (not a preposition).

(31) a. Wǒ sòng tā   yī běn shū.
          I   give s/he one CLF book
          'I gave him/her a book.'
      b. Wǒ sòng yī běn shū gěi tā.
          I   give one CLF book give him/her
          'I gave a book to him/her.'

[Mandarin, Huang and Ahrens 1999: 2, cited in Haspelmath 2011]

As our survey of varieties of English in Section 11.2.4 showed, non-standard varieties may exhibit different preferences for double object construction and indirect-object construction (Mukherjee and Hoffmann 2006). Cross-linguistically, the indirect-object construction is the most widely attested type, followed by double-object construction and secondary-object construction. The relevant figures are summarised in Table 11.5.

11.3.2   The order of direct objects and indirect objects

In double-object constructions, the recipient typically occurs before the theme, i.e. the indirect object precedes the direct object. This appears to be a cross-linguistically valid generalisation (Haspelmath 2011). It has been given a functional explanation, the argument being that animate noun phrases typically precede inanimate noun phrases.[4] English in most of its varieties appears to be consistent with this general trend. Mukherjee and Hoffmann (2006: 172) report very few cases with reverse order of recipient and theme.

This preferential ordering seems to be weakened for pronominal objects and clitics. As for object clitics, Gensler (2003: 197) cannot find a preferred ordering in his cross-linguistic sample. In German, the preferred order for full noun phrases is recipient before theme, though this ordering is reversed with pronominal objects. This reversal is illustrated in (32).

---

[4] This ordering preference is mirrored in the relative order of subject and object where subject-object order is vastly preferred to object-subject order. Subjects are more likely to be animate than objects.

(32) a. Er gab einem Bettler   eine Münze.
         he gave a   beggar.DAT a   coin.ACC
         'He gave a coin to a beggar.'
     b. Er gab es   ihm.
         He gave it.ACC him.DAT
         'He gave it to him.'
         [German, Gast 2007: 39]

We need to bear in mind that, in principle, German also permits the reverse ordering of recipient and theme in (32a) and (32b), but these orders would be pragmatically marked. Old English basically shows the same word order pattern as German, i.e. recipient-theme order, with full noun phrases and theme-recipient order with pronouns. This is shown in (33) and (34). Gast (2007) argues that the variation we find with pronominal objects in varieties of English today may be traced back to the kind of variation observable in older Germanic dialects.

(33) He [sealde [$_{REC}$þam geswenctum mannum] [$_{TH}$reste]].
     he gave   the   oppressed   people   rest
     'He gave the oppressed people rest.' [Old English, *Vercelli Homilies, volume IV*, 149–50, ed. Scragg; a1000, cited in Gast 2007: 49]

(34) He þe bæd   langes lifes, and þu hit$_{TH}$ him$_{REC}$ sealdest.
     he you asked long   life and you it.ACC him.DAT gave
     'He asked you for a long life, and you gave it to him.' [Old English, *Paris Psalter* 20, 4, ed. Stracke; a900, cited in Gast 2007: 49]

We may further note that the order of direct and indirect objects may be sensitive to the ditransitive construction in which the object noun phrases occur. For example, in Pero, a Chadic language spoken in Nigeria, full object noun phrases occur in the indirect-object construction, with the recipient noun phrases positioned behind the theme noun phrase. In contrast, pronominal recipients and themes occur in the double-object construction, their relative order being reversed. This is shown in (35).

(35) a. Músà mún-kò   júrà   tí D*íllà.
        Musa give-COMP peanut to Dilla
        'Musa gave peanuts to Dilla.'
     b. À-mún-tée-nò-té-m.
        NEG-give-VENT-1SG.OBJ-3SG.OBJ-NEG
        'He did not give it to me.'
        [Pero, Frajzyngier 1989: 167, 109, cited in Haspelmath 2011]

11.4   Summary and list of keywords

We began this chapter by introducing the two competing ditransitive constructions of English, i.e. the double-object construction and the prepositional construction, and by discussing some essential facts concerning syntactic and semantic transitivity. We also reviewed some important differences between the double-object construction and the prepositional construction. Our analysis of non-standard varieties of English produced interesting findings with regard to the double-object construction in which especially pronominal objects show alternative orderings. In the southern dialects of the United States, a double-object construction with highly idiosyncratic properties has developed. Moreover, varieties of English exhibit diverging preferences in their use of ditransitive constructions. With the double-object construction and the prepositional construction, English possesses two ditransitive constructions that enjoy a wide distribution cross-linguistically. What is more, even the special behaviour of pronominal objects in varieties of English has parallels in many other languages.

Keywords: alignment types, alternative double-object construction, benefactive dative, Binding Principles, canonical double-object construction, direct object, ditransitive, ditransitive construction, double-object construction, full noun phrase object, indirect object, indirect-object construction, intransitive, monotransitive, passivisation, prepositional construction, pronominal objects, recipient, reflexivity, secondary-object construction, semantic roles, Southern Double-Object Construction, theme, transitive, transitivity.

11.5   Exercises

Basic level

1. Determine the transitivity type of the verbs given below. Identify the semantic role of the given arguments of each sentence.

    a. *I run.*
    b. *Mary eats an apple.*
    c. *John gave Mary the book.*
    d. *It is raining.*

2. Summarise the major differences between the English double-object construction and the prepositional construction.
3. For each of the following verbs, construct a transitive and a ditransitive context. You may not use the prepositional construction.

    bring, buy, offer, show, tell.

Intermediate level

1. In this chapter, I distinguished carefully between the terms 'ditransitive construction' and 'double-object construction'. Can you see why?

2. In this corpus project, you are requested to investigate the distribution of pronominal objects in the double-object construction. I recommend using the *BNC* at http://corpus.byu.edu/bnc/, but you may also explore other online corpora.
   a. Draw up a list of all possible combinations of pronominal objects (*me it, it me, you it,* etc.).
   b. Identify the usage frequencies of the above pairs of pronominal objects.
   c. Can you identify preferences in the order of direct and indirect object? Explain your results.
   d. Which verbs are most common in the double-object construction?
3. Mukherjee and Hoffmann (2006) show that ditransitive verbs such as *give* and *send* have diverging complementation profiles in British English and Indian English. Extend this study so as to cover additional verbs and varieties of English.

Advanced level

1. The idea is to devise an experiment to test the usage of ditransitive constructions in a group of speakers of standard English and groups of speakers of non-standard varieties of English. The focus should be on the double-object construction, excluding the prepositional construction.

   The informants should carry out two tasks: (i) a sentence-completion task and (ii) a grammaticality-judgement task.

   a. Find some speakers of standard English and non-standard Englishes at your university.
   b. Devise a sentence-completion task in which you first introduce an animate as well as an inanimate referent through some discourse, and then ask your informants to complete the sentence inserting appropriate pronominal objects. Here are some examples:

   a. *John and Mary had coffee together. Mary ate all the cookies, except one. John stared at the cookie. Mary gave . . . (him it / it him).*
   b. *Mary and John went to the library yesterday. She wanted to reach for a certain book, but it was on a bookshelf that was too high up. John was tall enough, so he gave . . . (her it / it her).*
   c. *Mary and John still had to run some Christmas errands in the mall when John caught Mary staring at a beautiful silk blouse. Even though he already had enough gifts for her, he bought . . . (her it / it her).*

   c. For the grammaticality-judgement task choose three different ditransitive verbs (like *give*) and put them into appropriate sentential frames with pronominal objects in different orders. You may also try different person/number combinations. Embed these sentences into proper contexts. Let your informants evaluate these sentences.

   d. Analyse your results.

2. We learnt in Section 11.1.2 that ditransitive verbs of Romance origin are by and large not permitted in the English double-object construction. Consider the examples below again:

   a. *The mayor donated the university a large sum.*
   b. *The mayor donated a large sum to the university.*

   Try to think of ways to explain this restriction. Why should it be precisely verbs of Romance origin that show this restriction?

3. Consider the sentence in a. below. In terms of its meaning, does it correspond to sentence b. or c.? Can you make similar observations in your own language?

   a. *Ann stole John the book.*
   b. *Ann stole the book from John.*
   c. *Ann stole the book for John.*

11.6   References

Chomsky, Noam. 1981. *Lectures on Government and Binding*. Dordrecht: Foris.

Dench, Alan Charles. 1991. Panyjima. In R. M. W. Dixon and Barry J. Blake (eds.), *Handbook of Australian Languages, volume IV: The Aboriginal Language of Melbourne and Other Grammatical Sketches*, 124–243. Melbourne: Oxford University Press Australia.

Frajzyngier, Zygmunt. 1989. *A Grammar of Pero*. Berlin: Dietrich Reimer Verlag.

Gast, Volker. 2007. *I gave it him* – on the motivation of the alternative double-object construction in varieties of British English. In Anna Siewierska and Willem Hollmann (eds.), *Ditransitivity: Special Issue of Functions of Language* 14(1). 31–56.

Gensler, Orin. 2003. Object ordering in verbs marking two pronominal objects: Nonexplanation and explanation. *Linguistic Typology* 7(2). 187–231.

Haspelmath, Martin. 2011. Ditransitive constructions: The verb 'give'. In Matthew S. Dryer and Martin Haspelmath (eds.), *The World Atlas of Language Structures Online*. Munich: Max Planck Digital Library, chapter 105. Available online at http://wals.info/chapter/105. Accessed 22 December 2011.

Huang, Chu-Ren and Kathleen Ahrens. 1999. The function and category of *gei* in Mandarin ditransitive constructions. *Journal of Chinese Linguistics* 27(2). 1–26.

Hughes, Arthur, Peter Trudgill, and Dominic Watt. 2005. *English Accents and Dialects: An Introduction to Social and Regional Varieties of English in the British Isles*. London: Hodder Arnold.

Krifka, Manfred. 2004. Semantic and pragmatic conditions for the dative alternation. *Korean Journal of English Language and Linguistics* 4. 1–32.

Levin, Beth. 1993. *English Verb Classes and Alternations: A Preliminary Investigation*. Chicago University Press.

Malchukov, Andrej L., Martin Haspelmath and Bernard Comrie (eds.). 2010. *Studies in Ditransitive Constructions: A Comparative Handbook*. Berlin: Mouton de Gruyter.

Mukherjee, Joybrato and Sebastian Hoffmann. 2006. Describing verb-complementational profiles of New Englishes: A pilot study of Indian English. *English World-Wide* 27(2). 147–73.

Orton, Harold and Eugen Dieth (eds.). 1962–71. *Survey of English Dialects*, 13 volumes. Leeds: E.J. Arnold & Son Ltd.

Rappaport Hovav, Malka and Beth Levin. 2008. The English dative alternation: The case for verb sensitivity. *Journal of Linguistics* 44. 129–67.

Reh, Mechthild. 1985. *Die Krongo-Sprache (Nìinò Mó-Dì)*. Berlin: Dietrich Reimer Verlag.

Siewierska, Anna and Willem Hollmann. 2007. Ditransitive clauses in English with special reference to Lancashire dialect. In Mike Hannay and Gerald Steen (eds.), *Structural-Functional Studies in English Grammar: In Honour of Lachlan Macken-zie* (Studies in Language Companion Series 83), 83–102. Amsterdam: John Benjamins.

Topping, Donald M. (with the assistance of Bernadita C. Dungca). 1973. *Chamorro Reference Grammar*. Honolulu: University of Hawai'i Press.

Upton, Clive and J.D.A. Widdowson. 1996. *An Atlas of English Dialects*. Oxford University Press.

Webelhuth, Gert and Clare J. Dannenberg. 2006. Southern American English personal datives: The theoretical significance of dialectal variation. *American Speech* 81(1). 31–55.

See *General references* for Huddleston and Pullum 2002.

11.7   Further reading

Bresnan, Joan and Jennifer Hay. 2008. Gradient grammar: An effect of animacy on the syntax of *give* in New Zealand and American English. *Lingua* 118. 245–59.

Bresnan, Joan and Marilyn Ford. 2010. Predicting syntax: Processing dative constructions in American and Australian varieties of English. *Language* 86(1). 168–213.

Haspelmath, Martin. 2004. Explaining the ditransitive person-role constraint: A usage-based approach. *Constructions* 2. 1–49.

Hudson, Richard. 1992. So-called 'double objects' and grammatical relations. *Language* 68(2). 251–76.

Kittilä, Seppo. 2005. Recipient-prominence vs. beneficiary-prominence. *Linguistic Typology* 9(2). 269–97.

Mukherjee, Joybrato. 2005. *English Ditransitive Verbs*. Amsterdam: Rodopi.

12 Interrogative constructions

We can distinguish four major clause types in English: declaratives, interrogatives, imperatives, and exclamatives. We identify them primarily on the basis of their word order, as I will show below. The focus of this chapter lies on interrogatives, but it will be useful to introduce some background information on clause types and their associated functions. This will be done in Section 12.1. Interrogatives in varieties of English primarily differ from the corresponding standard specimens in terms of word order, both in main and embedded interrogative clauses. We will investigate these differences in Section 12.2. A cross-linguistic comparison of interrogatives that places standard and vernacular constructions of English in this domain into a larger picture will round off this chapter (Section 12.3).

12.1 Overview

Interrogative clauses as a grammatical phenomenon belong to the system of sentence types. We understand sentence types as the systematic pairing of the formal properties of a clause with some illocutionary function (see König and Siemund 2007). Let us first of all try to make clear what this means.

12.1.1 Illocutionary force and sentence types

In uttering a sentence, speakers can perform various communicative acts, such as making a statement, asking a question, issuing a command, or expressing surprise about an unexpected state of affairs. They may also want to apologise, promise something, or accuse or criticise somebody. There is scarcely a limit to the set of imaginable communicative acts, and speakers are likely to find extremely nuanced ways to express them.

However, the communicative acts of making a statement, asking a question, issuing a command, and expressing surprise, as introduced above, possess a certain priority in our communicative systems, since we find distinct sentential patterns to express them. The communicative act typically associated with a

Table 12.1 *Clause types and illocutionary force in English.*

	Pattern	Sentence type	Example	Force
1.	S V (O)	declarative	*John ate an apple.*	statement
2a.	AUX S V (O)	polar interrogative	*Did John eat an apple?*	yes/no question
2b.	WH AUX S V (O)	constituent interrogative	*What did John eat?*	open question
3.	V (O)	imperative	*Eat an apple, John!*	command
4.	WH S V (O)	exclamative	*What an apple John ate!*	exclamation

sentential pattern is usually referred to as its 'illocutionary force' or 'illocutionary force potential', using the terminology introduced by Austin (1962) and
Searle (1969). Realising some illocutionary force in communication is known
as a 'speech act'. In Table 12.1, you can find the four sentence types – subsum-
ing polar and constituent interrogatives under one type – that we can distinguish
in English according to their syntactic pattern, as well as the illocutionary force
prototypically associated with them. In Table 12.1 and throughout this chapter,
we will draw a very sharp distinction between sentence types and illocutionary
force, and also in terminology. Therefore, whenever we say 'statement' we
mean 'force', and when we say 'declarative' we refer to the relevant syntactic
pattern.

The neat typology shown in Table 12.1 is not without problems, though,
as the relationship between sentence type and illocutionary function is one of
prototypicality, and not categoriality. In other words, all the sentence types
listed in Table 12.1 can also be used with other illocutionary forces. This can
be seen in the examples below in (1), where (1a) is the declarative pattern used
as question, (1b) the interrogative pattern expressing a statement (a so-called
'rhetorical question'), and (1c) an exclamation resting on the syntactic structure
of a polar interrogative.

(1) a. Mary has bought another new car?
     b. Who wouldn't want to do that?
     c. Boy, is this cute!

Many additional examples could easily be constructed. Assuming that our
approach of relating sentential patterns to specific illocutionary forces (the so-
called 'literal force hypothesis'; Levinson 1983: 263) is correct, let us use the
term 'direct speech act' for those acts that involve the prototypical mapping of
force and sentential structure (as in Table 12.1), and 'indirect speech act' for
the cases illustrated in example (1).

The examples in (1) also point to the special role of intonation for the
identification of sentence types, as (1a) can be identified as a question owing to
its rising intonation. Since intonation can practically override the default force

Table 12.2 *Properties of interrogative clauses in English.*

Property	Polar interrogatives	Constituent interrogatives
subject-auxiliary inversion	yes	yes (non-subject)
wh-word(s)	no	yes
subordinators	*whether, if*	*wh*-word

of any sentence type, I here restrict myself to the morphosyntactic properties of a clause. Let us also define declaratives as the unmarked clause type against which to compare interrogative clauses.

12.1.2 The structure of interrogative clauses

We have defined interrogative clauses as clauses that are used with the intention of obtaining information, i.e. asking questions. In standard English, polar interrogatives and constituent interrogatives are marked – relative to declarative clauses – by subject-auxiliary inversion, *do*-periphrasis, and fronted *wh*-words (only constituent interrogatives). Declarative word order is kept if the subject of constituent interrogatives is replaced by a *wh*-word, as in (2).

(2) a. Who did John see? (who = direct object)
   b. Who saw John? (who = subject)

Interrogative clauses can occur as main clauses, or as embedded (subordinate) clauses. As one can see in examples (3) and (4), embedded interrogatives have a word order that is indistinguishable from that of main clause declaratives or embedded declaratives, i.e. there is no special syntactic pattern for embedded interrogatives.

(3) a. Is John the suspect? (main clause polar interrogative)
   b. I wonder if John is the suspect. (embedded polar interrogative)
(4) a. When did John leave for Singapore? (main clause constituent interrogative)
   b. I wonder when John left for Singapore. (embedded constituent interrogative)

We can identify the type of an embedded clause by virtue of the subordinator that introduces it. For example, the embedded polar interrogative in (3b) is introduced by the subordinator *if* (alternatively *whether*). Embedded constituent interrogatives are introduced by a *wh*-word, as in (4b). These properties are summarised in Table 12.2.

In concluding this section, we may note that – besides polar and constituent interrogatives – there is a third type of interrogative, usually referred to as 'alternative questions' (e.g. examples of the type *Would you like beer or wine?*).

Table 12.3 Wh-*words in English.*

who	whom	what	where	when	why	how
person	person	thing	place	time	reason	manner

Even though these have interesting properties both in standard English and also cross-linguistically, I have not seen them in discussions on varieties of English. They will therefore play no role in the following (but see Siemund 2001: 1012).

12.1.3   Interrogative words

A prominent diagnostic of constituent interrogatives is the presence of a *wh*-word. In English we find the *wh*-words shown in Table 12.3.

The *wh*-word for persons has both a subject and an object form, although the object form is perceived as slightly archaic. In addition to the *wh*-words shown in Table 12.3, there are the adjectival forms *which* and *whose*.

Most constituent interrogatives contain only one *wh*-word, which is positioned in sentence-initial position. If there is more than one *wh*-word, the additional *wh*-word occupies the syntactic position of the constituent it replaces in the corresponding declarative clause. Consider (5):

(5) a. Who showed what to whom?
     b. Paul showed the book to Mary.

In so-called echo-questions, *wh*-words regularly appear in the position of the corresponding constituents (*My goodness! You did what?*).

12.1.4   Interrogative tags (tag questions)

Standard English has a fairly complicated system of tag questions, which are full clausal units consisting of subject and verb and which assume a polarity opposite to that of the main clause in the typical case. The pronominal subject of the tag mirrors that of the main clause. In addition, the verb form in the tag question carries the same finiteness markers as the main verb (see also Chapter 9).

(6) a. The kids enjoy the winter, don't they?
     b. The kids do not enjoy the winter, do they?

Tags with a polarity opposite to that of the main clause are often referred to as 'reversed polarity tags' (Huddleston and Pullum 2002: 892). Tags with matching polarity, as in (7), are called 'constant polarity tags'. On the whole, constant polarity tags appear to be used less frequently than reversed polarity tags, with constellations consisting of negative main clause and negative tag, as in (7b), causing unhappiness for many speakers.

(7) a. The kids enjoy the winter, do they?
  b. The kids do not enjoy the winter, don't they?

We may analyse tag questions as a strategy to form polar interrogatives, as examples like (6) convey an illocutionary force similar to that of polar interrogatives formed by subject-auxiliary inversion. The question tag is appended to a declarative main clause. Such polar interrogatives convey a strong answer bias, asking for verification or confirmation depending on the intonation pattern used (Quirk et al. 1985: 811). Rising intonation triggers verification; falling intonation confirmation.

12.2 Varieties of English

Interrogative clauses across varieties of English may have several special properties that distinguish them from those found in the standard varieties. These special properties are primarily found in the post-colonial varieties (including Irish English) and to a lesser extent in traditional dialects, and mainly concern the word order patterns of interrogatives, though there are also differences in the form and use of question tags and the position of interrogative words in a clause.

As for word order, we can observe that questions are expressed with declarative word order, and, conversely, that embedded interrogatives show inversion of subject and verb. Trudgill and Hannah (2008: 137) give us the following pair of examples by way of illustration (see also Mesthrie and Bhatt 2008: 98):

(8) a. What this is made from?
  b. Who you have come to see?
(9) a. I asked him where does he work.
  b. I wonder where is he.

All these phenomena are unexpected from the point of view of the standard varieties. We will discuss them in what follows, starting with questions expressed by declarative word order.

12.2.1 No inversion in main clauses

We learnt in Section 12.1.2 above that English interrogative clauses are characterised by the inversion of subject and finite verb. The inverted pattern appears in both polar interrogatives and constituent interrogatives, and is only pre-empted in constituent interrogatives if the subject constituent is replaced by a *wh*-word (cf. *Who gave the book to Mary?*).

In the varieties spoken in India and Singapore, as we can see in the examples in (10), constituent interrogatives may begin with an interrogative word, but then proceed with declarative word order, i.e. subject-verb-object.

(10) a. When you are coming home? [Indian English, Bhatt 2004: 1020]

     b. Where he went? [Indian English, Bhatt 2004: 1020]

     c. Why you like give information? [Singapore English, *ICE*-Singapore: S1A-031]

     d. What you call that ... with auditor that one? [Singapore English, *ICE*-Singapore: S1A-018]

The sentences in (11) provide additional examples from many non-standard varieties around the world. What they have in common is that these are not traditional dialects.

(11) a. What you was thinking? [Hawai'i Creole, Sakoda and Siegel 2004: 749]

     b. Why you not want to stay in Savusavu? [Fiji English, Mugler and Tent 2004: 785]

     c. So whereabout in India she's? How many years she's there now? [Indian South African English, Mesthrie 2004b: 979]

     d. How they will come home? [Malaysian English, Baskaran 2004: 1078]

The example from Pakistani English in (12) illustrates the same phenomenon, additionally providing a case of present progressive overuse (see Chapter 7).

(12) Why so many are being killed? [Pakistani English, Mahboob 2004: 1051]

We need to bear in mind, though, that the use of the uninverted declarative word order, as illustrated in the above examples, is not categorical in these varieties. In other words, not all speakers do this, and those who do may not do so all the time. It is a statistical phenomenon that depends on various social variables (age, sex, socio-economic status, etc.) and parameters of the communication situation (degree of formality, spoken versus written language, in-group versus out-group, etc.).

Table 12.4 provides an idea of how frequent uninverted constituent interrogatives are in a selection of post-colonial varieties of English. The figures have been taken from Davydova et al. (2011) and are based on an analysis of the *ICE* (a collection of corpora from different English-speaking regions). As these corpora are roughly equal in size (about 1 million words), we can compare the absolute frequencies.

We can, first of all, note that the number of constituent interrogatives found in each of the varieties differs substantially, which is most certainly a consequence of the corpus design, i.e. of the data that went into the corpus. There is no reason to believe that speakers of Singapore English ask more questions than speakers of Indian English. When we look at the number of uninverted cases, we can see that Jamaican English has the highest absolute number (201 cases). Moreover, it

Table 12.4 *Inverted and uninverted main clause constituent interrogatives in the* ICE *(adapted from Davydova et al. 2011: 309).*

Type	Indian English	Singapore English	Jamaican English	East African English
inverted	552	1,050	732	767
uninverted	78	91	201	46
other	26	392	46	49
Total	656	1,533	979	862

appears that this variety also has the highest relative number of uninverted cases. In none of these varieties does the share of uninverted constituent interrogatives exceed 30 per cent.

As far as polar interrogatives are concerned, we also find several reports in the literature that they are realised as declarative sentences with rising intonation. Examples are shown in (13).

(13) a. You like banana? [Aboriginal English, Malcolm 2004: 675]
    b. You want me give him one empty [i.e. blank] disc? [Fiji English, Mugler and Tent 2004: 785]
    c. The children are studying? [Cameroon English, Mbangwana 2004: 904]
    d. I can go now? [Indian South African English, Mesthrie 2004b: 977]

In comparison with constituent interrogatives lacking subject-auxiliary inversion, as discussed above, the status of the yes/no questions in (13) is less clear, as these sentences are perfectly grammatical in standard English (ignoring other non-standard features). The uninverted constituent interrogatives in (10) and (11) are clearly ungrammatical in any of the standard varieties. Such 'polar declarative questions', as we may refer to cases like (13), typically express strong answer expectations in the standard varieties, with any of the questions shown in (13) expecting an affirmative answer. If they were used as neutral questions in the relevant non-standard varieties, they would carry no answer bias and they would also be more frequent than polar declarative questions in the standard varieties. I am not aware of any studies that would convincingly show this.

12.2.2 Inversion in embedded clauses

Post-colonial varieties, as stated in the introduction to Section 12.2, also provide us with a phenomenon that is complementary to missing inversion in main clauses, namely the inversion of subject and verb in embedded interrogative clauses. While the standard varieties only show inversion in main clause interrogatives, non-standard varieties exhibit exactly the same kind of inversion in embedded interrogatives, as the examples in (14) make clear. We find this phenomenon primarily in the so-called 'Celtic Englishes', as well as in several of the post-colonial varieties.

(14) a. I wonder what is he like at all. = = The leprechaun. = I don' know what is it at all. [Irish English, Filppula 1999: 168]

b. If they got an eight they had to decide where was the best place to put it. [Scottish English, Miller 2004: 58]

c. I don't know what time is it. [Welsh English, Penhallurick 2004: 104]

d. A Catholic bishop who asked me what would I do if he could pay for my studies. [Black South African English, Mesthrie 2004a: 965]

e. I wonder where does it go in winter? [Indian South African English, Mesthrie 2004b: 979]

f. I asked Ramesh what did he eat for breakfast. [Indian English, Bhatt 2004: 1020]

g. Ya every time I go for those government interviews a lot of them ask me why don't I go into teaching. [Singapore English, *ICE*-Singapore: S1A-046]

h. Have you measured how much how high is your cholesterol? [Singapore English, *ICE*-Singapore: S1A-013]

The examples in (14) show embedded inversion with constituent interrogatives. We also find the phenomenon with embedded polar interrogatives, as in (15).

(15) a. I asked her could I go with her. [Urban African American Vernacular English, Wolfram 2004b: 334]

b. Let me know did your sister send for Thomas. [Irish English, *Hamburg Corpus of Irish Emigrant Letters*, CaseyJ_02]

c. You ask me is Hamilton home from new Zealand. [Irish English, *Hamburg Corpus of Irish Emigrant Letters*, McCanc_08]

d. I don't know was it a priest or who went in there on time with a horse-collar put over his neck. [Irish English, Filppula 2004: 94]

e. I asked him did he want some tea. [North of England, Beal 2004: 129]

f. He asked could he get there about fifteen minutes late. [Colloquial American English, Murray and Simon 2004: 224]

On a methodological note, we need to distinguish embedded inversion from main clause inversion in direct speech. This is not trivial. Consider the examples in (16) and (17), which I adapted from the examples introduced above. I present them in writing in such a way that they are clearly marked as direct speech (namely in inverted commas).

(16) a. They asked me: 'Why don't you go into teaching?'

b. I wonder: 'What is he like at all?'

Table 12.5 *Inverted and uninverted embedded constituent interrogatives in the* ICE *(adapted from Davydova et al. 2011: 308).*

Type	Indian English	Singapore English	Jamaican English	East African English
inverted	130	67	30	45
uninverted	507	384	336	261
Total	637	451	366	306

(17) a. I asked her: 'Can I go with you?'

    b. You ask me: 'Is Hamilton home from new Zealand?'

Converting these instances of direct speech into reported speech, i.e. embedding the relevant main clauses, results in structural changes in the a-examples, though not in the b-examples. In (16a) the pronoun *you* changes to *I*, while (17a) requires a change from *can* to *could* and *you* to *her*. This is shown again in (18) and (19). Conversion to standard-like reported speech would also require a change in word order, but this is not at issue here.

(18) a. They asked me why don't I go into teaching.

    b. I wonder what is he like at all.

(19) a. I asked her could I go with her.

    b. You ask me is Hamilton home from new Zealand.

These considerations show that we can identify examples like (18a) and (19a) as unequivocal cases of embedded inversion, whereas the relevant b-examples remain ambiguous. Additional clues from the context (e.g. prosody, orthography, verbal context) would have to be consulted to settle these cases. If the ambiguities could not be resolved, we would have to exclude such examples from our analysis.[1]

There are some quantitative studies available that attempt to assess the extent to which embedded inversion occurs in varieties of English. For example, Davydova et al. (2011: 308) report the figures shown in Table 12.5 for constituent interrogatives.

In a similar way, Table 12.6 gives the corresponding figures for embedded polar interrogatives.

Both Table 12.5 and Table 12.6 make clear that embedded inversion can be encountered in the varieties sampled for this study. The absolute number of cases reported for constituent interrogatives is quite substantial, and we can expect many true cases of embedded inversion to be among them.

---

[1] Embedded inversion in varieties of English can also be found with matrix predicates that cannot control direct speech: *The police found out had the goods been stolen*; *We couldn't establish did he meet them.* (Henry 1995: 107). Such examples represent unambiguous cases of embedded inversion.

Table 12.6 *Inverted and uninverted embedded polar interrogatives in the* ICE *(adapted from Davydova et al. 2011: 310).*

Type	Indian English	Singapore English	Jamaican English	East African English
inverted	5	7	2	2
uninverted	87	134	79	23
Total	92	141	81	25

Let us also briefly compare the quantitative profiles of embedded inversion with the use of declarative word order in main clause interrogatives, i.e. the uninverted main clause structures discussed in the previous section. This concerns Table 12.4, Table 12.5, and Table 12.6. It is obvious that neither embedded inversion nor declarative word order in main clause questions represent categorical phenomena. As a matter of fact, the standard English word order patterns also seem to be the default option in non-standard varieties, as main clause constituent interrogatives show inversion in the majority of cases (Table 12.4) and subject and verb are typically not inverted in embedded interrogatives (Table 12.5 and Table 12.6).

12.2.3   Interrogative words

Non-standard interrogative words are interesting for two reasons. Firstly, they show positional differences in interrogative clauses and may not be fronted to sentence-initial position as in standard English, but instead appear in the structural position of the corresponding declarative clause. This so-called '*in situ*' position of interrogative words can be encountered in some post-colonial Englishes, as well as in Pidgin and Creole Englishes. This *in situ* property is amenable to an explanation in terms of language contact (see Section 12.3.2). Examples are provided in (20) and (21).

(20) a. He has sent the letter to who? [Cameroon English, Mbangwana 2004: 903]

   b. They are going where? [Malaysian English, Baskaran 2004: 1078]

   c. This bus go where? [Singapore English, Wee 2004: 1063]

(21) Yu   wokem   wanem?

   you do   what

   'What did you do?' [Bislama, Crowley 2004: 696]

The other reason non-standard interrogative words are interesting is that they may appear in different forms. Quite typically, these are semantically more transparent than the corresponding standard forms. They usually occur in Pidgin

Table 12.7 *Some non-standard interrogative words.*

Variety	Interrogative word	Meaning	Source
Creoles of Trinidad and Tobago	*huu-an-huu* *wich-paat*	'who' (plural) 'where'	James and Youssef 2004: 468
Australian Creoles and Aboriginal English	*hu blanga*	'whose'	Malcolm 2004: 666
Bislama	*wataem* *wijwan* *olsem wanem*	'what time' 'which one' 'why'	Crowley 2004: 696
Nigerian Pidgin English	*wating* *wichwe* *wεples* *wichtaim*	'what' 'how' 'where' 'when'	Faraclas 2004: 851

Table 12.8 *Interrogative words in Sranan (adapted from Winford and Migge 2004: 494).*

Meaning	Sranan	Early Sranan	Source
'who'	*suma*	*o suma*	*somebody*
'what'	*san*	*o sani*	*something*
'where'	*pe*	*o pe*	*place*
'how'	*fa*	*o fasi*	*fashion*
'why'	*(fu) san ede*	*fu san ede*	*for what head* (= reason)

and Creole varieties. A selection of such interrogative words drawn from the literature is shown in Table 12.7. It appears that the adverbial interrogative words are more likely to be replaced by semantically transparent forms, though this claim would need empirical verification.

A very special paradigm of interrogative words can be found in the Surinamese Creole Sranan, in which the entire paradigm was recreated. It is shown in Table 12.8. The rightmost column of this table provides the original lexical source of the interrogative words.

12.2.4 Interrogative tags and particles

The elaborate clausal agreement tags that we find in standard English (see Section 12.1.4 above) are typically substituted by some invariant particle-like tag in vernacular varieties. There is a plethora of competing forms, which I have tried to systematise in Table 12.9. Neither the list of tags nor the list of

Table 12.9 *Non-standard tags (based on Kortmann et al. 2004)*.

Tag	Variety
non-agreeing *isn't* or *innit*	several British dialects, Indian English, Nigerian English, Cameroon English, Malaysian English, etc.
e or *eh*	Scottish English, Aboriginal English, Fiji English, Australian Creoles
no, na	Scottish English, Jamaican English, Cameroon English, etc.
or not, can or not	Singapore English
ngi	Kriol

varieties from which they have been reported is complete. Completely unrelated varieties resort to similar strategies, even though the lexical sources of the tags may not necessarily be the same.

Some examples of non-agreeing *isn't* are shown in (22). Notice that this phenomenon does not seem to be restricted to any particular region or type of variety. It occurs in traditional dialects, just as in post-colonial varieties. Invariant *isn't* or *innit* is a good example of an angloversal (see Chapter 9).

(22) a. You like that, isn't it? [Nigerian English, Alo and Mesthrie 2004: 817]
   b. You said you'll do the job, isn't it? [Indian English, Bhatt 2004: 1022]
   c. They are coming, isn't it? [Malaysian English, Baskaran 2004: 1079]
   d. Yall didn buy no clothes from town, inni? [Gullah, Mufwene 2004: 368]

In Singapore English, we find the complex tag *can or not* that is apparently calqued on a similar structure in Chinese. It is also reported from Malaysian English.

(23) a. Can answer the question or not? 'Do you know the answer or not?' [Singapore English, Wee 2004: 1064]
   b. A: I want to go home. B: [no response] A: Can or not? [Singapore English, Wee 2004: 1064]
   c. You carry this for me, can or not? 'Will you carry this for me?' [Malaysian English, Baskaran 2004: 1079]

For Cameroon English, Mbangwana (2004: 905) provides us with a host of forms, as illustrated in (24). What they have in common is that they are invariant and non-clausal.

(24) a. You will pay the debt, na?
   b. She said it, not so?
   c. We should stop it, ein?
   d. Yaya finished the work, is that?
   e. You'll wait for me outside the courtyard, right?
   f. Mali will be on time, okay?
      [Cameroon English, Mbangwana 2004: 905]

12.3   Cross-linguistic comparison

In our cross-linguistic assessment of interrogative constructions in varieties of English, we will investigate the most important parameters of variation that have emerged from studying such constructions in the world's languages and position the phenomena reported from varieties of English against the matrix opened up by them. We will mainly consider three areas: firstly, the marking options encountered that distinguish interrogatives from declaratives; secondly, differences in the sets of interrogative words and the positions they may occupy in the clause, and thirdly, interrogative tags and particles.

12.3.1   The marking of interrogative clauses

To facilitate our cross-linguistic comparison, let us here assume that the marking strategies available for polar and constituent interrogatives are by and large the same. This, of course, is an oversimplification.

Perhaps the default strategy for marking interrogatives is intonation, with rising intonation usually signalling questions and falling intonation statements.[2] Languages frequently make use of this option on its own – for example, polar interrogatives in Spanish or Italian[3] – or in combination with other strategies (see below). As for varieties of English, it is especially the post-colonial varieties that use intonation together with declarative word order to signal questions. We encountered some examples in Section 12.2.1. This, of course, applies mainly to yes/no questions, as open questions contain interrogative words, i.e. another marker of questions. In the standard varieties, such declarative questions carry a strong answer expectation (as in *You smoked for 20 years?*).

Another fairly widespread strategy to mark questions is the addition of an interrogative particle to the clause, typically in clause-final position. The example in (25) shows this for Japanese, where the sentence without the particle *ka* expresses the corresponding statement.

(25) yamada-san wa   ginkoo de hataraite-imasu ka?
       yamada-Mr. TOP bank   at working   Q
      'Does Mr. Yamada work at the bank?' [Japanese, Hinds 1984: 158]

In the standard varieties of English, the default strategy for marking interrogatives – both polar and constituent – involves a change in the order of constituents such that the subject and the finite verb change position with one another. We

---

[2] Again, this is an oversimplification, as constituent interrogatives typically have falling intonation.

[3] The Spanish sentence *Usted habla español.* 'You speak Spanish.' is a declarative clause. The same syntactic pattern uttered with a rising intonation is interpreted as a question: *¿Usted habla español?* 'Do you speak Spanish?'

discussed this in Section 12.1.2. English shares this strategy with other Germanic languages. In addition, it has been reported from some Austronesian and Amazonian languages (Dryer 2011a). On the whole, however, this strategy is extremely rare, and thus it does not come as a complete surprise that many non-standard varieties of English do not use it, or, if they do so, do not use it consistently (e.g. Indian English, Singapore English). At the same time, however, we have learnt that it is precisely the varieties that use declarative word order in questions that manifest subject-auxiliary inversion in embedded interrogative clauses (embedded inversion). This, however, can only mean that trying to explain the underuse of main clause inversion for the marking of interrogatives in some varieties of English by pointing to its cross-linguistic rarity cannot be the full story.

We need to mention two additional marking strategies for interrogative clauses that do not, however, seem to play a role in varieties of English. The first strategy consists of a highly reduced alternative question ('is or is not') that can be appended to a declarative clause. Such a negative-disjunctive strategy can be found, *inter alia*, in Mandarin Chinese. This is illustrated in (26). The Singapore English tag *can or not* discussed in Section 12.2.4 above appears to be related to this strategy.

(26) tā   zài jiā   bu   zài jiā?
    3SG at   home NEG at   home
    'Is s/he at home?' [Mandarin, Li and Thompson 1984: 53]

The other strategy involves dedicated verbal morphology, i.e. some verbal affix, to signal questions. Such verbal morphology may functionally behave like an interrogative particle, but be a bound affix of the verb, as shown in example (27). This strategy seems to be relatively common.

(27) lɔ'ta wi-wa'nă-n
    run   2SG-want-Q
    'Do you want to run?' [Tunica, Haas 1940: 118, cited in Dryer 2011a]

Interrogative affixes may also exhibit higher degrees of fusion and be more tightly integrated into the mood system of a language, thus contrasting, for example, with imperative or declarative affixes. Such systems are attested in some Inuit languages (Siemund 2001: 1017–18). These strategies play no role in the discussion of English and its varieties.

Table 12.10 provides a quantitative overview of the attested marking strategies for polar interrogatives. The data has been taken from Dryer (2011a) and illustrates nicely how rare word order change for the marking of questions is.

12.3.2   Interrogative words

As far as interrogative words are concerned, there are two main parameters of interest here: firstly, their position in the clause and, secondly, their form and internal differentiation.

Table 12.10 *Strategies for marking polar questions (Dryer 2011a).*

Strategy	Number of languages
Question particle	584
Interrogative verb morphology	164
Question particle and interrogative verb morphology	15
Interrogative word order	13
Absence of declarative morphemes	4
Interrogative intonation only	173
No interrogative-declarative distinction	1
Total	954

In terms of position, the major cross-linguistic parameter is whether the interrogative words are fronted to clause-initial position or remain in the position of the constituent they replace. More precisely, what we mean is the position of the constituent in the corresponding declarative clause. Fronting of interrogative words is often called '*wh*-movement'; if they do not move, we may speak of '*wh-in situ*'. The standard varieties of English quite consistently show the fronting of interrogative words. In Section 12.2.3, we encountered some non-standard varieties in which interrogative words remain *in situ*. It appears reasonable to interpret this as structural influence from the relevant substrate languages.

The *in situ* position is clearly dominant cross-linguistically. Dryer (2011b) investigates this parameter in a sample of 901 languages and finds only 264 languages that move interrogative words to clause-initial position, as the English standard varieties do. The example in (28) shows such an *in situ* case from Lango, a Nilotic language spoken in Uganda. This language has SVO word order, just like English.

(28) òkélò ò-nènò   ŋà
     Okelo 3SG-see.PERF who
     'Who did Okelo see?' [Lango, Noonan 1992: 173, cited in Dryer 2011b]

Concerning the form and internal differentiation of interrogative words, languages vary with respect to the word classes for which they offer interrogative words. For example, the standard varieties of English possess nominal interrogative words (*who*, *what*), adverbial ones (*where*, *when*, *why*, *how*), and those that are adjectival (*which*, *whose*). There are none for numerals (*how many*), verbs, or prepositions, though there is in principle no reason they should not exist. Hagège (2008) reports examples of such less familiar interrogative words. König and Siemund (2012) postulate the (implicational) hierarchy of interrogative words shown in (29) that predicts the existence of interrogative words to the left of an attested point on it.

(29) noun > adverb > adjective/determiner > numeral/cardinal > ordinal >
     verb > preposition

Non-standard varieties of English, as we saw in Section 12.2.3, may substitute monomorphemic interrogative words such as *when* or *where* by more complex expressions like *what time* or *which place*. These are semantically more transparent and can be found especially in the Pidgin and Creole varieties. Such substitutions appear to be less common with the nominal interrogative words, but it is currently not clear if we can relate the phenomena reported from varieties of English to the hierarchy in (29).

Another implicational hierarchy that may turn out to be of relevance for the study of interrogative words in varieties of English is that shown in (30), taken from Mackenzie (2009: 1134). We can read it as the semantic counterpart to (29), even though it only covers nominal and adverbial interrogative words. Again, the idea is that if a language has an interrogative word encoding 'reason' (i.e. *why*), it will also have interrogative words for the other semantic domains.

(30) INDIVIDUAL > LOCATION > TIME > MANNER > QUANTITY >
     REASON

Interrogative words are frequently related to indefinite expressions (Haspelmath 1997). Let me illustrate this using data from German, even though the phenomenon is more common in non-standard language. As you can see in (31), the interrogative word *wen* translates into English as *who* in (31a), but as *somebody/anybody* in (31b).

(31) a. Wen hast Du gesehen?
        who have you seen
        'Who have you seen?'
     b. Hast Du wen   gesehen?
        have you somebody seen
        'Have you seen anybody?'
        [German, personal knowladge]

We encountered a similar formal relationship between interrogative words and indefinite expressions in Sranan (see Table 12.8 in Section 12.2.3 above). There, the interrogative words *suma* 'who' and *san* 'what' are etymologically related to the indefinite expressions 'somebody' and 'something'.

12.3.3   Returning to tags and particles

Particles, as we learnt in Section 12.3.1 above, can be considered the most prominent strategy of question formation cross-linguistically. Strictly speaking, this strategy is not attested in varieties of English, unless we decide to analyse one or more of the many invariant tags that we encountered in Section 12.2.4 as interrogative particles.

The main difference between interrogative particles and tags is that tags produce conducive questions, while interrogative particles yield neutral questions. Standard English tag questions (*You don't like that, do you?*) raise strong answer expectations. Questions formed by particles do not produce similar effects. Siemund (2001: 1015) draws attention to additional differences between particles and tags. For example, tags are typically clause-final, whereas interrogative particles can be clause-final or clause-initial, and may also occur in the second syntactic slot of a clause. Moreover, tags usually possess greater morphological substance than particles and are often (content) words, phrases, or complete clausal units, as in standard English.

The problem is that the distinction between interrogative particles and tags is typically not drawn in the literature on varieties of English, at least in the publications that I am aware of. The elements listed in Table 12.9 in Section 12.2.4 all seem to be conducive in one way or another. The best exemplar of an interrogative particle comes from the Creoles of Trinidad and Tobago, as shown in (32) below. There, the particle -*fa* apparently yields neutral questions (James and Youssef 2004: 471).

(32) a. We yu du dat -fa
   why you do that Q
   'Why did you do that?'
b. We yu a   bada mi -fa?
   why you PROG bother me Q
   'Why are you bothering me?'
   [Creoles of Trinidad and Tobago, James and Youssef 2004: 472]

12.4   Summary and list of keywords

To facilitate the identification of interrogative clauses, we began this chapter with a characterisation of sentence types, which we described as the systematic pairing of morphosyntactic properties with illocutionary forces. Interrogative clauses in English possess special word order patterns that correlate with the function of asking questions. Syntactically and also functionally, we can distinguish between polar and constituent interrogatives (yes/no and open questions). Non-standard varieties of English offer alternative pairings of form and function, namely declarative word order in main clauses for asking questions and interrogative word order in embedded questions, for which we find declarative word order in the standard varieties. In addition, non-standard varieties feature special interrogative words, particles, and tags. Our cross-linguistic comparison showed that the use of special word order patterns is not among the prominent marking strategies of interrogatives, particles being vastly more common. Interrogative words may be fronted or remain *in situ*, with the latter option being encountered in some non-standard varieties. Some non-standard interrogative words are semantically transparent and partially related to indefinite expressions.

Keywords: answer bias, conducive questions, constituent interrogatives, direct speech, direct speech act, embedded clause, embedded inversion, fronting of interrogative words, illocutionary force, indirect speech act, *in situ* interrogative words, interrogative particles, interrogative tags, interrogative words, interrogatives, intonation, main clause, open questions, polar interrogatives, questions, reported speech, sentence type, speech act, subject-auxiliary inversion, yes/no questions.

12.5   Exercises

Basic level

1. Summarise the basic sentential patterns of English and their associated illocutionary force potential.
2. Explain and illustrate the phenomenon of 'inversion in embedded clauses'. Do not forget to define 'embedded clause'.
3. Define the notion of 'interrogative particles'.

Intermediate level

1. Below you can find some authentic examples of non-standard English that show the invariable tag *innit* (taken from www.bbc.co.uk/voices).

   a. *'We need to decide what to do about that now innit.'*
   b. *'I can see where my REAL friends are, elsewhere innit!!'*
   c. *'I'll show young Miss Hanna round to all the shops, innit.'*

   a. Translate these sentences into standard English.
   b. Which changes do you have to make? Try to describe them as accurately as possible.
2. In non-standard varieties of English, the interrogative word *when* is frequently substituted by *what time*, as shown in the hypothetical example below:

   a. *When would you like to come? (standard)*
   b. *What time you want come? (non-standard)*

   a. Describe the relationship between the interrogative words in a. and b.
   b. Think of reasons why speakers may choose to say *what time* instead of *when*.

Table 12.11 *Inverted and uninverted main clause constituent interrogatives in the* ICE *(adapted from Davydova et al. 2011: 309).*

Type	Indian English	Singapore English	Jamaican English	East African English
inverted	552	1050	732	767
uninverted	78	91	201	46
other	26	392	46	49
Total	656	1533	979	862

3. The cross-varietal comparison of inverted and uninverted main clause constituent interrogatives reported in Davydova et al. (2011: 309) reveals the absolute numbers as shown in Table 12.11 above. Calculate the relative frequencies and display them as percentages.

Advanced level

1. An important problem in the analysis of embedded inversion is the overt identity of such examples with cases of direct speech.

   a. *I wonder what we should do. (embedding, no inversion)*
   b. *I wonder what should we do. (embedded inversion)*
   c. *I wonder 'What should we do?' (direct speech)*

   a. Develop a set of criteria that allows you to differentiate between embedded inversion and direct speech. You should consider such criteria as 'sequence of tense', 'changes of pronominal forms', and the 'embedding verb', among others.
   b. You may consult Henry (1995: 106–7) for inspiration.

2. Davydova et al. (2011), based on a cross-varietal comparison, conclude that embedded inversion in Irish English is different from that found in other contact vernaculars, in spite of the fact that Irish English superficially shows phenomena that look intriguingly similar.

   a. Read the article by Davydova et al. (2011).
   b. Which reasons do these authors advance in support of their conclusion?

3. It has been hypothesised that Indian English has the two non-standard grammatical properties listed below (Mesthrie and Bhatt 2008: 98):

   i. Indian English has no inversion in main clause interrogatives.
   ii. Indian English has inversion in embedded interrogatives.

    a. Test these hypotheses using the *ICE* (http://ice-corpora.net/ice/), Indian Component (*ICE*-India). What do the data tell us?

    b. Should we classify non-standard inversion in Indian English as a categorical or a statistical phenomenon?

12.6   References

Austin, John L. 1962. *How to Do Things with Words*. Oxford: Clarendon.

Davydova, Julia, Michaela Hilbert, Lukas Pietsch, and Peter Siemund. 2011. Comparing varieties of English: Problems and perspectives. In Peter Siemund (ed.), *Linguistic Universals and Language Variation*, 291–323. Berlin: Mouton de Gruyter.

Dryer, Matthew S. 2011a. Polar questions. In Matthew S. Dryer and Martin Haspelmath (eds.), *The World Atlas of Language Structures Online*. Munich: Max Planck Digital Library, chapter 116A. Available online at http://wals.info/chapter/112A. Accessed 22 December 2011.

Dryer, Matthew S. 2011b. Position of interrogative phrases in content questions. In Matthew S. Dryer and Martin Haspelmath (eds.), *The World Atlas of Language Structures Online*. Munich: Max Planck Digital Library, chapter 93A. Available online at http://wals.info/chapter/93A. Accessed 22 December 2011.

Filppula, Markku. 1999. *A Grammar of Irish English: Language in Hibernian Style*. London: Routledge.

Haas, Mary R. 1940. *Tunica*. New York: Augustin.

Hagège, Claude. 2008. Towards a typology of interrogative verbs. *Linguistic Typology* 12(1). 1–44.

Haspelmath, Martin. 1997. *Indefinite Pronouns*. Oxford University Press.

Henry, Alison. 1995. *Belfast English and Standard English: Dialect Variation and Parameter Setting* (Oxford Studies in Comparative Syntax). Oxford University Press.

Hinds, John. 1984. Japanese. In William S. Chisholm, Louis T. Milic, and John A.C. Greppin (eds.), *Interrogativity: A Colloquium on the Grammar, Typology and Pragmatics of Questions in Seven Diverse Languages*, 145–88. Amsterdam: John Benjamins.

König, Ekkehard and Peter Siemund. 2007. Speech act distinctions in grammar. In Timothy Shopen (ed.), *Language Typology and Syntactic Description, volume I: Clause Structue*, 276–324. Cambridge University Press.

    2012. Satztyp und Typologie. In Jörg Meibauer, Markus Steinbach, and Hans Altmann (eds.), *Satztypen des Deutschen*. Berlin: Mouton de Gruyter.

Levinson, Stephen C. 1983. *Pragmatics*. Cambridge University Press.

Li, Charles N. and Sandra A. Thompson. 1984. Mandarin. In William S. Chisholm, Louis T. Milic, and John A.C. Greppin (eds.), *Interrogativity: A Colloquium on the Grammar, Typology and Pragmatics of Questions in Seven Diverse Languages*, 47–62. Amsterdam: John Benjamins.

Mackenzie, J. Lachlan. 2009. Content interrogatives in a sample of 50 languages. *Lingua* 119(8). 1131–63.

Mesthrie, Rajend and Rakesh M. Bhatt. 2008. *World Englishes: The Study of New Linguistic Varieties*. Cambridge University Press.

Noonan, Michael. 1992. *A Grammar of Lango*. Berlin: Mouton de Gruyter.

Searle, John. 1969. *Speech Acts*. Cambridge University Press.

Siemund, Peter. 2001. Interrogative constructions. In Martin Haspelmath, Ekkehard König, Wulf Oesterreicher, and Wolfgang Raible (eds.), *Language Typology and Language Universals: An International Handbook, volume II*, 1010–27. Berlin: Walter de Gruyter.

Trudgill, Peter and Jean Hannah. 2008. *International English: A Guide to the Varieties of Standard English*. London: Hodder Education.

See *General references* for Alo and Mesthrie 2004; Baskaran 2004; Beal 2004; Bhatt 2004; Crowley 2004; Faraclas 2004; Filppula 2004; Huddleston and Pullum 2002; James and Youssef 2004; Kortmann et al. 2004; Mahboob 2004; Malcolm 2004; Mbangwana 2004; Mesthrie 2004a; Mesthrie 2004b; Miller 2004; Mufwene 2004; Mugler and Tent 2004; Murray and Simon 2004; Penhallurick 2004; Quirk et al. 1985; Sakoda and Siegel 2004; Wee 2004; Winford and Migge 2004; Wolfram 2004b.

12.7   Further reading

Croft, William. 1994. Speech act classification, language typology and cognition. In Savas L. Tsohatzidis (ed.), *Foundations of Speech Act Theory: Philosophical and Linguistic Perspectives*, 460–77. London: Routledge.

Filppula, Markku. 2000. Inversion in embedded questions in some regional varieties of English. In Ricardo Bermúdez-Otero, David Denison, Richard M. Hogg, and Chris B. McCully (eds.), *Generative Theory and Corpus Studies: A Dialogue from 10 ICEHL*, 439–53. Berlin: Mouton de Gruyter.

Hilbert, Michaela. 2008. Interrogative inversion in non-standard varieties of English. In Peter Siemund and Noemi Kintana (eds.), *Language Contact and Contact Languages*, 261–92. Amsterdam: John Benjamins.

2011. Interrogative inversion as a learner phenomenon in English contact varieties: A case of Angloversals? In Joybrato Mukherjee and Marianne Hundt (eds.), *Exploring Second-Language Varieties of English and Learner Englishes: Bridging a Paradigm Gap*, 126–44. Amsterdam: John Benjamins.

Huddleston, Rodney. 1994. The contrast between interrogatives and questions. *Journal of Linguistics* 30. 411–439.

Sadock, Jerrold M. and Arnold M. Zwicky. 1985. Speech act distinctions in syntax. In Timothy Shopen (ed.), *Language Typology and Syntactic Description, volume I: Clause Structure*, 155–96. Cambridge University Press.

Sand, Andrea and Daniela Kolbe. 2010. Embedded inversion worldwide. *Linguaculture* 2(1). 25–42.

13 The formation of relative clauses

The term 'relativisation' as a grammatical term refers to the modification of a noun phrase through a finite clause (*the book that I read*). Such modifying clauses are known as 'relative clauses' and typically occur after the noun they modify. The formation of relative clauses is a fascinating topic even in standard English, though various additional dimensions come into play once we extend the discussion to non-standard varieties. Moreover, relative clauses have been profoundly investigated from a cross-linguistic perspective, and principles of rather surprising generality have been proposed for this domain of grammar that inform the discussion of English and its varieties in interesting ways.

13.1 Overview

13.1.1 Some basic definitions

As stated above, relative clauses belong to the area of nominal modification. However, this categorisation does not do justice to the complex properties of these constructions, as there are non-trivial syntactic relations between the relative clause and the noun thus modified. Generally speaking, the modified noun, in addition to being modified, also plays a syntactic role in the relative clause. Let us consider a few examples, starting with the ditransitive sentence in (1).

(1) The postman gave the letter to the child.

This sentence can serve as the basis for the formation of a number of relative clauses, as shown in (2), and in each case we turn one of the basic constituents of the sentence into the head noun of the resulting relative clause. In (2a) it is the subject and in (2b) the indirect (prepositional) object. It is the direct object in (2c). As a consequence, the syntactic position thus relativised on (see below) remains empty in the original sentence, which we mark by the underscores in the examples. In other words, the noun phrase modified by the relative clause – in addition to serving as the head noun of the relative clause – also fulfils a syntactic function within the relative clause.

(2) a. The postman who ___ gave the letter to the child.
   b. The child to whom the postman gave the letter ___
   c. The letter that the postman gave ___ to the child.

If we embed the relative clause into a larger sentential frame, the head noun of the relative clause may serve two different syntactic functions at the same time. In (3), for example, the noun phrase *the postman* is the object of the main clause and the subject of the relative clause.

(3) John met the postman who had given the letter to the child.

Let us be clear about the terminology used: the noun phrase modified by the relative clause is called the 'head noun' of the construction. The syntactic position that this noun phrase occupies in the underlying non-relative clause is known as the 'position relativised on'. The linking element between head noun and relative clause is usually called the 'relative pronoun'. It has the more general function of a subordinator. In introducing these notions, we are positing a syntactic relation between a relative clause and the source sentence it is derived from.

You will probably be familiar with two distinct functions of relative clauses, namely 'defining' in contrast with 'non-defining' relative clauses. Examples of each relative clause type are shown in (4). A simple diagnostic test to distinguish between the two is whether they can be omitted or not. Non-defining relative clauses can be omitted.[1]

(4) a. The man who I met yesterday turned out to be my cousin. (defining)
   b. This man, who turned out to be my cousin, I met yesterday. (non-defining)

13.1.2   Strategies of relativisation

Relative clauses can be formed in different ways, and we will investigate the full cross-linguistic spectrum in Section 13.3. In English, we can distinguish essentially three strategies to form relative clauses. These are (i) relative pronouns, (ii) the subordinator *that*, and (iii) gapping (contact clauses). We will introduce them briefly in the following.

Relative pronouns We can analyse relative pronouns as elements that introduce relative clauses, thus linking the relative clause to the head noun. These relative pronouns agree with their respective head nouns in terms of certain features. There is a basic semantic contrast between persons and things encoded by *who* and *which*, as in (5).

(5) a. the man who came in from the cold
   b. the arguments which are most important

---

[1] Huddleston and Pullum (2002: 1034–5) prefer the terms 'integrated' and 'supplementary' relative clauses.

This semantic contrast is neutralised in the case of the possessive relative pronoun *whose* (Huddleston and Pullum 2002: 1049). In relative clauses such as (6), it is the modifier position of the genitive construction that is relativised on.

(6) a. She started a home for women whose husbands were in prison.

    b. The report contains statements whose factual truth is doubtful.

Additional relative pronouns include *where*, *when*, *why*, and marginally *while* and *whence* (Huddleston and Pullum 2002: 1050–1). They encode place, time, reason, duration, and source. Examples can be found in (7).

(7) a. She wanted to see the house where she had grown up.

    b. It happened at a time when I was alone.

    c. That's the main reason why they won't help us.

Relative marker that The second strategy of relative clause formation in English is based on the subordinating element *that*. Huddleston and Pullum (2002: 1056), correctly to my mind, insist that this is not just a variant of the relative pronoun strategy, since the subordinator *that* in relative clauses has the same function as in other subordinate clauses, namely to introduce such a subordinate clause. This parallel is illustrated in (8).

(8) a. She said that she could not come.

    b. I heard of the girl that could not come.

Subordinating *that* used as a relative clause marker occurs with a wide range of antecedents, unlike the relative pronouns discussed above, which occur with specific head nouns. The examples in (9) demonstrate this.

(9) a. the girl that spoke first

    b. the book that she was reading

    c. the day that she arrived

    d. the town that she went to

    e. the reason that she resigned

    f. the way that she controlled the crowd

Moreover, subordinating *that* cannot replace *whose* in the standard varieties (10a), even though examples such as (10b) are attested in non-standard varieties, as we will see in Section 13.2.

(10) a. the boy whose bicycle was stolen

    b. *the boy that's bicycle was stolen

Gapping In the third strategy of relative clause formation, the head noun and the ensuing relative clause are juxtaposed without an intervening relativising element. This strategy is known as 'gapping' or the 'gap strategy'. The relative clause in this construction may also be referred to as a 'contact clause', as it is in immediate contact with the head noun. As the examples in (11) show, this strategy can be found with a wide array of head nouns, except for those cases where the subject has been relativised on (11a).

(11) I remember...

    a. *the girl spoke first
    b. the book she was reading
    c. the day she arrived
    d. the town she went to
    e. the reason she resigned
    f. the way she controlled the crowd

The condition on subject relatives, as in (11a), is fairly robust, but even standard grammatical descriptions such as Huddleston and Pullum (2002: 1055) mention that exceptions can be found in vernacular speech, listing the examples in (12). We will investigate these cases in more detail in Section 13.2.2.

(12) a. It was my father did most of the talking.

    b. There is someone at the door wants to talk to you.

13.1.3   The syntactic function of the modified noun phrase

At the end of this brief introduction to relative clauses let us take a look at the syntactic function that the head noun plays in the relative clause (or the underlying non-relative clause). Put differently, the question is which noun phrases in a clause can be relativised on.

On the face of it, there seem to be few restrictions on the functional properties of such noun phrases. The examples in (13) show that noun phrases in subject position, object position, and indirect-object position can be relativised on (13a–c). Moreover, English allows us to relativise on obliques (13d), the modifier of a genitive construction (13e), and the object of a comparative construction (13f). As for relativisation, English turns out to be a fairly flexible language.

(13) a. This is the girl who ___ wrote the book. (subject)

    b. This is the girl who the painter portrayed ___. (object)
    c. This is the girl on whom they bestowed a fortune ___. (indirect object)
    d. This is the girl who John would like to dance with ___. (oblique)
    e. This is the girl whose father ___ died. (genitive)
    f. This is the girl who Mary is taller than ___. (object of comparative)

In our subsequent cross-linguistic survey in Section 13.3, we will learn that languages may exhibit rather tight restrictions in this domain. We have already encountered one such restriction in the context of the examples in (11), as standard English disallows the relativisation on subject noun phrases in the context of the gapping strategy (though not the other strategies).

13.2   Varieties of English

Relative clause formation in non-standard varieties of English differs from that found in the standard varieties with respect to mainly three parameters. Firstly, we find a greater range of relative markers, and that the standard relative markers occur in additional functions. Secondly, the strategy of gapping, i.e. connecting the relative clause to its head noun without an intervening relative marker, is more common and may be applied to subject constituents (*There's a man came to me and said...*). Thirdly, non-standard varieties of English illustrate the curious phenomenon of resumptive pronouns. These are pronominal copies of the head noun that appear in the position relativised on (*the boy I saw him; the place I went to there*).

We need to bear in mind that relative clauses are a means of noun modification that may be taken over by alternative expressive means. In the relevant literature, we encounter remarks suggesting that noun modification by subordination is typically replaced by coordinative structures in spoken vernaculars. This is certainly not unexpected. Some examples are shown in (14).

(14) a. The boy I was talking to last night – and he actually works in the yard – was saying it's going to be closed down. [Scottish English, Miller 2008: 315–16]

   b. ... and there were a man in there and he were a dowser. [Southwest of England, Wagner 2004: 165]

   c. I put a litee from Renishaw, I don't even know him, in the goals. 'I put a youngster, whom I don't even know, as goalkeeper.' [Indian South African English, Mesthrie 2004b: 982]

13.2.1   Relative markers (subordinators, relative pronouns)

Across varieties of English, relative clauses are typically introduced by a relative marker. There seems to be a strong preference for using *that* in many varieties. For example, *that* is the most frequent relative marker in northern English dialects and the English of Northern Ireland (Tagliamonte et al. 2005: 87).

Moreover, there is considerable variation with respect to the relative marker employed, as we find many forms that appear in none of the standard varieties. Table 13.1 presents a non-exhaustive selection of attested relative markers in non-standard varieties of English.

The relative markers *what, at, as*, and possessively used *that* are indicative of traditional dialects, even though they also seem to surface in some Pidgin and Creole Englishes. We can interpret the form *at* as a reduced variant of *that*. Here are some representative examples:

Table 13.1 *Non-standard relative markers based on a survey of Kortmann et al. (2004).*

Relative marker	Variety
a	Jamaican Creole
as	British dialects, Appalachian English, etc.
at	Orkney and Shetland, North of England, Appalachian English, etc.
di, pe, suma, san	Surinamese Creoles
one	Singapore English
possessive that	Scottish English, Appalachian English, etc.
weh, we, wε	Gullah, Jamaican Creole, Creoles of Trinidad and Tobago, Australian Creoles, Solomon Islands Pijin, Tok Pisin, Nigerian Pidgin English, Ghanaian Pidgin English, Cameroon Pidgin English, etc.
what	British dialects, Scottish English, Colloquial American English, Appalachian English, Newfoundland English, Bahamian English, Aboriginal English, Indian South African English, etc.
which one	Indian South African English

(15) a. He's the one what done it. [East Anglia, Trudgill 2004: 148]

    b. But the kind of boodle what I'm earning is grand, man. [Indian South African English, Mesthrie 2004b: 981]

(16) a. I know a man at will do it for you. [North of England, Beal 2004: 131]

    b. Tom Sparks has herded more than any man as I've ever heard of. [Appalachian English, Montgomery 2004: 266]

(17) a. The girl that her eighteenth birthday was on that day was stoned. [Scottish English, Miller 2004: 62]

    b. We need to remember a woman thats child has died. [Appalachian English, Montgomery 2004: 266]

The relative markers *weh*, *we*, and *wε*, which are probably related to *what* and/or *where*, can mainly be found in English Pidgin and Creole varieties. There, these forms typically occur with a broad range of antecedents.

(18) a. A di   tok fo   Lum weh I di   silip fo   trenja rum.
      I PROG talk PREP Lum REL he PROG sleep PREP guest room
      'I am talking to Lum who sleeps in the guest room.' [Kamtok, Ayafor 2004: 916]

    b. da gyal weh Clinton duh   look at
      the girl REL Clinton PROG look at
      'the girl Clinton is looking at' [Gullah, Mufwene 2004: 364]

Sentence (19) shows an example featuring the relative marker *a* of Jamaican Creole, apparently derived from *that*.

(19) Yu miin him a   wena   mek naiz mam?
     you mean him REL PAST.PROG make noise ma'am
     'Do you mean the one who was making noise, ma'am?' [Jamaican Creole,
     Patrick 2004: 426]

The examples in (20) through (22) illustrate the usage of the relative markers
in Surinamese Creoles. The form *di* is related to *this*, while *pe* is derived from
place. *Di* can occur with human and non-human head nouns. The relative
marker *san* (< *thing*) in (22) is an interrogative word that we have already
encountered, in Chapter 12.

(20) Luku a   uman di e   weli a   buuku.
     look DET.SG woman REL IMPFV wear DET.SG trouser
     'Look the woman who is wearing trousers.' [Surinamese Creoles, Winford
     and Migge 2004: 501]

(21) Na a   konde pe   a   e   tan.
     FOC DET country where she IMPFV stay
     'It's the village where she lives.' [Surinamese Creoles, Winford and Migge
     2004: 501]

(22) Den ben bigin ferteri yu wan sani san yu musu ben   sabi.
     they PAST begin tell   you one thing REL you must PAST know
     'They started to tell you things that you had to know.' [Surinamese Creoles,
     Winford and Migge 2004: 501–2]

I am aware of two varieties of English that employ the pronominal form *one* as
a relative marker. On the one hand, this is Indian South African English, as in
(23), where it occurs in combination with *which*, yielding *which one*.

(23) That's the maid which one was here . . . 'That's the maid who was here . . . '
     [Indian South African English, Mesthrie 2004b: 981]

On the other hand, *one* as relative marker has been reported from Singapore
English, especially Colloquial Singapore English. In this variety, it occurs at
the right periphery of the relative clause so that the relative clause is enclosed
by the head noun and the relative marker. Alsagoff and Ho (1998) argue
that these relative clauses are modelled on Chinese. Examples can be found
in (24).[2]

(24) a. When you see the church got stained glass one, you turn right.
     b. That man wear red shirt one Keng's cousin from Ipoh. You ever met
        him?
     c. The cake John always buy one very nice.
     d. I prefer the pen can put refill one.
        [Singapore English, Alsagoff and Ho 1998: 128]

---

[2] Wee and Ansaldo (2004: 66–73) cast some doubt on the analysis of *one* as a relative marker and,
following Gil (2003: 480), see it more generally as a nominaliser.

Singapore English may also enclose the relative clause by two relative markers, as in (25). A similar kind of bracketing of the relative clause is also known from Tok Pisin, even though the relative markers are difficult to compare. The Tok Pisin relative marker *ia* is apparently derived from *here*. This is shown in example (26).

(25) The man who do camera one not yet come. Can come back later?
     [Singapore English, Alsagoff and Ho 1998: 128]

(26) stereo ia   mitla putim lo kou ia   em no   lukim
     stereo REL we   put in coat REL he NEG see
     'The stereo which we put in the coat he didn't see.' [Tok Pisin, Smith
     2004: 736]

Even though the relative markers discussed in the foregoing paragraphs are indicative of certain varieties, as suggested by the correlations expressed in Table 13.1, it would be a gross oversimplification to believe that they represent the exclusive or even dominant markers in these varieties. The variety-specific relative markers typically compete with the standard markers, i.e. the *wh*-forms *who*, *which*, *whose*, etc., as well as the subordinator *that*.

The distribution of all relative markers is subject to a complicated interaction of several internal and external constraints. Tagliamonte et al. (2005), based on a large sample of northern British dialects, explore the interaction of relative markers with sentence structure (existential, possessive, cleft, etc.) and the type of antecedent (indefinite, definite, full noun phrase, pronoun), as well as the complexity and length of the relative clause. *Wh*-relative markers are nearly absent in these dialects, while the use of *that* is very common. The relative marker *that* also turned out to be the most common and, in this sense, unmarked form in D'Arcy and Tagliamonte's (2010) sociolinguistic study of Toronto English, whereas the *wh*-forms signal prestige, high style, and higher levels of education. These findings nicely mirror the historical development of relative markers and relative clause formation in English, as the *wh*-forms only gained momentum during the standardisation processes of Early Modern English.

13.2.2   Subject gapping

The juxtaposition of head noun and relative clause without intervening relative marker is here treated as a separate strategy of relative clause formation, as this facilitates cross-linguistic comparisons. In principle, we could alternatively postulate a zero relative marker, which would then allow the comparison of the zero marker with the other relative markers.

As pointed out in Section 13.1.2 above, the standard varieties do not permit the gap strategy for forming relative clauses on subjects (**the girl spoke first*). Subject gapping, however, is widespread in non-standard varieties, as the examples in (27) make clear.

(27) a. You know anybody ∅ wants some, he'll sell them. [Southwest of England, Wagner 2004: 166]

    b. They is people ∅ gets lost in these Smoky Mountains. [Appalachian English, Montgomery 2004: 278]

    c. There's no one ∅ pays any attention to that. [Newfoundland English, Clarke 2004: 315]

    d. It's a man ∅ come over here talking trash. [Urban African American Vernacular English, Wolfram 2004b: 334]

    e. I knew a girl ∅ worked in an office down the street there. [Australian Vernacular English, Pawley 2004: 637]

    f. I don't know anybody ∅ study as much as you. [Hawai'i Creole, Sakoda and Siegel 2004: 759]

    g. We talking about my friend ∅ lives down there. 'We're talking about my friend who lives down there.' [Indian South African English, Mesthrie 2004b: 981]

Subject gapping as in (27) does not seem to be completely unconstrained, as it can be typically found in presentational constructions that introduce new referents into the discourse. Tagliamonte et al. (2005: 96) find the gap strategy especially in existential constructions (28a), cleft sentences (28b), and possessive constructions (28c). These findings are not restricted to subject gapping, though.

(28) a. There's no many folk ∅ liked going to the pit to work.

    b. It was an earthen floor ∅ was in that house.

    c. I have a woman ∅ comes in on a Thursday morning.
    [Tagliamonte et al. 2005: 96]

13.2.3   Resumptive pronouns (pronoun retention)

Resumptive pronouns can be defined as pronominal copies of the head noun of a relative clause that occur in the position of the constituent relativised on. Thus, they fill the syntactic slot emptied by the process of relative clause formation. Resumptive pronouns can be found in many varieties of English across the globe and do not seem to be restricted to a specific variety type. In most cases they refer to the third person singular or plural, as illustrated in (29), though there are also adverbial resumptive pronouns, as we will see below.

(29) a. They jumped banks that time on the race-course that they wouldn't hunt over *them* today. [Irish English, Filppula 2004: 85]

    b. They're the ones that the teacher thinks *they*'re going to misbehave. [Scottish English, Miller 2004: 63]

    c. You know the software that I left *it* . . . the box that I left *it* on your desk. [Fiji English, Mugler and Tent 2004: 785]

    d. The guests whom I invited *them* have arrived. [Nigerian English, Alo and Mesthrie 2004: 818]

  e. Students discovered that the kind of education that these people are
     trying to give *it* to us . . . [Black South African English, Mesthrie 2004a:
     967]

Resumptive pronouns can be found in all major syntactic functions. The examples in (30) and (31) show them in subject position and direct object position
respectively.

(30) Well, it's what they fed, you used to put it [i.e. treacle, T.H.] on hay [that
     it was mouldy], you know, bad hay, and just sprinkle it on to give a better
     taste for t' cow to eat, you see. [North of England, Herrmann 2003: 149]

(31) And I have lots of letters which I discovered about five years ago, which I
     thought were probably letters [that my father had written *it*] . . . [Scotland,
     Herrmann 2003: 149]

The examples in (32) and (33) illustrate resumptive pronouns in prepositional
complement position and in the modifier position of a possessive (genitive)
construction. The latter case is slightly doubtful, as we could analyse *which its*
as a complex relative marker.

(32) . . . it was, you know, looked upon then you were, were public transport
     and the public team [that you belonged to *them*]. [East Anglia, Herrmann
     2003: 149]

(33) But (trunc) y you'd got to watch, there again, that er you didn't exceed
     the width of er of your waggon, [which *its* maximum limit was er would
     be er eight foot three, or er eleven foot six, high]. [English Midlands,
     Herrmann 2003: 149]

Resumptive pronouns may also copy head nouns with adverbial functions. Two
examples are provided in (34).

(34) a. they had the stallions down there then you see, they had stallions at
        the stud. <S: 0208> [[at] Which we were *there* often]. [East Anglia,
        Herrmann 2003: 149]

     b. The area where we find the capital *there* today is Yaounde. [Cameroon
        English, Mbangwana 2004: 906]

In the British dialect data investigated by Herrmann (2003), resumptive pronouns are quite infrequent. There are only twenty-one occurrences in her data
(Herrmann 2003: 150). Gisborne (2000: 364–5) discusses them in the context
of Hong Kong English, but it is unclear how firmly they are integrated into the
grammatical system. Mesthrie and Dunne (1990: 40) report them from South
African Indian English, though they describe the phenomenon as a 'discourse-
governed strategy that has not stabilized'.

13.3   Cross-linguistic comparison

Relative clauses have been extensively explored cross-linguistically, and three
main parameters have been identified that can be used to categorise the
observable spectrum of variation. These concern the order of relative clause

and head noun, the strategy of relative clause formation (with mainly four strategies being attested worldwide), and the syntactic function of the noun phrase relativised on. Especially the last point has given rise to rather interesting theoretical debates in relation to the so-called 'accessibility hierarchy'. We will investigate these points in what follows, trying to assess the position of English non-standard phenomena in the cross-linguistic matrix of variation.

13.3.1   Order of relative clause and head noun

Even though the order of relative clause and head noun is of no particular importance for English, as nearly all varieties of English – standard and non-standard – place the relative clause after the head noun, it appears worth mentioning that the reverse order is also relatively common cross-linguistically. Dryer (2011), relying on a sample of 825 languages, identifies 580 with an order of 'noun–relative clause', contrasting with 141 languages that have 'relative clause–noun' order. The two numbers do not add up to the entire sample size, as there are relative clauses to which this parameter does not apply.

English varieties follow the majority pattern, with the exception of South African Indian English, where the reverse order is attested. The examples in (35) show prenominal relative clauses apparently modelled on similar constructions in Dravidian languages.

(35) a. That's all [we had] trouble. 'That's all the trouble we had.'

   b. People who got [working-here-for-them] sons, like, for them nice they can stay. 'It is nice for people who have sons [who are] working for the company, since they are allowed to stay on in the barracks.'
   [South African Indian English, Mesthrie and Dunne 1990: 37]

Similar examples can be found in (36). According to Mesthrie and Dunne (1990: 38), these are based on the participial strategy of relative clause formation found in Indic languages.

(36) a. That Neela's-knitted jersey is gone white. 'That jersey which Neela knitted / knitted by Neela has gone white.'

   b. You can't beat Vijay's-planted tomato. 'You won't find better tomatoes than those which Vijay planted / which were planted by Vijay.'
   [South African Indian English, Mesthrie and Dunne 1990: 38]

13.3.2   Strategies of relative clause formation

The cross-linguistically attested spectrum of strategies for the formation of relative clauses is fairly limited and essentially amounts to four dominant

strategies plus a few minor ones that can be subsumed under the dominant strategies. They are listed below (Comrie and Kuteva 2011a):
– Relative Pronoun Strategy
– Non-Reduction Strategy
– Pronoun-Retention Strategy
– Gap Strategy
We are already familiar with the relative pronoun strategy, as it is common in standard English (see Section 13.1.2). This strategy places the noun phrase relativised on to the periphery of the relative clause – in English to the left of the relative clause – and connects head noun and relative clause with a relative pronoun. The relative clause is constructed as an embedded or subordinate clause. By and large, this strategy appears to be restricted to Europe. An example from German is shown in (37).

(37) Das Kind das da   spielt heißt   Paul.
      the child who there plays is named Paul
      'The child who is playing there is called Paul.' [German, personal knowl-
      edge]

The relative pronoun strategy is also very common in non-standard varieties of English, as we saw in Section 13.2.1. There is substantial variation in terms of the relative marker used, and in a few cases the relative marker appears at the end of the relative clause or encloses it.

Another strategy of relative clause formation consists in the combination of two main clauses (non-reduction strategy). The relative clause need not receive special marking, and its interpretation as a relative clause, i.e. modifying a noun, may become a matter of context. Example (38) shows a case from Pirahã, an Amazonian language spoken in Brazil.

(38) boitóhoi bogái-hiabis-aoaxái boitó báosa xigisai (hix)
      boat   come-NEG-Q   boat barge bring (Q)
      'Is the boat which tows barges not coming?' (lit.: Is the boat not coming,
      the boat tows barges?) [Pirahã, adapted from Everett 1986: 276]

For the non-reduction strategy, the typological literature distinguishes between 'correlative clauses', 'internally headed relative clauses', and 'paratactic relative clauses'. They are formed on the basis of parataxis (the conjoining of main clauses), rather than hypotaxis (the conjoining of main clause and subordinate clause). There are cases reported from South African Indian English that by and large correspond to what the typological literature refers to as 'correlative clauses', as shown in (39). The syntactic pattern appears like a direct import from Indic languages.[3]

---

[3] Mesthrie and Dunne (1990: 37) describe the properties of these correlative clauses as follows: 1. The relative clause is prenominal and is introduced by a *wh*-pronoun. 2. The main clause contains an anaphoric pronoun taking up the *wh*-pronoun. 3. The full noun phrase occurs in the relative clause or in both main and subordinate clause.

(39) a. But now, which-one principal came here, she's just cheeky like the other one. 'The principal who arrived recently is just as stern as the previous one.'

    b. But then, who wanted to stay, they didn't force them. 'They didn't force those who wanted to stay to leave.'

    c. Which-one I put in the jar, that-one is good. 'The ones [i.e., pickles] I put in the jar are the best.'

    [South African Indian English, Mesthrie and Dunne 1990: 37]

Comrie and Kuteva (2011a) illustrate paratactic relative clauses using the English example in (40), which can be interpreted as a relative clause, even though it lacks the requisite syntactic structure.

(40) That man just passed by us, he introduced me to the Chancellor of the University yesterday.

The third strategy of relative clause formation that can be distinguished cross-linguistically is referred to as 'pronoun retention', as the head noun of the relative clause is linked to a pronominal copy at the position relativised on. In other words, the syntactic position emptied through the formation of the relative clause is filled and thus explicitly marked by a pronoun. The resumptive pronouns that we encountered in various varieties of English qualify as cases of pronoun retention, even though they are usually not categorical and occur together with relative pronouns. Example (41) provides an illustration from Persian. The other example, in (42), is taken from Babungo, a Niger-Congo language spoken in Cameroon.

(41) mardhâi [ke ketâbhâ-râ be ânhâ dâde bud-id]
    men   that books-ACC to them given were-2SG
    'the men that you had given the books to' (lit. 'the men that you had given the books to them') [Persian, Comrie 1998: 63, cited in Comrie and Kuteva 2011b]

(42) mɔ́ yè   wɔ́   ntíə fáŋ ŋwɔ́ sí   sàŋ   ghɔ̂
    I   see.PFV person that who he   PST2 beat.PFV you
    'I have seen the man who has beaten you.' [Babungo, Schaub 1985: 34, cited in Comrie and Kuteva 2011a]

The fourth strategy of relative clause formation is known as 'gapping'. We have already encountered it in our introductory discussion of English relative clauses in Section 13.1.2. Its main diagnostic is that the relationship between the head noun and the relative clause receives no special marking, as the two are simply juxtaposed. The sentences in (43) and (44) show examples from Turkish and Korean. The gap strategy is difficult to distinguish from other types of noun modification in many languages.

(43) [kitab-ı   al-an]   öğrenci
    book-ACC buy-PTCP student
    'the student who bought the book' [Turkish, Comrie 1998: 82, cited in Comrie and Kuteva 2011a]

Table 13.2 *Strategies of relative clause formation (Comrie and Kuteva 2011a, b).*

	Relative pronoun	Non-reduction	Pronoun-retention	Gap	Total
Subject	12	24	5	125	166
Oblique	13	14	20	55	112

(44) [Hyənsik-i   kɨ kä-lɨl   ttäli-n]   maktäki
Hyensik-NOM the dog-ACC beat-REL stick
'the stick with which Hyensik beat the dog' [Korean, Comrie 1989: 151, cited in Comrie and Kuteva 2011b]

Relativisation on subject positions is different from that on obliques, with subject and oblique positions showing different preferences with regard to the strategies for relative clause formation introduced above. The term 'oblique' refers to syntactic functions other than direct or indirect objects, i.e. mainly adverbial functions. Sentence (45) shows an example from Russian in which a noun encoding an instrument is relativised on.

(45) Ja poterjal nož,   kotorym   ja narezal xleb.
I lose.PST knife.ACC which.INSTR I cut.PST bread
'I lost the knife with which I cut the bread.' [Russian, Comrie and Kuteva 2011b]

As one can see in Table 13.2 above, the gap strategy is more common on subject positions than on that of obliques. By contrast, pronoun retention is more frequent with obliques. Notice that obliques do not add up to 112 in Table 13.2, as they cannot be relativised on in 10 languages. Generally speaking, obliques are less prone to relativisation than subjects.

Standard English partially contradicts the general trend expressed in Table 13.2, as it disallows the gap strategy on subject positions. Section 13.2.2 showed that non-standard varieties are less restricted in this respect. They often permit subject gapping, albeit in particular contexts, and thus more closely follow cross-linguistic trends.

13.3.3   The accessibility hierarchy

In the typological literature it has been argued that relative clause formation is constrained by the so-called 'accessibility hierarchy' (Keenan and Comrie 1977). It is shown in (46) below. The idea is that languages differ in the range of syntactic functions available for the formation of relative clauses. The accessibility hierarchy is an implicational hierarchy and possesses the

Table 13.3 *Frequency of relative clause forming strategies (Herrmann 2003: 133).*

Subject	>	Direct object	>	Prep. complement	>	Genitive	>	Other
63.18 %		27.23 %		7.32 %		0.12 %		2.15 %

general properties introduced in Chapter 1. In keeping with these properties, the accessibility hierarchy claims that if a language permits the formation of relative clauses using a specific syntactic function or noun phrase position on this hierarchy, this will also be possible for all functions further to its left.[4]

(46) *Accessibility Hierarchy* [Keenan and Comrie 1977: 66]
    Subject > Direct Object > Indirect Object > Oblique > Genitive > Object of Comparative

As a language may have more than one strategy of relative clause formation, their fit to the accessibility hierarchy should be evaluated separately. For example, the formation of relative clauses using relative pronouns is possible along the entire hierarchy in English. The examples in (13) above illustrate this. Curiously enough, the gap strategy is blocked for subject constituents in English, though it works for the other position on the hierarchy (**the man ∅ attacked John*). Non-standard varieties typically allow the gap strategy on subjects, thus showing a closer fit to the accessibility hierarchy (see Section 13.2.2 above). We need to bear in mind, though, that subject gapping in non-standard varieties is restricted to a few specific constructions.

In view of the accessibility hierarchy, we also expect a correlation between noun phrase position (syntactic function) and frequency of use, such that relative clauses using the higher positions on the hierarchy are more frequent than those using the lower positions. Herrmann (2003: 133) confirms this expectation based on a corpus of British dialect data and a slightly modified version of the accessibility hierarchy. Table 13.3 summarises the results of her study.

In their cross-linguistic study, Keenan and Comrie (1977: 92–3) found that the accessibility hierarchy is practically reversed for pronoun retention, i.e. more languages show pronoun retention in the lower positions of the hierarchy, and fewer in the higher positions. They argue that pronoun retention can be understood as a mechanism that facilitates the relativisation on cognitively difficult noun phrase positions. Consequently, we would also expect frequency

---

[4] As a matter of fact, Keenan and Comrie (1977: 67) postulate the following, more specific hierarchy constraints: '1. A language must be able to relativize subjects. 2. Any RC-forming strategy must apply to a continuous segment of the AH. 3. Strategies that apply at one point of the AH may in principle cease to apply at any lower point.'

Table 13.4 *Resumptive pronouns in simple relative clauses (Herrmann 2003: 150).*

Subject	>	Direct object	>	Prep. complement	>	Genitive	>	Other
8		5		4		1		3

data that are the reverse of those shown in Table 13.3 above. This prediction, however, is not borne out by Herrmann's (2003) dialect data. Table 13.4 shows the same overall trend as Table 13.3.[5]

13.4   Summary and list of keywords

Relative clauses owe much of their complexity to the double function of the relativised noun phrase as head of the relative clause and basic constituent in the corresponding declarative clause, i.e. the clause relativised on. We spent large parts of Section 13.1 describing and motivating this relationship. A view of relative clauses in terms of constructions would be simpler, but substantially less interesting. Varieties of English offer relative clauses with several special properties, especially a wide range of non-standard relative markers, the gap strategy on subject noun phrases, and resumptive pronouns. Some varieties even show prenominal relative clauses and correlative clauses. As many non-standard Englishes are contact varieties influenced by typologically diverse languages, essentially all major strategies of relative clause formation can be encountered, even though correlative clauses, for example, are not very common and are basically restricted to South African Indian English. The strategy of pronoun retention may be recovered in terms of resumptive pronouns in varieties of English. Non-standard varieties of English appear to follow the accessibility hierarchy more closely, as the gap strategy can be used to relativise on subjects there.

Keywords: accessibility hierarchy, bracketing, coordination, correlative clauses, existential constructions, gap strategy, gapping, head noun, hypotaxis, internally headed relative clauses, non-reduction strategy, obliques, parataxis, postnominal relative clauses, prenominal relative clauses, pronoun retention, relative markers, relative pronouns, resumptive pronouns, subordination, subordinator, syntactic function, syntactic position, *wh*-pronouns.

---

[5] We here equate pronoun retention with resumptive pronouns, which most certainly is an over-simplification.

13.5   Exercises

Basic level

1. Which strategies of relative clause formation do we find in standard English?
2. Explain the term 'resumptive pronoun'.
3. Draw up a list of the differences between standard English and non-standard English in the domain of relative clauses.

Intermediate level

1. According to Tagliamonte et al. (2005), the subordinator *that* is the most widely employed relative marker in northern British English. Therefore, we would also expect it to be the most common relative marker in other non-standard varieties of English.

   Test this hypothesis on one or more of the post-colonial Englishes (Singapore English, Hong Kong English, etc.), basing your analysis on the relevant components of the *ICE* (http://ice-corpora.net/ice/).
2. Herrmann (2003: 159–65), following Keenan and Comrie (1977: 92–3), claims that pronoun retention or resumptive pronouns tend to occur in cognitively demanding contexts ('difficult environments'). You can find two examples below taken from Herrmann (2003: 159–60).

   a. *Er things like er <pause> crowbars and bull croppers and er rescue ropes and lines and things of that kind, which are very very simple, stuff [Ø you would buy in a hardware shop and probably be able to manage with it].*
   b. *... you know the decontamination side, the clearing up, the protecting of the environment from toxic chemicals er [which we've all heard about in newspapers, and read reports and seen it on television] ...*

   Write a short essay explaining what these authors mean by 'difficult environments'. Consult the relevant literature.
3. Explain and illustrate the term 'correlative clause'.

Advanced level

1. Standard English employs two strategies of relative clause formation: the use of relative pronouns and the so-called 'gap strategy', as shown below.

   a. *The man who I met disappeared. (relative pronoun)*
   b. *The man I met disappeared. (gapping)*

    a. Investigate the productivity of these strategies in relation to Keenan and Comrie's (1977: 66) accessibility hierarchy:
Subject > Direct Object > Indirect Object > Oblique > Genitive > Object of Comparative
Which observations can we make?

    b. In non-standard varieties, we can find relative clauses of the type shown in the examples below. Which conclusions can you draw from the existence of such examples?

    c. *I have a friend lives over there.*

    d. *We had this French girl came to stay.*

2. We learnt in Section 13.2.2 that non-standard relative clauses frequently exhibit the gap strategy on subject positions. However, this option is restricted to existential constructions, cleft sentences, and possessive constructions.
What could be the reason for this restriction? Try to find an explanation.

3. We would expect that the order of head noun and relative clause correlates with the word order type of a language. One could hypothesise, for example, that VO languages prefer the order noun–relative clause, while OV languages favour the order relative clause–noun.

    a. What is the conceptual basis of these hypotheses?

    b. Test these hypotheses based on the information you can find in the *World Atlas of Language Structures* (http://wals.info).

13.6   References

Alsagoff, Lubna and Chee Lick Ho. 1998. The relative clause in colloquial Singapore English. *World Englishes* 17(2). 127–38.

Comrie, Bernard. 1989. *Language Universals and Linguistic Typology*. Oxford: Blackwell.

    1998. Rethinking the typology of relative clauses. *Language Design* 1. 59–86.

Comrie, Bernard and Tania Kuteva. 2011a. Relativization on subjects. In Matthew S. Dryer and Martin Haspelmath (eds.), *The World Atlas of Language Structures Online*. Munich: Max Planck Digital Library, chapter 122. Available online at http://wals.info/chapter/122. Accessed 22 December 2011.

    2011b. Relativization on obliques. In Matthew S. Dryer and Martin Haspelmath (eds.), *The World Atlas of Language Structures Online*. Munich: Max Planck Digital Library, chapter 123. Available online at http://wals.info/chapter/123. Accessed 22 December 2011.

D'Arcy, Alexandra and Tagliamonte, Sali A. 2010. Prestige, accommodation, and the legacy of relative *who*. *Language in Society* 39(3). 1–28.

Dryer, Matthew S. 2011. Order of relative clause and noun. In Matthew S. Dryer and Martin Haspelmath (eds.), *The World Atlas of Language Structures Online*.

Munich: Max Planck Digital Library, chapter 90. Available online at http://wals. info/chapter/90. Accessed 22 December 2011.

Everett, Daniel L. 1986. Pirahã. In Desmond C. Derbyshire and Geoffrey K. Pullum (eds.), *Handbook of Amazonian Languages, volume I*, 200–325. Berlin: Mouton de Gruyter.

Gil, David. 2003. English goes Asian: Number and (in)definiteness in the Singlish noun phrase. In Frans Plank (ed.), *Noun Phrase Structure in the Languages of Europe*, 467–514. Berlin: Mouton de Gruyter.

Gisborne, Nikolas. 2000. Relative clauses in Hong Kong English. *World Englishes* 19(3). 357–71.

Herrmann, Tanja. 2003. Relative Clauses in Dialects of English: A Typological Approach. University of Freiburg PhD dissertation.

Keenan, Edward L. and Bernard Comrie. 1977. Noun phrase accessibility and universal grammar. *Linguistic Inquiry* 8. 63–99.

Mesthrie, Rajend and Timothy T. Dunne. 1990. Syntactic variation in language shift: The relative clause in South African Indian English. *Language Variation and Change* 2(1). 31–56.

Miller, Jim. 2008. Scottish English: Morphology and syntax. In Bernd Kortmann and Clive Upton (eds.), *Varieties of English: The British Isles*, 299–327. Berlin: Mouton de Gruyter.

Schaub, Willi. 1985. *Babungo*. London: Croom Helm.

Tagliamonte, Sali, Jennifer Smith, and Helen Lawrence. 2005. No taming the vernacular! Insights from the relatives in northern Britain. *Language Variation and Change* 17(1). 75–112.

Wee, Lionel and Umberto Ansaldo. 2004. Nouns and noun phrases. In Lisa Lim (ed.), *Singapore English: A Grammatical Description*, 57–74. Amsterdam: John Benjamins.

See *General references* for Alo and Mesthrie 2004; Ayafor 2004; Beal 2004; Clarke 2004; Filppula 2004; Huddleston and Pullum 2002; Kortmann et al. 2004; Mbangwana 2004; Mesthrie 2004a; Mesthrie 2004b; Miller 2004; Montgomery 2004; Mufwene 2004; Mugler and Tent 2004; Patrick 2004; Pawley 2004; Sakoda and Siegel 2004; Smith 2004; Trudgill 2004; Wagner 2004; Winford and Migge 2004; Wolfram 2004b.

13.7   Further reading

Ball, Catherine N. 1996. A diachronic study of relative markers in spoken and written English. *Language Variation and Change* 8. 227–58.

Hyltenstam, Kenneth. 1984. The use of typological markedness conditions as predictors in second language acquisition: The case of pronominal copies in relative clauses. In Roger W. Andersen (ed.), *Second Languages: A Crosslinguistic Perspective*, 39–58. Rowley: Newbury House.

Ihalainen, Ossi. 1980. Relative clauses in the dialect of Somerset. *Neuphilologische Mitteilungen* 81. 187–96.

Keenan, Edward L. 1985. Relative clauses. In Timothy Shopen (ed.), *Language Typology and Syntactic Description, volume II: Complex Constructions*, 141–70. Cambridge University Press.

Lehmann, Christian. 1986. On the typology of relative clauses. *Linguistics* 24(4). 663–
    80.
Newbrook, Mark. 1998. Which way? That way? Variation and ongoing changes in the
    English relative clause. *World Englishes* 17(1). 43–59.
Suñer, Margarita. 1998. Resumptive restrictive relatives: A crosslinguistic perspective.
    Language 74(2). 335–64.

14   Summary and outlook

In this final chapter, I will try to elaborate on essentially three areas that help
to position the present book in current research on varieties and variation.
These concern, firstly, cross-linguistically exceptional properties of standard
and non-standard varieties of English, secondly, the discussion of angloversals
and vernacular universals, and, thirdly, the apparent emergence of the new
research field of 'variationist' or 'sociolinguistic typology'.

14.1   Exceptional properties of English

As I pointed out in Chapter 1, the cross-linguistic approach adopted in this
book helps us to separate the wheat from the chaff and to see the patterns
of variation attested in varieties of English and their limitations more clearly.
In all of the chapters discussing grammatical phenomena, we could observe
morphosyntactic coding strategies that are common cross-linguistically, though
we also encountered strategies that need to be considered exceptional and rare.
In view of the fact that we focused on typological commonalities in the cross-
linguistic sections of the preceding chapters, we will here shift the focus to
those grammatical phenomena that appear idiosyncratic and infrequent from a
cross-linguistic perspective.

Standard English – just like any language – possesses several features that
are exceptional in the above sense. Some of them are listed in Table 14.1 below.
They have been taken from the *Rara Archive* maintained at the University of
Konstanz.

According to a frequently voiced claim, non-standard varieties of English
are often more consistent cross-linguistically, as the idiosyncrasies of standard
English tend to be levelled out. For example, subject-verb agreement may
be more regular, with the third person -*s* suffix being extended to the entire
paradigm or completely abandoned. In a similar way, some varieties of English
display case and/or number contrasts on second person pronouns as well as the
formal identity of definite article and demonstrative pronoun.

The listing of exceptional properties given in Table 14.1 may easily be
extended. Some additional idiosyncrasies of standard English, as they have

Table 14.1 *Exceptional properties of standard English, as portrayed by Frans Plank in* Das grammatische Raritätenkabinett *(http://typo.uni-konstanz.de/rara/intro/).*

Exceptional property	Example
verbal inflection with non-zero exponent for third person (subject or object agreement/cross-reference), but zero for all other persons	*I walk, you walk, s/he walk-s*
independent personal pronouns for first and third (animate) person inflecting for both number and case, but that for second person inflecting for neither category (defectiveness of second person pronouns in number alone being more common)	*I/me, he/him, she/her, we/us, they/them* versus *you/you*
(finite) verb-second word order in main declarative clauses only if the first constituent is an adverbial with strong negative force (such as *never before, hardly ever*)	*Never have I seen such a thing in my life.*
relative pronoun as the only target for agreement in animacy	*who* versus *which*
a definite article formally distinct from (one form or another of) any kind of pronoun – demonstrative, personal (free, clitic, or bound), possessive, relative, interrogative	*the* versus *these, he, his, whose,* etc.

Table 14.2 *Some additional exceptional properties found in standard English.*

Exceptional property	Example
two series of reflexive pronouns	*myself* versus *himself*
negation requires support by an auxiliary	*He doesn't eat enough.*
interrogative tags agreeing in person, number, gender, and tense	*She likes apples, doesn't she?*
relative clause formation strategy not permitted on subjects (gapping)	*The man who came.* versus **The man ___ came.*
categorical opposition between present perfect and simple past	*We have seen it many times.*
unmarked habitual non-past tense	*We eat porridge every day.*

emerged during our discussion of the foregoing chapters, can be found in Table 14.2.

Notwithstanding the idiosyncrasies of standard English, it would be a gross oversimplification to say that the grammars of non-standard varieties are generally more regular and transparent, or that they would follow the cross-linguistic mainstream more closely. The opposite seems to be the case. As we can see in Table 14.3, nearly all of the grammatical domains discussed in the present book yield phenomena that deserve to be categorised as exceptional in one of the above senses. Moreover, they can be found in all major types of English

Table 14.3 *Exceptional properties of non-standard varieties of English.*

Exceptional property	Variety (illustration)	Example
mass/count distinction expressed by gendered pronouns	Southwest of England, Newfoundland	*the tree – he* versus *milk – it*
case distinction on pronouns only in first person	Torres Strait Creole	*ai/mi* versus *em/em*
case distinction on pronouns only in third person	Surinamese Creoles	*mi/mi* versus *a/en*
subjective pronominal forms used as emphatic pronouns in object position (pronoun exchange)	Southwest of England	*I saw she.*
mass/count distinction encoded by determiners	Southwest of England	*thick tree* versus *that grass*
after-perfect	Irish English	*I'm after meeting the boss.*
six habitual aspects	Irish English	a. *do be* + V*ing*; b. *do be* + adjective; c. *do* + INF; d. *be* + V*ing*; e. *be's/bees* + V*ing*; f. *be's/bees* + adjective
one expression for negative *be*, *have*, and *do*	African American Vernacular English	*She ain't do it.*
Northern Subject Rule	North of England, Scotland	*They peel them and boils them.*
different copulas for affirmative and negative contexts	Great Britain	*I/you/he/she weren't* versus *I/you/he/she was*
Southern Double Object Construction	Southern United States	*Cindy sent her a letter to Sue yesterday.*
subject-verb inversion in embedded interrogative clauses, but not in main clause interrogative clauses	Indian English	*What this is made from?* versus *I asked him where does he work.*

varieties, namely traditional dialects, post-colonial Englishes, and Pidgin and Creole varieties.

We can assume that the features listed in Table 14.3 are the result of essentially two processes. On the one hand, they may be due to diachronic change representing spontaneous developments. On the other hand, they may have their origin in contact-induced change (interference, transfer). The bottom line of the foregoing discussion is that the grammars of all varieties contain idiosyncrasies (and are in this sense complex), albeit perhaps to different degrees.

14.2   Universals, angloversals, and vernacular universals

In the introductory chapter (Chapter 1), I established the notions of 'universals', 'angloversals', and 'vernacular universals', and over the course of the present book we have repeatedly addressed the relationship of English non-standard phenomena to universal aspects of languages. We achieved this in essentially two ways.

Firstly, it turned out that non-standard phenomena of English can be successfully related to various implicational universals or implicational hierarchies. In this context, we discussed the person hierarchy, the hierarchy of individuation (animacy hierarchy), the accessibility hierarchy, the agreement hierarchy, and the hierarchy of interrogative words. Implicational hierarchies are powerful tools, as they make strong predictions. Moreover, they reveal the status of English non-standard phenomena vis-à-vis related phenomena in standard English, as well as in other languages.

Secondly, in the cross-linguistic sections of the foregoing chapters, I tried to present the major parameters of variation governing the grammatical domains discussed. For example, we observed that strategies of relative clause formation in a large cross-linguistic sample can be reduced to essentially four types (relative pronoun strategy, non-reduction strategy, pronoun retention strategy, and gap strategy). We were able to map many – though by no means all – non-standard features of English onto these dominant coding strategies. Even though this procedure does not uncover universal traits of language, it allows us to separate common phenomena from uncommon ones. Table 14.4 provides a summary of these features.

Even though the features listed in Table 14.4 can hardly pass as linguistic universals, they represent compelling cross-linguistic trends. The listing in Table 14.4 contains two morphosyntactic non-standard features that Chambers (2004: 128) classifies as 'vernacular universals': default singulars (subject-verb non-concord) and multiple negation (negative concord). Additional vernacular universals introduced by Chambers which we have not discussed in this book include copula deletion (*She smart*) and conjugation regularisation (*Mary heared the good news*).

Chambers defines vernacular universals as 'a small number of phonological and grammatical processes [that] recur in vernaculars wherever they are spoken'. The notion is not restricted to English vernaculars, since universal vernacular features can be expected to exist in other languages, too. English vernacular universals have been termed 'angloversals', though the latter notion does not carry Chambers' claim to universality.

We may compare the cross-linguistically common coding strategies in Table 14.4 with the list of angloversals discussed in Kortmann and Szmrecsanyi (2004: 1154). Based on a comparison of 76 non-standard features in 46 varieties of English, they identify the following 11 features that are found in at least 75 per cent of all the varieties surveyed. They are shown in Table 14.5. The first column is the identifier in their data pool. The third column gives the

Table 14.4 *Non-standard features of English that follow the cross-linguistic mainstream.*

Feature	Variety (illustration)	Example
possessive pronominal forms in reflexives throughout the paradigm	South of England	*myself, yourself, hisself, ourselves, yourselves, theirselves*
body part reflexives	Nigerian Pidgin	*him bodi* 'himself'
no gender distinction in independent personal pronouns	Tok Pisin	*em* 'he/she/it'
no case distinctions	Solomon Islands Pijin	*mi* 'I/me'
determiners without dental fricatives	Irish English, Indian English	*di* 'the'
three distance contrasts encoded by demonstrative pronouns	Orkney and Shetland	*this, that, yon*
distance contrasts encoded by locative adverbials	Appalachian English	*this here rifle*
use of numeral 'one' as indefinite article	Hawai'i Creole	*wan pikap* 'a pickup'
perfect encoded by 'finish' or 'already'	Singapore English	*I eat already.*
less categorical simple past/present perfect distinction	Indian English	*I never felt alone.*
present tense expresses universal perfect	Irish English	*I live here all my life.*
go-future	Nigerian Pidgin	*A go waka.* 'I will walk.'
negative concord	Great Britain	*I couldn't see no one.*
regular subject-verb agreement	Great Britain	*I says, you says, he says* versus *I say, you say, he say*
distinction of second person singular and plural pronouns[1]	North American English	*you* versus *y'all*
non-initial interrogative words	Cameroon English, Singapore English	*This bus go where?*
no subject-verb inversion in interrogatives	Indian English	*What this is made from?*
interrogative particles	Cameroon English	*na, not so, ein*, etc.
invariant tags	colloquial English	*innit*
gap strategy of relative clause formation with subjects	Great Britain	*There's a girl wanted to see you.*

number of varieties where the feature is attested. The threshold of 75 per cent was set by the authors.

We need to disregard features 42, 43, and 19, as these have not been discussed in this book. As far as the remaining features are concerned, there is clear overlap between Table 14.4 and Table 14.5. The following features

---

[1] Even though we did not discuss this feature in this book, it is mentioned here for the sake of completeness.

Table 14.5 *Angloversals (adapted from Kortmann and Szmrecsanyi 2004: 1154).*

Feature		No.
74	lack of inversion in main clause *yes/no* questions	41
10	*me* instead of *I* in coordinate subjects	40
49	*never* as preverbal past tense negator	40
42	adverbs same form as adjectives	39
14	absence of plural marking after measure nouns	37
73	lack of inversion / lack of auxiliaries in *wh*-questions	36
44	multiple negation / negative concord	35
43	degree modifier adverbs lack *-ly*	35
3	special forms or phrases for the second person plural pronoun	34
25	levelling of difference between present perfect and simple past	34
19	double comparatives and superlatives	34

are angloversals (in the above sense) and are common cross-linguistically: no subject-verb inversion in interrogatives (74, 73), negative concord (44), and no categorical past/perfect distinction (25). Thus, angloversals overlap with common cross-linguistic features.

14.3 Variationist (sociolinguistic) typology

Over the past ten or so years we have been able to witness increasing interest among dialectologists and sociolinguists (scholars working on language variation) in typological questions. This interest is documented in several publications: Kortmann (2004), Siemund and Kintana (2008), Filppula et al. (2009), Siemund (2011), Trudgill (2011). The relevant scholars are asking how the variation that they observe within language relates to cross-linguistic variation. The present book clearly demonstrates this interest.

Curiously enough, comparable interest among typologists for language-internal variation is difficult to detect, with the exception of perhaps Walter Bisang's publications (see Bisang 2004). I can only speculate about the reasons for this unilateral interest, all the more so as typologists have always expressed an interest in the grammatical encoding of social information (address terms, honorifics, expressions reserved for males or females, politeness distinctions, etc.).

In view of this increasing interest among dialectologists and sociolinguists in typological matters, we may currently be witnessing the emergence of a new field that we might tentatively call 'variationist typology' or 'sociolinguistic typology', with a recent book by Peter Trudgill (2011) bearing the latter title.

Trudgill (2011) argues for a correlation between degree of language contact and the degree of complexity that a language exhibits. Language contact reduces linguistic complexity, while languages spoken by isolated communities may develop astonishing degrees of internal complexity. This approach presupposes a view of language that acknowledges differences in complexity between them, i.e. that some languages are more complex than others. Not everybody shares this assumption. Notwithstanding this general controversy, it appears plausible to argue that the existence of many grammatical irregularities, non-transparent relationships between form and function, and the redundant encoding of grammatical information make a language more complex to learn and to maintain (see Trudgill 2011: 20–4).

We need to be careful about language contact and the reduction of complexity, though, as several studies have demonstrated an increase in complexity through language contact (see the contributions in Siemund and Kintana 2008). Trudgill (2011: 34) observes that language contact between adults, especially short-term contact that involves second language learning, leads to simplification. Complexification, in contrast, can be expected 'in long-term co-territorial contact situations involving child bilingualism'. In other words, depending on the type of contact, languages may grow in complexity or lose it.

English has been in contact with other languages throughout its history. There was extensive contact with Celtic and Scandinavian languages during the Old English period and with French in the Middle English period. The ensuing British colonial expansion led to massive contact between English and a host of other languages. In its role as a world language today, English is in a situation of constant language contact. Crucially, all the contact situations that English has been through have involved high degrees of adult second language learning. The fact that English has constantly been losing grammatical, especially morphological, complexity during its history seems to support Trudgill's (2011) hypothesis. There can be no doubt that English is well on its way from a more synthetic to a more analytic language type.

Even though I am happy to follow Trudgill's line of thinking, we may note that the trend towards less synthetic structures has mainly affected the inflectional morphology of English (see Siemund 2004). Its derivational morphology is still heavily synthetic, and one wonders why this kind of complexity appears to pose no problem for adult second language learners. English morphophonemics, in particular, is astonishingly complex. Having said that, there also seems to be a certain trend towards more analytic structures in derivational morphology (Haselow 2011).

Kortmann and Szmrecsanyi (2011), in their study of analytic and synthetic tendencies in varieties of English, are able to confirm Trudgill's (2011) hypothesis on the relation between intensity of language contact and linguistic complexity. In subjecting seventy-six morphosyntactic features of forty-six varieties to a principal component analysis (see Figure 14.1), they are able to show that varieties cluster according to their type, namely Pidgin Englishes, Creole Englishes, second language varieties, and traditional dialects. Evidently, Pidgin Englishes are high-contact varieties, while traditional dialects can be regarded as low-contact varieties. Creole Englishes and second language varieties range in between. Furthermore, Kortmann and Szmrecsanyi (2011: 277) propose to analyse the two components in terms of complexity, with component one standing for 'increasing degrees of L2-acquisition difficulty' and component two for 'increasing degrees of transparency', i.e. lower structural complexity.

14.4   Where to go from here

In concluding this book, I would like to suggest three areas of research that offer themselves for future work. Firstly, there are several additional grammatical phenomena that can be subjected to a cross-varietal and cross-linguistic comparison. Notice that the present book is exclusively about morphosyntax and does not address issues of phonology, phonotactics, and prosody. Comparative studies of that kind would seem highly rewarding. Additional morphosyntactic phenomena include number marking and agreement, copula deletion, serial verb constructions, complementation, and perhaps others.

Secondly, with the exception of Irish English, there is practically no research addressing the diachrony of post-colonial varieties. Certainly, the varieties of Indian English, Singapore English, Hong Kong English, and other such new Englishes possess extensive histories in the relevant territories, but little is known about their development through time and the emergence of their diagnostic features.

Thirdly, we may note that all speakers of varieties of English are unique in terms of their language biographies. In the minds of these speakers, non-standard varieties co-exist with standard English and other languages and varieties thereof. Knowing more about these speaker language biographies would enable us to understand the non-standard features of English that the relevant speakers produce in their social context. Instead of generalising across one corpus containing data from many different speakers, it may be more fruitful in the future to analyse data of smaller, yet more coherent, groups of speakers.

14.5   Summary and list of keywords

My aim in this summary was to oppose the exceptional or idiosyncratic features found across varieties of English with those that more closely follow the cross-linguistic mainstream. In addition, I attempted to relate these features to current debates about universals, angloversals, and vernacular universals. Finally, I

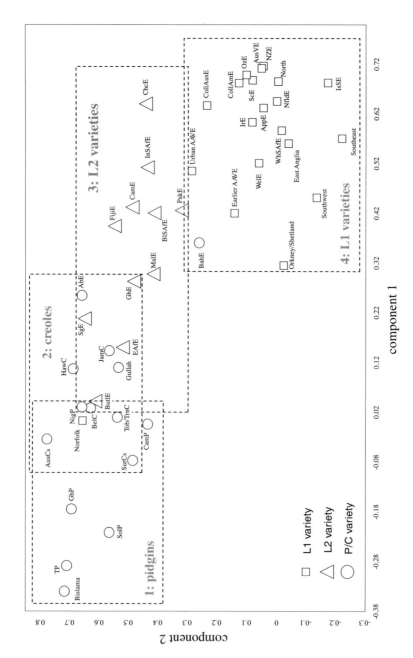

Figure 14.1 Visualisation of principal components of variance in the 76 × 46 database. Dotted boxes indicate group memberships (Kortmann and Szmrecsanyi 2011: 276). Reproduced with permission.

wished to direct your attention towards the emerging field of variationist or sociolinguistic typology, hoping that it will spark your interest in carrying out more research in the future.

Keywords: angloversals, complexification, complexity, cross-linguistic trends, exceptional properties, high-contact societies, implicational hierarchies, language contact, low-contact societies, rara, regularity, simplification, sociolinguistic typology, transparency, universals, variationist typology, vernacular universals.

14.6   Exercises

Basic level

1. List five exceptional properties of standard English. Moreover, find five exceptional properties that occur in non-standard varieties of English. Why do you consider them exceptional?
2. Explain the term 'regular' in its linguistic sense, using illustrative exemplification.
3. Name five high-contact varieties of English and five low-contact varieties.

Intermediate level

1. We can define a *transparent* relationship between linguistic forms and their functions as one in which each form expresses exactly one function and each function is expressed by exactly one form. Moreover, grammatical information should be expressed at the location where it is relevant.
   a. Try to find three examples that illustrate a transparent form–function relationship.
   b. In addition, look for three grammatical phenomena that you would consider non-transparent. Explain exactly why you consider them non-transparent.
2. It has often been claimed that the second person plural form *y'all* is a distinct feature of American English. Try to corroborate this claim using the *BNC* and the *Corpus of Contemporary American English*. You can access these corpora at http://corpus.byu.edu/.
3. In Table 14.1 above, it was stated that the standard English verb-second word order in main declarative clauses following adverbials with strong negative force is highly exceptional in cross-linguistic terms. However, as the minimal pair below shows, this rule is not without exceptions.

a. *With no job would John be happy.*
b. *With no job John would be happy.*

a. The two examples given above have slightly different meanings. Try to find suitable paraphrases that make this difference explicit.
b. Try to find a reason for the resulting difference in meaning.

Advanced level

1. Linguistic complexity is a controversial notion that is difficult to pin down. Trudgill (2011: ch. 4) discusses the following dimensions that help to operationalise this difficult notion:
   (I) opacity: non-transparent relations between form and function
   (II) irregularity: paradigms containing exceptions
   (III) number of morphological categories
   (IV) syntagmatic redundancy: repetition of information.
   a. Read chapter 4 in Trudgill (2011) and note down one example of each of the dimensions introduced above.
   b. In a short academic essay, discuss the notion of 'complexity'. Base your analysis on Trudgill's dimensions and use sufficient illustration. You may also want to include examples from the present book.
2. In a short research paper, investigate copula deletion (*she happy*) across varieties of English. You may use the general structure of the chapters in the present book as a template for your paper. More specifically:
   a. Investigate in which varieties of English and in which contexts copula deletion can be found.
   b. Compare English copula deletion with the cross-linguistic feature of present/absent copulas. The *World Atlas of Language Structures* contains a chapter entitled 'Zero Copula for Predicate Nominals'.
3. Greenberg (1960) proposed to capture the morphological complexity of languages in terms of a so-called 'synthesis index' that measures the number of grammatical morphemes in relation to the number of words across a representative text segment. For example, the sentence below contains nine words comprising six grammatical morphemes (possessive -*s*, plural -*s*, past -*ed*, *to*, comparative -*er*, *than*). This yields a synthesis index of 1.5 (9 devided by 6).

John's brothers turned out to be taller than me.

In this exercise, we would like to compare a representative text segment of standard English with a comparable text segment taken from an English Pidgin or Creole variety. The task is to measure the respective synthesis indexes.
   a. Familiarise yourself with Greenberg's (1960) original article. Some comments on Greenberg's paper can be found in Siemund (2004).

b. Below you can find a short passage of Tok Pisin and its standard English translation. Compute the relevant synthesis indexes. Interpret your results.

Mi laik story long taim mi liklik yet na mi bin statim Tok Pisin. Papa bin stap long bus, em bin tich lo bus na mi bin gro lo bus. Mi bin liklik yet, long eich long abaut faif, na mi bin statim Tok Pisin. Papa wantem mama save tok ples, tasol mipla no sawe kechim tok ples blo ol, mipla sa Tok Pisin tasol, i kam i kam, mi bikpla.

'I'd like to tell you about the time I was still small and I started (to speak) Tok Pisin. Dad lived in the bush, he taught in the bush and I grew up in the bush. I was still small, at the age of five, when I started to speak Tok Pisin. My father and mother knew the local language, but we couldn't catch their language, we only learned Tok Pisin right up to the time we were big.' [Smith 2002: 1]

14.7   References

Bisang, Walter. 2004. Dialectology and typology – an integrative perspective. In Bernd Kortmann (ed.), *Dialectology Meets Typology: Dialect Grammar from a Cross-Linguistic Perspective*, 11–45. Berlin: Mouton de Gruyter.

Chambers, Jack K. 2004. Dynamic typology and vernacular universals. In Bernd Kortmann (ed.), *Dialectology Meets Typology: Dialect Grammar from a Cross-Linguistic Perspective*, 127–45. Berlin: Mouton de Gruyter.

Filppula, Markku, Juhani Klemola, and Heli Paulasto (eds.). 2009. *Vernacular Universals and Language Contacts: Evidence from Varieties of English and Beyond*. London: Routledge.

Greenberg, Joseph H. 1960. A quantitative approach to the morphological typology of language. *International Journal of American Linguistics* 26. 178–94.

Haselow, Alexander. 2011. *Typological Changes in the Lexicon: Analytic Tendencies in English Noun Formation*. Berlin: Mouton de Gruyter.

Kortmann, Bernd (ed.). 2004. *Dialectology Meets Typology: Dialect Grammar from a Cross-Linguistic Perspective*. Berlin: Mouton de Gruyter.

Kortmann, Bernd and Benedikt Szmrecsanyi. 2011. Parameters of morphosyntactic variation in World Englishes: Prospects and limits of searching for universals. In Peter Siemund (ed.), *Linguistic Universals and Language Variation*, 264–90. Berlin: Mouton de Gruyter.

Siemund, Peter 2004. Analytische und synthetische Tendenzen in der Entwicklung des Englischen. In Uwe Hinrichs (ed.), *Die europäischen Sprachen auf dem Wege zum analytischen Sprachtyp*, 169–96. Wiesbaden: Harassowitz.

Siemund, Peter (ed.). 2011. *Linguistic Universals and Language Variation*. Berlin: Mouton de Gruyter.

Siemund, Peter and Noemi Kintana (eds.). 2008. *Language Contact and Contact Languages*. Amsterdam: John Benjamins.

Smith, Geoff P. 2002. *Growing up with Tok Pisin: Contact, Creolization, and Change in Papua New Guinea's National Language*. London: Battlebridge Publications.

Trudgill, Peter. 2011. *Sociolinguistic Typology: Social Determinants of Linguistic Complexity*. Oxford University Press.

See *General references* for Kortmann and Szmrecsanyi (2004).

14.8   Further reading

Dahl, Östen. 2004. *The Growth and Maintenance of Linguistic Complexity*. Amsterdam: John Benjamins.

McWhorter, John H. 2001. The world's simplest grammars are Creole grammars. *Linguistic Typology* 5(2/3). 125–66.

Miestamo, Matti, Kaius Sinnemäki, and Fred Karlsson (eds.). 2008. *Language Complexity: Typology, Contact, Change*. Amsterdam: John Benjamins.

Sampson, Geoffrey, David Gil, and Peter Trudgill (eds.). 2009. *Language Complexity as an Evolving Variable*. Oxford University Press.

Siemund, Peter. 2009. Linguistic universals and vernacular data. In Markku Filppula, Juhani Klemola, and Heli Paulasto (eds.), *Vernacular Universals and Language Contacts: Evidence from Varieties of English and Beyond*, 321–46. London: Routledge.

Siemund, Peter. 2011. Universals and variation: An introduction. In Peter Siemund (ed.), *Linguistic Universals and Language Variation*, 1–20. Berlin: Mouton de Gruyter.

General references

Aceto, Michael. 2004. Eastern Caribbean English-derived language varieties: Morphology and syntax. In Bernd Kortmann, Kate Burridge, Rajend Mesthrie, Edgar W. Schneider, and Clive Upton (eds.), 439–53.

Alo, Moses A. and Rajend Mesthrie. 2004. Nigerian English: Morphology and syntax. In Bernd Kortmann, Kate Burridge, Rajend Mesthrie, Edgar W. Schneider, and Clive Upton (eds.), 813–27.

Anderwald, Lieselotte. 2004. The varieties of English spoken in the southeast of England: Morphology and syntax. In Bernd Kortmann, Kate Burridge, Rajend Mesthrie, Edgar W. Schneider, and Clive Upton (eds.), 175–95.

Ayafor, Miriam. 2004. Cameroon Pidgin English (Kamtok): Morphology and syntax. In Bernd Kortmann, Kate Burridge, Rajend Mesthrie, Edgar W. Schneider, and Clive Upton (eds.), 909–28.

Baskaran, Loga. 2004. Malaysian English: Morphology and syntax. In Bernd Kortmann, Kate Burridge, Rajend Mesthrie, Edgar W. Schneider, and Clive Upton (eds.), 1073–88.

Bayley, Robert and Otto Santa Ana. 2004. Chicano English: Morphology and syntax. In Bernd Kortmann, Kate Burridge, Rajend Mesthrie, Edgar W. Schneider, and Clive Upton (eds.), 374–90.

Beal, Joan. 2004. English dialects in the north of England: Morphology and syntax. In Bernd Kortmann, Kate Burridge, Rajend Mesthrie, Edgar W. Schneider, and Clive Upton (eds.), 114–41.

Bhatt, Rakesh M. 2004. Indian English: Syntax. In Bernd Kortmann, Kate Burridge, Rajend Mesthrie, Edgar W. Schneider, and Clive Upton (eds.), 1016–30.

Bowerman, Sean. 2004. White South African English: Morphology and syntax. In Bernd Kortmann, Kate Burridge, Rajend Mesthrie, Edgar W. Schneider, and Clive Upton (eds.), 948–61.

Burridge, Kate. 2004. Synopsis: Morphological and syntactic variation in the Pacific and Australasia. In Bernd Kortmann, Kate Burridge, Rajend Mesthrie, Edgar W. Schneider, and Clive Upton (eds.), 1116–31.

Clarke, Sandra. 2004. Newfoundland English: Morphology and syntax. In Bernd Kortmann, Kate Burridge, Rajend Mesthrie, Edgar W. Schneider, and Clive Upton (eds.), 303–18.

Collins, Peter and Pam Peters. 2004. Australian English: Morphology and syntax. In Bernd Kortmann, Kate Burridge, Rajend Mesthrie, Edgar W. Schneider, and Clive Upton (eds.), 593–610.

Crowley, Terry. 2004. Bislama: Morphology and syntax. In Bernd Kortmann, Kate Burridge, Rajend Mesthrie, Edgar W. Schneider, and Clive Upton (eds.), 682–701.

Dryer Matthew S. and Martin Haspelmath (eds.). 2011. *The World Atlas of Language Structures Online*. Munich: Max Planck Digital Library.

Escure, Geneviève. 2004. Belize and other central American varieties: Morphology and syntax. In Bernd Kortmann, Kate Burridge, Rajend Mesthrie, Edgar W. Schneider, and Clive Upton (eds.), 517–44.

Faraclas, Nicholas G. 2004. Nigerian Pidgin English: Morphology and syntax. In Bernd Kortmann, Kate Burridge, Rajend Mesthrie, Edgar W. Schneider, and Clive Upton (eds.), 828–53.

Filppula, Markku. 2004. Irish English: Morphology and syntax. In Bernd Kortmann, Kate Burridge, Rajend Mesthrie, Edgar W. Schneider, and Clive Upton (eds.), 73–101.

Hosali, Priya. 2004. Butler English: Morphology and syntax. In Bernd Kortmann, Kate Burridge, Rajend Mesthrie, Edgar W. Schneider, and Clive Upton (eds.), 1031–44.

Huber, Magnus. 2004. Ghanaian Pidgin English: Morphology and syntax. In Bernd Kortmann, Kate Burridge, Rajend Mesthrie, Edgar W. Schneider, and Clive Upton (eds.), 866–78.

Huber, Magnus and Kari Dako. 2004. Ghanaian English: Morphology and syntax. In Bernd Kortmann, Kate Burridge, Rajend Mesthrie, Edgar W. Schneider, and Clive Upton (eds.), 854–65.

Huddleston, Rodney D. and Geoffrey K. Pullum. 2002. *The Cambridge Grammar of the English Language*. Cambridge University Press.

James, Winford and Valerie Youssef. 2004. The creoles of Trinidad and Tobago: Morphology and syntax. In Bernd Kortmann, Kate Burridge, Rajend Mesthrie, Edgar W. Schneider, and Clive Upton (eds.), 454–81.

Jourdan, Christine. 2004. Solomon Islands Pijin: Morphology and syntax. In Bernd Kortmann, Kate Burridge, Rajend Mesthrie, Edgar W. Schneider, and Clive Upton (eds.), 702–19.

Kautzsch, Alexander. 2004. Earlier African American English: Morphology and syntax. In Bernd Kortmann, Kate Burridge, Rajend Mesthrie, Edgar W. Schneider, and Clive Upton (eds.), 341–55.

Kortmann, Bernd. 2004. Synopsis: Morphological and syntactic variation in the British Isles. In Bernd Kortmann, Kate Burridge, Rajend Mesthrie, Edgar W. Schneider, and Clive Upton (eds.), 1089–103.

Kortmann, Bernd and Benedikt Szmrecsanyi. 2004. Global synopsis: Morphological and syntactic variation in English. In Bernd Kortmann, Kate Burridge, Rajend Mesthrie, Edgar W. Schneider, and Clive Upton (eds.), 1142–202.

Kortmann, Bernd, Kate Burridge, Rajend Mesthrie, Edgar W. Schneider, and Clive Upton (eds.). 2004. *A Handbook of Varieties of English, volume II: Morphology and Syntax*. Berlin: Mouton de Gruyter.

Mahboob, Ahmar. 2004. Pakistani English: Morphology and syntax. In Bernd Kortmann, Kate Burridge, Rajend Mesthrie, Edgar W. Schneider, and Clive Upton (eds.), 1045–57.

Malcolm, Ian G. 2004. Australian creoles and Aboriginal English: Morphology and syntax. In Bernd Kortmann, Kate Burridge, Rajend Mesthrie, Edgar W. Schneider, and Clive Upton (eds.), 657–81.

Mbangwana, Paul. 2004. Cameroon English: Morphology and syntax. In Bernd Kortmann, Kate Burridge, Rajend Mesthrie, Edgar W. Schneider, and Clive Upton (eds.), 898–908.

McCormick, Kay. 2004. Cape Flats English: Morphology and syntax. In Bernd Kortmann, Kate Burridge, Rajend Mesthrie, Edgar W. Schneider, and Clive Upton (eds.), 993–1005.

Melchers, Gunnel. 2004. English spoken in Orkney and Shetland: Morphology, syntax and lexicon. In Bernd Kortmann, Kate Burridge, Rajend Mesthrie, Edgar W. Schneider, and Clive Upton (eds.), 34–46.

Mesthrie, Rajend. 2004a. Black South African English: Morphology and syntax. In Bernd Kortmann, Kate Burridge, Rajend Mesthrie, Edgar W. Schneider, and Clive Upton (eds.), 962–73.

2004b. Indian South African English: Morphology and syntax. In Bernd Kortmann, Kate Burridge, Rajend Mesthrie, Edgar W. Schneider, and Clive Upton (eds.), 974–92.

2004c. Synopsis: Morphological and syntactic variation in Africa and Southeast Asia. In Bernd Kortmann, Kate Burridge, Rajend Mesthrie, Edgar W. Schneider, and Clive Upton (eds.), 1132–41.

Miller, Jim. 2004. Scottish English: Morphology and syntax. In Bernd Kortmann, Kate Burridge, Rajend Mesthrie, Edgar W. Schneider, and Clive Upton (eds.), 47–72.

Montgomery, Michael. 2004. Appalachian English: Morphology and syntax. In Bernd Kortmann, Kate Burridge, Rajend Mesthrie, Edgar W. Schneider, and Clive Upton (eds.), 245–80.

Mufwene, Salikoko S. 2004. Gullah: Morphology and syntax. In Bernd Kortmann, Kate Burridge, Rajend Mesthrie, Edgar W. Schneider, and Clive Upton (eds.), 356–73.

Mugler, France and Jan Tent. 2004. Fiji English: Morphology and syntax. In Bernd Kortmann, Kate Burridge, Rajend Mesthrie, Edgar W. Schneider, and Clive Upton (eds.), 770–88.

Murray, Thomas E. and Beth Lee Simon. 2004. Colloquial American English: Grammatical features. In Bernd Kortmann, Kate Burridge, Rajend Mesthrie, Edgar W. Schneider, and Clive Upton (eds.), 221–44.

Patrick, Peter. 2004. Jamaican Creole: Morphology and syntax. In Bernd Kortmann, Kate Burridge, Rajend Mesthrie, Edgar W. Schneider, and Clive Upton (eds.), 407–38.

Pawley, Andrew. 2004. Australian Vernacular English: Some grammatical characteristics. In Bernd Kortmann, Kate Burridge, Rajend Mesthrie, Edgar W. Schneider, and Clive Upton (eds.), 611–42.

Penhallurick, Robert. 2004. Welsh English: Morphology and syntax. In Bernd Kortmann, Kate Burridge, Rajend Mesthrie, Edgar W. Schneider, and Clive Upton (eds.), 102–13.

Quirk, Randolph, Sidney Greenbaum, Geoffrey Leech, and Jan Svartvik. 1985. *A Comprehensive Grammar of the English Language*. London: Longman.

Reaser, Jeffrey and Benjamin Torbert. 2004. Bahamian English: Morphology and syntax. In Bernd Kortmann, Kate Burridge, Rajend Mesthrie, Edgar W. Schneider, and Clive Upton (eds.), 391–406.

Sakoda, Kent and Jeff Siegel. 2004. Hawai'i Creole: Morphology and syntax. In Bernd Kortmann, Kate Burridge, Rajend Mesthrie, Edgar W. Schneider, and Clive Upton (eds.), 742–69.

Schmied, Josef. 2004. East African English (Kenya, Uganda, Tanzania): Morphology and syntax. In Bernd Kortmann, Kate Burridge, Rajend Mesthrie, Edgar W. Schneider, and Clive Upton (eds.), 929–47.

Schneider, Edgar W. 2004. Synopsis: Morphological and syntactic variation in the Americas and the Caribbean. In Bernd Kortmann, Kate Burridge, Rajend Mesthrie, Edgar W. Schneider, and Clive Upton (eds.), 1104–15.

Sebba, Mark. 2004. British Creole: Morphology and syntax. In Bernd Kortmann, Kate Burridge, Rajend Mesthrie, Edgar W. Schneider, and Clive Upton (eds.), 196–208.

Singler, John V. 2004. Liberian Settler English: Morphology and syntax. In Bernd Kortmann, Kate Burridge, Rajend Mesthrie, Edgar W. Schneider, and Clive Upton (eds.), 879–97.

Smith, Geoff P. 2004. Tok Pisin: Morphology and syntax. In Bernd Kortmann, Kate Burridge, Rajend Mesthrie, Edgar W. Schneider, and Clive Upton (eds.), 720–41.

Swan, Michael. 2005. *Practical English Usage*. Oxford University Press.

Trudgill, Peter. 2004. The dialect of East Anglia: Morphology and syntax. In Bernd Kortmann, Kate Burridge, Rajend Mesthrie, Edgar W. Schneider, and Clive Upton (eds.), 142–53.

Wagner, Susanne. 2004. English dialects in the Southwest: Morphology and syntax. In Bernd Kortmann, Kate Burridge, Rajend Mesthrie, Edgar W. Schneider, and Clive Upton (eds.), 154–74.

Wee, Lionel. 2004. Singapore English: Morphology and syntax. In Bernd Kortmann, Kate Burridge, Rajend Mesthrie, Edgar W. Schneider, and Clive Upton (eds.), 1058–72.

Wilson, Sheila and Rajend Mesthrie. 2004. St Helena English: Morphology and syntax. In Bernd Kortmann, Kate Burridge, Rajend Mesthrie, Edgar W. Schneider, and Clive Upton (eds.), 1006–15.

Winford, Donald and Bettina Migge. 2004. Surinamese creoles: Morphology and syntax. In Bernd Kortmann, Kate Burridge, Rajend Mesthrie, Edgar W. Schneider, and Clive Upton (eds.), 482–516.

Wolfram, Walt. 2004a. Rural and ethnic varieties in the southeast: Morphology and syntax. In Bernd Kortmann, Kate Burridge, Rajend Mesthrie, Edgar W. Schneider, and Clive Upton (eds.), 281–302.

2004b. Urban African American Vernacular English: Morphology and syntax. In Bernd Kortmann, Kate Burridge, Rajend Mesthrie, Edgar W. Schneider, and Clive Upton (eds.), 319–40.

Index of languages, varieties, and areas

Abkhaz 15
Aboriginal English 1, 121, 126, 243, 247, 248, 263
African American English 142, 143
African American Vernacular English 73, 151, 178, 179, 189, 280 *see also* Urban African American Vernacular English
Afrikaans 141, 145
Amele 167
American English 3, 7, 8, 26, 51, 114, 160–1, 169, 198, 199, 207, 287
  Colloquial American English 27, 116, 162, 178, 180, 208, 244, 263
  North American English 53, 124, 130, 180, 282
  Southern American dialects 222, 228, 233
  Southern American English 8, 227, 228
  Southern American Vernacular English 226–7
Amharic 36
Andoke 15
Appalachian English 1, 8, 26–7, 29, 70, 77–8, 93, 94, 96, 97, 104, 115, 119, 141, 142, 149, 162, 178, 179, 263, 266, 282
Appalachians 94, 95
Arabic 36, 39
Australia 2, 8–9, 10, 27, 59, 75, 93, 96, 98, 121
Australian Creoles 1, 247, 248, 263
Australian English 3, 7, 52, 70, 124, 139, 161, 198, 199, 205, 207
  Australian Vernacular English 1, 27, 70, 71, 178, 185, 208, 266
  Colloquial Australian English 54

Babungo 270
Bahamas 8
Bahamian Creole 143
Bahamian English 100, 143, 145, 179, 263
Barbados 8
Basque 36
Belizean Creole 49

Bengali 10
Bislama 1, 49, 74, 93, 97, 122, 246, 247
Bolton 29, 72
British Creole 49, 74, 121, 200
British English 3, 6, 7, 8, 31, 41, 83, 114, 130, 160–1, 169, 171, 191, 198, 199, 207, 224, 228–9, 234
  British dialects 81, 159, 248, 263
  northern British English 8, 162, 224, 265, 274
  southern British dialects 181
  standard British English 41, 224
British Isles 8, 27, 159, 203, 204, 212
Butler English 74, 98, 160

Cameroon 131, 270
Cameroon English 178, 182, 243, 246, 248, 267, 282
Cameroon Pidgin English 75, 263
Canada 8, 15, 57
Canadian English 7
Cantonese 118
Cape Flats English 29, 95, 124, 201, 208
Caribbean 1, 8, 9, 121, 160, 178
Caribbean English *see* Eastern Caribbean English
Celtic Englishes 10, 119, 244
Celtic languages 8, 142, 284
Chamorro 230
Cheshire 205
Chicano English 185
Chinese 6, 10, 38, 118, 161, 165–6, 231, 248, 250, 264
Colloquial English 282
Creoles of Trinidad and Tobago 75, 76, 247, 253, 263

Danish 58, 166
Devon 51, 204
Dorset 142
Dutch 34, 58–9, 63, 141, 149, 166, 201

Earlier African American English 72, 73
Early Modern English 9, 81, 96, 155, 168,
    189, 190, 265
East African English 98, 99, 139, 243, 245,
    246, 255
East Anglia 1, 77, 98–9, 179, 200–1, 208, 263,
    267
Eastern Caribbean English 128, 143
English Midlands 73, 267
English Pidgin and Creole varieties *see* Pidgin
    and Creole Englishes

Fiji English 94, 116, 127, 178, 242, 243, 248,
    266
    Pure Fiji English 49–50
Finnish 36, 39, 101, 127, 135, 185, 186
French 104, 124, 127, 128, 165, 187–8, 190,
    201, 284

Georgian 39
German 25, 34, 35–6, 38, 45–7, 66, 101, 103,
    104, 124, 134, 149, 163, 165–6, 170, 185,
    209, 231–2, 252, 269
Germanic 35, 36, 57–8, 120, 165–6, 169, 228,
    232, 250
Ghana 8, 121
Ghanaian English 99–100, 108, 115, 164, 179
Ghanaian Pidgin English 76, 77, 92, 94, 263
Glasgow English 7
Great Britain 1, 6, 27, 72, 200–1, 217, 280,
    282
Greek 34
Greenlandic 101
Gullah 92, 98, 122, 142–3, 162, 178, 182, 248,
    263

Harar Oromo 166
Hawai'i Creole 26, 73, 92, 94, 103, 120–2,
    138, 242, 266, 282
Hawai'i English 149
Hebrew 36, 39
Hindi 6, 10, 125, 152
Hokkien 118
Hong Kong English 115, 217, 267, 274, 285
Hungarian 36, 79
Hunzib 79, 105

Icelandic 38, 166
Igbo 39
Imbabura Quechua 186
India 6, 8, 10, 183, 242
Indian English 6, 8, 92, 115, 116, 124, 125,
    139–40, 151, 182, 228–9, 234, 242,
    243–6, 248, 250, 255–6, 280–2, 285
Indonesian 101, 122–3

Indonesian English 7
Ireland 8, 9, 117, 119, 120
Irish 36, 117, 120, 149
Irish English 1, 6, 10, 27, 30–1, 32, 41, 42, 51,
    92, 97, 114, 115, 116, 117, 119–20,
    123–4, 129, 131, 139, 141–2, 145, 149,
    150, 164, 184, 241, 244, 255, 266, 280,
    282, 285
Italian 135, 149, 165, 189, 211, 249
Izi 188

Jamaica 8
Jamaican Creole 49–50, 75, 92, 94, 121, 141,
    143, 160, 162, 178, 263, 264
Jamaican English 26, 75, 97, 160, 242, 243–6,
    248, 255
Japanese 35, 103, 249
Jutland 58

Kamtok 75, 121, 128, 131, 143, 144, 178, 200,
    263
Kannada 183
Kiowa 101
Kolyma Yukaghir 184
Korean 270–1
Kriol 144, 248
Krongo 230

Lakhota 101
Lancashire 202, 203, 224, 226
Lango 251
Latin 65–6, 68
Latvian 78, 101
Lavukaleve 167
learner Englishes 91
Leicestershire 202
Liberia 8
Liberian Settler English 73–4, 122, 144,
    186

Ma 188
Maba 39
Malagasy 101
Malay 10
Malaysian English 7, 98, 99, 139, 242, 246,
    248
Mandarin 38, 118, 231, 250
Middle English 67, 72, 81, 189–90, 284
Mitla Zapotec 34
Modern English 47, 67–8, 190
Modern German 47, 58, 103

New Englishes 6, 10, 191, 285
New Zealand 8, 9, 10
New Zealand English 7, 70, 139, 161

Newfoundland 51, 53, 59, 77, 94, 119, 120,
    178, 280
Newfoundland English 1, 51, 53, 54, 72, 92,
    94, 97, 117, 119, 120, 126, 141, 142, 145,
    178, 185, 263, 266
Nigeria 10, 93, 121, 126, 188, 232
Nigerian English 3, 7, 103, 121, 126, 139, 164,
    248, 266
Nigerian Pidgin 28, 143, 178, 282
Nigerian Pidgin English 26, 39, 76, 92, 93,
    122, 178, 247, 263
non-native Englishes 9
non-standard English 84, 130, 170, 234, 254,
    273, 274, 287
Norfolk Island 178
North America 1, 8–9, 10, 217
North Frisian dialects 58
north of England 2, 70, 72, 73, 77, 95, 161–2,
    181, 199, 223, 244, 263, 267, 280
northern England 202, 223
Northern Ireland 199, 202, 203, 262
northwest of England 224

Old Dravidian 183
Old English 29–30, 33, 36, 47, 58, 67, 72,
    101–2, 103, 169, 189–90, 197, 232,
    284
Old Swedish 166
Orkney and Shetland 94, 95, 97, 160, 162,
    263, 282
Orkney and Shetland English 51, 94–6, 160,
    162
Ozark English 141, 143

Pakistan 10
Pakistani English 99, 115, 242
Panyjima 230
Pero 232
Persian 103, 270
Pidgin and Creole Englishes 1, 6, 10, 18, 26,
    27–8, 30, 39, 49, 56, 60, 73, 75, 77, 79,
    81, 92, 93, 94, 96, 98, 100, 103, 119, 120,
    121, 124, 128, 141, 143, 151, 159, 160,
    178, 200–1, 212, 246, 262, 263, 280, 285,
    288
Pirahã 269
Plains Cree 57
Polish 34
post-colonial Englishes 6, 9, 10, 18, 91, 92,
    97, 98, 102, 115, 119, 124, 159, 179,
    205, 217, 241–4, 246, 249, 274, 280,
    285

Russian 2, 34, 66–7, 100, 101, 146, 152, 189,
    271

Saamaka 93
Saramaccan 28
Scandinavian languages 101, 284
Scotland 9, 119, 120, 181, 199, 202, 267, 280
Scots 159
    Hawick Scots 162, 163
Scottish English 7, 10, 95, 97, 116, 119, 139,
    140, 161, 162–3, 164, 178, 184–5, 244,
    248, 262, 263, 266
Shetland English 72, 120 see also Orkney and
    Shetland English
Singapore 6, 10, 242
Singapore English 3, 5–6, 7, 10, 92, 97–8, 99,
    102, 117–19, 125, 129, 130, 143, 144,
    161, 201, 217, 242–6, 248, 250, 255, 263,
    264–5, 274, 282, 285
    Colloquial Singapore English 99, 264
Solomon Islands Pijin 49, 74–5, 98, 102, 125,
    127, 138, 263, 282
Somerset English 7
South Africa 8–9, 95, 141, 182
South African English 3, 7, 115, 205
    Black South African English 116, 139, 244,
    267
    Indian South African English 94, 98, 119,
    124, 178, 185, 242, 243, 244, 262–3, 264,
    266, 273
    South African Indian English 267, 268,
    269–70
    White South African English 95, 141
south of England 282
southeast of England 26–7, 71, 72, 77, 92,
    178, 179, 182
southeast of the United States 72, 120, 178,
    208
Southern United States 162, 280
southwest of England 26, 27, 51–3, 58–60, 61,
    77, 94, 96, 97–8, 100, 141, 142, 159, 262,
    266, 280
Spanish 2, 25, 34, 47, 101, 124, 135, 144–5,
    146, 165, 189, 209, 211, 249
Sranan 28, 30, 39, 247, 252
    Early Sranan 247
Sri Lanka 10
St Helena English 73, 121, 126
Standard English 2, 23, 24, 28, 30, 41, 50, 51,
    52, 56, 57, 59, 62, 65, 67–9, 71, 73, 77,
    79, 80, 81, 83, 84, 87, 91, 93–4, 95–6,
    97–9, 102, 103, 104, 106, 107, 117, 118,
    121, 126, 128, 129, 131, 150, 155, 162,
    163, 169, 170, 177, 179, 180, 181, 182,
    184, 185, 191, 192, 195, 196, 204, 210,
    213, 217, 219, 234, 239, 240, 243, 246,
    247, 253, 258, 261, 269, 271, 274,
    278–81, 285, 287, 288, 289

Straits Salish 15
Surinamese Creoles 75–6, 81, 92, 93–4, 247,
    263, 264, 280
Swahili 213
Swedish 124

Tamil 10, 183
Tasmania 51, 59
Tasmanian Vernacular English 51, 54
Teochow 118
Texan English 7
Tok Pisin 28, 39, 49, 74–5, 102, 104, 119, 120,
    122, 143, 178, 263, 265, 282, 289
Toronto English 7, 265
Torres Strait Creole 26, 75, 81, 93, 98, 138,
    280
Trinidad and Tobago see Creoles of Trinidad
    and Tobago
Tunica 250
Turkish 34, 35, 36, 270
Tyneside English 8
Tzotzil 39

Ulster English 7
United States 6, 8, 27, 225
Urban African American Vernacular English
    73, 74, 162, 186, 244, 266
Urdu 101

Wales 9
Welsh English 10, 140, 142, 159, 182,
    244
West African Englishes 121, 125, 147
West Frisian dialects 58
West Jutish 58

Xhosa 10

York English 205
Yorkshire 202, 203, 205
Yorkshire English 29
Yoruba 125

Zimbabwe 8, 182
Zulu 10

Index of names

Abbott, Barbara 109
Aceto, Michael 128, 143
Ahrens, Kathleen 231
Algeo, John 9
Alo, Moses A. 103, 121, 126, 139, 164, 248, 266
Alsagoff, Lubna 99, 264
Ammann, Andreas 166–7
Anderwald, Lieselotte 26, 27, 71, 72, 92, 159, 176–84, 187, 191, 193, 205, 208
Ansaldo, Umberto 264
Audring, Jenny 59, 60, 63
Austin, John L. 174, 238
Ayafor, Miriam 75, 121, 128, 143, 144, 178, 200, 263

Ball, Catherine N. 276
Bao, Zhiming 117–19, 129, 130, 143, 153, 161–2, 166
Barnes, William 142
Baskaran, Loga 98, 99, 139, 242, 246, 248
Bately, Janet M. 67
Battistella, Edwin 172
Bauer, Brigitte L. M. 109
Bauer, Laurie 22
Baugh, Albert C. 216, 217
Baugh, John 153
Bayley, Robert 185
Beal, Joan 27, 70, 72, 77, 92, 94, 95, 161–2, 244, 263
Bechert, Johannes 64
Bendor-Samuel, John 193
Bernstein, Cynthia 172
Bhatt, Rakesh M. 115, 124, 139, 182, 241–2, 244, 248, 255
Bickerton, Derek 149
Binnick, Robert 132
Bisang, Walter 18, 283
Blake, Barry J. 85
Boertien, Harmon S. 172

Bowerman, Sean 95, 141
Boye, Kasper 171
Bresnan, Joan 236
Brinton, Laurel 153
Brown, Keith 162, 163, 184
Bryan, Margret A. 188
Burchfield, Robert 3, 9
Burridge, Kate 21, 27, 70
Butt, Miriam 85
Bybee, Joan 132

Cable, Thomas 216, 217
Chambers, Jack K. 6, 72, 73, 206, 217, 281
Cheshire, Jenny 27
Chesterman, Andrew 88
Chomsky, Noam 227
Christian, Donna 29
Clarke, Sandra 1, 48, 72, 77, 92, 94, 117, 119, 120, 126, 145, 178, 185, 266
Cole, Peter 186
Coleman, William L. 162
Collins, Peter 71, 124, 153, 161
Comrie, Bernard 14, 78, 79, 111, 112, 126, 129, 134, 140, 146, 147–9, 152, 236, 269, 270–2, 274, 275
Corbett, Greville G. 56, 57, 64, 195–6, 198, 199, 207–15, 216–17
Cornips, Leonie E. A. 12
Corrigan, Karen 12
Croft, William 17, 19, 42, 59–60, 63, 257
Crowley, Terry 1, 49, 74, 93, 96–7, 122, 246, 247
Crystal, David 8, 22
Curzan, Anne 64

D'Arcy, Alexandra 173, 265
Dahl, Östen 46, 123–4, 125–6, 127–8, 132, 146, 184, 290
Dako, Kari 99, 100, 115, 164, 179
Dannenberg, Clare J. 44, 226–7
Davies, Diane 22

Davies, Mark 83, 130, 170, 171, 216
Davydova, Julia 7, 21, 34, 67, 100, 116, 125, 140, 193, 242, 243–6, 255
de la Cruz, Juan 172
Declerck, Renaat 113
Dench, Alan Charles 230
Di Paolo, Marianna 172
Diessel, Holger 104, 105, 107, 109
Dieth, Eugen 224
Dolberg, Florian 60
Dollinger, Stefan 172
Donaldson, Bruce 59
Dryer, Matthew S. 13, 16, 56, 101, 103, 107, 184, 185, 188–9, 250–1, 268
Dunne, Timothy T. 267–70
Dutton, Thomas E. 43

Edmont, Edmond 20
Edwards, Viv 27, 42, 201
Edwards, Walter F. 153
Elsness, Johan 114
Enger, Hans-Olav 166
Escure, Geneviève 49
Evans, Nicholas 15, 16, 17
Everett, Daniel L. 269

Faltz, Leonard M. 35
Faraclas, Nicholas G. 26, 28, 76, 92, 93, 122, 178, 247
Felser, Claudia 141
Fennell, Barbara 172
Fillmore, Charles J. 67
Filppula, Markku 1, 9, 30, 31, 97, 98, 115, 116, 117, 120, 124, 132, 139, 142, 145, 164, 244, 257, 266, 283
Ford, Marilyn 236
Frajzyngier, Zygmunt 232

Gabriel, Christoph 189
Gachelin, Jean-Marc 58
Gass, Susan M. 178
Gast, Volker 34, 44, 158, 223, 224, 232
Gensler, Orin 231
Gil, David 89, 102, 264, 290
Gilliéron, Jules 11
Gisborne, Nikolas 267
Gleason, Johanna L. 90–1, 101
Godfrey, Elizabeth 204, 212
Grant, William 31
Green, Lisa J. 73
Greenberg, Joseph H. 16–17, 56, 288

Haas, Mary R. 250
Hagège, Claude 251

Hancock, Jan 86
Hannah, Jean 3, 241
Harris, John 153
Haselow, Alexander 284
Haspelmath, Martin 16, 56, 107, 110, 189, 193, 230–1, 232, 236, 252
Hawkins, John A. 88, 90–1
Hay, Jennifer 218, 236
Heine, Bernd 108, 131
Hengeveld, Kees 17
Henry, Alison 12, 245, 255
Hernández, Nuria 32
Herrmann, Tanja 267, 272–3, 274
Hilbert, Michaela 20, 256, 257
Hinds, John 249
Ho, Chee Lick 99, 264
Ho, Mian Lian 109, 152
Hoffmann, Sebastian 223, 228–9, 231, 234
Hollmann, Willem 223–4, 226
Horn, Laurence R. 193
Hosali, Priya 74, 98, 160
Howe, Darin M. 194
Huang, C.-T. James 38
Huang, Chu-Ren 231
Huber, Magnus 76, 92, 94, 99–100, 115, 164, 179
Huddleston, Rodney D. 24, 32, 41, 47–8, 70, 84, 87, 88, 89, 107, 113, 156, 197–9, 219, 240, 257, 259, 260, 261
Hudson, Richard 68, 84, 181, 199, 236
Hughes, Arthur 223
Hyltenstam, Kenneth 276

Iggesen, Oliver A. 79, 80
Ihalainen, Ossi 276

Jackendoff, Ray S. 175
James, Winford 74, 75, 76, 247, 253
Jantos, Susanne 218
Jenkins, Jennifer 22
Jespersen, Otto 184, 189–90
Jourdan, Christine 74, 98, 102, 125, 127, 137, 138
Juvonen, Päivi 101

Kachru, Braj B. 7, 9, 19
Kallen, Jeffrey 153
Karjalainen, Merja 185
Karlsson, Fred 290
Kautzsch, Alexander 26, 72, 73
Keenan, Edward L. 271–2, 274, 275, 276
Kintana, Noemi 283, 284
Kittilä, Seppo 236
Klein, Wolfgang 111, 112, 130, 137
Klemola, Juhani 20, 132, 289

Kolbe, Daniela 257
König, Ekkehard 31, 36, 37, 44, 140, 158, 237, 251
Kortmann, Bernd 3, 26, 27, 51, 72, 73, 77, 92, 113, 132, 137, 151, 248, 263, 281, 283, 284–6
Koster, Jan 42
Krifka, Manfred 221–2
Krug, Manfred 169, 182, 191
Kruisinga, Etsko 64
Kuno, Susumo 105
Kuteva, Tania 108, 131, 269, 270–1

Labov, William 12, 194
Lawrence, Helen 276
Leech, Geoffrey 172
Lehmann, Christian 277
Levin, Beth 221
Levin, Magnus 198–9, 207, 215
Levinson, Stephen C. 15–17, 238
Li, Charles N. 166, 250
Lindstedt, Jouko 132, 153
Liu, Dilin 90, 91, 101

Mackenzie, J. Lachlan 252
Madison, Ian 15
Mahboob, Ahmar 99, 115, 242
Maier, Georg 21, 43, 193
Mair, Christian 6
Malchukov, Andrej L. 230
Malcolm, Ian G. 1, 93, 96, 98, 121, 126, 144, 243, 247
Martin, Stefan 189
Mashburn, Carolyn 172
Maslova, Elena 184
Mathiassen, Terje 78
Mathiot, Madeleine 64
Mazzie, Claudia 110
Mbangwana, Paul 182, 243, 246, 248, 267
McArthur, Tom 22
McCafferty, Kevin 153, 218
McCormick, Kay 29, 95, 124, 201, 208
McWhorter, John H. 290
Meier, Ingeborg 188
Meier, Paul 193
Melchers, Gunnel 22, 72, 94–6, 120, 160, 162
Meriläinen, Lea 21
Mesthrie, Rajend 21, 73, 94, 95, 103, 115, 116, 119, 121, 124, 126, 139, 164, 185, 241–4, 248, 255, 262, 263, 264, 266–70
Miestamo, Matti 183, 186–7, 189, 290

Migge, Bettina 75–6, 92, 93, 94, 247, 264
Millar, Martin 184
Miller, Jim 94–5, 98, 116, 119, 133, 140, 153, 159, 161, 162–3, 164, 185, 244, 262, 263, 266
Mishoe, Margaret 173
Montgomery, Michael 1, 26, 29, 70, 77, 93, 94, 96, 98, 104, 115, 119, 141, 162, 173, 179, 263, 266
Moravcsik, Edith A. 80
Morgan, Jerry 207
Mortelmans, Tanja 165–6
Mufwene, Salikoko S. 92, 98, 122, 143, 162, 178, 182, 248, 263
Mugler, France 50, 94, 116, 127, 242, 243, 266
Mühlhäusler, Peter 28, 74
Mukherjee, Joybrato 223, 228–9, 231, 234, 236
Murison, David D. 31
Murray, Thomas E. 27, 141, 143, 178, 180, 208, 244
Muysken, Pieter 28

Nagle, Stephen J. 173
Nevalainen, Terttu 189
Nevins, Andrew 206
Newbrook, Mark 277
Nichols, Patricia 149
Nolan, David W. 194
Noonan, Michael 251

O'Donnell, William Robert 131
Orton, Harold 11, 224
Owens, Jonathan 166

Paddock, Harold 53, 54, 86
Palmer, Frank 156, 164, 165, 166, 170
Parrott, Jeffrey K. 206
Parry, David R. 159
Patrick, Peter 49, 50, 75, 92, 94, 98, 121, 141, 160, 162, 264
Paulasto, Heli 6, 20, 132, 289
Pawley, Andrew 1, 27, 48, 51–2, 54, 71, 185, 208, 266
Payne, John R. 194
Penhallurick, Robert 140, 159, 182, 244
Peters, Pam 71, 124, 161
Pietsch, Lukas 20, 36, 117, 119, 124, 131, 133, 153, 201–4, 205, 217, 256
Plank, Frans 173, 279
Platt, John 99, 149
Pullum, Geoffrey K. 24, 32, 41, 47–8, 70, 84, 87, 88, 89, 107, 113, 156, 197–9, 219, 240, 259, 260, 261

Quinn, Heidi 86
Quirk, Randolph 47, 48, 67–8, 87,
  90, 107, 112, 156, 158, 168, 170, 175,
  241

Ranta, Elina 21
Rappaport Hovav, Malka 221
Rastall, Paul 133
Reaser, Jeffrey 100, 143, 145,
  179
Reh, Mechthild 230
Reichenbach, Hans 112, 130–1
Reuland, Eric 42
Rickford, John 151
Roberts, John R. 167
Roberts, Marjorie 64
Romaine, Suzanne 43
Rupp, Israel D. 229

Sadock, Jarrold M. 257
Şahingöz, Yasemin 35
Sakoda, Kent 26, 73, 92, 94, 103, 120–2, 138,
  242, 266
Sampson, Geoffrey 290
Sand, Andrea 110, 257
Sankoff, Gillian 110
Santa Ana, Otto 185
Sasse, Hans-Jürgen 60
Schaub, Willi 270
Schilling-Estes, Natalie 205
Schladt, Matthias 39
Schlauch, Margaret 149
Schlegel, August 12
Schleicher, August 12
Schmied, Josef 99
Schneider, Edgar W. 10, 21, 51
Schreier, Daniel 218
Schweinberger, Martin 43
Searle, John 174, 238
Sebba, Mark 49, 74, 121, 200
Selinker, Larry 178
Sharma, Divyani 133
Shaw, Philip 22
Shields, Kenneth 194
Shnukal, Anna 26, 75, 93, 138
Shorrocks, Graham 29, 72, 86
Siegel, Jeff 26, 73, 92, 94, 103, 120–2, 138,
  242, 266
Siemund, Peter 3, 12, 20, 25, 31, 32, 36, 37,
  44–51, 52–4, 57–60, 96, 133, 154, 182,
  237, 240, 250, 251, 253, 256, 283, 284,
  288, 290
Siewierska, Anna 56–7, 223–4, 226
Silverstein, Michael 59, 80

Simon, Beth Lee 27, 141, 143, 178, 180, 208,
  244
Singler, John V. 73–4, 122, 144, 186
Sinnemäki, Kaius 290
Smith, Geoff P. 49, 74, 102, 104, 119, 120,
  122, 178, 265, 289
Smith, Jennifer 181, 218, 276
Smith, Norval 28
Spencer, Andrew 86
Stathi, Katerina 34
Stenroos, Merja 64
Sulkala, Helena 185
Suñer, Margarita 277
Svartengren, T. Hilding 60
Swan, Michael 90, 139, 140
Szmrecsanyi, Benedikt 26, 27, 72, 92, 281,
  283, 284–6

Tagliamonte, Sali 173, 181, 204–5, 212, 218,
  262, 265, 266, 274
Tang, C.-C. Jane 38
Taniguchi, Jiro 31
Tent, Jan 50, 94, 116, 127, 242, 243,
  266
Terrill, Angela 167
Thompson, Sandra A. 166, 250
Thráinson, Höskuldur 38
Todd, Loreto 131
Topping, Donald M. 230
Torbert, Benjamin 100, 143, 145, 179
Trudgill, Peter 1, 3, 9, 12, 72, 73, 77, 99, 179,
  200–1, 218, 235, 241, 263, 283–4, 288,
  290
Tucker, Archibald N. 188

Upton, Clive 21, 225

van den Berg, Helma 79, 105
van den Berg, Margot C. 28, 30
van der Auwera, Johan 166–7, 171, 190
van Gelderen, Elly 102
van Rooy, Bertus 154
Velupillai, Viveka 123–4, 125–6, 127–8, 133,
  146
von der Gabelentz, Georg 12
von Humboldt, Wilhelm 12

Wagner, Susanne 26, 27, 48, 51, 53, 77, 94, 98,
  100, 159, 262, 266
Wahrig-Burfeind, Renate 58
Wakelin, Martyn 72, 73
Watt, Dominic 235
Webelhuth, Gert 44, 226–7
Weber, Heidi 109, 152

Wee, Lionel 98, 99, 144, 201, 246, 248, 264
Wenker, Georg 11
Whittle, Pamela 42
Widdowson, J. D. A. 225
Wilson, Sheila 73, 121, 126
Winford, Donald 10, 75–6, 92, 93, 94, 133, 154, 247, 264

Wolfram, Walt 72–3, 120, 149, 178, 186, 189, 205, 208, 244, 266
Wright, Joseph 11, 29

Youssef, Valerie 75, 76, 247, 253

Zupitza, Julius 30
Zwicky, Arnold M. 257

Subject index

a-prefixing 140–1, 150
absolute tense 112
absolute universals 16, 17, 80
absolutive 78–9
abstract nouns 52, 58, 99
accessibility hierarchy 268, 271–3, 275, 281
accusative 35, 65–7, 68, 69, 78–80, 81, 135
adjacency 203, 207, 214, 215
adjuncts 31, 38
adverbials of time 94, 115, 125, 126, 127
after-perfect 114, 117, 123, 129, 280
agglutinating 12, 13, 19
agreement *see* canonical agreement, conditions on agreement, controller, features, formal agreement, semantic agreement, syntactic agreement, target
agreement hierarchy 198, 214, 217, 281
ain't 177–8, 183, 185, 187, 190
aktionsart 113, 123, 137, 151 *see also* lexical aspect
alignment 78–9, 80, 81, 230–1
already 117–19, 125–30, 282
alternative double object construction 222–3, 224
analytic 9, 12, 13, 19, 141, 145, 284
anaphoric uses of pronouns 46, 89, 209, 269
anaphors 29, 227
angloversals 6, 7, 17, 278, 280–3, 285
animacy 46, 214, 279
animacy hierarchy 56, 59, 80–1, 281 *see also* hierarchy of individuation
answer bias 241, 243
antecedent 23, 35, 37–8, 42, 48, 197, 209, 213, 214, 260, 263, 265
argument 23, 25, 28, 30–1, 35, 40, 78, 111, 137, 220, 221, 226–7, 229–30, 233 *see also* co-argument
aspect *see* aktionsart, completive, continuous, *done*, habitual, imperfective, lexical aspect, perfective

asymmetries 3, 78, 80–1, 177, 182–3, 184, 187, 190
auxiliary contraction 176, 180–1, 190
auxiliary verbs 117, 120, 128, 144, 145, 155–7, 159, 160, 163, 164–5, 167–8, 176–7, 180–1, 184, 185, 186, 188, 196–7, 279, 283

bare infinitive 155, 156, 165, 168
be-perfect 120, 123
benefactive dative 29, 228
binding domain 37–8
Binding Principles 227
body-part nouns 27–8, 37, 39, 42, 282
boundedness 134, 136
bracketing 265
British Empire 8, 12

canonical agreement 210, 211, 215, 217
canonical double object construction 222–4
case alignment *see* alignment
case marker 65, 67, 78 *see also* nominative, accusative, genitive, dative
central modals 155, 166, 168, 169, 170
circumfixal negation 184, 188
circumstantial modality 157
clause polarity 188, 206, 215
clause type 208, 237, 238, 239
cleft sentences 199, 265, 266, 275
clefting 15, 33, 70, 83
cliticisation 159, 180
closed class 155, 169
co-argument 24
co-indexation 23–4, 28, 29, 37
collective nouns 48, 198
colonial expansion 12, 284
common gender 48, 58–9
completion 119, 129, 134, 136, 140, 143, 150
completive 118, 138, 143
complex reflexives 35, 38

complexification 284
complexity 93, 265, 284–5, 288
conditions on agreement 196, 208, 210–11, 214
conducive questions 253
consonant systems 15
constative utterances 174
constituent interrogatives 238, 239–40, 241–3, 245–6, 249, 255
constituent negation 175
constituent structure 15–16
construal 135, 136 *see also* metonymic construal
continuous 147, 148
continuity 134, 137
contraction 121, 159, 177, 180, 189, 190 *see also* auxiliary contraction, negative contraction
controller 45, 46–7, 61, 195, 196, 198, 208, 210, 211–12, 213–14
coordination 33, 38, 41, 68, 70, 199
coreference 28, 30, 41, 227
correlative clauses 269, 273, 274
count nouns 52, 57–8, 59, 95, 99
covariance 45, 195, 196
cross-linguistic trends 271, 281
cultural/situational uses of definite articles 91, 98, 101, 105, 106
current relevance 123, 135

dative 35, 65–7, 78, 221, 226
definite articles 45, 87–8, 90–1, 93, 94, 97–103, 105–6, 108, 278, 279 *see also* cultural/situational uses of definite articles
definiteness 93, 99–101, 106, 214
deictic centre 31, 38, 88–9, 105
deictic uses of pronouns 46, 89
deixis 112, 137, 150
demonstrative pronouns 67, 87, 88–9, 92–3, 94–6, 100–2, 104–6, 107–8, 195, 202, 278, 279, 282
dental fricatives 92, 282
deontic modality 157–8, 159, 161–2, 166–7, 169
dependent 66, 68
dialectology 11–13, 18
direct object 25, 29, 30, 38, 69, 78, 119, 219–20, 223, 229, 230, 231, 239, 258, 267, 272, 273, 275
direct speech 244–5, 255
direct speech act 238
distance contrasts 104, 106, 107, 282
distance-oriented systems 104–5
do-support 157, 168, 176, 177, 190, 191
done 119, 143, 151

double modals 159, 162–3, 170, 171
double negation 187–9, 192
dual 26, 96–7
dual gender nouns 47–8, 62

embedded clause 6, 37, 38, 70, 239, 243, 250, 254, 269
embedded inversion 6, 244–6, 250, 255
emphasis 77, 81, 142, 181, 186–7
emphatic reflexives 25, 35 *see also* intensifying *self*-forms
epistemic modality 157–8, 159, 161–2, 166–7, 169
epistemic *mustn't* 161, 170
ergative 78–9
event verbs 116
existential constructions 201, 266, 275
existential perfect 113, 123, 130
experiential perfect 113, 123

features 46, 47, 196, 208, 209, 210, 211, 212, 213–14, 259
feminine 45, 46–8, 51, 52–5, 57, 59, 60, 83
finish 117–19, 125, 129, 143, 151, 282
first language acquisition 7, 10, 178
formal agreement 46, 57
fronting of interrogative words 251
full noun phrase object 223, 229, 232
function words 155
functional typology 1, 10–11, 12–14, 18
future 112, 113, 121–3, 127–9, 130, 282
future perfect 112

gap strategy 259, 260–2, 265–6, 269, 270–3, 274–5, 279, 281, 282
gapping *see* gap strategy
gender assignment 46, 47, 61
genitive 65, 68, 79, 80, 260, 261, 267, 272, 273, 275
grammatical relations 14, 79
grammaticalisation 102, 103, 108, 122, 123, 129, 131, 151, 164, 167–9, 184
Great Vowel Shift 27, 72

habitual 137–8, 140, 141–5, 147, 148, 150, 204, 279, 280
habituality 138, 140–3, 144, 147, 150
head 66, 209, 258–9, 260–2, 264, 265, 266, 267–8, 269, 270, 273, 275
hierarchy of individuation 56, 59–61, 63, 80, 81, 281 *see also* animacy hierarchy
high-contact societies 9
hypotaxis 269

identifiability 88, 90, 100–1, 105
illocutionary force 237–8, 241, 254
imperfective 134–5, 137, 138, 143, 144–5,
  146–9, 150, 152
implicational hierarchies 17, 217, 224, 251–2,
  271, 281
implicational universals 16–17, 19, 35, 80,
  281
in situ interrogative words 246, 251, 253
inception 134
inchoative 118, 138
incompletion 136, 143, 146
indefinite articles 87–8, 93–4, 99, 100–1,
  102–3, 105–6, 108, 282
indefiniteness 103
indirect object 35, 38, 41, 68, 69, 219–20,
  222–3, 229–30, 231–2, 234, 261, 271, 272,
  275
indirect speech act 238
indirect-object construction 230–1, 232
inflectional marking 35, 47, 67, 128, 144–5,
  165, 200, 284
intensifying *self*-forms 25, 31, 35–7, 40
internally headed relative clauses 269
interrogative particles 252–3, 254,
  282
interrogative tags 3, 177, 181–2, 190, 191,
  202, 208, 240–1, 247–9, 250, 252–3, 254,
  279, 282
interrogative words 90, 240, 241, 242, 246–7,
  249, 250–2, 253–4, 264, 281, 282 *see also*
  fronting of interrogative words, *in situ*
  interrogative words
interrogatives *see* constituent interrogatives,
  polar interrogatives
intonation 175, 238, 241, 243, 249, 251
intransitive 78, 120, 220
irrealis 186, 187
iteration 140, 144

Jespersen Cycle 184, 189–90, 191

language contact 6, 7, 9–10, 18, 117, 118, 119,
  145, 160, 246, 284
language shift 7, 9–10, 19
levelling 183, 204–5, 213, 283
lexical aspect 113, 137 *see also* aktionsart
lexical gender 47, 56, 58
linguistic universals 11, 14–17, 129, 280–3,
  285 *see also* absolute universals,
  implicational universals, statistical
  universals, vernacular universals
locality 213
locative adverbials 92, 107, 282
locative expressions 144, 145, 148–50

long-distance reflexives 38, 42
low-contact societies 9

marginal modals 168, 170
marker of middle situation types 25
masculine 45, 46–8, 49, 51–2, 54–5, 57, 59,
  83
mass nouns 52, 57–9
mass/count distinction 57–8, 61, 96, 280
measure nouns 100, 283
medial object perfect 119–20, 123, 124,
  131
metonymic construal 28, 121
modality *see* circumstantial modality, deontic
  modality, epistemic modality, epistemic
  mustn't, root modality, situational modality
monotransitive 230
mood 38, 138, 155, 187, 250
morphological negation 184
multiple negation 1–2, 4, 6, 177, 179–80, 185,
  187–8, 190, 191, 281, 283
mutative verbs 120

narrative tense 124
negation *see* circumfixal negation, constituent
  negation, double negation, morphological
  negation, multiple negation, negative
  auxiliaries, negative concord, negative
  modals, sentence negation, subtractive
  negation, syntactic negation
negative auxiliaries 185
negative concord 188–9, 190, 191, 192, 195,
  209, 282, 283 *see also* multiple negation
negative contraction 3, 176, 177, 180–1,
  190
negative indefinite expressions 189
negative modals 159
negative polarity items 175, 180
neuter 45, 46–8, 51, 55, 58–60, 71, 77
nominative 65–7, 68, 69, 78–9, 80, 81
non-canonical agreement *see* canonical
  agreement
non-finite forms 156, 165, 168
non-reduction strategy 269, 271, 281
Northern Subject Rule 2, 3, 4, 199, 201–4,
  207, 212, 214–15, 216, 217, 280
numeral 'one' 103, 106, 108, 282
numeral bases 13, 14

object *see* direct object, indirect object
obligatory marking 210
obliques 261, 271–2, 275
omission of articles 91, 97, 98–9
on-goingness 135, 136, 144, 148, 150
open questions 238, 249, 253

optional marking 135, 212
overuse and underuse of articles 87, 91,
    97–100, 101, 105, 106

parataxis 269
participant roles 66–7
passivisation 15, 220
past 111–16, 120–1, 123, 124, 125–7, 129–30,
    134–7, 143, 144–5, 155–6, 161, 165, 169,
    178, 183, 185, 195–7, 201, 204, 205, 211,
    213, 215, 216, 279, 282, 283
past perfect 112, 114, 116, 126
perfect see after-perfect, already, be-perfect,
    existential perfect, experiential perfect,
    finish, medial object perfect, possessive
    perfect, resultative perfect, universal perfect
perfective 118, 134, 135, 137, 144–5, 146,
    152
performative utterances 112, 174
periphrastic marking 144–6
person hierarchy 35, 281
person-oriented systems 105
perspectivisation 38
polar interrogatives 238–9, 241, 243–6, 249,
    250
politeness 164, 182, 283
polysynthetic 9, 12, 19
positive anymore 180, 192
possessive 's 65, 80, 81
possessive determiners 94, 96
possessive perfect 124–5
postnominal relative clauses 268
postpositions 16, 19, 138
predication 16, 155, 156, 181, 220, 227
prenominal relative clauses 268, 269,
    273
prepositional construction 134, 221–2, 223–4,
    228, 229, 230, 232–3, 234
preterite presents 165
productivity 213, 275
progressive 113, 121, 128, 134–5, 136–7,
    138–41, 143, 144–9, 150, 151, 242
pronominal objects 222–4, 228, 229, 231–2,
    233, 234
pronoun exchange 65, 73, 77, 81, 280
pronoun retention 269–73, 274, 281
pronouns see anaphoric uses of pronouns,
    deictic uses of pronouns, demonstrative
    pronouns, pronoun exchange, pronoun
    retention, relative pronouns, resumptive
    pronouns

quantifiers 87, 89, 95, 175, 179, 184, 188, 202
questions see answer bias, conducive
    questions, open questions, yes/no questions

rara 278, 279
reduplication 144, 145
referential gender 46, 48, 56, 58
referential properties 87
reflexive markers see complex reflexives,
    emphatic reflexives, intensifying self-forms,
    marker of middle situation types,
    untriggered reflexives
reflexive relations 23–4, 25–9, 33, 34, 38, 39,
    40
regularisation 27, 200–1, 215, 281
regularity 278–9
relative markers 202, 260, 262–5, 267, 269,
    273 see also relative pronouns
relative pronouns 71, 198, 199, 201, 214,
    259–60, 262, 269, 271, 274, 279, 281
relative tense 112
remoteness distinctions 125–7
repetition 134, 288
reported speech 245
resultative perfect 113, 130
resumptive pronouns 262, 266–7, 270, 273,
    274 see also pronoun retention
root modality 157

scope of negation 158, 159, 171, 175, 180, 191
second language acquisition 6, 7, 9, 10, 19, 99,
    178, 200–1, 212, 284–5
secondary-object construction 229–31
semantic agreement 46, 198, 211, 214
semantic roles 79, 220, 233
semi-modals 155
sentence negation 174, 175–6, 177–8, 183,
    184, 185
sentence type 237–9, 253
simplification 74–6, 284
situation time see time of situation
situational modality 157
sociolinguistic typology 278, 283–7
sociolinguistics 1, 10–13, 18
Southern Double Object Construction 225–8,
    280
speech act 238 see also direct speech act,
    indirect speech act
state verbs 113, 115
statistical universals 17
subject type 202–3, 206, 215
subject-auxiliary inversion 6, 157, 239, 241,
    243, 250
subject-type hierarchy 206, 212, 217
subjunctive 38, 160–1, 169, 170
subordination 262
subordinator 239, 259, 260, 262, 265, 274
subtractive negation 183
suppletion 197, 216

syncretism 67, 197
syntactic agreement 211, 214
syntactic function 67, 79, 219, 259, 261, 271–2
syntactic negation 184–5
syntactic position 32, 65, 71, 240, 258, 259, 270
synthetic 12, 13, 19, 145, 284
systemic substratist hypothesis 118

tags *see* interrogative tags
target 45, 46, 61, 80, 195, 196, 198, 208–10, 211–14, 279
tense *see* absolute tense, future, future perfect, narrative tense, past, past perfect, relative tense
tertium comparationis 11, 19
third language acquisition 7
third person singular *don't* 183, 207–8
time of reference 112, 130
time of situation 112–13, 130, 135–7, 150
time of utterance 112, 127, 130, 134, 137
topic time 137
transitivity 220–1, 233
transparency 285, 287
trial 96–7

triple gender nouns 47–8
truth-value 174
typology *see* functional typology

unboundedness 136, 137, 146
unique referents 88
universal perfect 113, 123, 130, 282
universals *see* linguistic universals
untriggered reflexives 32–3, 37, 38, 40, 42

variationist typology 278, 283–7
verbal inflection 155
vernacular universals 6, 278, 280–3, 285
vowel systems 15

was/were-generalisation 201, 204–6
wh-pronouns 71, 239, 240, 241, 269 *see also* interrogative words
word class distinctions 14–15, 17
word order 6, 13–14, 15–16, 79, 100, 101, 102, 219, 232, 237, 239, 241–2, 245, 246, 249–51, 253, 275, 279, 287

yes/no questions 238, 243, 249, 253, 283

zero marking 28, 200–1